A MATERIALIST
THEORY OF THE MIND

International Library of Philosophy and Scientific Method

Editor: Ted Honderich

A catalogue of books already published in the
International Library of Philosophy and Scientific Method
will be found at the end of this volume

A MATERIALIST THEORY
OF THE MIND

by
D. M. ARMSTRONG

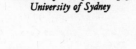

Challis Professor of Philosophy
University of Sydney

LONDON
ROUTLEDGE & KEGAN PAUL
NEW YORK : HUMANITIES PRESS

First published 1968
by Routledge & Kegan Paul Ltd
Broadway House, 68-74 Carter Lane
London, EC4V 5EL
Reprinted 1969
Reprinted 1971
Reproduced and Printed in Great Britain by
Redwood Press Limited
Trowbridge & London
© *D. M. Armstrong* 1968
ISBN 0 7100 3634 5

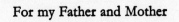
For my Father and Mother

CONTENTS

vii

Contents

Contents

Contents

PART THREE: THE NATURE OF MIND

ACKNOWLEDGEMENTS

PROFESSOR J. J. C. SMART converted me to the view, defended in this book, that mental states are nothing but physical states of the brain. He in his turn has acknowledged the influence of U. T. Place. In the book I make certain criticisms of some of the views that Smart and Place have put forward in print. But for the most part I conceive myself only to be filling out a step in the argument to which they have devoted little attention: the account of the *concept* of mind. My intellectual debt to them remains profound.

Professor C. B. Martin, now my colleague at Sydney University, first made me aware of the central role played by the concept of *causality* in an account of the mental concepts. Previously I had assigned the central place to the notion of dispositions, conceived of as Ryle conceives them in *The Concept of Mind*. My change of view on this question was a turning point in my conception of philosophical psychology, and, although Martin does not accept a physicalist account of the mind, I owe him no less than I owe Smart and Place.

The following have read various drafts of all or some of the manuscript, and have helped me greatly with criticism and comment: Dr. J. Beloff, Professors A. G. N. Flew, D. A. T. Gasking, D. M. McCallum, J. L. Mackie, B. Medlin, G. C. Nerlich, J. J. C. Smart, Mr. D. C. Stove and Dr. W. A. Suchting. Other acknowledgements are made in the text. I am indebted in particular for a number of suggestions, at once ingenious and profound, to Professor M. J. Deutscher. I have learnt a great deal from students at Yale, Melbourne, Sydney and Stanford Universities in the course of presenting to them portions of the material in this book.

Acknowledgements

My thanks are also due to Roswitha Duffy for typing the manuscript.

I have indeed received so much valuable help from so many persons that I cannot be certain that I am responsible for every error that the book may contain.

D. M. A.

University of Sydney

INTRODUCTION

WHAT is a man? One obvious thing to say is that he is a certain sort of material object. A man's body functions in a more complex and curious way than any other known material object, natural or artificial. But it is a material object. The question then arises: 'Is man nothing but his material body? Can we give a complete account of man in purely physical terms?'

In the past, there seemed to be two great objections to giving a purely physical account of man. In the first place, man had a property which he shared with animals and plants, but which ordinary material objects lacked: he was *alive*. Could life be nothing but a purely physical property? In the second place, man had a property which he shared with many animals, but with nothing else in the physical world: he had a *mind*. He perceived, felt, thought and had purposes. Could mentality be nothing but a purely physical property?

Increasing scientific knowledge has largely answered the first objection. It is now very probable, even if not certain, that life is a purely physico-chemical phenomenon. We do not need to postulate 'vegetative souls' or 'vital entelechies' to explain life. What of the second objection? More and more psychologists and neurophysiologists explicitly or implicitly accept the view that, so far as mental processes are concerned, there is no need to postulate anything but purely physical processes in man's central nervous system. If we take the word 'mind' to mean 'that in which mental processes occur' or 'that which has mental states', then we can put this view briefly and not too misleadingly as: the mind is nothing but the brain. If scientific progress sustains this view, it seems that man is nothing but a material object having none but physical properties.

I

Introduction

Most *philosophers*, however, believe that there are conclusive reasons for rejecting such a physicalist theory of mind. That is the occasion for writing this book. It is written by a philosopher, and written primarily for philosophers. Its object is to show that there are no good philosophical reasons for denying that mental processes are purely physical processes in the central nervous system and so, by implication, that there are no good philosophical reasons for denying that man is nothing but a material object.

It does not attempt to prove the truth of this physicalist thesis about the mind. The proof must come, if it does come, from science: from neurophysiology in particular. All it attempts to show is that there are no valid philosophical or logical reasons for rejecting the identification of mind and brain. Like John Locke, I conceive my task negatively. I am an underlabourer carting away rubbish from the path along which I conceive, or guess, that scientific progress lies.

For this reason, the importance of this work for psychology, if any, is mainly indirect. To vary Locke's metaphor, what I am doing is trying to protect those psychologists who explicitly or implicitly identify mind and brain against a harassing action on their flank, a harassment, perhaps, that some of them do not take very seriously anyway. If there is anything I say that is of assistance to psychologists in dealing with the logical problems involved in the consideration of our ordinary mental concepts, I shall be happy. But this will be an intellectual bonus over and above what I conceive to be the special importance of this work for psychology.

The first five chapters consider and criticize what I take to be the important alternatives to an identification of mind and brain. I regard the difficulties that beset these alternatives as a most compelling reason for believing that my own theory is on the right track. Nevertheless, some readers may wish to omit these chapters in an already long book. Although a few references are made back to the early chapters in the later course of the work, readers should have no great difficulty if they begin at Chapter 6.

I should also warn that some of the things I say in the first five chapters are provisional. This arises because, if the position sketched in Chapter 6 is correct, certain old positions and old arguments concerning mind and body appear in a new light.

Part One

THEORIES OF MIND

I

A CLASSIFICATION OF
THEORIES OF MIND

THERE are many possible ways of classifying theories of mind. The classification to be put forward here is based upon different conceptions of the relationship of mind to *body*.

Some theories of mind and body try to reduce body to mind or some property of mind. Such theories may be called *Mentalist* theories. Thus according to Hegel and his followers, the Absolute Idealists, the whole material world is really mental or spiritual in nature, little as it may appear so. According to Leibniz, material objects are colonies of rudimentary souls. These are both mentalist theories. It may be plausibly argued that Bishop Berkeley and his philosophical descendants the Phenomenalists, who hold that physical objects are constructions out of 'ideas' or sense-impressions, are putting forward mentalist theories of matter.

In opposition to these mentalist theories, we have *Materialist* theories which try to reduce mind to body or to some property of body.

Between mentalist and materialist theories we find two sorts of compromise theories. In the first place, there are *Dualist* theories which treat mind and matter as two independent sorts of thing. In the second place, we have theories like Spinoza's, which treat mind and matter as different attributes of the same underlying stuff, or *Neutral Monism*, which holds that mind and matter are different arrangements of a single sort of stuff.

However, if we consider the tradition of modern analytical

philosophy, within which this book is written, we find that many of these views are not living intellectual options. Some analytical philosophers have accepted Phenomenalism. But most have taken the common sense view that physical objects are not mental in nature, nor are they attributes of, nor constructions out of, something neutral in nature. For this reason, the only theories of mind and body that I will actually examine in this first part of the book are those that accept the irreducibly physical nature of physical things. I have two reasons for ignoring Phenomenalism. In the first place, its intellectual credit has been shaken in recent years. In the second place, I have already said what I have to say in criticism of Phenomenalism in *Perception and the Physical World* (Routledge, 1961, Chs. 5 and 6).

Having in this way limited the field of theories to be examined, a new classification is required for those theories that remain. We may distinguish between *Dualist* theories of mind and body, *Attribute* theories and *Materialist* theories.

A Dualist theory is one that holds that mind and body are *distinct things*. For a Dualist a man is a compound object, a material thing—his body—somehow related to a non-material thing or things—his mind. There are two main types of Dualist theory.

In the first place, we have *Cartesian* Dualism. For the Cartesian Dualist the mind is a *single* non-material or spiritual substance somehow related to the body. Although the term 'Cartesian' refers to Descartes, and we find this view of the mind and body expounded by Descartes in his *Sixth Meditation*, the term, as I use it, is not to be restricted to the exact theory put forward by Descartes. It is to be applied to any view that holds that a person's mind is a single, continuing, non-material substance in some way related to the body.

(Since this is the first time that the term 'substance' has been used in this work, and since it will be used frequently in the future, it will be convenient to say a word about the notion of substance here. Locke conceived of substance as the unknowable substratum of objects. Those who came after him often rejected the doctrine of such a substratum, but the unfortunate effect was not to revise Locke's conception of substance, but to give the whole notion of substance a bad odour. But when I present the Cartesian view as the view that the mind is a non-material substance, I do not regard the Cartesians as necessarily committed to a doctrine of an unknowable mental substratum. I understand by a substance nothing more than a thing that is *logically capable of independent existence*.)

In the second place, we have what may be called 'Bundle' Dualism, the term 'bundle' echoing Hume's notorious description of the mind as a 'bundle of perceptions'. This form of Dualism characteristically arises out of reflection on the difficulties of Cartesian Dualism. When the great Empiricist philosopher, David Hume, turned his gaze inward upon himself, he found that he could discern no continuing spiritual principle within himself. In his discussion of the nature of the self in his *Treatise of Human Nature*, Bk. I, Pt. IV, Sect. 6, he says:

> For my part, when I enter most intimately into what I call *myself*, I always stumble on some particular perception or other, of heat or cold, light or shade, love or hatred, pain or pleasure. I never can catch *myself* at any time without a perception, and never can observe any thing but the perception. (p. 252, ed. Selby-Bigge, Oxford University Press, 1888)

Hume is arguing here that there is no continuing object in the mental sphere corresponding to the body in the physical sphere. Nobody ever observes such a spiritual principle within himself. All that observation of what goes on in our minds reveals is a succession of what Hume calls 'perceptions': that is, perceptions, sensations, emotions, thoughts and so on. So the 'Bundle' Dualist takes the mind to be a succession of non-physical particulars or items distinct from, although related to, the body.

Although 'Bundle' Dualism is closely linked with Hume's name, it is not absolutely clear whether or not Hume himself was a 'Bundle' Dualist. His view of the mind certainly fits our definition, but it is legitimate to doubt whether he holds a Materialist theory of the body. For sometimes he seems to hold a view of physical objects similar to that of Berkeley, making them nothing but our perceptions 'of' them. This would imply that minds and bodies are both constructed from perceptions. However, at other times Hume's view seems to be less radical, and closer to common sense. Then he talks as if a man were a material thing somehow united to a bundle of non-material items: perceptions or experiences.

There is another important way of classifying Dualist theories which cuts across the distinction between Cartesian and 'Bundle'

Dualism. This classification is based on the particular nature of the relationship thought to hold between the mind and the body: it is the distinction between *Interactionist* and *Parallelist* theories.

The difference between Interactionist and Parallelist theories may be brought out by considering the causal relations between (i) a room and its thermostat; (ii) a room and its thermometer. A room and its *thermostat* act upon each other. A rise in the temperature of the room brings about changes in the thermostat; the changes in the thermostat in turn affect the room, bringing back its temperature to a certain level. If this action and reaction did not occur, the thermostat would not be acting as a thermostat. The Dualist who is an Interactionist thinks of body and mind as related like room and thermostat. The body acts on the mind, the mind reacts back on the body.

On the other hand, although a room acts upon its *thermometer*, a rise in the temperature of the room causing a rise in the mercury of the thermometer, the thermometer does not react back upon the room. (In fact it does so to a very small extent, but we may ignore this point.) If the thermometer affected the temperature of the room, as a thermostat does, it would be no use as a thermometer. Now the Dualist who is a Parallelist thinks of body and mind as related like room and thermometer. The body acts on the mind, but the mind is incapable of reacting back on the body in any way at all.

There is a still more extreme form of Parallelism according to which not only is the mind incapable of acting on the body, but the body is also incapable of acting on the mind. Instead they run in two parallel series like the two rails of a railway line, or two perfectly synchronized clocks. However, I do not propose to consider this form of Parallelism explicitly. My reason is that I do not think that it is seriously considered by present-day thinkers. Here we concern ourselves only with those theories of Mind and Body which are living options for the thought of our time.

It is sometimes argued that if we accept a Uniformity theory of causation, for which causation is nothing but regular sequence, then the distinction between Interactionism and Parallelism disappears. And it is true that acceptance of a Uniformity theory would blur the distinction between the mild and the extreme forms of Parallelism. But it is clear that, even on a Uniformity theory, there is a distinction between the way a room's temperature is related to its thermostat, and the way it is related to its thermometer. The uniformities involved in the first sort of relation are much more complex than the uniformities involved in the second sort. Now the relations of the room's temperature to thermostat and thermometer respectively are the same as the relations of body to mind envisaged by Interactionism and Parallelism respectively.

I said that the distinction between Interactionism and Parallelism cuts across our original distinction between Cartesian and 'Bundle' Dualism. Descartes himself was an Interactionist, although he did think that there was difficulty in conceiving of the interaction of spiritual and material substance. His successors, however, gave up the doctrine of Interaction, and so became Cartesian Parallelists. In his Dualist mood, Hume believed in the interaction of mind and body. Later 'Bundle' Dualists, however, became sceptical about the possibility of such interaction, and so we have 'Bundle' Dualists who are Parallelists. This is the important position known as *Epiphenomenalism*, that finds its classical exposition in T. H. Huxley's paper 'On the Hypothesis that Animals are Automata and its History' (to be found in his *Methods and Results*, Macmillan, 1894). For Huxley, consciousness is thought of as a mere by-product of the operation of the brain. We do have experiences which are, in themselves, something more than the workings of the brain, but they are incapable of influencing the operation of the brain in any way. Experience is, in Huxley's phrase, the smell above the factory, or, as the American philosopher Santayana put it more poetically, the motes above the stream. It is clear that Epiphenomenalism will have a great appeal to anybody who is sympathetic to Materialism, but who still thinks that there is something irreducible about mental states with which Materialism cannot deal.

Some philosophers would wish to use the term 'Epiphenomenalism' to cover any form of the 'thermometer' view of the mind, whether the mind is conceived of as a bundle of items or as a spiritual substance. They would restrict the term 'Parallelism' to what I called the extreme form of Parallelism: the 'railway-line' view. But the term 'Epi-*phenomenalism*' clearly suggests that the mind is conceived of not merely as totally passive but also as a mere collection of phenomena. So I restrict the term to the *intersection* of 'bundle' and 'thermometer' Dualist theories.

This completes our classification of Dualist theories. In sharp opposition to any form of Dualism we have *Materialist* or *Physicalist* theories of mind. For a Materialist, man is nothing but a physical object, and so he is committed to giving a purely physical theory of the mind. There are two types of Materialist theory. In the first place, there are various forms of *Behaviourism*. The Behaviourist denies that the mind is any sort of *object*, or collection of objects, arguing that to have a mind is simply to behave physically in a certain way, or to have tendencies to behave physically in a certain way. On this theory, the difference between a living man with a mind, on the one hand, and a corpse or a stone, on the other, is simply that the living man behaves, or has tendencies to behave, in a different way from the corpse or the stone.

Behaviourism originates with the psychologist J. B. Watson (see his *Behaviour*, New York: Holt, 1914 and his *Behaviourism*, University of Chicago Press, 1924). In recent times the American psychologist B. F. Skinner has defended a Behaviourist theory of mind (see his *Science and Human Behaviour*, New York: Macmillan, 1953). Turning to the philosophers, it is very easy to interpret Gilbert Ryle's *The Concept of Mind* (Hutchinson, 1949) as a defence of Behaviourism, although this interpretation is denied by some philosophers. It seems to be denied by Ryle himself in the course of the book, but I think that this is only because he gives the word 'Behaviourism' a particularly narrow meaning. Some philosophers, of whom I am one, think that Wittgenstein's very important, but very difficult, *Philosophical Investigations* (Blackwell, 1953) also expounds a Behaviourist account of the mind. But in some quarters one risks being torn to pieces for interpreting the book in this way.

The second form of Materialism is what the American philosopher Herbert Feigl has called the *Central-state* theory of the mind. Mental states are identified with physical states of the organism that has the mind, in particular, with states of the brain or central nervous system. Such a view has always been attractive to many psychologists, but until recent years most *philosophers* have thought that there were obvious and conclusive objections to this sort of theory. But in the last decade or so, the Central-state theory has been revived by philosophers in a very interesting way. The revival is associated with such names as Herbert Feigl,

Paul Feyerabend, U. T. Place, Hilary Putnam and J. J. C. Smart.

Before the modern revival, the most conspicuous defender of a Central-state theory was Thomas Hobbes. But his defence of the theory lacks philosophical sophistication, and in any case he seems to waver between a Central-state theory and Epiphenomenalism. The object of this book is to defend a particular form of the Central-state theory of the mind.

Instead of speaking of the Central-state theory, some philosophers speak of the *Identity* theory, that is, the theory that the mind and the brain are identical. The label is less explicit than 'Central-state theory', although it is briefer. In any case, the term seems sometimes to be applied to Attribute as well as to Central-state theories.

We have now mentioned the main forms of Dualist and Materialist theory. Some philosophers are dissatisfied *both* with Dualism and with pure Materialism. They try to get the best of both theories in the following way. They agree with the Materialists, against the Dualists, that a man with a mind is but a single substance. There is no question of the mind being a non-material substance, or a collection of non-material items, distinct from the body. But the compromisers argue that this single substance, the man, has further *properties* beyond those conceded by the Materialists. For a Materialist, a man is a physical object, distinguished from other physical objects only by the special complexity of his physical organization, and the special complexity of his physical capacities. He does not have any non-physical properties. But the theory we are describing argues that men, besides having physical properties, have further properties quite different from those possessed by ordinary physical objects. It is the possession of these unique properties that gives men a mind. I shall call such theories *Attribute* theories of the mind. Some modern philosophers have spoken instead of *Double-Aspect* theories, and have seemed to mean by the term what I mean by Attribute theories. But the term 'Double-Aspect' is unsatisfactory, because all it suggests is that mind and body are the one identical thing observed in two different ways, or from two different points of view. This might even be compatible with Central-state Materialism, and so the term blurs the distinction between a pure Materialism and a compromise theory.

Aristotle's doctrine, put forward in *De Anima*, that the mind is the 'form' of the body is perhaps a version of the Attribute theory. Spinoza certainly held that mind is an attribute of the body. But he does not really fit into our classification, because he holds that *everything* has mental as well as material attributes. This means that he does not accept the framework within which our discussion of theories of mind is placed: the purely Materialist or Physicalist account of ordinary physical objects. Samuel Alexander's theory in *Space, Time and Deity* (Macmillan, 1920) is an Attribute theory, although one that comes very close to Materialism. The late John Anderson, of Sydney University, held a somewhat similar view. (See his *Studies in Empirical Philosophy*, Angus and Robertson, 1962, especially the paper 'Mind as Feeling'.) Locke's case is an interesting one. Locke is a Cartesian Dualist, holding that the mind is a non-material substance. Nevertheless, on a number of occasions he says that it is not beyond the power of God, if he should please, to endow matter with consciousness. He seems to be saying that, although Dualism is true in fact, the Attribute theory of mind is a logically possible one. (I think it is very unlikely that he thought that a purely Materialist theory of mind is logically possible.)

Is the Thomist theory of the relation of mind and body an Attribute theory? The Thomist insistence that a man is a single substance points in this direction, but the assertion that the soul can continue to exist independently of the body, even if in an unnatural state, points back towards a Dualist theory. I am inclined to see in Thomism an uneasy and somewhat confused oscillation between an Attribute theory and Dualism, although I lack space here to substantiate the accusation.

I cannot see any clear and important way of sub-dividing Attribute theories.

It is important for the subsequent argument to realize that the object, or collection of objects, with which the *Dualist* identifies the mind is not in space although it is in time. It may then be objected to our classification that it has ignored the possibility that the mind is an object or collection of objects distinct from the body but nevertheless spatial. But to this view we may put a dilemma. Either this spatial mind is in the same place as part or the whole of the body, or it is not. If it is not, we have an eccentric and implausible form of physicalism. If mind and body are spatially coincident, we have not got a Dualism but an Attribute theory. For two spatial things cannot be at the same place at the same time. To attempt to speak of two spatial things with different properties at the same place at the same time is to speak of just one thing with both sets of properties.

This completes our scheme of classification. I hope it will cover most of those theories of mind and body that are seriously held today, always remembering the limitation to what I have called Materialist or Physicalist accounts of matter. But it will be wise to make some qualifications to prevent misunderstanding.

In the first place, it may well be possible to find theories of mind which stand on the border-line of our divisions. In particu-lar there may be certain theories which could be classified in-differently either as Attribute theories, or as forms of Materialism.

In the second place, closely connected with the first point, there is the possibility of combining two or more of these differ-ent views of the nature of mind to produce a mixed theory. Thus, in recent philosophy there have been many triumphs for Be-haviourist and Behaviourist-oriented analyses of psychological concepts. At the same time, those who acknowledged these triumphs were, very often, understandably reluctant to say that Behaviourism was the whole truth about the mind. This led to the idea of an account of mind which would combine Behaviourism with one of the other theories. A 'Bundle' Dualist, for instance, might admit that when we ascribe mental predicates to persons we are very often speaking only of the way they behave. On a certain occasion, for instance, what we mean by saying that a man 'thought fast' may simply be that he *acted* in the right way very promptly. But, the 'Bundle' Dualist would add, besides behaviour there is a succession of non-material experiences dis-tinct from, although related to, the behaving body. Such a 'Bundle' Dualist would be taking the notion of the mind to be, as it were, a portmanteau notion: a concept that straddles the non-material and the material world. Such a view of mind may seem to get the best of both realms, avoiding the difficulties that beset a purely spiritual or a purely material account of the mind. In the same way, we could combine Behaviourism with Cartesian Dual-ism, with an Attribute theory, or with Central-state Materialism.

One philosopher who adopts such a mixed theory is P. F. Strawson. (See the chapter on 'Persons' in his book *Individuals*, Methuen, 1959.) Unfortunately, however, from the point of view of our classification, it is not clear whether it is a 'Bundle' Dualism, or a form of Attribute theory, that he is attempting to combine with Behaviourism.

This leads on to the third warning that must be given about our classification of theories of mind. When we consider modern philosophers who write about the mind, it is often difficult to determine just how their view of mind fits into the classification offered. This might be taken to be a criticism of the classification, but in fact I do not think that it should be so taken. I believe there are two other reasons why it is so hard to place their views. In the first place, there is no doubt that the question of the nature of the mind is one of the utmost difficulty. When we add this to the tentative and piecemeal character of a great deal of modern philosophizing, it is not surprising that many philosophers have simply not come to a clear decision about their view of the mind.

There is, however, what I think is a much darker and less intellectually honourable reason for the difficulty that there often is in discovering their view. Since the work of Wittgenstein, it has been fashionable to maintain that philosophy does not issue in any theories at all about the nature of reality. Hence it is not the *business* of the philosopher to maintain any theory of mind. I think that this doctrine has proved intellectually corrupting, for in fact it is quite impossible to be in such a theory-free state if you think at all extensively on philosophical topics. Those philosophers who believe that they are in such a theory-free state are really being moved by obscure and ill-formulated theories which escape any criticism or correction because they are never brought out into the open where they can be clearly considered.

2

DUALISM

HAVING placed Central-state Materialism in relation to its rivals, I turn to a criticism of these rivals. By appreciating their difficulties, the strength of the Materialist view will be seen more easily. I begin with a critique of 'Bundle' Dualism.

I. CRITICISM OF 'BUNDLE' DUALISM

A 'Bundle' Dualist conceives of the mind as a temporal series of non-physical items: 'perceptions' or 'experiences' somehow linked with a particular body. The mind is a succession of such things as thoughts, feelings, desires, mental images, sensations and, above all, sense-impressions or sense-perceptions, all conceived of as non-physical particulars.

There is one particular version of 'Bundle' Dualism according to which this list can be abbreviated to sensations, sense-impressions and mental images. This is the *Sensationalist* theory of mind, for which all mental events can be analysed in terms of the having of sensations. (The theory made no very clear distinction between sensation, sense-impression and mental image.) But a 'Bundle' Dualist need not be a Sensationalist, and it will be simpler to ignore the special difficulties of Sensationalism. The two well-known difficulties now to be brought forward are difficulties for any form of 'Bundle' Dualism.

(a) *What is the uniting principle of a mind?*

Why is it that I group together all my mental experiences, and call them my mind? What makes my experiences today part of one and the same mind as my experiences yesterday, and marks them off from your experiences today and yesterday? The Cartesian Dualist will answer, 'Because my experiences today and my experiences yesterday are both states of that one, continuing, non-physical substance that is the real I.' Whatever the difficulties in this answer, at least it has the merit of simplicity. The 'Bundle' Dualist has no such simple answer.

His problem can be understood by considering a similar, but much easier, problem. Suppose that there are two long chains, each composed of the same sort of links, which are entangled with each other in a confused heap, although the four ends are left running out of the tangle. Taking up two of these ends, we say 'Here are two ends of the one chain.' What does this statement mean? The answer is obvious. If we start with one of the ends, and if we advance each time to a link connected with the previous link, we shall eventually reach the other end that we are holding, and not one of the other two ends. This explains what we mean by 'the one chain'.

Now the problem for the 'Bundle' Dualist is to find a uniting principle which will link together the collection of non-physical particulars that he takes to constitute the mind. Just as we found a relation that united all the different links of the one chain, but which did not hold between any link of that chain and any other chain, so the 'Bundle' Dualist needs to find a relation that unites all those particulars that constitute one mind, and which does not hold between any of those particulars and the particulars that belong to other minds. To use John Stuart Mill's phrase, the 'Bundle' Dualist has to point to the 'thread of consciousness' that threads together all those particulars, and only those particulars, which make up one mind. The relationship need not be a link-by-link connection like that between the parts of a chain. It may be more like the relation between the different beads on the same thread, or it may be some quite different sort of relation. But the 'Bundle' Dualist must discover some principle that unites the collection of non-physical particulars.

In writing about personal identity in his *Treatise*, Hume relies on the relations of *resemblance* and *causation*. Let us consider resemblance first. There is no doubt that the mental experiences that a person has at different times will tend to resemble each other rather more closely than they will resemble the experiences of others. But it seems perfectly possible that we should have quite novel experiences which resemble nothing that we have experienced before. If resemblance were an important mark of identity, there should be difficulty in identifying such experiences as *ours*. Again, two people might have mental experiences of almost exactly the same sort, say when looking at the same picture, yet this would give us no inclination to say that the two experiences belonged to the one mind. Causation is no better than resemblance. My experiences are, no doubt, in a great part determined by the nature of my experiences in the past. But some experiences seem to be produced solely by external causes: they seem to be experiences I would have had even if my past experiences had been quite different from what they in fact were. Again, the fact that I have certain experiences may determine the nature of your experiences, as well as my own. So the relations of resemblance and causation fail to separate off experiences into those collections which the 'Bundle' Dualist identifies with minds. It was reasons such as these, I presume, that led Hume in the Appendix to the *Treatise*, to confess that he could not solve the problem of finding a uniting principle for the mind.

Some philosophers have sought the uniting principle in *memory*. And the suggestion has this much to recommend it: it is quite obvious, whatever theory of the nature of the mind that we hold, that memory is involved in our ordinary concept of the identity of a mind. Suppose we try to imagine a mind with no memory at all. Would it be what we call a mind? Would it not rather be a *mere* succession of mental states? So perhaps memory is the uniting principle that the 'Bundle' Dualist seeks.

But even waiving many other problems, there is an obvious difficulty that was pointed out by Hume. Many of our mental experiences, perhaps the vast majority, pass like a shadow. They neither involve any memory of past mental states, nor are they remembered later on. (Consider our more casual perceptions.) Yet such items are part of the history of our minds. On what principle are they included in the mind? We could try to bring them in by going back to the relations of similarity and causation, but, even then, there seems to be no way of getting *all* our un-remembered mental states, and no others, within the net.

It has been suggested that we might meet Hume's objection by demanding only the *possibility* of memory-links to link together a particular bundle. Where direct or indirect memory-links are possible, there we have mental items belonging to the one mind.

But what does 'possible' mean here? Do we mean empirical possibility, for instance, the possibility of a man running a mile in four minutes? Or do we mean bare logical possibility, for instance, the possibility of a man running a mile in four seconds? If we mean empirical possibility, then it still seems that there can be mental events that escape the net. May not memory of past mental events be lost *irrecoverably*? It is at least an intelligible notion. But if we mean logical possibility, then may not any two mental events be linked in this way, regardless of what mind they belong to?

John Mackie has objected that there is a fourth relation that the 'Bundle' Dualist can appeal to here. He points out that in any normal continuous waking period there is continuity of experience. One mental event runs into another, and it is only by arbitrary division that they can be broken up into discrete events. Now is not this felt continuity the relation that binds together the 'bundle' of experiences? Resemblance, causation and memory need be appealed to only where such continuity breaks down.

But what is this continuity of which we are aware? To speak of continuity is to say nothing at all: anything that continues to exist has continuity, and when we are aware of its continuing existence we are aware of its continuity. The question we want to answer is what *constitutes* the continuity of experience. The appeal to resemblance, causation or memory is at least an attempt to answer the question, even if an unsatisfactory attempt. An appeal to mere awareness of continuity is not. The continuity might be, as the Cartesian claims it is, the continuity of a substance. It may, of course, be said that the continuity involved is a special, unique, kind of continuity that cannot be further defined. This answer we will consider in a moment, but in the meanwhile let us consider a different attempted line of solution.

So far we have looked for some *internal* bond of unity among the collection of items that are supposed to form a mind. But perhaps we should look to the *body* associated with a particular mind to provide the uniting principle, or some part of the uniting principle, of the collection of items. Just as the uniting principle of a ship's company is that they all stand in a special relation to the one ship, so perhaps we call a particular collection of mental events 'one mind' because they all stand in a special relation to the one body. The advantage of such a course is obvious: it gives us a clear and simple uniting principle.

Difficulties might be raised about the nature of the relation holding between the individual mental items and the body, but they need not be discussed here because they will come up again when we examine the problems faced by both Interactionism and Parallelism. Here I will confine myself to pointing to a problem about *disembodied existence*.

The first point to be made is that the existence of a mind in a disembodied state seems to be a logical possibility. Whether disembodied existence is empirically possible is another matter; it may well be argued that it is empirically impossible for the mind to exist without a body. Indeed, a Central-state Materialist is committed to so arguing. But disembodied existence seems to be a perfectly intelligible supposition. It may be that a good deal of perception in some sense presupposes that we have a body or at least a position in space. For instance, we see things as oriented in space with respect to *us*, and it is hard to see what 'us' refers to here if not to our body. But consider the case where I am lying in bed at night thinking. Surely it is logically possible that I might be having just the same experiences, and yet not have a body at all? No doubt I am having certain somatic, that is to say, bodily, sensations. But if I am lying still these will be not very detailed in nature, and I can see nothing self-contradictory in supposing that they do not correspond to anything in physical reality. Yet I need be in no doubt about my identity.

I believe that we should say, therefore, that it is a criticism of any theory of mind if it is unable to allow the logical possibility of disembodied existence. I will admit, however, that the situation is not completely clear. On the one hand, there are various theories of mind which do not permit the logical possibility of disembodied existence, for instance, Behaviourism and perhaps the Attribute theory. Supporters of these theories claim that we simply have to accept the fact that, surprising as it may seem, disembodied existence is a meaningless notion even although we did not realize this until we had thought the matter through. The situation has arisen where a *general theory* clashes with a *particular case*. We are faced with the question whether we give up the theory in the face of the case, or whether we give the theory so much weight that we let it persuade us that we have made a mistake about the case. There is no general formula for deciding such a question, but, in this particular clash, it seems so difficult to deny that disembodied existence is a conceivable possibility that I think we are entitled to back the case against the theory. I admit, however, that I can give no argument for the intelligibility of the notion of disembodied existence except by appealing to cases such as the one described.

(Incidentally, the reader may be thinking here that Central-state Materialism cannot admit that disembodied existence is a meaningful notion. But we shall see later that the form of Central-state Materialism to be defended in this book does not rule out disembodied existence as something meaningless, but only as something false.)

Now the suggestion that the 'Bundle' Dualist can solve his problem about the 'thread of consciousness' by tying the collection of mental items to the body, runs into just this difficulty about disembodied existence. For if the continuing identity of my mind is logically dependent upon all my experiences being related in a certain way to a particular body, then *dis*embodied existence of a mind must be a meaningless notion. But, I claim, disembodied existence *is* a meaningful notion. So the body cannot be the 'thread of consciousness'.

Faced with the difficulty of finding either an internal or an external relation to link up the 'bundle of perceptions', some 'Bundle' Dualists have become desperate. They have tried to solve their problem by suggesting that there is a unique and indefinable relationship which holds between items that form part of the same consciousness, and between no other items. It is not similarity, it is not causation, it is not memory, it is not relationship to a body, it is something else, something we are all aware of, but which we cannot explain in terms of anything else. Added to memory, this unique relation serves to mark off one mind from another.

The genius of Hume disdained this line of escape. He preferred, surely rightly, to confess his incapacity to solve the problem of the unifying principle. For what a triumph this postulation of a unique relation represents for the Cartesian over the 'Bundle' Dualist! 'You objected to my spiritual substance on the grounds that you could observe no such mysterious object when you looked into your mind. Yet here you are *forced* by your need to find a uniting principle among experiences to postulate a mysterious unique and indefinable relation. Why did you boggle at my postulating of a spiritual substance? You yourself are postulating a spiritual principle, so my position is at least as plausible as yours.'

So the 'Bundle' Dualist must either (i) appeal to relations like similarity, causation and memory, which seem to be insufficient; (ii) tie the bundle of mental items to the body, implausibly making the notion of a disembodied mind a contradiction in terms; (iii) postulate a special spiritual tie between experiences, similar to the Cartesian postulate of a spiritual substance. It is an unhappy choice.

(b) *Experiences are not capable of independent existence*

But there is another difficulty for 'Bundle' Dualism, one that Hume never noticed, which, if it is a difficulty at all, is a refutation of the theory.

If the mind is conceived of as a succession of non-physical items: if these are the things that make up the mind, that are the building-blocks out of which it is constructed, that constitute its substance: then it must be a conceivable possibility for any individual item in the collection to exist, not merely in independence of any material body, but also in independence of the other items that make up the collection. Such individual items should not be called '*mental* experiences' because, for the 'Bundle' Dualist, the mental is essentially a *collection* of items, but it must be conceivable that the items should exist outside the collection. (Compare the case of an army. It is made up of soldiers, who could not be called 'soldiers' apart from their membership of an army. But it is possible for the individuals we call soldiers to exist in independence of any army.)

So far, so good. This consequence would have been accepted by Hume, indeed it was explicitly drawn by him. In the *Treatise* he says that if substance is defined as 'something which may exist by itself' then all our distinct perceptions (that is to say, distinct mental items) are distinct substances (Vol. I, Bk. I, Pt. IV, Sect. 5, p. 244, ed. Selby-Bigge). But he fails to realize that this is a *reductio ad absurdum* of his own theory of mind. For is it meaningful to conceive of a single twinge of pain, a single sense-perception, a single after-image, a single thought or a single feeling of grief existing by itself independently of anything else? It certainly seems possible that a mind should begin to exist, have only the one experience, say a twinge of pain, and then be extinguished before it has any other experiences. (Though we might say that it existed for too brief a time to be called 'a mind' or for what happened to it to be called 'pain'.) But is this the same as the supposition of a twinge of pain that exists independently of anything else? I do not think it is. For the twinge of pain demands some further background, something to *have* the twinge of pain. But to say this is to go beyond 'Bundle' Dualism, which admits nothing but the experiences. The difficulty is really already present when the mind is said to be a collection or bundle of mental items, but it is concealed because it is possible to think of the *having* of the twinge of pain as simply being the relation that one mental item bears to the whole collection of items.

There can be faces without grins but there cannot be grins without faces. Grins are not capable of independent existence. The universe could not consist of a grin, and absolutely nothing else. A grin demands a background, something to have the grin. There are substances that have soporific virtue, that is to say, the power of putting people to sleep. But there cannot be soporific virtues that inhere in no substance. Soporific virtues are not capable of independent existence. The universe could not consist of an instance of soporific virtue, and absolutely nothing else. The soporific virtue demands a background, a thing to have the soporific virtue. Mental experiences, I am arguing, like grins or soporific virtues, require something further to have them. But this is incompatible with 'Bundle' Dualism.

I must admit again that, just as in the case of the intelligibility of the notion of disembodied existence, I can produce no further argument for saying that after-images, pains, thoughts, etc., are incapable of independent existence. All I can do is ask any philosophers who might be inclined to deny the incapacity to contemplate the case. It seems that we can imagine a universe which contains only one object, say, one electron. But is there not a repugnancy in the idea of a universe which contains nothing but a thought, with nothing to have the thought? If this contemplation of the case does not convince, I know of no further argument.

II. CRITICISM OF CARTESIAN DUALISM

It now becomes clear that Cartesian Dualism has important advantages over a 'Bundle' Dualism. The enduring spiritual substance provides the principle of unity between mental states for which the 'Bundle' Dualist searches in vain. Still more importantly, the spiritual substance provides the necessary background to mental states, which by themselves are incapable of independent existence. As grins stand to faces, or soporific virtues stand to physical substances, so mental states can stand to spiritual substances.

Nevertheless, there is something curiously formal and empty about the Cartesian solution. What is this spiritual substance which has these mental affections? One seems able to say nothing positive about it except that it has the mental affections. One can say negative things about it, that it lacks spatial properties, for instance, but its positive nature remains a mystery. By contrast, we can easily describe faces apart from their grins, or physical substances apart from their soporific virtues. Spiritual substance looks like something invented to be the solution of Dualist problems.

This emptiness of the Cartesian hypothesis is brought out in an interesting way in a dispute between Descartes and Locke. (I am indebted to C. B. Martin for pointing this out to me.) Descartes seems to be half-aware of the fact that, apart from the mental experiences, there is no way of characterizing the spiritual substance. It seems in part to be this that makes him say that 'thought' (by which he means any sort of mental happening) is the essence of the soul. His problem is not really solved then, but at least it is concealed. For now the spiritual substance is never *completely* indescribable, for we can always point to the 'thought' that the soul is having. Unfortunately, however, it follows from this view that we are 'thinking' at every moment of our existence. This revolted the common sense of Locke. Surely there is nothing going on in our minds at all when we are sleeping dreamlessly?

'Thus, methinks, every drowsy nod shakes this doctrine, who teach that the soul is always thinking' (*Essay*, Bk. II, Ch. 1, p. 13). But like Descartes, Locke is also a Cartesian Dualist, and he never faces up to the problem of what properties the soul has when there is no thought going on. It seems that he would have found it impossible to say.

Cartesian Dualism, then, may have formal advantages over 'Bundle' Dualism, but it is a doctrine of a very empty sort. We may now go on to consider difficulties that arise for *any* Dualist theory of mind, whether a Cartesian or a 'Bundle' theory.

III. DIFFICULTIES FOR ANY DUALIST THEORY

(a) *Can a Dualist account for the unity of mind and body?*

In his book *Individuals* P. F. Strawson has emphasized how natural it is to ascribe mental and physical properties to the same subject. We say 'I am thinking' and 'I am angry', but we also say 'I am lying down' and 'I am twelve stone' and seem to have no consciousness of using the word 'I' in two different senses. ('I was lying down thinking.') Yet if a Dualist account of mind and body is correct, then in the first two cases the word 'I' refers to a spiritual substance or to a collection of non-physical items, while in the second set of cases the word refers to a certain physical object.

I do not think that this argument is very strong as it stands. The Dualist can very well reply that, in ordinary speech, personal pronouns such as 'I' refer to a *compound* object 'spiritual object (or objects) related in a certain way to a certain physical object.' Consider the case of a motor-car. For certain purposes we might regard a car as a compound of two substances, the engine and the chassis. Now we say 'The *car* is back-firing' although we could speak more strictly and say 'The *engine* of the car is back-firing'. Again, we say 'The *car* is squeaking and rattling' although we could speak more strictly and say 'The *chassis* of the car is squeaking and rattling'. In the same way, the Dualist might urge, to say 'I am angry' could be put in a stricter way as 'The spiritual part of me is angry', while 'I am lying down' could be put in a stricter way as 'The physical part of me is lying down'. As the example of the car shows, we can attribute to wholes properties which are, strictly speaking, only properties of proper parts of the whole.

Such a line of defence would be greatly strengthened if Dualism were combined with Behaviourism. If the concept of mind involved *both* a spiritual substance (or spiritual events) and certain sorts of bodily behaviour, then it would be easy to see why ordinary speech makes no sharp distinction between a spiritual subject and a material subject, but instead attributes both mental and physical characteristics to the same subject: the person.

Nevertheless, there is an underlying point to this objection to Dualism which is not so easy to deal with. The difficulty is this: does a Dualist theory provide for a sufficiently close connection between the spiritual and the physical components of man? We ordinarily think of the connection between the mind and the body as very close indeed. Man is a unity. Dualism is unsatisfactory because it breaks up that unity.

To develop this point. We could solve the problem by postulating, or claiming to observe, a unique and indefinable relation that holds together the spiritual and physical components of man. But if we disdain to resort to this manoeuvre, there remain only the relations of *temporal simultaneity* and *causal relationship* to tie the spiritual object or objects to the body. It is not easy to see clearly that these are the only known relations we can appeal to, because the imagination is tempted, quite illegitimately from the Dualist standpoint, to add a further relation. It is very natural to think of the mind as actually situated inside the body: as an inner realm. But this is to put the mind into physical space, and the essential point about Dualism is its denial that the mind is a spatial thing. And once we are rid of this picture of the mind as literally inside the body, there are only the relations of temporal simultaneity and causal connection to bind the mind and the body together.

In the *Sixth Meditation*, Descartes denies that his mind is in his body simply as a pilot is in his vessel. He says that the relationship of mind and body is much closer than this. The remark is a tribute to Descartes' philosophical honesty, but it is difficult to reconcile with his Dualism. For the pilot is not only causally related to his vessel, acting on it and being acted on by it, but he is also spatially inside the vessel. But without resort to completely *ad hoc* postulation of some further relation, a Dualist can only appeal to the causal relations of mind and body. So a *Dualist* ought to say that the relation of mind to body is in some ways more distant than that of pilot to vessel.

It might be suggested that the Dualist can provide a closer relationship in the following way. It is characteristic of our sensory field, in particular of our visual field, that *we* are in the centre of it. We perceive things as nearer or further from *ourselves*. Now our body is also perceived to be in the centre of our sensory field. So, in some sense, it seems that we are located in the same place as our body.

But what is the 'I' that is where my body is? I do not think it is anything more than *the body itself* as given to sense-perception. We perceive things as nearer or further from our body: it is our body that is the centre of our sensory field. So as far as this point goes, all that a Dualist can say by way of linking the mind and the body more closely is that the body is a central object in our perceptual field, the central material object on which our attention is directed. The relationship between mind and body remains a remarkably distant one, and the Dualist cannot explain why we think the two are so closely connected.

The existence of bodily sensations may also be thought to point to a specially intimate relationship between a particular mind and a particular body. For bodily sensations (such as pains and itches) seem to have the two following characteristics. In the first place they are mind-dependent: there could not be a pain or itch without a mind to have it. In the second place, however, they have a bodily location: in the hand or behind the ear. So here mind and body seem to be commingled.

But does this apparent combination of mental being and physical location really assist the *Dualist's* case? It might show that there was a close link between mind and body, but to the extent that it did this, it would show that Dualism was false. For Dualism cannot locate the mind, or any part of the mind, in the body.

It is true, as has already been said, that the Dualist can claim that there is a special and unique relation, with which we are all acquainted, but which is quite distinct from causal connection, that binds together spiritual and bodily objects. And it should be emphasized that there is no logical difficulty in solving the problem in this way. But it can hardly be said to be a *plausible* solution.

Dualism

(b) How do we numerically differentiate spiritual objects?

Another serious difficulty for any Dualist theory of mind is the question whether it can provide for the numerical difference of spiritual objects. If we consider two physical objects that exist at the same time, we can say that what makes them two, that is to say makes them numerically different, is that they are in different places. However alike they may be, their difference of place makes them distinct from each other. Difference of place *individuates* them. If they are in exactly the same place at the same time, they are not two objects but only one.

But now let us consider the possibility that there are two spiritual substances, or collections of spiritual items, which are exactly the same in nature at a certain time. What makes two such objects, or sets of objects, *two*? We cannot appeal to their spatial separation because, by hypothesis, they are not in space.

It might be replied that they can be differentiated by differences in their past history. But this reply is insufficient. For, *firstly*, it is a meaningful possibility that two spiritual substances, or collections of spiritual items, should exist like two perfectly synchronized clocks, having exactly the same past spiritual history. *Secondly*, even in a case where this is not so and the spiritual histories are identical in character for a limited time, what differentiates the objects during that time? What difference is there between the case where we have two different spiritual substances, or collections of spiritual items, and the case where the two substances, or sets of items, 'coalesce' temporarily?

It might be thought that two such spiritual substances, or collections of spiritual items, can be differentiated from each other in the following way. One is connected to *this* body, while the other is connected to *that* body. For, unlike the two spiritual substances or collections of spiritual items, however much the bodies resemble they are nevertheless made different by being in different places.

But suppose the spiritual substance, or collection of spiritual items, were disembodied? The Dualist would have to admit that this was a meaningful possibility on pain of making nonsense of his Dualism, even if he thought that such disembodied entities should not be called 'minds'. What would make the two different then? And even if the spiritual substance or collections of spiritual items, were not disembodied, reference to the bodies would not really help. For might there not be just *one* spiritual substance or collection of spiritual items, identically related to the *two* bodies? How would the Dualist differentiate between this case, and the case where *two* spiritual substances or collections of spiritual items, were identical in nature and each related to their own body?

The problem just considered is that of the individuation of spiritual objects that exist at the same time. In what does their difference consist? There is a parallel problem about the identity of one spiritual object or collection of objects over a stretch of time. What makes a spiritual object that exists now the very same one as a spiritual object that existed in the past? Resemblance cannot be the mark of identity, because there might be two or more spiritual objects identical in character and history. In the case of ordinary physical objects we can appeal to *spatio-temporal* continuity. My body is spatio-temporally continuous with my body yesterday, but not with my twin's body. This spatio-temporal continuity is what makes it one body. But in the case of the spiritual objects postulated by the Dualist, there can be no question of any spatial continuity. So what is the principle of continuity for spiritual objects?

It is interesting to notice that these problems troubled St. Thomas Aquinas. The problem came up for him in connection with angels. Angels are disembodied intelligences, and therefore raise the question what makes them numerically different from each other. Aquinas' solution was to say that each angel was of a separate species, a different *sort* of object from any other angel. Among angels, difference of number is simply difference of kind. (See *Summa Theologica*, Pt. 1, Q. 50, Art. 4.) But Aquinas' resolution of the difficulty is clearly a makeshift. Why should not God create two identical angels? It is surely an intelligible possibility. And what would differentiate the two then?

As usual, the argument might be met by postulation. One could postulate a 'principle of individuation' of a non-spatial nature to ensure the numerical difference of spiritual objects. And, indeed, I think that the existence of such a principle of distinction is an intelligible conception. This last point has been denied by some modern philosophers. They seem to maintain that if we suppose two distinct objects that exist at the same time, then the only meaning we can give to this supposition is that the objects are in different places. If we accepted what they say, then it would seem to be a logically necessary truth that objects that are in time are also in space. But if this is so, a logically necessary truth seems to be giving us positive information about the nature of the world, viz. that whatever is temporal is also spatio-temporal. Now I do not believe that mere logic is capable of providing this information. I believe that it is a *fact* about the world that every object that is in time is also in space (indeed, I believe that it is a fact about the world that every object there is is in space and time), but I cannot think that this is a matter of logical necessity. We cannot rule out the existence of a non-spatial or even a non-temporal 'principle of individuation' *a priori*.

Nevertheless, it does seem likely that the only 'principle of individuation' with which we have any *concrete acquaintance* is that of being in different times and places. The inability of the Dualist to say anything at all about his spiritual 'principle of individuation' strongly suggests that the only way he can understand his notion is a negative way: as 'a non-spatial principle of individuation'. It seems that he is not in fact acquainted with such a principle, nor is there any reason to postulate it.

The position taken here is very similar to Immanuel Kant's view in the *Critique of Pure Reason*. For reasons that need not be discussed here, Kant speaks of space and time as the 'forms of intuition'. He recognizes, also, that it is space and time which secure the numerical difference of distinct objects. (See, *e.g. Critique*, A263/264 = B319/320.) But although space and time are the *human* forms of intuition, Kant thinks it is perfectly possible that there might be other forms of intuition, although we have no concrete acquaintance with any. (See, *e.g. Critique*, B72.) Presumably, then, he would have said that, if such other forms of intuition existed, they would differentiate objects one from the other just as space and time do.

(c) *Is the Dualist account of the origin of the mind a plausible one?*

Let us now consider whether Dualism is a plausible theory in the light of modern scientific knowledge, in particular, in the light of knowledge or plausible guesses about the working of the brain.

We may begin by considering the question of exactly when the mind emerges in the growth of men and animals.

It seems that the Dualist must conceive of the emergence of mind in the following way. At some time after conception, when the nervous system of man and the higher animals reaches a certain level of physiological complexity, a completely new, non-spatial entity is brought into existence in a certain completely new sort of relation to the body. The emergence of this new existent could not have been predicted from laws that deal with the physical properties of physical things.

Already the account is highly implausible from the scientific point of view. It is not a particularly difficult notion that, when the nervous system reaches a certain level of complexity, it should develop new properties. Nor would there be anything particularly difficult in the notion that when the nervous system reaches a certain level of complexity it should affect something that was already in existence in a new way. But it is a quite different matter to hold that the nervous system should have the power to create something else, of a quite different nature from itself, and create it out of no materials. Admittedly, there is no contradiction in the notion that the nervous system should have these powers, but what we know of the workings of the world makes the hypothesis a very unlikely one.

The need for the creation of a spiritual object or objects by the nervous system would be ruled out if we assumed that the mind existed before it was embodied, and was simply brought into a special relation to the body at a certain level of physiological development. But, of course, this removes one scientific implausibility only to create another. There is very little evidence for believing that the mind pre-exists its body.

But whether we assume that, at a certain point, the body creates the spiritual object or objects, or whether mind and body are simply brought together at this point, there is a further difficulty for the Dualist to surmount. At what point in the development of the organism shall we say that such a momentous event occurs? The difficulty is that there seems to be nothing in the physiological development of the organism to suggest any point of sharp break. Instead we have a gradual growth from complexity to further complexity, and there is no point of which we can say 'There is such a sharp physiological change here, that this is probably the point at which the body acquires a mind'. Organisms develop by insensible gradations, and so it is natural to say the mind develops in the same way. But because the Dualist sets up so sharp a gap between the material and the mental, he must find a definite point when the mental comes into existence.

The problem we are discussing here is closely connected with one that used to be discussed (perhaps still is?) by theologians: 'When does the infant acquire a soul?' This question may appear academic or scholastic in the worst sense, but it is one that those who believe in the soul as something distinct from the body have to consider. Equally, the Dualist has to consider the question when his spiritual object or objects come into existence. To treat the question as frivolous, while still holding to a Dualist theory of mind and body, would itself be intellectual frivolity.

(d) *Do mind and body interact?*

We may now consider the dispute between the Interactionist and the Parallelist forms of Dualism, the dispute between what we called the 'thermostat' and the 'thermometer' models of the relations between mind and body.

The first thing to be said is that the Interactionist view is the natural one, and only most compelling reasons should drive anybody to accept a Parallelist account. For consider the following sequence. I am struck on the hand, I feel pain, I wring my hand. It is completely natural, and surely correct, to say that the blow *causes* me to feel pain, and the pain in turn *causes* me to wring my hand. It appears obvious that, in a case like this, body and mind interact. A bodily event causes a mental event which causes a further bodily event. There are, however, difficulties for the Dualist in accepting the interaction of body and mind.

Before considering these difficulties, however, we must be quite clear that there is no *logical* difficulty in the notion that non-physical events may cause physical events, or vice-versa. It is a purely *empirical* question, to be decided by experience, what is capable of acting on what. As Hume says, discussing this very point:

> ... to consider the matter *a priori*, any thing may produce any thing ... (*Treatise*, Vol. I, Pt. IV, Sect. 5, p. 247, ed. Selby-Bigge)

(Acceptance of Hume's negative point here, by the way, does not require acceptance of his notorious positive analysis of the causal relationship in terms of constant conjunction. The word 'anything', of course, must not be understood to mean 'absolutely anything'. The number 4, for instance, cannot be a cause. It must mean 'anything of the sort that it is intelligible to speak of as a cause'—for instance, an event.) If the mind is a spiritual substance, or collection of spiritual items, there is no contradiction in supposing that it acts on the body or is acted on by the body. But, as we shall now see, there are weighty *empirical* reasons which make a Dualist theory of interaction difficult to sustain.

The difficulties arise when we try to think out an Interactionist theory in a concrete way. It seems that the mind will have to act on the body by acting on the *brain*. Now, to a physiologist, the brain is an enormously complex and highly organized material system to which physical stimuli of various sorts are applied, and which in turn has certain physical effects on the rest of the body. Inside the brain one physical event is followed by, and is the cause of, another physical event. If the Dualist is to be an Interactionist two conditions must be satisfied. In the first place, there must be last physical events in the brain which are followed by, and are the causes of, mental events. (Fulfilment of just this condition does not mark off Interactionism from Parallelism.) In the second place, there must be last mental events which are followed by, and are the causes of, events in the brain.

Let us now consider the situation where a physical stimulus of some sort, say the sounds of a human voice, brings about certain mental events, say perceptions and thoughts, which then issue in further physical action. On the 'way up' there must be a last physical event in the brain before the mental events ensue. The mental events must then bring about a first physical event in the brain on the 'way down'. So this second event will have to be an event that is not solely determined by the previous physical state of the brain and physical environment. This means that there will be, as it were, a 'gap' between the state of the brain before the mental event has had its effect and the state of the brain after the mental event has had its effect. The transition between the two states will not take place solely as a result of the physical workings of the brain and physical environment.

Now, with the gradual advance of knowledge of the operation

Dualism

of the brain and nervous system, physiologists are becoming increasingly unwilling to think that there is any such gap.

If the mind acts on the brain, there must be one or more *points d'appui* in the brain where the first physical effects of mental events occur. Descartes, both Dualist and Interactionist, saw that he must look for such a place and thought that he had found it in the pineal gland. He was taking his own Interactionism seriously, to his eternal intellectual credit. But later research has not backed him up about the pineal gland, nor has any other plausible candidate been found for the point or points in the brain where the first physical effects of the mental appear. This suggests that the spiritual component of man cannot act on the material one, which explains why so many Dualists have not accepted Interactionism and have turned reluctantly to Parallelism.

One modern neurophysiologist, Sir John Eccles, has accepted a Dualist Interactionism. (See his *The Neurophysiological Basis of Mind*, Clarendon Press, 1953, Ch. 8, 'The Mind–Brain problem'.) But beyond making the suggestion that, if the mind could affect the pattern of discharge of relatively few neurones in a systematic manner, it could quite easily produce quite large alterations in the total patterns of stimulation in the brain, he does nothing in the way of producing a worked-out theory of how interaction occurs. Nevertheless, his idea that discharges might occur in neurones that could not be predicted by any physical laws, but which, occurring systematically, would bring about relatively big alterations in the state of the brain, is scientifically testable, at least in theory. But most neurophysiologists, I imagine, would be astounded to find any such non-physical interference in the workings of the brain. A puzzling feature of Eccles' view is that he says it demands a 'spatio-temporal patterning of the mind'. Apparently he regards the mind as both non-physical, yet somehow in space.

On the Parallelist view, instead of the spiritual affecting the physical, events in the brain and events in the soul are *correlated* with each other, running in double-harness with each other, or, in the language of logicians, in one-to-one correlation. Whenever there are events in the brain of a certain sort, spiritual events are brought into being 'beside' the brain-events, but do not modify them. On this Parallelist view, a complete science treating of the relation of the brain to the mind would consist of a huge 'dictionary', allowing us to pass from the current existence of a certain state in the brain to a certain state of mind, and *vice-versa*. But the dictionary would be a dictionary of contingent truths, for it would be experience that had taught us what the correlations were.

But, of course, Parallelism escapes the arguments (or perhaps we should say, more modestly, the intuitions) of modern physiology only to fall foul of ordinary experience. If we consider the sequence (i) a blow on the hand; (ii) a pain in the hand; (iii) wringing of the hand; it seems impossible to deny that, not only is the first event the cause of the second event, but also that the second event is the cause of the third event. If this is not a causal sequence, what is? Yet the Parallelist must, quite implausibly, deny that the pain makes me (causes me to) wring my hand.

It may be objected, however, that the Parallelist can provide for the interaction of mind and body in the following way. When my hand is struck, I feel distress. Equally, when my hand is struck, certain processes occur in my brain. Whenever these processes occur, I feel distress; and whenever I feel distress, these processes occur. The next thing that happens is that I wring my hand, and the physiologist would say that the wringing was caused by the processes in the brain. But, the Parallelist may say, is it not equally correct to say that the wringing was caused by my distress? In order to assert that this was not so, we would have to find a case where the same sort of brain-process occurs, the felt distress does not, but I still wring my hand. But, on the Parallelist hypothesis, we never get such a case. Whenever we have that sort of brain-process, we feel distress.

The objection to this ingenious rejoinder is that, granted there is no 'gap' in the chain of physical causation in the brain (and it is the accepting of this consequence that leads to the unwilling acceptance of Parallelism), then we can in theory deduce the wringing of the hand given no more than the physical state of the brain, the body, the environment and the physical laws by which they operate. This implies that the existence of the spiritual object, and the correlation between brain-processes and spiritual states, has no effect on the way the physical world operates. And to assert this is to deny that mind acts on body.

There is, however, one other line that a Parallelist can take.

He can argue that mind and body do seem to interact, but that this interaction is an illusion, an illusion brought about by the observed fact that wringing the hand in a certain way is regularly preceded by having a sensation of pain. The sequence is mistaken for a causal sequence, a mistake that is discovered as a result of modern neurophysiological knowledge. Ordinary speech ('the pain made me wring my hand') bears witness to the time before the mistake had been discovered.

This is a possible line of defence. But it must be realized how very extensive the 'error' turns out to be. We are constantly speaking, in all sorts of contexts, of mental events giving rise to bodily happenings ('An idea crossed my mind, *so* I said . . .'). If other evidence is sufficiently pressing, we may have to write off all these ways of expressing ourselves as embodying a mistake. But a theory that would allow for the interaction of mind and body would be preferable.

Before leaving this discussion of Interactionism and Parallelism, a further objection to Parallelism may be mentioned briefly. Everything in the physical world interacts with its environment. No material thing is purely passive: it is acted on, but it also acts. The Parallelist is maintaining that the spiritual component of man is different in this respect. Unlike everything else in the universe, the spirit is powerless. We should certainly hesitate to believe that this exception occurs.

So a Dualist Interactionism cannot be squared with physiology and a Dualist Parallelism is incompatible with ordinary experience. Yet a Dualist must either be an Interactionist or Parallelist.

There seem, then, to be serious objections to any form of Dualism. Nevertheless, there is an important distinction to be made between 'Bundle' and Cartesian Dualism. It was argued that 'Bundle' Dualism is not merely implausible, but that it is logically incoherent. For the 'objects' out of which it seeks to build the mind have not got the capacity for independent existence which the theory requires. In this respect, they are like grins or soporific powers. There must be something, with further characteristics of its own, that has the grin or the power to cause sleep. In the same way, there must be something, with further characteristics of its own, that has a perception or a sensation. But this contradicts 'Bundle' Dualism. Now there is no such logical incoherence in

Cartesian Dualism. If the Cartesian is prepared to postulate, or claim to observe, a spiritual substance; if he is prepared to postulate, or claim to observe, a unique relationship that ties particular spiritual substances to particular bodies; if he is prepared to postulate, or claim to observe, a principle of numerical differentiation to secure the numerical difference of spiritual substances; if he is prepared to accept the scientific implausibilities involved in the hypothesis of the emergence of spiritual substance; and if he is prepared to accept either the scientific implausibilities involved in Interactionism, or the conflict with ordinary experience involved in Parallelism; then no actual contradiction can be shown in his position. But if we could find an account of the mind that avoids such awkward consequences, it would be preferable.

Our discussion has not merely uncovered difficulties for Dualism, but has the following positive value. It has shown us that a completely satisfactory theory of mind should meet a number of demands. (i) It should allow for the logical possibility of the disembodied existence of a mind. (ii) It should treat mental happenings as things incapable of independent existence. (iii) It should account for the unity of mind and body. (iv) It should provide a principle of numerical difference for minds. (v) It should not be scientifically implausible. (vi) It should allow for the causal interaction of mind and body. Here we have some useful touchstones with which to test the worth of different theories of mind.

3

THE ATTRIBUTE THEORY

WE have now to examine those theories of mind which reject both Dualism and pure Materialism. A pure Materialist allows man nothing but physical, chemical and biological properties which, in all probability, he regards as reducible to physical properties only. But Attribute ('Double-Aspect') theories of mind hold that man, although a single substance, has other, non-material, properties which cannot be reduced to material ones. It is possession of these extra properties that allows us to say that man has a mind. (As will emerge, we should not say that these properties *are* the mind.)

As has already been pointed out, an Attribute theory can be combined with Behaviourism. For it might be held that our mental concepts *straddle* these special properties, on the one hand, and our behaviour or dispositions to behave, on the other. That is to say, it might be held that to have a mind a man must both possess these special properties and behave, or be disposed to behave, in a certain way. As has also been remarked, P. F. Strawson's theory of mind *may* be an Attribute theory combined with Behaviourism.

Some Attribute theories take the single substance that constitutes a man to be a material thing—the body—which is then endowed with these further special properties. But Strawson says that we should take as fundamental the notion of a *person*, and that we should attribute both material and mental properties to the person. It is the person that has the material property of being six feet tall, or the mental property of being slow-thinking.

However, if Strawson's theory really is an Attribute theory, I think that this apparent disagreement whether it is a material thing or a person that has the mental properties turns out to be nothing but a verbal dispute. The reason for this is that we determine what sort of a substance a thing is by what sort of properties it has. And, since any thing will have many, perhaps even infinitely many, different properties, the sort of substance we say it is will depend upon the properties that we consider especially important, or that we have a special interest in. (*Pace* Aristotle.) What properties these are will differ from person to person, and even for the same person at different times. What sort of a thing is arsenic? Is it primarily a poison, or a chemical? It depends on whether we are concerned with murder or chemistry. In the same way, if living human beings are substances having both material and non-material properties, it seems to be a verbal matter whether we say that a man is a material object having certain additional non-material properties, or whether we think that the possession of such extra properties should make us stop talking about material objects and start speaking of persons instead. Are we especially interested in the resemblance between men and ordinary material objects? Then we call a man a material object, even if one having special properties. Or are we concerned with the differences between men and ordinary material objects? Then we treat men as a separate sort of object, and talk about persons or human beings. But the two ways of talking are not contradictory. For my own convenience, while we are discussing the Attribute theory I shall formulate the theory in the materialistic way: man is a material substance having certain extra, non-material, attributes.

One of the great difficulties for an Attribute theory is to understand just what is meant by non-material properties and how they are connected with the body. So let us begin by trying to clear up this point.

In the first place, should these special attributes be taken to be a special sort of relation that the body, or parts of the body, have to other things in the world, or should they be thought of as non-relational properties of the body? I shall present an argument to show that they cannot be thought of as such relations.

In the case of many mental states, it seems at first sight quite plausible to say that they are, or involve, a unique sort of relation to other things in the world. If I am looking at a tree, it seems very natural to say that my looking is, or involves, an unique irreducible relation holding between me and the tree. If I remember an event in my childhood, it may still seem plausible to say that there is an unique irreducible relation holding between myself at the present time and my childhood state. However, such a relation to the past seems more peculiar. Again, when I look forward to dinner one might say that this involves an unique irreducible relation holding between me now and the dinner to come, although once again the relation seems a peculiar one.

However, there is a most serious objection to this attempt to construe mental states as relations to things in the world. Suppose, as is perfectly imaginable, that I have exactly the same perceptual experience as I had when I looked at the tree, but suppose that this time there is no tree there. Or suppose that I have exactly the same memory-experiences, as I had when I remembered the event in my childhood, but no such event ever took place. Or suppose that I am in exactly the same mental state as when I anticipated dinner, but I never get any dinner. In all these cases, there is, by hypothesis, nothing in the world for me to be 'mentally related' to. So no unique, irreducible, relation can be involved. Yet, also by hypothesis, the mental state is no different from the mental state in the first set of cases. So no relation of ourselves to things in the world is ever involved. It is true, of course, that we do not normally use the *words* 'perceive' and 'remember' unless what is perceived or remembered really exists or existed. But this only means that the notions of perceiving or remembering involve something more than a reference to mental states, viz. the fact that something in the world or in the past corresponds to these states.

This argument does not strictly disprove the view that mental states essentially involve unique and irreducible relations to objects lying outside the body. But once such things as 'what is perceived' and 'what is remembered' are rejected as the other term of these relations it is hard to find plausible substitutes.

Realist philosophers like Samuel Alexander tried to deal with the problem in the following way. They argued that in the case, say, of a false memory, although the situation remembered had no real existence, nevertheless the *constituents* of the situation did have a real existence. The event in my childhood never occurred, but I did have a childhood and the event, or the constituent parts of the event, did occur—perhaps in somebody else's childhood. My false memory is therefore a relation holding between myself and these scattered constituents.

But this account of memory as a many-termed relation to the memory-constituents faces incredible problems. How can my current relation to a past A and a B be a belief that A *was* B? Nothing in the relational situation seems to correspond to this copulation. Another difficulty is that B, at least, may be simply a property, such as a colour. What are we to make of a relation that relates a particular mind to a universal in this way?

It seems, then, that the Attribute theory must say that mental states are some sort of *non-relational* property of the body. Perhaps mental states involve relations, but if they do they will not be relations to anything lying beyond the body of which they are attributes. (The fact that my head is above my trunk is a relation of one part of my body to another part. But it is not a relational property of my body, because it is not a relation my body has to *something else*. Equally, mental attributes could involve relations without being relational properties of the body.)

But before we turn to consider the view that mental states are non-relational properties of bodies, it must be noted that here we have stumbled upon a very important property of mental states. What it is easy to think of as a relation of the mental state to something in the world is, in fact, what has been called the *intentionality* of such states. This word was used by the Scholastic philosophers, and again by the Austrian philosopher Franz Brentano at the turn of the century, to express the peculiar 'pointing' character of mental states. In the present day, J. N. Findlay in England, and R. M. Chisholm in the U.S.A., have followed Brentano here. (See Findlay, *Values and Intentions*, Allen & Unwin, 1961, Ch. 1, Pt. III; and Chisholm, *Perceiving*, Cornell, 1957, Ch. 11.) Some, perhaps all, mental states 'point' beyond themselves. The visual experience of a tree 'points' to a tree. The intention to have a dinner 'points' to the dinner. The thought of Vienna 'points' to Vienna. The thought of a unicorn 'points' to a unicorn. But, although I have used the graphic word 'pointing', the relation involved cannot be construed as a relation between the person in that mental state, and some object in the world. For, as we saw above, there may be no such object. As Brentano said, I can hang a man only if he exists, but I can think of him even if he does not. This is a quite special characteristic of mental states which is not possessed by ordinary physical states or by physical objects. A knife does not 'point' to cutting, although it may suggest cutting to somebody, and the word 'knife' may be a word applied only to things that cut.

The term 'intentionality' is somewhat unhappy. It suggests a special link between intentionality and intentions which does not exist. Intentions do have intentionality, for they 'point' to what is intended. But they are not distinguished herein from other mental states. An alternative term is 'intensionality'. But this may lead to confusion with the (not unconnected) logician's notion of intension. Despite disadvantages, it seems better to stick to the commoner usage.

Now any theory of the mind must be able to give some account or analysis of the intentionality of mental states, or else it must accept it as an ultimate, irreducible, feature of the mental. Brentano takes the second course, and he is followed in this by Findlay and Chisholm. What is more, Brentano thinks that intionality is the *mark* of the mental. For not only is intentionality peculiar to mental states, but, according to Brentano, every mental state possesses intentionality. (See 'The Distinction between Mental and Physical Phenomena', translated by D. B. Terrell, in the collection edited by R. M. Chisholm: *Realism and the Background of Phenomenology*, Glencoe Free Press, 1960.) It is clear that no physicalist can accept the irreducibility of intentionality, although he could accept Brentano's view that intentionality is the mark of the mental.

The notion of intentionality, incidentally, enables a defender of the Attribute theory to make clear what he means by a nonphysical property of the physical body. If the intentionality of mental states is irreducible then mental states clearly have a special status. The Attribute theory can mark this special status by speaking of mental states as non-material states of the material body.

In terms of our present purposes, however, we have been digressing. At present we are concerned only with the point that the mental attributes postulated by the Attribute theory cannot be relations between the body and other things in the world. The next question that arises is whether these mental properties are properties of the body as a whole, or whether they are simply properties of some part, and, if so, which part? This question may seem to be rather a peculiar one, but I think it is one that a supporter of the Attribute theory has got to answer. For if he says that the properties are neither properties of the whole body nor of some proper part, his position seems to have become indistinguishable from Dualism. For it has simply become a matter of the mental states being somehow related to the body, although distinct from the body.

The answer that a defender of the Attribute theory must give seems pretty clear. The mental properties will have to be, as a matter of contingent fact, properties of the brain, or the central nervous system. The reason for this is simply that we find by scientific investigation that no other part of the body is connected with the operation of the mind in such an intimate way. If we lack a heart or lungs we soon lack a mind, but this is only because heart and lungs supply the brain with blood and oxygen. If the brain could be given these supplies by other means our mind would continue to exist. And so with all the rest of the body, except the central nervous system. So it seems that an Attribute theory must say that, as a matter of empirical fact, it is only the central nervous system that has the mental properties. (If 'the mind is the form of the body' is interpreted as a version of the Attribute theory, then, in the light of modern physiological knowledge, it must now be amended to 'the mind is the form of the central nervous system'.)

Can we say anything further about the nature of the mental properties postulated by the Attribute theory? If we consider properties of physical objects like temperature or sweetness then questions whether the object has that property *all over* or not are always appropriate. Is the lump of metal hot all over? Is the apple sweet all through? Whatever the answers may be, these questions are intelligible. But there are other properties where this question is inappropriate. If an object is spherical, we cannot ask whether it is spherical all over. The question is meaningless. Again, if it weighs two pounds, then we cannot ask if it weighs two pounds all over. Now, if mental states are special non-physical properties of the central nervous system, are they properties of the first or the second sort?

Once the question is posed, I do not think that there can be much doubt of the answer. If thinking a certain thought is a matter of a certain property belonging to a portion of our body (as a matter of empirical fact, part of the central nervous system), then the question 'Does this portion of the body have this property all over or not?' seems absurd. A complex thought may perhaps be divided into simpler thoughts, but we quickly reach thoughts that cannot be further sub-divided into thoughts. If thinking this thought is a property of a part of the central nervous system then how can a part of this part have the mental property? A part of a thought, if the notion is intelligible at all, is not a thought. It seems that the mental properties would not permit the question 'All over or not?'

So it seems that the Attribute theory must conceive of its mental properties in the following way. They are non-relational properties of the body or portions of the body, and properties of the sort of which it makes no sense to ask 'Does the body or portion of the body of which they are predicated have these properties all over or not? And it seems that, as a matter of contingent fact, these properties are properties of the central nervous system.

At the end of our discussion of Dualism we drew up a number of demands that any satisfactory theory of mind should be able to meet. Having now gained a somewhat clearer view of the nature of the Attribute theory, let us see whether it can meet these demands. Let us consider first the demands that give the theory no particular trouble.

(i) We saw from our discussion of 'Bundle' Dualism that we must treat mental states not as substances, but as things incapable of independent existence.

There seems to be no particular difficulty for an Attribute theory here. The theory could happily admit that the notion of an object which had the mental properties and no others was an impossible one. The demand for a wider context for the mental properties is met by pointing out that the mental properties are properties of a physical object: the body.

(ii) We said that any theory of mind and body must account for their *unity*. It must account for the ease with which we pass between 'I am thinking of Vienna' and 'I am sitting in this chair': the close relationship that we think holds between the mental and material components of man.

By making mental states attributes of the body this problem is solved very simply.

(iii) We saw that Dualist theories find difficulty in discovering a principle of numerical differentiation that differentiates two minds that exist at the same time. Difference in the nature of their mental states will not suffice, because we can easily conceive of minds having exactly the same sort of experiences at the same time. And the Dualist cannot appeal to difference of place because, for him, minds are not in space.

But if mental states are attributes of the body the problem is simply solved. However alike mental states, and the bodies of which they are attributes, may be, they are distinguished by being in different places.

(iv) Our preliminary discussion of the Attribute theory unearthed a further demand that we must make of any theory of mind: that it explain the *intentionality* of mental states. Here, at least, the theory seems to be in no worse position than other theories of mind. In particular, it seems in no worse (although no better) position than Dualism.

But there remain some serious problems for the Attribute theory.

(i) In the first place, we agreed that any theory of mind ought to provide for the *logical* possibility of disembodied existence. But the Attribute theory appears to make disembodied existence logically impossible. We have seen that instances of mental states considered in abstraction from anything else are incapable of independent existence. And if the non-physical properties of man postulated by the Attribute theory are identified with mental states then there cannot be objects which have these properties, and these properties alone. So disembodied existence would become logically impossible if the Attribute theory is true. Yet it seems to be a meaningful conception.

This argument might just possibly be escaped in the following way. Suppose that a defender of the Attribute theory denied the identification between mental states and the non-material properties that he postulates. Supposing he says instead that mental states are simply *certain features* of the non-material properties (attributes of attributes, as it were). He could then maintain that, although instances of mental states considered in abstraction from anything else are incapable of independent existence, the non-material properties of the body from which the mental states are abstractions might be instantiated in objects that had no other properties. Consider a parallel case. Ordinary physical objects have both visual and tactual properties, they are, for instance, both coloured and solid. Now we can certainly imagine an object which is solid, and has other tactual properties, but is perfectly invisible. (The simplest thing to imagine is that it is perfectly transparent.) Equally, it seems conceivable that there should be objects which have all ordinary visual properties, but which have no tactual properties at all. Now, an Attribute theorist might say, in the same way we can imagine objects which lacked all ordinary material properties but did have the non-material properties that the Attribute theory attributes to a body that has a mind. The difficulty that instances of mental states are incapable of independent existence is then met by saying that mental states are mere incomplete aspects or attributes of these non-material properties.

Perhaps in this way the Attribute theory can provide for the logical possibility of a mind without a body. But, even if no other difficulties are raised, it is clear that a great price has been paid: the same sort of price that is paid by Cartesian Dualism. The spiritual substance of the Cartesian Dualist serves as a background for mental states. Mental states can then be conceived of as modifications of the spiritual substance. But the Cartesian Dualist is unable to give any concrete description of the spiritual substance except as 'that which has mental states'. This lays him under the strongest suspicion of postulation of a purely *ad hoc* sort. In the same way, if the Attribute theory makes its special properties something more than the experienced properties of mental states, it also lies under the same suspicion of manufacturing entities in an *ad hoc* manner in order to solve a difficulty for the Attribute theory.

(ii) We saw that any theory of mind must allow for the interaction of mind and body, and yet at the same time must be scientifically plausible. Can the Attribute theory meet this demand?

At first sight it seems that an Attribute theory will be forced to adopt something like a Parallelist theory of the relation of mind and body. For the Parallelist, there is a one-one correlation between current states of the brain and current states of the mind. If the brain is in a particular state, a corresponding mental state is automatically and invariably produced, just as a room at a certain temperature automatically produces a certain reading on a thermometer. But for the Interactionist there is no such one-one correlation between current states of the brain and states of the mind. Given a certain brain-state it does not follow automatically that the mind is then in a certain state. For the state of the mind depends not only upon the current state of the brain, but also upon what state of mind preceded the action of the brain. If the brain is in state x and the mind in state y this will bring about one result, but if the brain is in state x but the mind in a different state, z, that will bring about another.

Now if we think of mental states as a set of attributes of the brain it is very difficult to deny that the state of the mind is uniquely determined by the current state of the brain. For if it is not, then we will be faced with certain properties of the brain *varying independently of the current physical state of the brain*. This may be a conceivable possibility, but it is one that we would require an enormous amount of persuasion to accept. So it seems that an Attribute theory must embrace something very like a Parallelist theory, and in discussing Dualism we have already seen the affront to ordinary experience involved in Parallelism.

However, this is not the end of the matter. In order to see that it is not, we must realize that an upholder of the Attribute theory is entitled to maintain that, on his theory, as a matter of empirical fact, the mind is the brain. According to his theory of mind, the very same object that has the physical properties of being a brain also has the mental properties. This object can therefore be described as 'the mind' just as much as 'the brain'. So the Attribute theory can share with the Central-state theory the slogan 'The mind is the brain'. (The Central-state theory only differs from the Attribute theory in denying that the brain has any non-physical properties.) This at once puts a new complexion on the question whether a supporter of the Attribute theory can accept the interaction of mind and body. For there is no doubt that the body acts on the brain and the brain reacts back on the body. But if body and brain interact, and if an Attribute theory is entitled to say that the mind is the brain, then do not the body and the mind interact? So the Attribute theory can claim that it allows for the interaction of mind and body, while still allowing that the mental properties are uniquely determined by the current physical state of the brain.

However, I think that this reply is only valid if we take a certain view of the way the brain works. Suppose it were shown that the brain operated solely in accordance with those physical, chemical and biological laws that explain the workings of the rest of the body. Suppose, that is, that the special workings and powers of the brain were shown to be simply a result of the tremendous complexity of its physical structure, and not at all a result of radically new modes of operation. Surely we would be forced to say that the extra mental properties postulated by the Attribute theory are causally idle ('piggy-back properties', to use a phrase of Wilfred Sellars); and that the characteristically Parallelist thesis that the mental is unable to affect the physical order in any way is completely correct? The fact that the situation was one where properties were predicated of the brain instead of a situation where non-physical items were correlated with states of the brain would seem to be an irrelevant distinction.

This means that, if we are to have a form of the Attribute theory that is to allow a genuine interaction of mind and body, then it must claim that the portions of the brain which have these special mental properties are also distinguished by operating in a way that could not be predicted on the basis of the laws governing other, ordinary, matter. The emergence of new 'mental' properties in the brain must carry with it the emergence of new laws of physical working in the brain. Only thus could the Attribute theory save the specifically mental from a mere spectator-role.

This means that, in order to save the common sense view that what is specifically mental plays a causal role in the physical world, the Attribute theory will be forced to take a certain view of the scientific facts about the workings of the brain. But, as we saw in discussing the difficulties for a Dualist Interactionist, this view contradicts the findings, or at any rate the intuitions, of most modern neurophysiologists. For there is increasing evidence that the workings of the brain involve nothing more than the physical, chemical, and biological laws that govern the rest of organic matter. To be forced to oppose this view of the brain, or else to condemn the specifically mental properties to impotence, is the unhappy choice that the Attribute theory must make.

(iii) We saw that one of the difficulties for Dualism is that it must assign the coming into existence of the immaterial mind to a definite point of time in the development of the organism, although there seems to be no natural point at which such an entity could emerge. The same difficulty holds for the Attribute theory. At what point in the gradual growth of an organism do these new, non-material, properties of the substance appear? If intentionality is to be reckoned an irreducible feature of mental processes there is a great metaphysical gulf fixed between physical and mental properties. (And if intentionality is not an irreducible feature of the mental, what analysis of intentionality can the Attribute theory offer?) Yet on the physical side we seem to have no more than a gradual increase in physical complexity without a break at any point that might betoken the emergence of something new.

It must be admitted that this difficulty is less serious for the Attribute theory than for the Dualist. For in the case of the Attribute theory we have only the emergence of irreducibly new properties; while in the case of the Dualist theory we have the creation of a new sort of substance. But the problem is still a serious one even for at Attribute theory.

(iv) The final criticism to be brought against the Attribute theory is a very simple one. It is just that the notion of these unique properties of the brain is a mysterious one. We are to think of the central nervous system as somehow stippled over with a changing pattern of these special properties. They are properties of which it makes no sense to ask 'Does the portion of the brain that has the property have it all over or not?' They have, or are bound up with, intentionality. Just how do these properties attach to the brain? I, at any rate, can form no clear conception of such properties and their attachment.

It will be seen, then, that the Attribute theory is in a stronger position than any form of Dualism. It is not faced with many of the difficulties that beset the Dualist. Nevertheless, it is in difficulty on the question of disembodied existence, on the interaction of mind and body, and the emergence of the mental attributes in the development of the organism. And the theory itself is a somewhat mysterious and unclear one. If we had to choose between Dualism and an Attribute theory, it seems clear that we ought to choose the Attribute theory. But it would be preferable to have to choose neither.

4

A DIFFICULTY FOR ANY
NON-MATERIALIST THEORY
OF MIND

BEFORE leaving the Dualist and Attribute theories of mind I shall mention a difficulty which has recently been canvassed on a number of occasions by J. J. C. Smart. I can add nothing to what he has said, but the argument is too important to be ignored. We have already come near it, but only near it, when we discussed the difficulties facing an Interactionist theory.

It seems increasingly likely that biology is completely reducible to chemistry which is, in its turn, completely reducible to physics. That is to say, it seems increasingly likely that all chemical and biological happenings are explicable in principle as particular applications of the laws of physics that govern non-chemical and non-biological phenomena.

Consider what this means for a non-Materialist theory of the mind. It means that the whole world studied by science contains nothing but physical things operating according to the laws of physics *with the exception of the mind*. Only psychology is forced to recognize a new thing, or at any rate a new sort of property of things, in the world. Given the laws of physics alone, and the initial configuration of the things physics deals with, the future seems to be predictable in theory. (Of course, if the fundamental laws of physics are statistical only, as is sometimes claimed, then only a statistical prediction will be possible.) Mental happenings, and

49

mental happenings alone, would escape. They, and they alone, could not be predicted, even in principle, by physics.

This conclusion would hold, be it noted, even if there were the strictest *parallelism* between physical events in the brain and mental events. For even in this case a supreme physicist would need, besides his knowledge of physics, a physiological–psychological 'dictionary'. By means of this dictionary, having first worked out what the physical state of a particular subject's brain must be at a certain time, he could then say what the corresponding mental event in the subject's mind must be. But the 'dictionary' could never be compiled in the first place simply on the basis of a knowledge of *physics*.

Now is this a credible picture of the world? Until relatively recently, it did not seem scientifically likely that biology was completely reducible to chemistry, and chemistry completely reducible to physics. Under those circumstances, it was quite plausible to think that psychology dealt with quite new entities and quite new laws, which emerged when we had organisms of a sufficiently complex biological structure. But if all the sciences except psychology are, in theory, very complex particular cases of the fundamental science of physics, it seems very unlikely that psychology is an exception. It would follow that some Materialist theory of the mind is the true one.

Even this has not done full justice to the scientific implausibility of a non-Materialist account of the mind. Consider the nature of the connections that must be assumed to exist between the brain and the non-material mind. The processes that go on in the brain when I feel a pain in my hand are known to be incredibly complex. But, if we can trust to introspection, the pain itself is a relatively simple affair. Now the non-Materialist must postulate laws connecting these incredible physiological complexities with the relatively simple mental events. The existence of such laws fits in very ill with the rest of the structure of science.

These arguments are not *logically* compelling ones. There is nothing self-contradictory in saying that all other sciences are reducible to physics, but that psychology is not so reducible. Nor is there anything self-contradictory in connecting the complexities of brain-processes with the relative simplicities of mental events. It is only being argued that it is a very implausible hypothesis that there are irreducibly novel events associated with the operation of that enormously complex mechanism, the central nervous system, while no such 'emergent' entities are found anywhere else in the universe. We may baptize this argument the 'Argument from the supremacy of physics'.

There are various objections that may be made to this argument, and the rest of this chapter will be devoted to a brief consideration of them.

In the first place, some philosophers will be inclined to protest that it is impossible for a scientific argument of this sort to affect a point of philosophy. (This protest may also be made about some of the arguments advanced in the two previous chapters.) They argue in the following way. Philosophy is not concerned with things, but with our concepts of things. Now conceptual truths are true independently of any scientific discovery. Philosophical questions about the mind are therefore questions about the concept of mind, and scientific findings have no bearing on these questions.

Now it may be questioned whether this is the whole truth about philosophy, and, indeed, if the doctrine of mind to be put forward in this book is correct, philosophy is not solely conceptual analysis. But at present I will grant that philosophy is concerned solely with concepts because, even if this is true, I think the objection is still invalid. Here it is worth considering G. E. Moore's procedure in another context. Certain philosophers have advanced *a priori* arguments for disbelieving in the existence of the physical world, or of time. But, Moore pointed out, we are actually far more certain of the existence of the physical world and of time, than we are of the validity of these difficult philosophical arguments. He drew the conclusion that it would be rational to accept the existence of the physical world and of time, rather than the philosophical arguments, *even if we cannot see what is wrong with the arguments.*

The situation is similar here. It is obviously a very difficult philosophical question to determine the true analysis of the concept of mind. Certainty will be hard to obtain. In such circumstances we may well take scientific results and likelihoods to be as good *pointers* to the truth as any other consideration. We are quite right to let such considerations influence us, and influence us strongly, in the same way that we are right to let our belief in the existence of physical objects, or of change, outweigh *a priori* argumentation. So objections to non-Materialist theories of the mind drawn from empirical science not merely are, but ought to be, considerations that influence the philosophical intellect.

In the second place, however, a still more general objection to our procedure may be raised. Let it be granted that an argument like the 'Argument from the supremacy of physics' has some force. But where is its *special* force? In considering the philosophy of mind, why should we give special weight to the findings or intuitions of science? Why not pay at least as much heed to religious or moral or artistic or even philosophical intuitions? Is it not an act of arbitrary intellectual choice to give special weight to the scientific vision when we are seeking to give an account of the nature of man?

But there is in fact, however, a very simple reason for giving special weight to scientific considerations. Historically, scientific investigation has proved to be the only way that a *consensus* of opinion about disputed matters of theory has ever been achieved among those who have given the matters serious and intelligent attention. Only science has settled disputed questions. This is why the seventeenth century is a landmark in the intellectual history of the human race. From that time onwards there has been a steady growth of knowledge in fields where there was previously only wrangling speculation. And the reason for this is the application of scientific method to these fields. It follows that scientific considerations should be given a quite special weight in considering questions of theory which are still in dispute, such as the nature of mind.

It may be replied that the fields in which science can give us reliable knowledge are limited, so that in some fields we must of necessity trust to less reliable guides. This may be so, but I hardly think that it has been made out. In particular, it has not been made out for the question of the nature of mind. On the contrary, as I have tried to show in this chapter, following Smart, scientific considerations do point in a certain direction. Should not these considerations be given special weight?

In the third place, descending from these matters of high generality, it may be objected that there is one body of alleged scientific evidence, of a highly controversial nature, which may show that the realm of mind is not governed solely by the laws of physics: viz. psychical research. Although the whole question is very controversial, there is some scientific evidence for the existence of telepathy and perhaps evidence for other 'paranormal' powers of mind also. The existence of such powers would not necessarily contradict a purely materialist account of man: all that might be necessary would be the admission that this material object, man, had very special abilities. But there is difficulty for the view that this object is behaving solely in accordance with the laws of physics. For it is not at all easy to see how these special powers, if they do exist, could be reconciled with our present conceptions of physics.

I refer only briefly to this point here: in the final chapter a little more will be said. But the consideration of psychical research must introduce a note of caution into the use of the 'Argument from the supremacy of physics'. For it raises a real doubt whether physics is supreme.

In the fourth place, it may be objected that there is at least one group of properties that cannot be fitted into the structure of physics: the secondary qualities such as colour, sound, taste and smell. It does not matter for this objection whether the secondary qualities are conceived of as qualifying physical objects or mental items such as sense-impressions. All that is essential for this objection to maintain is that they are ultimate properties, irreducible to the properties of objects with which physics concerns itself. If this is granted, we will need extra correlation-laws to correlate these properties with such things as the wave-length of light, or a certain sort of neural electro-chemical discharge. It will then be much more plausible to maintain that the emergence of mind involves the emergence of special qualities or entities, correlated with the existence of physical states of the brain.

But the very scientific evidence appealed to in this chapter gives us reason to suspect that the secondary qualities are not in fact irreducible. In Chapter 12, therefore, it will be argued that there is nothing illogical in identifying them, as scientists often do identify them, with purely physical properties of physical objects and events. If this (obviously controversial) line of argument is successful, the fourth objection to the 'Argument from the supremacy of physics' fails.

5

BEHAVIOURISM

I. PRELIMINARY

IT has been argued that 'Bundle' Dualism is an incoherent theory, that Cartesian Dualism involves many implausibilities, and that the Attribute theory, although more satisfactory than Cartesian Dualism, still involves serious difficulties. We are now ready to consider purely physicalist accounts of the nature of mind. And first it is natural to turn to *Behaviourism*, and in particular the highly sophisticated form of Behaviourism which has emerged in recent philosophy, which may be called *Analytical* Behaviourism. According to this view we can give an account of all mental processes in terms of the physical behaviour and tendencies to behave of men's bodies.

To be completely precise, Behaviourism does not entail Materialism. For it is conceivable that a philosopher should give an account of the mind solely in terms of behaviour and dispositions to behave, yet think that the behaviour that betokens mind is so complex and sophisticated that it could not have a purely material *cause*. In practice, however, I suppose that no Behaviourist would take this line. One who reduces the mind to behaviour and tendencies to behave will in fact also hold that the brain is capable of bringing this behaviour about. He will therefore give a purely Materialist account of man.

Gilbert Ryle's book *The Concept of Mind* seems to be a defence of Analytical Behaviourism. I think the same is true of Wittgenstein's *Philosophical Investigations*, although this interpretation is hotly denied by many disciples. The problem of interpreting Wittgenstein's book may perhaps be reduced to the problem of interpreting a single sentence:

580. An 'inner process' stands in need of outward criteria.

When Wittgenstein speaks of 'outward criteria' he means bodily behaviour. The phrase 'inner process' refers to mental happenings of the sort that, *prima facie*, seem quite different from bodily behaviour: such things as thoughts and sensations. In saying that 'inner processes' stand in need of outward criteria Wittgenstein seems to be saying that there is a logically necessary connection between the former and the latter. But if this is so, Wittgenstein seems committed either to asserting the existence of a logically necessary connection between 'distinct existences', which seems an implausible interpretation of his view, or else to saying that 'inner processes' are not really anything distinct from bodily behaviour, although there may be two different ways of talking about what men do. But this is a form of Behaviourism. This interpretation is strengthened if we notice the quotation marks that enclose the phrase 'inner process', marks absent in the case of the phrase 'outward criteria'.

But there is one difficulty in interpreting Wittgenstein and Ryle as Behaviourists. Both writers deny that they hold this doctrine! I think, however, that the only reason that these philosophers denied that they were Behaviourists was that they took Behaviourism to be the doctrine that there are no such things as minds. Since they did not want to deny the existence of minds, but simply wanted to give an account of the mind in terms of behaviour, they denied that they were Behaviourists.

But this raises a further problem. Why did these philosophers interpret Behaviourism in this strange way: an interpretation that it would be difficult to find any actual Behaviourist to endorse? I think the reason for this was the doctrine held by Wittgenstein (and apparently accepted by Ryle) that philosophy, when done properly, issues in illuminations, but not in doctrines. In order to maintain this curious view it is necessary to persuade oneself that any philosophical doctrine one holds is not really a doctrine. If the doctrine in question is Behaviourism, then it will be a help to re-define Behaviourism in such a way that entails that one is not a Behaviourist. One's own view will lack a name, and then it will be easier to overlook that it, too, is a doctrine. In this way, I think, these philosophers wrongly persuaded themselves that they were not Behaviourists.

However, whether this piece of interpretation is right or not does not really matter. The accounts of mental processes given by these philosophers were certainly very close to Behaviourism, and it is useful to consider them as Behaviourists. If they are not Behaviourists, we may challenge them or their followers to tell us in what way their view differs from Behaviourism.

As a theory of mind, Behaviourism has certain advantages.

(i) It is clear that Behaviourism can account for the close unity that we think holds between mind and body. For according to this theory, the mind is just the body in action.

(ii) Like the Attribute theory, Behaviourism can easily give an account of the numerical difference between two minds. For the minds are distinguished by the two bodies involved, two bodies which must be in different places to be two.

(iii) Behaviourism is compatible with modern scientific knowledge of body and brain.

On the other hand, however, Behaviourism has certain disadvantages.

(i) It is clear that a Behaviourist cannot allow the logical possibility of the disembodied existence of a mind. Yet we saw that this seemed to be a meaningful conception.

(ii) What can the Behaviourist make of the *interaction* of mind and body? As we have already argued, the following sequence appears to be a causal one: (*a*) my hand is hit; (*b*) I feel pain; (*c*) I wring my hand. We want to say that the blow makes me feel pain, and the pain in turn makes me wring my hand. Can the Behaviourist treat this as a causal sequence? For him the pain is simply a disposition or tendency, a disposition or tendency manifested in things like wringing one's hand. Can he say that the blow causes the disposition (which is the pain) which causes the wringing? Since the whole point of Behaviourism is to deny the existence of inner mental events between the physical stimulus and the physical response, he cannot. In order for there to be interaction there must be things to interact. The Behaviourist denies that the mind is a thing. So it cannot interact with the body. Yet the case of the struck hand is naturally construed as a case of interaction.

(iii) It is not at all clear how the Behaviourist is going to explain the *intentionality* or 'pointing' character of mental processes. Here he may claim that he is in no worse position than a Dualist or a defender of the Attribute theory. But this is not quite true, for no Materialist can claim that intentionality is an unique, unanalysable property of mental processes and still be consistent with his Materialism. A Materialist is forced to attempt an *analysis* of intentionality. But a non-Materialist is under no such obligation, so that he has more freedom of manoeuvre when he is trying to deal with the problem.

(iv) These difficulties for Behaviourism are all manifestations of one central difficulty. Most implausibly, the Behaviourist denies the existence of *inner* mental processes. There seems to be something more going on in us than mere outward physical behaviour. The great problem for the Behaviourist is to say why, if his view is correct, we are so wildly misled in this matter.

Now I do not think that this problem can be solved, but there is no doubt that heroic efforts were made to solve it. What is more, these efforts led to new insights into the nature of the mental concepts which are of permanent value for the philosophy of mind. Before embarking on further criticism of Behaviourism, therefore, it will be well worthwhile to look at the various considerations by which the Analytical Behaviourists tried to make the denial of inner mental processes plausible. There is much to be learnt from their ingenious excuses for Behaviourism.

II. BEHAVIOURISM AND THE MENTAL CONCEPTS

In the *first* place, the Behaviourists emphasized the tremendous importance of dispositions in unfolding the nature of the mental concepts. Consider the case of belief. When it is said truly of somebody that he believes that the earth is flat, it is clear that he need not be behaving in any significant way. He may even be asleep. We may therefore be tempted to think that, in speaking of the belief, we are referring to some inner psychical state which persists in him as long as he holds the belief, sleeping or waking. But what we have to realize, the Behaviourists maintained, is that to believe that the earth is flat does not imply that we are in any state at all. To hold this belief is simply to be disposed to act in a certain way. Once we see this point we shall lose the desire to postulate mysterious inner states. We shall say instead that to believe that the earth is flat is to be disposed to carry out certain *bodily* actions: uttering, and speaking in defence of, the statement 'the earth is flat', and many similar things.

As we have mentioned earlier, dispositional predicates are not applied to people only. We say that a glass is brittle—that it is disposed to break easily—and if we can apply dispositional predicates to a glass then we can apply them to a human body. It is true that when we say glass is brittle we believe that there is some current *state* of the glass which accounts for its brittleness. (The molecular structure of the glass, perhaps.) In the same way, if a man believes that the earth is flat, no doubt the current state of his brain differs from the state of the brain of one who does not believe this. But, the Behaviourist maintains, the existence of such states of the brain is not involved in the concept of belief.

The recognition of the importance of dispositions in attributions of mental state allows us to see, the Behaviourists maintained, that many *explanations* of human conduct are dispositional in nature. It is tempting to construe 'He drinks because he is thirsty' after the model of 'He falls because he is pushed'. Being pushed is an event which precedes, and brings about, his fall. So, the Behaviourist argues, when we consider 'He drinks because he is thirsty' we are inclined to look for an event preceding the drinking, which is its cause. We may fail to find such an event in the subject's behaviour, and so we conclude that 'being thirsty' is an inner psychical event which brings about the drinking. But, the Behaviourist goes on, once we are alive to the importance of dispositions in an account of the mind we shall construe 'being thirsty' as a mere disposition to drink. We shall compare 'He drinks because he is thirsty' to 'The glass breaks because it is brittle' and not to 'He falls because he is pushed'. And then the need to postulate an inner event will be gone.

In the *second* place, the Behaviourists pointed to an asymmetry between my knowledge of my own dispositions, and another person's knowledge of my dispositions. It is an empirical fact that I am very often able to make true statements about my own current dispositions which nobody else can make *and not on the basis of any evidence*. I may be able to say truly 'I am thirsty now', meaning that I am disposed to drink if occasion offers, yet not be engaged in any other behaviour that I could construe as drink-

searching, nor have any other evidence to go on. Another person would not have the power to make such true dispositional statements about me without evidence, but I have. My power here is something like my power to say where my left hand is even when my eyes are shut and I have not touched my hand to see where it is. (Suppose I am blindfolded, and somebody moves the hand about.) But, in the case of the thirst, what I know is not that my body is in a certain state, but that it has a certain disposition.

This 'privileged access' to our own dispositions is probably the most important suggestion that Analytical Behaviourism has to make for the solution of the mind–body problem. (Indeed, I believe it comes very close to the heart of the mystery.) It enables the Behaviourist to explain the origin (or at any rate one origin) of what he takes to be the myth of inner mental processes in the following way. If I have a power of making true statements about my own dispositions that other people lack, it is natural to think that my statements are based on some evidence. The evidence is clearly no bodily happening, for no relevant bodily happening may be occurring. Hence we wrongly conclude that the evidence must be some inner psychical process which we alone observe. But, *in fact*, Behaviourism maintains, my 'privileged access' to my own dispositions is knowledge that is not based on any evidence at all. It is only our incurable tendency to think that all knowledge is based upon evidence that has deceived us.

(Of course, the Behaviourist will not deny the existence of a *causal mechanism* that is responsible for our special ability to make statements about our own current dispositions to behave on the basis of no evidence at all. If there were no such mechanism, this ability would be magical. What happens, the Behaviourist can say, is that the disposition is contingently associated with a certain non-dispositional state, presumably a state of the brain. In suitable circumstances this brain-state is a causal factor that enables us to make true statements about our current dispositions, statements, however, that we are unable to back up by any evidence.)

In the *third* place, the Behaviourists maintained, to apply correctly the same predicate to a number of mental performances does not necessarily mean that they have some common feature in virtue of which the predicate is applied. If we consider the class of individuals covered by the word 'giraffe', then it is plausible to say that the word is applied to individual giraffes in virtue of features that are common and peculiar to them all. Now it is easy to go on to think that this is the case with *all* general words. The assumption lies behind Socrates' search for definitions, was inherited by Plato, and through him became an unquestioned assumption of Western philosophy. But Wittgenstein argued that the assumption is not always true (cf. *Philosophical Investigations*, Sect. 66). He says that if we consider a word like 'game' we cannot find any common and peculiar feature in virtue of which the word is correctly applied. Instead we shall find only a 'family-resemblance' between different sorts of games (children's games, board-games, Olympic games, and so on). There are, as it were, paths connecting certain species of game: that is to say, they resemble one another in certain respects; but these paths are not the same paths which link them to other species: they resemble these other species in different respects. And in the case of some species of game, they may be connected only *via* their resemblance to an intermediate species, and hardly resemble each other in any relevant respect.

Wittgenstein said that the word 'game' was a 'family-word', or that games form a 'family'. Perhaps we can put his contention another way by saying that the concept of game has a certain 'scatter'. Now the whole topic of 'family-words' demands a great deal more investigation than has yet been given to it. But one thing does seem obvious: if there is anything in the notion at all, then concepts can exhibit this 'scatter' *in greater or less degree*. Now, the Behaviourist claimed, it is a special feature of the majority of the mental concepts that they exhibit such 'scatter' in a high degree: that they are families of resembling instances held together in a particularly loose way. Suppose, for instance, that we look for a single sort of behaviour that constitutes a man's being angry. We shall not find it. If I am angry with Jones I may strike him, speak ill of him, work against his interests, or simply ignore him. But none of these things is necessary for me to be angry with Jones. Now, the Behaviourist argues, if we are still under the Socratic delusion that the word 'anger' is applied in virtue of some single feature that all cases of anger have in common, then we shall certainly have to reject any behaviouristic account of anger. We shall be forced to say that anger is a single *inner state* which, under different circumstances, gives rise to different sorts of behaviour. But once we see the possibility that anger is a family-concept, a Behaviourist account of anger will seem more plausible. The *medley* of types of behaviour that we call angry behaviour have a loose family-resemblance, and that is all that the one word 'anger' requires.

Some mental concepts may be *both* dispositional (or involve dispositional elements) and also be 'family-concepts'. A plausible case in point is the concept of intelligence. It seems clear that intelligence is a dispositional concept. An unconscious man can be called intelligent, but he is not called intelligent because of anything that he is doing currently. And the performances which we account manifestations of intelligence seem to have no more than a loose family-resemblance to each other.

In the *fourth* place, the Behaviourists drew a distinction between *central* cases falling under a certain concept, and *peripheral* ones. In terms of the image of the family, we could say that they drew a distinction between members of the immediate family circle, and distant relatives. This enabled them to give an account of cases that fall under a certain mental concept, but which involve little or no behaviour. In some cases, for instance, we are prepared to accept a man's word that he was very angry on a certain occasion, although his behaviour differed only slightly from ordinary non-angry behaviour. If one has no distinction between central and peripheral cases of anger, such cases drive one towards saying that anger is an inner process, and that in this case the inner process occurred without the behaviour it usually brings about. But the Behaviourist argues that these cases of unexpressed anger are *peripheral* members of the family of behaviours we call 'being angry'. The central cases are those where there is a clear and unambiguous pattern of behaviour: striking somebody, for instance, after being insulted by him. And if there had been no central cases we could never have admitted the peripheral cases as cases falling under the concept, just as, if there had been no family circle, there could have been no distant relatives. Our concept of anger is tied to certain clear and unambiguous patterns of behaviour, in a way that it is not tied to cases where we say (quite sincerely and truly) that we were very angry but our behaviour did not resemble the paradigm patterns of anger. Such cases are accounted cases of anger, but they are accounted members of this family only by a certain courtesy.

The point may be brought out, the Behaviourists thought, by considering that, although unexpressed anger is a case of anger, it is not the sort of case we can use to teach a child the meaning of the word 'anger'. For such teaching we must go to cases where there is overt and unambiguous angry behaviour. This indicates that these latter cases are the central cases, and the cases of un-expressed anger are peripheral.

In the *fifth* place, the Behaviourists argued that, even although there are central cases of behaviour falling under a certain mental concept, it is almost impossible to find behaviour which is a *completely* unambiguous instance falling under a certain mental concept. A man is insulted, and strikes his tormentor. Was he angry? It is possible to entertain this doubt. The behaviour does not actually *entail* anger. In spite of the insult, the blow might have been given for some other reason than anger. This point may again lead us to think that the anger is an inner mental state distinct from the behaviour. But, the Behaviourist argues, the fact that it is almost impossible to describe a pattern of behaviour that actually entails anger means only that we can conceive of further *behaviour*, or a wider context for the original behaviour, which would rule the original behaviour out as a case of anger.

The point made here is really the mirror-image of the point made just previously. There we said that we can find peripheral cases of behaviour which we count as falling under a certain mental concept, although the behaviour is not what we associate with central cases falling under that concept. Such cases could not be typical. Only if there are central cases can there be peripheral ones. Contrariwise, it is possible to find cases where the beha-viour involved is that associated with the central cases falling under a certain concept, but the behaviour is not ranked under that concept. But again we may add that such exceptions could not be typical.

In the *sixth* place, the Behaviourists pointed out that it is a special feature of the mental concepts that there is no sharp boun-dary between instances that fall under a certain concept, and in-stances that do not. If we ignore the evolutionary past for the sake of simplicity, we can say of any animal that it is either a giraffe, or it is not. The class of giraffes has a sharp boundary. But if we consider the sorts of behaviour that, according to the Analytical Behaviourists, we call angry behaviour we shall quickly find that

certain sorts of behaviour can hardly be classified as angry behaviour, nor yet be described as behaviour that is not angry.
(This was the point of Wittgenstein's question 'Can you play
chess without the queen?') Even if we are *fully* apprised of the
facts of the situation we may still be doubtful beyond any remedy
save that of a linguistic decision whether to call certain behaviour
'angry' or not. Of course, this is a feature of other concepts besides the mental ones, but it is a specially prominent feature of the
mental concepts.

This feature of mental concepts is clearly linked with, but is
nevertheless distinct from, the 'family-nature', or 'scatter' that
they also characteristically exhibit. It is very likely that a 'family'
concept will delimit a class that is also without fixed boundaries,
but a concept could have one feature without the other. The
concept of number may be a concept that is a 'family' one, but the
class of things we call 'numbers' has a pretty definite boundary.
Many different sorts of things count as numbers: natural numbers,
real numbers, imaginary numbers, infinite numbers, etc. And it
might be hard to find anything common and peculiar to all these
different sorts of number. But the class of numbers may still have
a definite boundary: there need not be things of which we cannot
say whether they are numbers or not. Contrariwise, colour-
concepts do not seem to be family concepts, but the class of
shades picked out by the word 'blue', for example, does not have
a definite boundary. There are shades that make us doubtful
whether to call them blue or not.

It is easy to overlook the fact that the class picked out by most
mental concepts has this vague boundary. And then it is easy to
go on asking fruitlessly 'Was it *really* anger, or not?' If we do this,
the Behaviourists argue, we shall not find it easy to accept an account of mental concepts in terms of behaviour, for behaviour is
fluid, and there is an absence of any sharp breaks between one
sort of behaviour and another. Instead we shall mistakenly postulate some inner item which is either present or not, and which is
the cause of certain sorts of behaviour. But once we do see that
mental concepts delimit classes with very vague boundaries, we
shall find it much easier to accept a Behaviourist account of the
mind.

In the *seventh* place, the Behaviourists pointed to the extent to
which the use of the mental concepts is built upon certain

empirical presuppositions. If we consider the concept of giraffe once again, we can say that it sets up a clear-cut division in the animal kingdom. Among present-day animals, at any rate, either an animal is a giraffe or it is not. We can, however, imagine cases where, in a cant phrase, 'we should not know what to say'. We can imagine cases where a linguistic decision would have to be taken as to whether the object in question was a giraffe or not. This is what Waismann meant by saying that a concept such as giraffe has 'open texture'. (See his article 'Verifiability', reprinted in *Logic and Language*, First Series, ed. A. G. N. Flew, Blackwell, 1951.) The class of giraffes has a precise boundary, but in different circumstances which do not obtain, but which are imaginable, it would not have a precise boundary. It is an unnoticed *presupposition* of our ordinary and familiar handling of concepts like 'giraffe' that such circumstances do not occur.

Now, like the question of 'family-resemblance', the question of 'open texture' has received relatively little attention for its own sake, although there seems to be a field of inquiry here well worth cultivating. It would be interesting, and important, to know whether every empirical concept has 'open texture', and, if so, whether this is a necessary truth about empirical concepts or not. But however these questions are decided, it is clear that in the case of the mental concepts, even where we ignore actual vagueness of boundary, it is peculiarly easy to imagine cases where normal principles of classification would break down: cases where 'we would not know what to say'. Or, to put what is the same point in another way, the empirical presuppositions of our ordinary use of the mental concepts are extraordinarily extensive. If many of the empirical facts about human beings were otherwise, much of our discourse about minds would go to ruin.

Now, the Behaviourists claimed, recognition of this feature of the mental concepts helps to explain, yet at the same time helps to overcome, the difficulty that an account of the mental concepts in terms of behaviour seems such a 'thin' one. If, for instance, we say that a person knows how to continue the series 1, 3, 6, 10, 15 . . ., if he can actually write down further numbers of the series, this analysis seems disappointingly slight. It seems to lack the full-bloodedness that belongs to the concept of 'knowing how to continue the series'. It is this that tempts us to postulate an inner process. The Behaviourist, however, points out that knowing how to go on in this case also involves the disposition to complete similar series correctly in appropriate conditions. This fills out his picture a little. But more than this, he can say, there are certain very extensive empirical presuppositions involved in saying of somebody that he 'knows how to continue the series'. We suppose, for instance, that, unless circumstances are pretty exceptional, one who gets it right once will be able to repeat the feat later; will be able to do simpler series of the same sort; will not come to a sudden complete halt at the ninth term or adopt what normal people would call entirely new rules for the expansion of the series at this point; and so on. If extraordinary happenings of this sort occurred, we might be at a loss to say whether the person in question really 'knew how to continue the series' or not. Our use of the concept 'knowing how to continue the series' presupposes the existence of all sorts of uniformities and semi-uniformities in human behaviour which give a greater 'fullness', and thus a greater plausibility, to a Behaviouristic account of the mental concepts.

In the *eighth* place, closely connected with the last point, and, indeed, with all the points already made, the Behaviourists stressed the importance of the past, present and future context surrounding a piece of behaviour when we apply a certain mental concept to that behaviour. If, for instance, I claim to remember a piece of information, then my claim to remember does not rest solely upon what I say now. We so use the word 'remember' that I can only claim to remember what I have previously learnt. Unless there was a previous learning, I am not remembering now. The correct application of the phrase 'he remembers . . .' depends in part, therefore, on a context supplied by the past. Again, when a man faced by the series 1, 3, 6, 10, 15 . . ., says suddenly 'Now I know how to go on' what makes his moment of illumination a moment of *illumination* is not anything that goes on at the time he is speaking. It is a moment of illumination, if it is one, because he can go on successfully afterwards. If we do not realize this, we shall be wrongly tempted to look for an inner process occurring at the time he spoke his words.

In the case we have mentioned, the context which makes a piece of behaviour the sort of thing it is, is given by the subject's past and present behaviour. But in some cases the context is something lying beyond the subject altogether. If somebody is said to *know* that *p* is true one of the things that is necessary if this is to be true is for *p* to be actually the case. Now this may be something quite independent of the subject's behaviour. Again, the very same behaviour that is properly described as angry behaviour in one social context may not be angry behaviour in another. Consider the difference between hitting a man after an argument, and hitting him in a boxing-ring. The pattern of action might be the same, but the difference of context makes all the difference. This is at least part of what Wittgenstein meant when he spoke of some mental predicates as only having application within whole 'ways of life'.

In the *ninth* place, the Behaviourists emphasized that a great deal of ordinary speech involving the mental concepts does not have a *descriptive* function, or at any rate a purely descriptive function. They thought this point was of especial importance in the case of 'first person statements of current mental state'. If I say I am in pain now, or that I think it will rain, or that something looks green to me now, or that I am angry now, or that I intend to go now, it is tempting to a philosopher to say that in each case I am reporting an inner state.

And, certainly, if these remarks are taken as *reports*, it is easy to think that they are reports of inner occurrences. But need we take them as reports? Consider the remark 'I am in pain now' in the sort of context that it is actually made. Does it really report the occurrence of something going on 'within' me? Does it not rather, as Wittgenstein suggested, function as *a piece of behaviour*: something within language which serves as conventional substitute for behaviour that naturally expresses pain: a sophisticated linguistic substitute for a wince or a groan? Consider again the statement 'I think it will rain'. Does this really report that there is an item or event going on 'within' me? Is not the statement rather a way of making a remark about the weather and not about me: a way of saying 'It will rain'? After all, it is natural for someone else to contradict 'I think it will rain' by saying 'It will not rain', and not by saying 'You do not think it will rain'. This suggests that I am talking about the rain, and not about some inner item. Again, to say 'It looks green to me now' is very naturally construed as an expression of a belief, or of a tendency to believe, that an object before me is green. It is a tentative way of saying 'It is green', not a report on inner happenings. Yet again, to say 'I am angry with

66

you' is not naturally construed as a report on an inner happening, but is itself a part of my anger. To say 'I intend to go' is most naturally taken as simply a conventional sign preparatory to going. And so on.

If it is objected to the Behaviourist that these sentences can have a purely descriptive use, or even that such a descriptive use is regularly present in discourse alongside the non-descriptive function, he can agree to the objection. But when these sentences are used descriptively, he will say, they describe only the speaker's actions, or his dispositions to act. And in the case where we are reporting mere dispositions, the disposition may well be one of those dispositions to which the speaker has a 'privileged access', that is to say, is able to report correctly on the basis of no evidence whatever.

In the *tenth* place, very closely connected with almost all the points that have gone before, the Behaviourists emphasized that it was impossible to provide exact *translations* of statements about mental happenings into statements about physical bodily happenings. If we demand *translations* then Behaviourism seems enormously implausible. It proves quite impossible to get rid of all mental expressions. But why should we demand translation? We will do better if we think of mental language, on the one hand, and language about bodily behaviour, on the other, as two separate and differently constructed grids drawn upon, or throwing their shadows upon, one and the same surface. Transformation from one grid to another, that is to say, from one way of speaking to another, might be impossible in any but a rough way. But this is not to say that the two grids are projected upon different surfaces. Talk about minds and talk about the physical behaviour of our bodies may be two languages, but, the Behaviourist claims, they are languages that have as their subject-matter the physical actions of the same physical thing.

III. CRITICISM OF BEHAVIOURISM

Armed with these new doctrines about the nature of our concepts in general, and our mental concepts in particular, philosophers such as Wittgenstein and Ryle (assuming that they were Behaviourists) were able to make Behaviourism more plausible than it had ever seemed before. And the detailed analyses of mental

concepts that they offered include many epoch-making philosophical achievements. Even if we do not accept Behaviourism I
think that there is no doubt that we must grant this much: outward physical behaviour and tendencies to behave do in some way
enter into our ordinary concept of mind. Whatever theory of the
mind is true, it has a debt to pay, and a peace to be made, with
Behaviourism. Nevertheless, Behaviourism cannot be accepted as
a complete theory of the mind. It may cover some, but it does not
cover all, the facts.

First, however, I will mention an attempt to refute Behaviourism which I think is invalid. The argument is simple. Behaviourism tries to give an account of my mind and others in terms of
observed behaviour. But what is the term 'observed' doing here?
'Observe' is a mental word, one of those words that Behaviourism
promises us an account of in behavioural terms. But if we give an
account of observation in terms of observed behaviour, we are
involved in flagrant circularity.

The refutation looks too quick and easy, and so I think it is. For
the Behaviourist can reply that, while it is true that he gives an
analysis of what it is to have a mind in terms of bodily happenings
that are observed, or, if not observed, could easily have been observed, nevertheless, the fact that the happenings are observed is
not part of the *analysis* of the concept of mind. He gives an account of the mind in terms of certain bodily happenings and dispositions for bodily happenings. It is a contingent fact that these
happenings are observed, or, when not observed, could easily have
been observed. This contingent fact accounts for the fact that we
know of the existence of our own mind, and of other minds, without any very arduous research, but it is not part of the definition
of a mind. In just the same way, to *define* a cat as the offspring of
two cats is to be guilty of circularity of definition. But it is a well
known *fact* about cats that each of them is the offspring of two
cats. According to Behaviourism, the mind is a matter of behaviour, actual or potential. It is a fact about this behaviour that
it is readily accessible to observation.

The difficulty for Behaviourism is of a more empirical sort: the
theory seems to clash with the plain 'evidence of introspection'.
It may cover some, but it does not cover all, the facts.

Suppose that, in response to a task that is set, somebody does a
calculation 'in his head'. How can we give an account of what went

on in purely behavioural terms? Let us suppose, for the sake of argument, that the subject exhibits no relevant overt behaviour at the time. The really important thing, the Behaviourist will say, the thing that makes the time between question and overt response the time when he was *calculating*, is what he says afterwards. If at time T_1 the subject is incapable of giving the right answer to a quite complex sum; but if he afterwards falls silent and exhibits 'signs of concentration' and at T_2 he is for the first time capable of giving the right answer, and if he is further capable of giving some account of how the calculation should go; then he has given us what we need for saying that between T_1 and T_2 he did the calculation 'in his head'.

Now let us admit to the Behaviourist, for the sake of argument, that only if a person could exhibit behaviour of this general sort could we say that he had made 'calculations in his head'. But is this all there is to it? Is 'calculation in the head' little more than a period of silence followed by an intelligent answer? At least sometimes when we 'calculate in our heads' are we not aware of a *current event*: something that goes on in us at the time of the calculation? And what account can the Behaviourist give of this happening? By hypothesis, it is not a piece of overt behaviour.

It may be replied that during the 'calculation' we were disposed to say and to do certain things, and that we are afterwards able to report the existence of these dispositions. But, granting this, was there not something *actual* going on, of which we were aware at the time?

Behaviourist psychologists have been tempted by the suggestion that what was going on in such a case is *covert* behaviour. (See B. F. Skinner, *Science and Human Behaviour*, Ch. XVII, 'Private events in a natural science'.) And there is no doubt that such covert behaviour often does accompany such things as 'calculating in the head'. For instance, movements may occur in the larynx which resemble the movements that bring about actual speech. But the difficulty about this suggestion is that it always makes sense to assert that there was no such behaviour, and yet that there were mental processes going on.

The only attempt to answer this problem that I know of is to be found in Wittgenstein's *Investigations*, Sect. 364. There he considers the objection that when somebody does a sum in his head 'There surely must have been calculation going on . . .'. He

answers, 'But what if I said: "*It strikes him as if* he had calculated." '
I think the suggestion here is that after the 'calculation in the
head', during which nothing actual goes on, we find ourselves
with an impression as if calculation (overt calculation) had gone
on, although in fact it had not.

But what about 'its striking him as if he had calculated'? Is not
this an inner mental *event*? It is just as implausible to give a purely
dispositional account of this event as it is of the original 'calculation in the head'. But in that case Wittgenstein has got rid of
the inner mental event at one place only to have it reappear at
another. He is like a man who smoothes out one bulge in the
carpet only to have it pop up again at another point.

(As John Mackie has pointed out to me, it is possible that
Wittgenstein is here simply using the argument he uses elsewhere
in connection with other mental events: the contention that, since
there is no possible way of distinguishing real inner calculation
from merely seeming to have calculated internally, there can be no
such process. If so, he has left quite unexplained our impression
that in 'calculation in the head' actual calculation occurs. He has
simply offered an *a priori* argument against the occurrence of an
inner process. As for that argument itself, in Section X of the
next chapter it will be contended that it *is* possible to be radically
mistaken about the nature of one's current mental states. If this
is correct, this argument of Wittgenstein is based on a false
premiss.)

'Calculating in the head' is a species of thinking to oneself.
The same argument will apply to all other sorts of thinking to
oneself. And similar considerations apply to other forms of
mental activity: forming an intention, feeling an emotion, having
a perception or a sensation or a mental image. In all these cases,
it is true that outward behaviour plays a vital part in our concept
of these activities, but in each case it is impossible to believe it is
the whole story. In the case of sense-impressions, sensations and
mental images it is particularly hard to deny the existence of
inner happenings. When we have a mental image, in particular,
the *primary* thing seems to be the inner happening. Current and
subsequent behaviour is unimportant.

One field of mental life where the denial of inner happenings is
peculiarly implausible is the case of *dreams*. In his book *Dreaming*
(Routledge, 1959) Norman Malcolm, following up hints by Witt-

genstein in the *Investigations*, makes a gallant attempt to argue that what constitutes going to sleep and dreaming is simply being disposed, after waking, to tell certain stories of how things seemed to be. (There is a remarkable parallel here to Wittgenstein's remarks about 'its striking him as if he had calculated' already quoted.)

Now *perhaps* the linguistic institution of 'telling one's dreams' is part of our ordinary concept of dreaming. Perhaps it can be said that the concept of a dog's or a young child's dream is different from the concept of the dream of a being who can talk. But it is impossible to accept 'telling one's dreams' as the whole truth about dreaming. We think that, when we dream, certain things go on in our minds during sleep. All Malcolm can allow is that, if we had been woken up at various different times during our sleep, the stories we would have told would have differed from occasion to occasion.

Malcolm's difficulties come to a head over the following problem: sometimes, during a dream, the thought occurs to us that we are dreaming. (It can be a reassuring thought, preparatory to awakening from a nightmare.) Now, for Malcolm, the sentence 'I am dreaming' is one that has no meaning. When we wake up from sleep we may say 'I dreamt . . .', meaning by this that we have woken up with an inclination to tell a story about happenings in the immediate past, which, however, we recognize did not happen. But there is no intelligible use for the sentence 'I am dreaming' on Malcolm's view. But if this is so, what account can we give of the sentence that may occur during the dream-story: 'But then I thought to myself "It is only a dream" '? Malcolm has to say that this is a piece of *nonsense* that crops up in dream-stories, something like 'And then they suspended the Law of Contradiction'. But, of course, the sentence does not *seem* to be nonsense. It took a philosopher defending a theory to argue that it was nonsense, whereas everybody recognizes that the story about the Law of Contradiction is nonsense. It seems, therefore, that it ought to be admitted that dreams are events that occur in the mind during sleep. But this falsifies Behaviourism.

We can try to bring to a head the whole doctrine of Behaviourism by considering a perfectly imaginary, but perfectly intelligible, case. Suppose that we were able to make a complete record of the impulses in a man's central nervous system during the whole of his life. Suppose we artificially create an exact copy of this central nervous system, but separate it from any body. Suppose we then arrange for what happens to this artificial system to be *exactly* the same in every detail as what happened to the person's central nervous system in life. Surely it is likely that this brain would have a mind, and *subjectively* its experiences would be likely to be exactly the same as those of the person whose central nervous system was copied. Yet, by hypothesis, the brain would be incapable of *behaviour*, except for the electrical impulses emerging from it.

What can the Behaviourist say about this case? If he is a Materialist (and if he is not, what view of man is he taking?) he must agree that this is a conceivable case. All he can say is that in such a case we must give an account of the mental events involved purely in terms of contrary-to-fact conditionals, that is to say, in terms of the behaviour that would have occurred if the brain had had a body. Yet surely there would be *actual* mental states associated with this brain, something that could not be analysed away in terms of mere unfulfilled possibilities?

This is simply the extreme case where there is no behaviour at all during the whole term of the existence of a mind. I think it shows us, in very clear fashion, the impossibility of putting forward Behaviourism as the *whole* truth about the concept of mind. To deny inner mental states is, as A. J. Ayer put it, 'to pretend to be anaesthetized'. It is true that 'not being anaesthetized' is not simply the having of experiences. It also involves acting in certain ways, or being disposed to act in certain ways. But it is one of the most important things about the anaesthetized that they do not have experiences.

Our examination of Behaviourism, then, has taught us two things. (i) We cannot deny the existence of inner mental states. (ii) Outer behaviour is, nevertheless, in some way involved in the concept of mind.

6

THE CENTRAL-STATE THEORY

BUT now we must examine the second form of Materialism, the view which identifies mental states with purely physical states of the central nervous system. If the mind is thought of as 'that which has mental states', then we can say that, on this theory, the mind is simply the central nervous system, or, less accurately but more epigrammatically, the mind is simply the brain.

I. IS THE THEORY REALLY PARADOXICAL?

Many philosophers still regard this theory of mind as a very extraordinary one. In 1962, for instance, A. G. N. Flew wrote:

> In the face of the powerful and resolute advocacy now offered *this admittedly paradoxical view* can no longer be dismissed in such short order. (*Philosophical Review*, Vol. LXXI, 1962, p. 403, my italics)

At the risk of seeming ungrateful to Professor Flew, it is interesting to notice that, even while conceding that the theory merits serious discussion, he calls it 'admittedly paradoxical'. I think his attitude is shared by many philosophers. Certainly I myself found the theory paradoxical when I first heard it expounded.

But it is important to realize that this opinion that the Central-state theory is paradoxical, is confined almost exclusively to philosophers. They are usually taught as first-year University students that the mind cannot possibly be the brain, and as a result they are inclined to regard the falsity of the Central-state theory as self-evident. But this opinion is not widely shared. Outside philosophy, the Central-state doctrine enjoys wide support.

In the first place, there is evidence from modern idiom. We speak of 'brains', 'brain-child', 'brain-storm', 'racking one's brains' and 'brain-washing', and in each case we are speaking about the mind. If one follows this up, as I have done, by asking people of general education, but no philosophical training, whether they think the mind is the brain or not, many say it is. Some even treat the matter as closed, asking what else it could be. Those who deny that the mind is the brain usually do so for *theological* reasons.

If we then turn to those scientists who are most directly concerned with the problem, viz. the psychologists, we find no tendency to say that the Central-state theory is paradoxical or far-out. D. O. Hebb may be fairly quoted as representative. Now in his *Textbook of Psychology* (Saunders, 1958, p. 3) he writes:

> There are two theories of mind, speaking very generally. One is animistic, a theory that the body is inhabited by an entity—the mind or soul—that is quite different from it, having nothing in common with bodily processes. The second theory is physiological or mechanistic, it assumes that mind is a bodily process, an activity of the brain. Modern psychology works with this latter theory only. Both are intellectually respectable (that is, each has support from highly intelligent people, including scientists), and there is certainly no decisive means available of proving one to be right, the other wrong.

These appeals to the authority of the unphilosophic man and the psychologists are, of course, not intended to do anything to settle the substantive question. They are made only with the hope of moderating philosophical dogmatism. It may be that the unphilosophic man and the psychologists are seriously confused. But it may also be that, as so often in the past, the philosophers have been misled by plausible arguments. The reasonable man ought to regard the question as open.

II. THE THEORY MEASURED AGAINST DEMANDS ALREADY FORMULATED

Getting down to more serious business, let us measure the theory against the various demands that a satisfactory theory of mind must meet as they have emerged in the last four chapters, beginning with the demands that create no difficulty.

(i) It is clear that this theory accounts very simply for the unity of mind and body. The brain is physically inside the body. It is the pilot in the vessel. This fits in remarkably well with ordinary talk about the mind. It is completely natural to speak of the mind as 'in' the body, and to speak of mental processes as 'inner' processes. Now 'in' is primarily a spatial word. The naturalness of this way of speaking is strikingly, and the more strikingly because quite unconsciously, brought out by Hume. For in the course of putting forward a theory of mind according to which it is not in physical space, he says:

> Suppose we could see clearly into the *breast* of another and observe that succession of perceptions which constitutes his mind or thinking principle . . . (*Treatise*, Bk. I, Pt. IV, Sect. 6, p. 260, ed. Selby-Bigge, my italics)

Hume's way of talking here, indefensible on his own theory, seems to us *all* to be a natural way of talking, although we might now say 'head', not 'breast'. But a Dualist must say that the mind is not in the body in any gross material sense of the word 'in'. What his own refined sense of the word is, is a mystery.

(ii) Central-state Materialism can provide a simple principle of numerical difference for minds, viz., difference of place, just as the Attribute and the Behaviourist theory can.

(iii) Central-state Materialism can explain very simply the interaction of mind and body. Brain and body interact, so mind and body interact.

(iv) Central-state Materialism allows us to say that the mind comes into being in a gradual way, and that there is no sharp break between not having a mind and having one. For in the evolution of the species, and in the development of the individual, the brain comes into being in a gradual way. The simplification of our world-picture that results is the especial advantage of Materialist theories (including Behaviourism).

(v) But unlike Behaviourism, a Central-state theory does not deny the existence of inner mental states. On the contrary, it asserts their existence: they are physical states of the brain.

Nevertheless, a Central-state theory seems to face some serious objections.

(i) We argued that any satisfactory theory of mind ought to allow for the logical possibility of disembodied minds. If the mind is the brain, it might seem that a mind logically cannot exist in a disembodied state in any but the crudest sense, that is to say, as a brain without a body. This is not what we mean by a disembodied mind.

(ii) In criticizing the 'Bundle' theory, we saw that mental states are incapable of independent existence. It is not clear how the Central-state theory can account for this. Brain-states or processes seem to be things that could be conceived to exist independently of anything else. They do not even require a brain, for we could conceive them as, *e.g.* patterns of electrical discharge in space.

(iii) It is not clear what account a Central-state theory can give of the 'intentionality' or 'pointing' nature of mental processes. It is true that no theory we have examined has cast any particular light on this problem so far. But, as we noticed when discussing Behaviourism, Materialist theories are at a special disadvantage in dealing with 'intentionality', because they cannot treat it as an irreducible, unanalysable, feature of mental processes on pain of contradicting their Materialism.

(iv) In discussing Behaviourism, we conceded that behaviour and dispositions to behave do enter into the concept of mind in some way. It is not clear how a Central-state theory does justice to this feature of the mental.

III. A FURTHER DIFFICULTY FORMULATED, AND AN ANSWER SKETCHED

But the difficulties considered in the previous section pale before one powerful line of argument that may seem to be a conclusive reason for denying that the mind is the brain. Take the statement 'The mind is the brain'. ('Mental processes are brain-processes' may be substituted if preferred.) Does the statement purport to be a logically necessary truth, or is it simply claimed to be contingently true? Does a defender of the Central-state theory want to assimilate the statement to 'An oculist *is* an eye-doctor' or '7 + 5 *is* 12', on the one hand, or to 'The morning star *is* the evening star' or 'The gene *is* the DNA molecule', on the other?

It is perfectly clear which way the cat must jump here. If there is anything certain in philosophy, it is certain that 'The mind is the brain' is not a logically necessary truth. When Aristotle said that the brain was nothing but an organ for keeping the body cool, he was certainly not guilty of denying a necessary truth. His mistake was an empirical one. So if it is true that the mind is the brain, a model must be found among contingent statements of identity. We must compare the statement to 'The morning star is the evening star' or 'The gene is the DNA molecule', or some other contingent assertion of identity. (The statement 'The gene is the DNA molecule' is not a very exact one from the biological point of view. But it will prove to be a useful example in the development of the argument, and it is accurate enough for our purposes here.)

But if 'The mind is the brain' is a contingent statement, then it follows that it must be possible to give logically independent explanations (or, alternatively, 'ostensive definitions') of the meaning of the two words 'mind' and 'brain'. For consider. 'The morning star is the evening star' is a contingent statement. We can explain the meaning of the phrase 'the morning star' thus: it is the very bright star seen in the sky on certain mornings of the year. We can explain the meaning of the phrase 'the evening star' thus: it is the very bright star seen in the sky on certain evenings of the year. We can give logically independent explanations of the meanings of the two phrases. 'The gene is the DNA molecule' is a contingent statement. We can explain the meaning of the word 'gene' thus: it is that thing or principle within us that is responsible for the transmission of hereditary characteristics, such as colour of eyes. We can explain the meaning of the phrase 'DNA molecule' along the following lines: it is a molecule of a certain very complex chemical constitution which forms the nucleus of the cell. We can give logically independent explanations of the word 'gene' and the phrase 'DNA molecule'.

Now if it is meaningful to say that 'The mind is the brain' it must be possible to treat the words 'mind' and 'brain' in the same way.

The word 'brain' gives no trouble. Clearly it is possible to explain its meaning in a quasi-ostensive way. The problem is posed by the word 'mind'. What verbal explanation or 'ostensive definition' can we give of the meaning of this word without implying a departure from a physicalist view of the world? This seems to be the great problem, or, at any rate, one great problem, faced by a Central-state theory.

The object that we call a 'brain' is called a brain in virtue of certain physical characteristics: it is a certain sort of physical object found inside people's skulls. Yet if we say that this object is also the mind, then, since the word 'mind' does not mean the same as the word 'brain', it seems that the brain can only be the mind in virtue of some *further* characteristic that the brain has. But what can this characteristic be? We seem on the verge of being forced back into an Attribute theory.

Put the problem another way. Central-state Materialism holds that when we are *aware* of our mental states what we are aware of are mere physical states of our brain. But we are certainly not aware of the mental states *as* states of the brain. What then are we aware of mental states as? Are we not aware of them as states of a quite peculiar, mental, sort?

The problem has so daunted one physicalist, Paul Feyerabend, that he has suggested that the materialist ought simply to recognize that his world-view does not allow statements that assert or imply the existence of minds. A true physicalism will simply talk about the operation of the central nervous system, and will write off talk about the mind as an intellectual loss. (See his 'Mental events and the Brain', *The Journal of Philosophy*, Vol. LX, 1963.)

I think that if the situation is as desperate as this it is desperate indeed. It is at least our first duty to see if we can give an explanation of the word 'mind' which will meet the demands that have just been outlined. In order to do this, let us turn to a way of thinking about man that has been popularized by psychology. Psychologists very often present us with the following picture. Man is an object continually acted upon by certain physical stimuli. These stimuli elicit from him certain behaviour, that is to say, a certain physical response. In the causal chain between the stimulus and the response, falls the mind. The mind is that which causally mediates our response to stimuli. Now the Central-state theory wants to say that between the stimulus and the response fall physical processes in the central nervous system, and nothing else at all, not even something 'epiphenomenal'. At the same time the theory cannot mention the central nervous system in its account of the concept of mind. If we now think of the psychologist's picture, the outline of a solution is in our hands. As a first approximation we can say that what we mean when we talk about the mind, or about particular mental processes, is nothing but the effect within a man of certain stimuli, and the cause within a man of certain responses. The intrinsic nature of these effects and causes is not something that is involved in the concept of mind or the particular mental concepts. The concept of a mental state is the concept of that, whatever it may turn out to be, which is brought about in a man by certain stimuli and which in turn brings about certain responses. What it is in its own nature is something for science to discover. Modern science declares that this mediator between stimulus and response is in fact the central nervous system, or more crudely and inaccurately, but more simply, the brain.

IV. VIEWS OF PLACE AND SMART

If we now consider the two papers that are already 'classical' expositions of Central-state Materialism: U. T. Place's 'Is Consciousness a Brain Process?' (*British Journal of Psychology*, Vol. XLVII, 1956, pp. 44–50) and J. J. C. Smart's 'Sensations and Brain Processes' (*Philosophical Review*, Vol. LXVIII, 1959, pp. 141–56), we find that they give the problem we grappled with in the previous section only very brief consideration. So far as they do consider it, they come down on the side of the stimulus, not the response. Smart wrote:

> When a person says, 'I see a yellowish-orange after-image', he is saying something like this: '*There is something going on which is like what is going on when* I have my eyes open, am awake, and there is an orange illuminated in good light in front of me, that is, when I really see an orange.'

Here the having of an orange after-image is explicated in terms of the stimulus: an orange acting on a person in suitable conditions. Place took a similar line.

Now if we consider some other mental processes it is at once clear that this sort of analysis solely in terms of the effects of a stimulus can have no hope of success. Suppose I form the intention to go out and get a drink. There may well be no typical physical situations which have the effect of creating this state in me. The account of intentions must clearly proceed instead in terms of the behaviour that such an intention initiates. The intention is an inner cause of a certain sort of response, not the inner effect of a certain sort of stimulus. Of course, the intention *is* an effect of certain causes, but it cannot be *defined* in terms of these causes.

In fact, however, the point just made about intentions would constitute no criticism of Place's and Smart's position as put forward in these articles. For with respect to things like intentions they are not Central-state Materialists, but Behaviourists. Place wrote:

> In the case of cognitive concepts like 'knowing', 'believing', 'understanding', 'remembering', and volitional concepts like 'wanting' and 'intending', there can be little doubt, I think, that an analysis in terms of dispositions to behave is fundamentally sound. On the other hand, there would seem to be an intractable residue of concepts clustering around the notions of consciousness, experience, sensation, and mental imagery, where some sort of inner process story is unavoidable.

Smart took the same view.

Against Place and Smart, however, I wish to defend a Central-state account of *all* the mental concepts. We do naturally distinguish between the thought or belief, and its expression in words or action, between the emotion and its expression in action, between the aim or intention and its expression in action. Taking the word literally, something is 'expressed' when it is squeezed out, as oil is expressed from olives. Applied to the mind, this yields the picture of an inner state bringing about outward behaviour. Surely some strong reason (as opposed to mere current prejudice) must be advanced if this picture is to be rejected? In default of such a reason it should be accepted.

It may be said that all we are ever aware of in introspection are sense-impressions, sensations and mental images. Now it may perhaps be granted that they are the most obtrusive sort of inner item, but it is far from clear that we are not sometimes aware of thoughts and intentions, for example, without accompanying imagery and sensations. Putting the matter at its lowest, it certainly seems to make sense to say 'I was aware of thoughts going through my mind. An inner event occurred, but no relevant images went through my mind, nor did I have any relevant sense-impressions or sensations.' Perhaps such statements are never true, but, again, perhaps they sometimes are. I think, indeed, that Place's and Smart's position is a mere hang-over from the Sensationalism of the British Empiricists which attempts to reduce all actual mental items to impressions, images and sensations. But once we have accepted any sort of inner mental item, strong arguments should be needed to exclude what are, *prima facie*, also items.

Smart has in fact changed his view on this matter. He now accepts a Central-state account of all the mental concepts. His original position was in fact, I think, an interesting example of a quite false spirit of economy. The motive was clear: if we have to admit inner items, let us admit as few as possible. But in fact once one has admitted the necessity for a certain sort of entity in one's theoretical scheme then it will often lead to a more economical theory if this sort of entity is postulated to explain the widest possible range of phenomena. Theoretical economy about entities is not like being economical with money. To be economical with money is to spend as little quantity of money as is consistent with one's purposes. But theoretical economy about entities is a matter of postulating the smallest number of *sorts* of entity that will explain the phenomena. Its analogue with respect to money would be a coinage that had the minimum number of *types* of coin consistent with all the sorts of financial operation that had to be undertaken. So once one admits inner mental states at all it is actually a theoretical economy to give a Central-state account of all the mental concepts.

But even if we confine ourselves to the ground originally chosen by Place and Smart, it is clear that their account of such things as perceptions in terms of the characteristic effects of certain stimuli is inadequate. I am not denying that what they say is part of the truth. As we shall see when we come to discuss the concept of perception in detail, it *is* part of our notion of seeing or seeming to see something yellow that it is the sort of inner event characteristically produced in us by the action of a yellow physical object. But a full account of the visual experience involves more than this. To show us that he can perceive, a man must show us that he can do certain things: that he can systematically discriminate in his behaviour between certain classes of objects. As Anthony Kenny remarks in his *Action, Emotion and Will* (Routledge, 1963, p. 59) we pick a man's lack of perceptual powers by a certain inefficiency in conduct. So, even in such a case as perception, reference to certain sorts of *responses* for which the perception gives us a capacity is at least as important for elucidating the concept as reference to certain sorts of stimuli.

V. THE CONCEPT OF A MENTAL STATE

The difficulties in Place's and Smart's position incline me to look to the response rather than the stimulus in seeking a general account of the mental concepts. The concept of a mental state is primarily the concept of *a state of the person apt for bringing about a certain sort of behaviour*. Sacrificing all accuracy for brevity we can say that, although mind is not behaviour, it is the *cause* of behaviour. In the case of some mental states only they are also *states of the person apt for being brought about by a certain sort of stimulus*. But this latter formula is a secondary one.

It will be advisable to dwell rather carefully on this first formula: state of the person apt for bringing about a certain sort of behaviour.

In the first place, I attach no special importance to the word 'state'. For instance, it is not meant to rule out 'process' or 'event'. I think that in fact useful distinctions can be made between states, processes and events, and that mental 'items', to use a neutral term, can be variously classified under these quite separate heads. This point will emerge in Part II (cf. in particular, Ch. 7, Sect. I). But in the meanwhile 'state' is not meant to exclude 'process' or 'event'.

In the second place, I call attention to the word 'apt'. Here there are two points to be made: (*a*) By saying only that mental states are states *apt* for bringing about behaviour we allow for some mental states being actual occurrences, even although they result in no behaviour. (*b*) The formula is intended to cover more than one sort of relationship between mental state and behaviour. If we consider intentions, for instance, then they are naturally construed (*pace* Ryle) as causes within our minds that tend to initiate and sustain certain courses of behaviour. But it is most implausible to say that perceptions, for instance, are causes tending to initiate certain courses of behaviour. Suppose I see a magpie on the lawn. It may well be that magpies are things which I can take or leave, and that no impulse to do anything at all is involved in the perception. What must be said about perception (as will be elaborated later) is that it is a matter of acquiring capacities to make systematic physical discriminations within our environment *if we should be so impelled.* (If intentions are like pressures on a door, perceptions are like acquiring a key to the door. You can put the key in your pocket, and never do anything with it.) Other mental states will turn out to stand in still different causal relations to the behaviour which constitutes their 'expression'. In some cases, indeed, it will emerge that certain sorts of mental states can only be described in terms of their *resemblance* to other mental states that stand in causal relations to behaviour. Here the relation to behaviour is very indirect indeed.

A closely connected point is that, in many cases, an account of mental states involves not only their causal relation to behaviour, but their causal relation to other mental states. It may even be that an account of certain mental states will proceed solely in terms of the other mental states they are apt for bringing about. An intention to work out a sum 'in one's head' would be a case in point. The intention is a mental cause apt for bringing about the thoughts that are the successive steps in the calculation. So all that is demanded is that our analysis must *ultimately* reach mental states that are describable in terms of the behaviour they are apt for.

In the third place, the 'bringing about' involved is the 'bringing about' of ordinary, efficient, causality. It is no different in principle from the 'bringing about' involved when the impact of one billiard-ball brings about the motion of another ball. But the mention of Hume's paradigm should not mislead. I do not wish to commit myself for or against a Humean or semi-Humean analysis of the nature of the causal relation. I am simply saying that causality in the mental sphere is no different from causality in the physical sphere.

The further assumptions I will make about the nature of the causal relation in this work will only be two in number. In the first place, I will assume that the cause and its effect are 'distinct existences', so that the existence of the cause does not logically imply the existence of the effect, or *vice-versa.* In the second place, I will assume that if a sequence is a causal one, then it is a sequence that falls under some law. The stone causes the glass to break. There may be no law connecting the impact of stones on glass with the breaking of the glass. But in speaking of the sequence as a causal sequence, we imply that there is *some* description of the situation (not necessarily known to us) that falls under a law. These assumptions are not entirely uncontroversial, but at least are relatively modest.

In the fourth place, the word 'behaviour' is ambiguous. We may distinguish between 'physical behaviour', which refers to any merely physical action or passion of the body, and 'behaviour proper', which implies relationship to the mind. 'Behaviour proper' entails 'physical behaviour', but not all 'physical behaviour' is 'behaviour proper', for the latter springs from the mind in a certain particular way. A reflex knee jerk is 'physical behaviour', but it is not 'behaviour proper'. Now if in our formula 'behaviour' were to mean 'behaviour proper', then we would be giving an account of mental concepts in terms of a concept that already presupposes mentality, which would be circular. So it is clear that in our formula 'behaviour' must mean 'physical behaviour'. (And it is clear also that this is going to make our projected account of the mental concepts that much more difficult to carry through.)

It will be seen that our formula 'state of the person apt for bringing about a certain sort of behaviour' is something that must be handled with care. Perhaps it is best conceived of as a slogan or catch-phrase which indicates the general lines along which accounts of the individual mental concepts are to be sought, but does no more than this.

This leads on to a final point to be made about the formula. It should not be regarded as a guide to the producing of *translations* of mental statements. It may well be that it is not possible to translate mental statements into statements that mention nothing but physical happenings, in any but the roughest way. It may be still true, nevertheless, that we can give a satisfactory and complete account of the situations covered by the mental concepts in purely physical and topic-neutral terms.

I think the situation is as follows. We apply certain concepts, the mental concepts, to human beings. That is to say, we attribute mental states to them. Then the question arises whether it is possible to do full justice to the nature of these mental states by means of purely physical or neutral concepts. We therefore try to sketch an account of typical mental states in purely physical or neutral terms. The account might fall indefinitely short of giving translations of mental statements, yet it might still be plausible to say that the account had done justice to the phenomena.

Of course, this does leave us with the question how, lacking the test of translation, we can ever know that we have succeeded in our enterprise. But this is just one instance of the perennial problem of finding a decision-procedure for philosophical problems. I think in fact that all we can do is this: we produce an account of a certain range of phenomena in terms of a favoured set of concepts; we then try to test this account by looking for actual and possible situations falling within this range of phenomena which seem to defy complete description in terms of the favoured concepts. If we can deal successfully with all the difficult cases, we have done all that we can do. But there is unlikely to be any way of *proving* to the general satisfaction that our enterprise has been successful. If there was, philosophy would be easier.

VI. DISTINCTION BETWEEN OUR VIEW AND BEHAVIOURISM: THE NATURE OF DISPOSITIONS

I turn to a question that may be worrying some readers. Now that I have given an account of the concept of a mental state, does it not appear that I am a Behaviourist in disguise? Admittedly, there is one great divergence from Behaviourism: the mind is not to be identified with behaviour, but only with the inner principle of behaviour. But, in elucidating our formula, there has been talk about tendencies to initiate, and capacities for, behaviour. And are not these perilously close to the Behaviourist's dispositions?

There is some force in this. In talking about dispositions to behave Behaviourism did come quite close to the version of the Central-state theory being defended here, far closer than it came when it talked about behaviour itself. But Behaviourism and the Central-state theory still remain deeply at odds about *the way dispositions are to be conceived.*

Speaking of dispositional properties in *The Concept of Mind* Ryle wrote (p. 43):

> To possess a dispositional property *is not to be in a particular state, or to undergo a particular change*; it is to be bound or liable to be in a

particular state, or to undergo a particular change, when a particular condition is realized. (My italics)

We might call this the Phenomenalist or Operationalist account of dispositions. A still more striking statement of this view is provided by H. H. Price in his *Thinking and Experience* (Hutchinson, 1953, p. 322), although Price is no Behaviourist. He said:

> There is no *a priori* necessity for supposing that *all* dispositional properties must have a 'categorical basis'. In particular, there may be mental dispositions which are ultimate . . .

To this we may oppose what may be called a Realist account of dispositions. According to the Realist view, to speak of an object's having a dispositional property entails that the object is in some non-dispositional state or that it has some property (there exists a 'categorical basis') which is responsible for the object manifesting certain behaviour in certain circumstances, manifestations whose nature makes the dispositional property the particular dispositional property it is. It is true that we may not know anything of the nature of the non-dispositional state. But, the Realist view asserts, in asserting that a certain piece of glass is brittle, for instance, we are *ipso facto* asserting that it is in a certain non-dispositional state which disposes it to shatter and fly apart in a wide variety of circumstances. Ignorance of the nature of the state does not affect the issue. The Realist view gains some support from ordinary language, where we often seem to identify a disposition and its 'categorical basis'. ('It has been found that brittleness is a certain sort of molecular pattern in the material.')

I will now present an *a priori* argument which purports to prove the truth of the Realist account of dispositions. Let us consider the following case. Suppose that, on a number of occasions, a certain rubber band has the same force, F, applied to it, and that on each occasion it stretches one inch. We can then attribute a disposition to the band. It is disposed to stretch one inch under force F.

Now one essential thing about dispositions is that we can attribute them to objects even at times when the circumstances in which the object manifests its dispositions do not obtain. Suppose, now, that I say of the band that, if it had been subjected to force F at T_1, a time when it was not so subjected, it would have stretched one inch. What warrant have I for my statement? Consider first the answer that a Realist about dispositions will give. He will say that there is every reason to believe that the categorical state of the band which is responsible for its stretching one inch under force F obtains at T_1. Given that it does obtain at T_1, then, as a matter of physical necessity, the band must stretch one inch under force F.

But what answer can the Phenomenalist about dispositions give? For him, a disposition does not entail the existence of a categorical state. The only reason he can give for saying that the band would have stretched one inch under force F at T_1 is that numerically the same band behaved in this way on other occasions. But now we may ask the Phenomenalist 'What is the magic in numerical identity?' A thing can change its properties over a period of time. Why should it not change its dispositional properties? How does the Phenomenalist know what the band's dispositional properties are at T_1? He may reply 'We have every reason to think that the relevant categorical properties of the object are unchanged at T_1, so we have every reason to think that the dispositional properties are unchanged.' But since he has asserted that the connection between 'categorical basis' and dispositional property is not a necessary one, he can only be arguing that there is a *contingent* connection between categorical properties and the fact that the band has that dispositional property at T_1. But how could one ever establish a contingent connection between categorical properties and unfulfilled possibilities? It is not as if one could observe the unfulfilled possibilities independently, in order to see how they are correlated with the categorical properties! It seems that the Phenomenalist about dispositions will be reduced to utter scepticism about dispositions, except on occasions that they are actually manifested.

I think we can imagine the possibility that the band should be acted upon by force F on different occasions, and behave quite differently on these occasions, although there was no relevant difference in the categorical properties of the band on these occasions. That is to say, I think we can imagine that the Principle of Sufficient Reason may be false in the case of the band. But it is only to the extent that we accept the Principle of Sufficient Reason that we can introduce the notion of disposition. It is only to the extent that we relate disposition to 'categorical basis', and difference of disposition to difference of 'categorical basis', that we can speak of dispositions. We must be Realists, not Phenomenalists, about dispositions.

All this is of central importance to the philosophy of mind. Thus, if belief, for instance, is a disposition, then it is entailed that while I believe *p* my mind is in a certain non-dispositional state, a state which in suitable circumstances gives rise to 'manifestations of belief that *p*'. The fact that we may not know the concrete nature of this state is irrelevant.

The tremendous difference between this and the 'Phenomenalist' account of disposition emerges when we consider that, on this 'Realist' view of dispositions, we can think of them as *causes* or *causal factors*. On the Phenomenalist view, dispositions cannot be causes. To say the glass breaks because it is brittle is only to say that it breaks because it is the sort of thing that does break easily in the circumstances it is in. But if brittleness can be identified with an actual *state* of the glass, then we can think of it as a cause, or, more vaguely, a causal factor, in the process that brings about breaking. Dispositions are seen to be states that actually *stand behind* their manifestations. It is simply that the states are *identified* in terms of their manifestations in suitable conditions, rather than in terms of their intrinsic nature.

Our argument for a 'Realist' account of dispositions can equally be applied to capacities and powers. They, too, must be conceived of as states of the object that has the capacity or power.

It will now be seen that a Behaviourist must reject this account of mental predicates involving dispositions, capacities or powers. For if he subscribed to it he would be admitting that, in talking about the mind, we were committed to talking about inner states of the person. But to make this admission would be to contradict his Behaviourism. It would contradict the *peripheralistic* or *positivistic* drive that is involved in Behaviourism. Behaviourism concentrates on the case of other minds, and there it substitutes the evidence that we have for the existence of other minds—behaviour—for the mental states themselves. To admit dispositions as states lying behind, and in suitable circumstances giving rise to, behaviour is to contradict the whole programme. If, however, the reader still wishes to call my view a form of Behaviourism, this is no more than a matter of verbal concern. For it remains a 'Behaviourism' that permits the contingent identification of mind and brain.

The Central-state Theory

Suppose now we accept for argument's sake the view that in talking about mental states we are simply talking about states of the person apt for the bringing about of behaviour of a certain sort. (The detailed working out and defence of this view will in fact occupy the major part of this book—Part Two.) The question then arises 'What in fact is the nature of these inner states? What are these inner causes like?' And here no logical analysis can help us. It is a matter of high-level scientific speculation.

At this point we have one of those exciting turn-arounds where old theories appear in a quite new light. We suddenly get a new view of Dualism and of the Attribute theories, not to mention any wilder views that may be proposed. They are not, as we have insisted upon treating them up to this point, accounts of the *concept* of mind at all. Given that the concept of a mental state is the concept of a state of the person apt for bringing about certain sorts of (physical) behaviour, then we should view the different accounts of the mind that have been advanced through the ages as different *scientific* answers to the question of the intrinsic nature of these states.

Take the primitive view that the mind or spirit is breath. Consider the difference between a living man and a corpse. A living man behaves in a quite different, and far more complex, way than any other sort of thing, but a corpse is little different from any other material object. What is the inner principle of the living man's behaviour? One obvious difference is that the living man breathes, the corpse does not. So it is a plausible preliminary hypothesis that the inner principle of man's unique behaviour— his spirit or mind—is breath or air.

Again, it is a meaningful suggestion that the mind is a flame in the body, or a collection of specially smooth and mobile atoms dispersed throughout the members. It is a meaningful suggestion that it is a spiritual substance, or a set of special properties of the body or central nervous system which are not reducible to the physico-chemical properties of matter. Or perhaps, as Central-state Materialism maintains, it is the physico-chemical workings of the central nervous system.

(Some theories, of course, do have to be rejected for conceptual reasons. We have argued that 'Bundle' Dualism is logically in-coherent. Behaviourism is unacceptable because, since the mind is the inner principle of behaviour, it cannot *be* behaviour. Any Parallelist theory must be rejected because the essential thing about the mind is that it stands and operates in the causal chain between stimulus and response. But these are unnatural views of the mind, only adopted unwillingly under the stress of great intellectual difficulties.)

At this point we see that the statement 'The gene is the DNA molecule' provides a very good model for many features of the statement 'The mind is the brain'. (I am greatly indebted to Brian Medlin for this very important model.) The concept of the gene, when it was introduced into biology as a result of Mendel's work, was the concept of a factor in the person or animal apt for the production of certain characteristics in that person or animal. The question then arose what in fact the gene was. All sorts of answers were possible. For instance, the gene might have been an im-material principle which somehow brought it about that my eyes are the colour they are. In fact, however, biologists have con-cluded that there is sufficient evidence to identify that which is apt for the production of hereditary characteristics as the sub-stance to be found at the centre of cells: deoxyribo-nucleic acid. This identification is a theoretical one. Nobody has directly ob-served, or could ever hope to observe in practice, the details of the causal chain from DNA molecule to the colouring of the eye. But the identification is sufficiently certain.

It may now be asserted that, once it be granted that the con-cept of a mental state is the concept of a state of the person apt for the production of certain sorts of behaviour, the identification of these states with physico-chemical states of the brain is, in the present state of knowledge, nearly as good a bet as the identifica-tion of the gene with the DNA molecule.

VIII. OBJECTIONS OUTSTANDING ANSWERED

This completes the preliminary sketch of my version of the Central-state theory. It will be noticed that the argument has two distinct 'movements'. As the first step, a certain logical analysis of the mental concepts is proposed. This is a conceptual thesis. It must be established, or refuted, in the same way (whatever that may be!) that any other piece of purported logical analysis is established or refuted. It may perhaps be called the *Causal analysis* of the mental concepts. It does not entail, but neither does it exclude, Materialism. The second step of the argument is to identify these inner states with physico-chemical states of the brain. This is a contingent or scientific identification, and it yields *Central-state Materialism*.

But once these two steps in the argument are clearly distinguished it becomes evident, I think, that recent defenders of a Central-state theory, such as Smart, have concentrated on defending the second step. I think that there is little to add to what they have said, so my discussion of this second step—in Part Three—will be brief. But it seems to me that there is much work to be done on the first, or conceptual, step. Part Two, which is a detailed working out of the Causal analysis of the mental concepts, is therefore the intellectual centre of this book.

Now no doubt the reader already has many objections to propose to this projected programme of argument. Some of the objections will be considered in the following sections. In the meanwhile, I will try to show that what has already been said answers almost all the difficulties for a Central-state Materialism that were mentioned in Section II. It will be remembered that in earlier chapters a series of demands was assembled, demands which it seemed desirable that a theory of mind be able to meet. In Section II of this chapter we mentioned four of these demands that the Central-state theory seemed to have difficulty with.

(i) The first difficulty was that Central-state Materialism seemed to be incompatible with the apparent logical possibility of disembodied existence.

Inside the context of our theory, somebody who asserts the logical possibility of a disembodied mind is only asserting that mental states (which are states of the person apt for the bringing about of certain sorts of behaviour) are not really states of the brain, but are states of a spiritual substance capable of existence after the dissolution of the body. And since we have allowed the logical possibility of non-physical substance, and since for Central-state Materialism it is a mere contingent fact that the mind is the brain, there is no bar to such a logical possibility. It is incompatible with the truth of Central-state Materialism, but that theory is, at best, only contingently true.

(ii) The second difficulty was that Central-state Materialism seemed incompatible with the admission that mental states are logically incapable of independent existence. For processes in the brain might have independent existence.

But if a mental state *qua mental state* is nothing but 'a state of the person apt for the bringing about of certain sorts of behaviour' then it is easy to see that there could not be objects which just had the characteristic of being mental states, and no others. For no thing or event can be simply apt for bringing about other events: it must have further independent characteristics of its own. So mental states, *qua* mental states, are incapable of independent existence.

(iii) We said that a Central-state Materialism must give an analysis of the 'intentionality' of mental processes. This is a demand that we will be able to meet only as our detailed analysis of the mental concepts unfolds.

(iv) Finally, in summing up our discussion of Behaviourism, we said that a satisfactory theory of mind ought both to allow the existence of inner mental events, yet also preserve a logical connection between these inner events and outward behaviour. It is clear that an account of mental states as states apt for the production of certain sorts of behaviour will fulfil this demand.

Indeed, it is startling to observe that Wittgenstein's dictum, 'An "inner process" stands in need of outward criteria', might be the slogan of a Causal analysis of the mental concepts. Mental processes have a nature of their own, although this nature is not directly given to us. Yet, *qua* mental processes, they 'stand in need of outward criteria', that is to say, they are the mental processes they are in virtue of the behaviour they are apt for bringing about. But, unlike Wittgenstein, we can remove the quotation marks from the phrase 'inner process'.

IX. THE NATURE OF CONSCIOUSNESS

It will seem obvious to some philosophers that the account of mental states given in the previous sections is unsatisfactory because it leaves out consciousness or experience. Their protest might take the following form. The argument, so far, they would say, has a quite unsatisfactory other-person character. It is as if we took the very complex behaviour of other persons, and said that this behaviour must be assumed to have a cause within the persons, a cause which may be called a mental state, and we then went on to identify these postulated 'mental states' with states of the brain. This is the procedure that occurs in the case of the gene. Complex patterns of inherited characteristics are observed; an inner cause is postulated; and finally this inner principle is identified with the DNA molecule. But, unlike the gene, the mind is not a mere theoretical concept. In our own case, at least, we have a direct awareness of mental states. We are conscious, we have experiences. Indeed, it was this very fact that led to the rejection of the physicalist programme with respect to the mind sponsored by Behaviourism. Consciousness is something more than the occurrence of an inner state apt for the production of certain sorts of behaviour.

There is something in this protest. Consciousness *is* something more than an inner state apt for the production of certain sorts of behaviour. But what more? Before we try to answer this question, let us try to become a bit clearer, by means of cases, about what is meant by 'consciousness' here. A continuum of cases could be constructed, but perhaps three members of this continuum will suffice.

Case 1. This is something that can happen when one is driving very long distances in monotonous conditions. One can 'come to' at some point and realize that one has driven many miles without consciousness of the driving, or, perhaps, anything else. One has kept the car on the road, changed gears, even, or used the brake, but all in a state of 'automatism'.

Case 2. One is thinking furiously about a problem, so furiously that one is 'lost to the world'.

Case 3. Under the direction of an old-fashioned psychologist, one is self-consciously trying to scrutinize what goes on from moment to moment in one's mind.

Now when critics say that an account of the mind of the sort we have adumbrated leaves out consciousness or experience, I think they have in mind the distinction between cases like Case 1, on the one hand, and Cases 2 and 3, on the other. Despite all the differences between Cases 2 and 3, in both cases there is consciousness. In Case 1 it is lacking. A Materialist account of the mind, they say, cannot explain Cases 2 and 3.

In Case 1 one must *in some sense* have been perceiving, and acting purposively. Otherwise the car would have ended in a ditch. But one was not conscious of one's perceptions and one's purposes. It may be surmised that animals spend much of their life in that state of automatism enjoyed by the long-distance driver.

By contrast, in Cases 2 and 3 one is conscious of one's thoughts and of the current contents of one's mind. I have deliberately chosen two very different cases to indicate that consciousness need not involve the special 'self-consciousness' present in Case 3. When I am 'lost in thought' I am, nevertheless, conscious of my thoughts. It is just that I am paying no attention to the fact that they are *my* thoughts. I am interested in them simply as thoughts. But when I am asked to introspect and to report my findings, this is normally not the case.

I hope I have now correctly characterized, by means of examples, what an opponent means when he says that an account of mental states as nothing but states of the person apt for the production of certain sorts of behaviour is deficient because it leaves out consciousness. Consciousness is something more. But, agreeing with this, I suggest that consciousness is no more than *awareness* (perception) of inner mental states by the person whose states they are.

If this is so, then consciousness is simply a further mental state, a state 'directed' towards the original inner states. Now why should we not give an account of this further mental state along the same general lines that we gave of the mental states towards which it is 'directed'? That is to say, why should not it, too, be an inner state apt for the production of certain behaviour? If I perceive a physical situation, then we have an inner mental state 'directed' in a certain way towards a certain physical situation. The exact unfolding of this 'directedness' is something that we shall try to give an account of when we discuss perception in detail. Now if I am aware, not only of the physical situation, but also of the fact that I am perceiving, then we have a further mental state 'directed' in the same sort of way (a relation still to be elucidated in detail) towards the original mental state. And if this further mental state, which *qua* mental state is simply a state of the person apt for the production of certain behaviour, can be contingently identified with a state of the brain, it will be a process in which one part of the brain scans another part of the brain. In perception the brain scans the environment. In awareness of the perception another process in the brain scans that scanning.

Further awareness of that awareness would also be possible: a further scanning of the original inner scanning.

Consciousness, or experience, then (as opposed to completely unselfconscious mental activity which is perfectly possible, and which occurs in the case of the 'automatic driving') is simply awareness of our own state of mind. The technical term for such awareness of our own mental state is 'introspection' or 'introspective awareness'. It is true that the term 'introspection' is sometimes reserved for the particular sort of self-inspection involved in our third case. But since the difference seems to be no more than one of degree, I shall in this work use the term to cover all consciousness of mental state, however little 'self-consciousness' is involved.

A completer elucidation of the nature of introspection must await Part Two. But it will be helpful here to discuss some of its features. I believe that Kant suggested the correct way of thinking about introspection when he spoke of our awareness of our own mental states as the operation of 'inner sense'. He took sense-perception as the model for introspection. By sense-perception we become aware of current physical happenings in our environment and our body. By inner sense we become aware of current happenings in our own mind.

It may be thought that there is no need to liken introspection to perception. All we need postulate is a capacity to make true statements about mental happenings. But it seems clear that it is possible to be aware of one's mental states without saying anything. Nor does such awareness seem to be a mere disposition or capacity to make a statement. It seems likely that animals, who cannot speak, have some rudimentary awareness of their own inner states. At any rate, it is an intelligible supposition. So I think we should reject an account of introspection purely in terms of statements.

It is sometimes argued that introspection cannot be compared to sense-perception because no sense-organ is involved. We say 'I see with my eyes', but there is nothing with which I can say that I discover I am thinking. Now I do not believe that this objection would carry much weight, even if the difference from sense-perception could be made out. But in any case there is one sort of sense-perception where we do not say that we perceive with anything: bodily perception. When I become aware that I am hot, or that my limbs are moving, and I do not gain this knowledge by touch, there is no organ that I can say that I perceive these things *with*. Yet any psychology textbook would take these to be cases of sense-perception.

Bodily perception, indeed, serves as an excellent model with which to grasp the nature of introspection, for it has a further important resemblance to 'inner sense'. In introspection we are aware only of states of our own mind, not of other people's minds. In bodily perception we are aware only of states of our own body, and not of other people's bodies. The biological usefulness to the organism of a special knowledge of its own bodily and mental state is obvious in both cases.

Some philosophers respond to these points about bodily perception by saying that these differences prove that it is wrongly called bodily *perception*. But then they are left with no way to classify such things as our direct (although not infallible) awareness of such things as bodily posture and temperature. In any case, as will emerge in our discussion of the nature of a sense-organ in Part Two (Ch. 10, Sect. II) there must be some perceptions that do not involve the *use* (as opposed to the mere stimulation) of an organ.

So much for certain general objections to the account of introspection as 'inner sense'. It may still be objected that if we accept the Causal analysis of mental states (the first step in our argument for Central-state Materialism) introspection cannot possibly be compared to sense-perception, even bodily sense-perception. For consider what we would be introspectively aware of. (i) We would be directly aware of an extraordinarily abstract, and purely relational, state of affairs. We would be aware that something of whose non-relational properties we had no direct awareness at all was operating to produce certain behaviour. (ii) The awareness would be a direct awareness of *causes*: a direct awareness that certain behaviour was being produced. Indeed, in some cases, the direct awareness would be a direct awareness of the mere possibility of the behaviour being produced if circumstances were different. It would be a direct awareness of counter-factual truths. Now, it may be objected, this is incredibly far from the detailed awareness of the intrinsic properties of objects that is yielded by sense-perception.

When philosophers think of perception they are all too liable to think of vision. But if we will turn from vision to touch we shall find, to our surprise, that a model is available which largely duplicates the features of introspective awareness as conceived by a Causal analysis of mental states. The case in point is the perception of pressure.

Suppose I feel a pressure in the small of my back. What am I aware of? It may be that I am aware of no more than this: something I know not what is pressing upon my back. I might say it was something material, but what is a material object in this context except 'that which is capable of exerting pressure'? I might not even know whether it was something solid, something liquid (such as a jet of water), or something gaseous (a jet of air). My awareness of the object is simply awareness of 'something which has the relation to me of pressing on me'. Here is a perceptual parallel to the abstract and relational awareness that is being attributed to 'inner sense'.

But this is not the only value the case of pressure has as a model. Pressure is a causal notion: it involves one body that is in contact with another body making this second body move in some way. Yet is there any more direct or non-inferential tactual perception than the perception of pressure? It is hard to see what simpler tactual perceptions the perception of pressure could be an inference from. This is not to imply that an inexperienced infant will have as clear a perception of pressure as an adult. Presumably this is not the case. But the adult's perception of pressure seems to be a completely non-inferential one, as non-inferential as the visual perception of colour and shape in a clear light. (On this see A. Michotte, *The Perception of Causality*, Ch. XIII, translated by T. R. and E. Miles, Methuen, 1963.) So it seems that touch involves a direct, or non-inferential, awareness of causes. Here is a perceptual parallel to the awareness of causal relation that our account attributes to 'inner sense'.

(What importance this has for our concept of cause I shall not stop here to inquire. I am inclined to argue that causes are one thing, and awareness of causes is another, so that the fact, if it is a fact, that in perception and introspection we have a non-inferential knowledge of causes is compatible with almost any theory of the nature of causation. But we cannot go into this fascinating and difficult question any further here.)

But the parallel can be extended even further. When something presses upon us we are aware, sometimes, that pressure is being exerted in a greater or lesser degree, even although our body is not yielding to the pressure. In this case we can say that we are aware that the object is exerting a force apt for the bringing about of motion in our body, although it is not actually bringing about such motion.

It may be objected that, in such a case, although our body as a whole is not being moved, nevertheless parts of our flesh are actually being moved by the object exerting the pressure. The greater the pressure, the greater the distortion of the flesh. If there were no different degrees of distortion of the flesh, how could we be aware of different degrees of pressure?

However, although there is no doubt that it is the different degrees of distortion of the flesh that cause us to be aware of different degrees of pressure, it is far from clear that what we are aware of is the distortion of the flesh. (In my discussion of the perception of pressure in *Bodily Sensations*, Routledge, 1962, pp. 22–3, I failed to notice this point.) Sometimes, at any rate, are we not aware of pressure on our body, of greater or lesser degree, yet not aware of *any* movement of our flesh? If so, all we are actually *aware* of is a process *apt* for bringing about a motion in our body, without being aware of any actual effect. The parallel with our account of introspection is then complete.

It must be admitted here that the parallel between introspective awareness and the tactual perception of physical pressure would fail if the latter were no more than an *inference* (no matter how automatic and unselfconscious) from independently given *sensations* of pressure. But in my view, which I will revert to briefly in Chapter 14, tactual perceptions of physical pressure are no more inferences from sensations of pressure than visual perceptions of coloured physical surfaces are inferences from visual colour-impressions.

It must also be admitted that the parallel between the perception of pressure and the direct awareness of our own mental states is more plausible in the case of some mental states than others. Intentions, desires, etc., may be plausibly construed as standing in the same causal relation to the thing intended or desired as the pressure does to its effect or potential effect. As has already been pointed out, *this* causal relation does not seem to hold between such mental states as perceptions and the behaviour in which they are expressed. Nevertheless, these other mental states stand in causal relations to behaviour, although different and more indirect causal relations from those involved in intentions. Now if we have made direct awareness of one sort of causal relation plausible, by calling attention to certain perceptions, then it becomes easier to see the possibility of direct awareness of other sorts of causal relation.

It is clear that there are good biological reasons why introspection should give us such meagre information about the intrinsic nature of mental events. Knowledge of the presence within us of potential causes of behaviour is obviously valuable in the conduct of life. If I know that I am set towards hitting you before I hit you, I may be able to control my impulse, in a way that I could not do if I knew nothing about the impulse until it manifested itself. But to know the intrinsic nature of the process, or even where in the body the process was, would be of little value in the state of nature. For the neural (or spiritual!) causes that control behaviour are processes far too delicate for a man to manipulate directly. (If I could control my impulse by putting a probe in my brain, that would be a different matter.)

In modern philosophy we are accustomed to distinguish between observational concepts such as 'blue-eyed', and theoretical concepts such as 'gene'. Genes are things that are not observed, but are postulated in order to explain things that are observed, such as blue eyes. The intrinsic nature of the gene is not given by the concept of gene: the nature has to be discovered by scientific research and theorizing. The peculiar feature of the concept of mind is that, in a way, it straddles this distinction between observational and theoretical concepts. Like theoretical concepts, the mind is a mere 'that which brings about certain effects'. Yet, like entities falling under observational concepts, there can be direct awareness of mental happenings. However, I hope the analogy with the tactual perception of pressure has shown that there are other cases which yield a not too distant parallel.

But all this time, however, we have been neglecting the most important argument of all against treating awareness of our own minds as 'inner sense', an argument that, if valid, would simultaneously refute any form of Central-state Materialism. This objection deserves a new section.

(The next two sections are based on a paper 'Is Introspective Knowledge Incorrigible?', *Philosopical Review*, Vol. LXII, 1963, pp. 417–32. But I have made many additions and alterations.)

X. THE ALLEGED INDUBITABILITY OF CONSCIOUSNESS

Many philosophers argue, in Cartesian fashion, that we logically cannot be mistaken about our own current mental states. We have indubitable or incorrigible knowledge concerning our own mental states. (The words 'indubitable' and 'incorrigible' will be used interchangeably from now on.)

In modern philosophy, the doctrine of indubitability is supported in the following way. If mistakes were possible about the current contents of our own consciousness, then it would make sense to say things like 'I think I am in pain now, but perhaps I am wrong' or 'I think I seem to be seeing something green now, but perhaps I am wrong.' But such sentences are nonsense, it is said, and so introspection is indubitable. (Notice that, having already rejected Analytical Behaviourism, we are assuming that there are inner mental states and that we can be directly aware of them. The only question before us is whether this awareness is logically indubitable or not. We are therefore assuming the falsity of the doctrine that first person statements of current mental state cannot *ever* function as reports.)

(a) *Definition of indubitability*

Before going on to show how the truth of this doctrine would refute Central-state Materialism, it may be advisable to try to define the notion of indubitability more carefully. This is particularly important in view of the widespread tendency to confuse the notion of indubitability with that of logical necessity. In fact, however, a little thought suffices to see that the two notions are distinct. If I think I am in pain now, perhaps I cannot be mistaken. But the statement 'I am in pain now' is certainly not logically necessary. We can conceive of a world in which I do not even exist, much less am in pain. Contrariwise, a logically necessary statement need not be indubitable. For we can think that something is not logically necessary when in fact it is.

Even if I have indubitable awareness of my own mental state, other people lack indubitable awareness of that state. This suggests that it is most convenient to define the notion of indubitable-for-A rather than simple indubitability. So let us say that p is *logically indubitable for A* if, and only if:

(i) A believes p,
(ii) (A's belief that p) logically implies (p).

The definition employs the notion of logical necessity, but is itself a distinct notion from logical necessity. Those who accept the indubitability of introspective awareness will go on to say that these conditions are satisfied when p is a proposition about A's current state of mind. I am assuming that if these conditions are satisfied we are entitled to speak of A's belief as a piece of indubitable *knowledge*. (I should acknowledge my debt to G. C. Nerlich in arriving at this definition.)

This definition of logical indubitability or incorrigibility suggests a parallel definition of a notion that, following Gilbert Ryle, I shall call 'self-intimation'. We can say p *is self-intimating for A* if, and only if:

(i) p,
(ii) (p) logically implies (A believes p).

Many philosophers have wished to argue that if p is a proposition about A's current state of mind, then the conditions for self-intimation laid down here are satisfied.

The notion of 'self-intimation' has not always been clearly distinguished from the notion of incorrigibility, the latter notion being taken to cover both. But there are great advantages in distinguishing the two. Using our definitions, in saying that introspective awareness is incorrigible we are simply saying that any belief we have about our own current mental state is inevitably true. Error is thus ruled out, but not ignorance. In saying that our current mental states are self-intimating we rule out this possibility of ignorance. We rule out the possibility of unconscious mental states: mental states that we are not aware of at the time of having them. We also rule out the possibility of features of mental states of which we are not aware.

If we say both that our introspective awareness of our current mental states is incorrigible, and that our current mental states are self-intimating, we have what may be called the doctrine of 'the perfectly transparent mind'. What we see in our own mind at the present moment we see rightly, and we see everything there is.

The current state of our mind is perfectly transparent to us. This doctrine is associated with Descartes, among others, but it stands in no necessary relation to Cartesian *Dualism*. It is not logically necessary that a spiritual substance be 'perfectly transparent to itself' in this way.

Before leaving this question of the meaning of indubitability or incorrigibility we should consider a notion that is similar to, but weaker than, incorrigibility. This is the notion that each of us has a *logically privileged access* to our own current mental states. Behavioural and physiological evidence logically cannot prevail against introspective awareness. It may seem that this is the doctrine of incorrigibility all over again, but this need not be so. In his 1959 British Academy lecture, 'Privacy', A. J. Ayer conceded that introspective reports are not incorrigible, but went on to maintain the doctrine of privileged access. I could be wrong in thinking that I seem to be seeing something green now, but if I am wrong, correction could only come, if it came at all, from my further introspective awareness.

(b) *The contradiction with Central-state Materialism*

It must now be shown that these doctrines of incorrigible awareness of, logically privileged access to, and self-intimating nature of, our own current mental states entail the falsity of Central-state Materialism.

As a preliminary point, notice that if any of these doctrines is true there is a wide gulf between introspection and perception. Perceptual statements make a claim about the physical world, and it is always logically possible that such a claim is mistaken. 'I think I see something green, but perhaps I am wrong' is perfectly intelligible. Nor is any perceiver in a logically privileged position with regard to anything he perceives. Nor is there any feature of the world which it is logically impossible for perceivers to overlook.

But far worse follows. If mental processes are states of the person apt for the bringing about of certain sorts of behaviour, and if these states are in fact physical states of the brain, then introspection itself, which is a mental process, will have to be a physical process in the brain. It will have to be a self-scanning process in the brain. Now it is at once clear that it is always logically possible, at the very least, for such a self-scanning mechanism to yield the wrong result. For any mechanism can fail to operate properly. So if introspective knowledge is incorrigible, as is alleged, then Central-state Materialism is false. Nor is it possible to see how such a self-scanning process could yield a logically privileged access. Again, it is impossible to conceive of a mechanism which logically ensures that all states of the brain that are mental states are scanned. (An argument of this same general sort was developed by Kurt Baier in 'Smart on Sensations', *Australasian Journal of Philosophy*, Vol. 40, 1962.)

But even if we are only concerned to defend the view that the concept of a mental state is the concept of a state of the person apt for the production of certain sorts of behaviour, it still seems that we cannot hold simultaneously that introspection is incorrigible. For can any knowledge of *causes* be incorrigible? Surely any statement that one thing is a cause, or potential cause, of another thing, however *arrived* at, is subject to the tests of future observation and experiment? And if it is so subject, how can it be incorrigible? So, since our analysis of the concept of a mental state involves causation, if introspective knowledge is incorrigible, as is alleged, then our account of the concept of a mental state is untenable. Nor, it seems, could there be logically privileged access to causal truths, nor could causal truths have a self-intimating character.

It is essential, therefore, for the defender of a Central-state Materialism to show that there can be no logically indubitable knowledge of, or logically privileged access to, or self-intimation by, our current mental states. As a matter of fact, however, once we find the courage to question these doctrines, compelling arguments against them are easily discovered. These arguments are quite independent of Central-state Materialism, so that what is about to be said about these old and respected dogmas may be true even if the main theses of this book are false. I should just add that in two previous books I misguidedly gave (somewhat half-hearted) support to these doctrines. (See *Perception and the Physical World*, Routledge, 1961, Ch. 4; and *Bodily Sensations*, Routledge, 1962, Ch. 9.) In this section I will be primarily concerned with the doctrines of incorrigibility and privileged access. Detailed discussion of self-intimation will be reserved to the next section.

(c) *Arguments against indubitable introspective knowledge*

I begin by advancing two closely connected arguments which do not strictly *disprove* the existence of incorrigible introspective knowledge, but which do cast the most serious doubt on its existence.

(i) It is clear that if there is incorrigible knowledge of our own mental states, then it cannot apply to the past, but only to the present. Put the mental state even a fraction of a second in the past, and error becomes logically possible. Two events that occur at different times must be 'distinct existences': it is always logically possible that one event might occur but the other not occur. If I think that I was in pain a fraction of a second ago, then, despite the brevity of the time-gap, the thought and the pain must be 'distinct existences'. So it must be logically possible for there to have been no pain to correspond to my thought.

But if we consider the knowledge that I was in pain a fraction of a second ago, it is clear that this is a paradigm of *empirically* indubitable knowledge. We can hardly imagine, in any concrete way, what it would be like to make a mistake in such a case. The mistake is only logically possible. Now what the upholder of the logical indubitability of current introspective knowledge must maintain is that the logical character of our certainty changes as we move from this immediate past to the present. From being empirically impossible, error becomes logically impossible. Now are we really prepared to say that a fraction of a second changes the nature of our certainty? Is our certainty that we are in pain now really any different from our certainty that we were in pain an instant ago? Yet the latter cannot be better than empirical certainty.

Nothing I have said here is a strict disproof of the thesis of indubitability, but consideration of the case of the immediate past should, I think, make us suspect the thesis.

(ii) A second, closely-connected, argument shows that it is (empirically) impossible that our ordinary *reports* of our current mental state should be indubitable.

Suppose I report 'I am in pain now'. If we take the view that the latter reports a piece of indubitable knowledge, to what period of time does the word 'now' refer? Not to the time before I started speaking, for there I am depending on memory, which can be challenged. Not to the time after I finish speaking, for then I depend on knowledge of the future, which can be challenged too. The time in question must therefore be the time during which the report is being made. But then it must be remembered that anything we say takes time to say. Suppose, then, that I am at the beginning of my report. My indubitable knowledge that I am in pain can surely embrace only the current instant: it cannot be logically indubitable that I will still be in pain by the time the sentence is finished. Suppose, again, that I am just finishing my sentence. Can I do better than *remember* what my state was when I began my sentence? So to what period of time does the 'now' refer?

At this point it seems that the defender of indubitable introspective knowledge will have to introduce the notion of the 'introspective instant'. Let us consider first the more obvious notion of a 'perceptual instant'. Suppose a light is switched on and off very rapidly, so that we are just, and no more than just, able to follow every step in the cycle. We can say that, within this situation, the time that the light remains switched on or off is a 'perceptual instant'. It is the smallest unit of time visually discernible within that situation. In parallel fashion, the 'introspective instant' would be the smallest unit of time discernible with respect to inner experiences. Now I think that the defender of indubitable introspective knowledge would have to say that our knowledge is indubitable only while it is knowledge of the current 'introspective instant'. During that instant we know indubitably what is going on in that instant; but past instants are only remembered and future instants only foreseen, so that doubt would be at least meaningful.

But the consequence of this is that the defender of incorrigibility will have to admit that it is in practice, if not in theory, impossible to make a *statement* of the required logical status about one's mental states. For, by the time one has finished speaking, the moment to which one was referring is in the past. Only if one could complete the statement within the 'introspective instant' would it be beyond challenge. So what becomes of the alleged indubitability of the statement 'I am in pain now' when I speak at ordinary speed? Is it in any different position from the empirically indubitable statements 'I have a hand now' or 'I was in pain a moment ago'? Logical indubitability has to retreat from speech to the instant's awareness. But at that point we may well become sceptical whether there is any such logically indubitable awareness. After all, the alleged indubitability was supposed to be established by a consideration of *statements*. Certainly, 'incorrigibility of the instant' would still be sufficient to refute Central-state Materialism. But does it seem likely that there is such a thing?

(iii) I now put forward an argument which is meant to be an apodeictic disproof of the thesis of indubitability. (A similar argument was hit upon independently by J. J. C. Smart. See his reply to Baier in the *Australasian Journal of Philosophy, loc. cit.*) But, as will emerge, at a critical point in the argument I have been unable to *demonstrate* that what I say is necessarily true, although I believe it to be necessarily true, and can offer some arguments for its being necessarily true. In a certain sense, therefore, this is also a probable argument.

It has already been pointed out that, if the mental state lies in the past, then our awareness that we were in that mental state is a 'distinct existence' from the mental state itself. It follows that there is a logical possibility that the awareness is a false awareness. Suppose, however, that our pain (say) and our awareness that we are in pain lie within the same 'introspective instant'. Are the pain and the awareness of pain still 'distinct existences'? If they are, the logical possibility of awareness of pain without the pain is still present, and the doctrine of indubitability falls.

It follows that the incorrigibilist must say that awareness of pain is not a 'distinct existence' from the pain itself. How is this necessary connection to be conceived? The incorrigibilist might maintain that 'pain' and 'awareness of pain' are simply two different phrases having the same meaning. However, he need not take this extreme and implausible view. 'Shape' does not mean the same thing as 'size', yet if X has a shape, X logically must have a size. X's shape is not a 'distinct existence' from X's size, in the way that X's colour and X's smell could be said to be 'distinct existences'. Again 'colour' does not mean 'extension', but if X has a colour then X logically must have an extension. Now, the incorrigibilist can claim, awareness of a pain stands to the pain as a thing's shape stands to its size, or its colour stands to its extension.

But now let us consider the mechanical analogue of awareness of our own mental states: the scanning by a mechanism of its own internal states. It is clear here that the operation of scanning and the situation scanned must be 'distinct existences'. A machine can scan itself only in the same sense that a man can eat himself. There must remain an absolute distinction between the eater and the eaten: mouth and hand, say. Equally, there must be an absolute distinction between the scanner and the scanned. Consider an eye (taken solely as a mechanism) scanning itself by means of a mirror. Certain features of the eye, such as its colour and shape, will register *on* the eye. But the registering will have to be something logically distinct from the features that are registered.

Now what reason is there to think that awareness of its own states in the case, of, say, a spiritual substance, will differ in its logical structure from that of a self-scanning device in a mechanism? Why should the substitution of spiritual for material substance abolish the need for a distinction between object and subject? I must admit that I can see no way to prove that there must be such a parallelism, which is a *lacuna* in my argument. But it seems clear that the natural view to take is that pain and awareness of pain are 'distinct existences'. If so, a false awareness of pain is at least logically possible.

It will be seen, incidentally, that if the argument here is valid it equally shows that there can be current mental states of which we are not aware. We have refuted the doctrine of self-intimation as well as that of incorrigibility.

The best that the defender of indubitability can now do is score a verbal victory by saying that he will not speak of 'pain' unless the mental state involved is correctly apprehended. But since the very same state might have been mistakenly apprehended, the point is worthless, and we would do best not to follow such a usage.

(d) *Rejection of logically privileged access*

At this point, somebody may concede that it has been proved that no introspective awareness can be logically guaranteed to be free from mistake, but still maintain that we have a logically privileged access to our own current inner states. It may be maintained, that is, that we are the logically ultimate authorities on our inner states, even while it is allowed that even we can be mistaken.

It seems clear, however, that this compromise is inadmissible. Once it has been admitted that I can be wrong about my current inner states, then we must allow the possibility that somebody else reaches a true belief about my mental state when I reach a false one. Now might not this person have *good reason* to think that a mistake had occurred? Suppose that certain sorts of neurological processes were necessary for the occurrence of pain. Suppose a person reported that he was in pain, but in fact he was not in pain, and that an observer discovered that the requisite brain-process had not occurred. If brain-theory were in a sufficiently developed state, might not the observer conclude with good reason that the subject was not in pain? It might be objected that the observer would have no way of ruling out two other hypotheses: (i) the subject had made an insincere report; (ii) the brain-theory previously developed had been falsified. Now no doubt the logical possibility of these hypotheses could never be ruled out, but if enough were known about the behavioural and physiological correlates of mental states might not these hypotheses be ruled out for all practical purposes? And, if so, the observer would be a better authority than the subject on the subject's mental state. So it seems that, once incorrigibility is given up, logically privileged access cannot be sustained. No doubt we have a privileged access (at times) to our own mental states, but it is an *empirically* privileged access.

Some philosophers may attempt a rather different line of compromise. They may distinguish between having knowledge of our mental experiences and simply having the mental experiences. Allowing that there is no logically indubitable knowledge of experiences, there are experiences themselves. Mental experiences, *qua* mental objects, are not indubitable, nor are they dubitable, because they are not that sort of thing. They are no more true or false than a stone. But 'privileged access' is still involved, because only I can have my own experiences.

The question is what 'mental experience' means here. If all that is meant by the phrase is 'mental state' then it is true that they simply occur. But then to say that only I have my own experiences is to utter the pointless tautology that only I have my own mental states. The same holds for my own physical states. I think, however, that to talk of 'mental experiences' normally brings in the further suggestion that they are not only mental states, but mental states of which we are conscious or aware. They are experien*ced*. But once this suggestion is made, the possibility of false consciousness or awareness of the states is introduced.

The situation is complicated by a further verbal ambiguity. In speaking of mental states as experiences we might simply be saying that they, or some of them, are experienc*ings*. Thus, suppose I feel cold. This may be said to be an experienc*ing* because it involves my body feeling to me to be cold, a bodily perception that may or may not correspond to physical reality. But that does not necessarily mean that the feeling cold is an experience in the sense of something experienc*ed*. It may be an 'experiencing of cold' which I am not aware of having.

(e) *Objections considered*

I now consider three objections to what has been said so far.

(i) Somebody may say: 'What would it be like to be mistaken about our current mental states? Only if you can describe cases where we would be inclined to say that introspective error had occurred will your position have any plausibility.'

Now there do seem to be cases where we are confused about the nature of our current experiences, and we could quite plausibly construe some of these as cases where error occurred. But these empirical cases are not very satisfactory for our purpose here, because it is not often plausible to regard them as involving major error about the nature of our mental states. So it may be better to consider imaginary cases. Consider the case of a brain technician who has a perfect understanding of the correlation between states of my brain and my mental states. Suppose, then, that I report 'I seem to be seeing something green', using the sentence as a phenomenological report on my visual experience. The brain technician is able to say from his knowledge of brain patterns that (*a*) I am not lying; (*b*) my brain is in the appropriate state for some other mental state; (*c*) there are disturbances in the brain-processes responsible for introspective awareness which would account for my mistake. On the evidence offered by the technician it ought to be concluded that I have made a mistake.

It may be objected again to this example that there is no reason why we should side with the brain technician. If the brain technician and I disagree, should we not rather conclude that there is something wrong with brain theory? Now there is no doubt that this is a *possible* rejoinder, and that if brain theory were not well founded it would be the rational rejoinder; but why is it the rejoinder that we must accept? Any hypothesis whatever may be 'protected' if we are prepared to make a sufficient number of *ad hoc* assumptions, but to protect a hypothesis indefinitely is not a rational attitude. The fact that we could cling to every deliverance of introspection even against the best-attested brain theory does nothing to show that it would be incorrect to side with the brain technician. In fact, I think, it would be rational to side with the technician against the deliverance of introspection, provided that the brain theory was well founded. This does not mean that we logically must accept the evidence of the brain technician. But there is no logically absolute need to accept the deliverance of of introspection either.

It is true, of course, that the brain technician would have to build up his theory in the first place by accepting people's introspective reports and correlating them with brain states. But a well-established brain theory could still be used to cast doubt on some of these introspective reports. In the same way, our knowledge of the physical world is got by perception but this in no way prevents us casting doubt on some perceptions.

Consider another case. I am asked if my hand is hurting. I say, perfectly sincerely, that it is not. Yet the hand is physically damaged, and my behaviour in respect of the hand is as if the hand is hurting. I protect it, favour it and perform tasks with it in a gingerly fashion. One possible interpretation of this evidence is that I think I am not in pain when in fact I am. Perhaps other explanations are possible, but I can see no reason, except the dogma of incorrigibility, to exclude this explanation.

This purports to be a possible case where I think I am not in pain but really am in pain. A case can also be described which could be interpreted as a case where I think I am in pain but am not. If asked, I say, perfectly sincerely, that my hand hurts. But my behaviour seems no more than a perfunctory imitation of a man with a hurt hand. I wring the hand briefly, but the next moment I behave as if it were not hurt at all. Perhaps I only think I am in pain?

It may be objected at this point that if extraordinary situations like the three I have just considered were to arise, we should not be so much convinced of introspective error as reduced to a state of total confusion. If evidence seems to suggest that I can be wrong in thinking I am in pain now, or that I seem to see something green, then the possibility of rational discourse has ceased. The conceptual reorganization necessary to accommodate such error would burst our system of thought.

I have some sympathy with this point, but I do not think that it does anything to prove the incorrigibility of current intro-spective reports. The discovery that I was under an illusion in thinking that I now have two hands, or, still better, that I now have a head on my shoulders, would be an even greater shock to thought and the conceptual system. But surely it is clear that the statements 'I have two hands now' or 'I have a head' are not *logically* indubitable?

Indeed, I think that the illusion of the special status of current introspective reports has been largely created by what Wittgenstein, in other contexts, spoke of as 'a one-sided diet of cases'. Philosophers have brooded upon statements like 'I am in pain now' and have wondered how we could possibly be wrong about them. They have failed to brood upon statements like 'I have a head now' which are really more difficult to deny than statements about our current mental state. But in each case there is the bare logical possibility of error.

(ii) I pass on to consider another difficulty. It may be objected that if somebody denies that the report 'I am in pain now' is indubitable, then he will be forced to admit indubitability at the next level. For if 'I am in pain now' is not indubitable, then it must be admitted that 'It seems to me that I am in pain now' *is* indubitable. But, the objection goes on, once indubitability is admitted anywhere there is no point in denying it to the original report.

Now there is no doubt that, if introspective knowledge is not incorrigible, then the sentence 'It seems to me that I am in pain now' must be admitted to be a straightforward, if unusual, state-ment. And it must be possible to use the sentence simply as a phenomenological report on what seems to me to be the case. But why need we say that such a report of our belief in the truth of a report about our own mental state is indubitable? It need be no more than *true*. (I owe this point to J. E. McGechie.)

If I am in doubt whether horses eat grass or not, at least I presuppose, and so do not doubt, that there are such things as horses and grass. (Consider 'I doubt whether unicorns would beat centaurs over seven furlongs'. Since we think that there are no such things as unicorns and centaurs the doubt cannot get started.) But this does not mean that the existence of horses and grass is logically indubitable. It is simply the presupposition of my starting-point. In the same way, when Descartes set out to examine his thoughts, to see if any were logically indubitable beliefs, he presupposed that he had thoughts. For he could not examine his thoughts unless he had some to examine! But, *pace* Descartes, this did not make his statement 'I am thinking now' a logically indubitable one. It was simply the presupposition of his starting point: Descartes only got out what he put in. In the same way, if it is given that I make the sincere report 'I am in pain now', then that presupposes that I believe that I am in pain now. But this does not make my belief an indubitable one. It is simply a presupposition of the given starting-point: I get out what I put in.

So reports of our current mental state can include 'I believe that I am in pain now', 'I believe that I believe that I am in pain now', and so on indefinitely, as far as logic is concerned. That is to say, there is no logical objection to the introspective awareness of mental states, to the simultaneous introspective awareness of that awareness, and so on as far as we please. But there will be no logically guaranteed freedom from error at any point. How far such awareness goes in fact is an empirical question, to which the answer seems to be 'Not very far'. We can speak of awareness of awareness of awareness of awareness of . . . x, but no psychological reality seems to correspond to our words.

Because our awareness cannot be an awareness of itself, there must always be ultimate awareness which is not itself an *object* of awareness. In Materialist terms, although the brain may contain self-scanners which scan the rest of the brain, and scanners which in turn scan the self-scanners, and so on as far as we please, we must come in the end to unscanned scanners. This seems to cast light on what philosophers have called the 'systematic elusiveness of the subject'. When we look into our own mind, they have complained, something always escapes us. We observe particular mental states, but where is that which is doing the observing? We find a doctrine of this sort in Kant when he speaks of the 'I think' that accompanies every judgement that we make, yet says that we are unable to give any sort of description of this 'I'. Its nature eludes us. Now at least one logical basis of this doctrine is simply that awareness is distinct from the object of awareness, so that in being aware of a particular mental state we are not automatically aware of the awareness. But the conclusion to be drawn from this is far less sweeping than the one Kant draws, because it is always possible that there is a new and distinct awareness of the original awareness.

(iii) But now it may be objected that if introspective reports about our current inner state are not indubitable, then they really lack any authority with us. For there is no way of checking on my introspective claims. But if claims cannot be checked, how can we claim to know? Yet in fact we do think we have introspective knowledge. In order to explain how it can be knowledge without checks, we must say it is indubitable.

I believe that this objection rests on a false doctrine of the nature of knowledge. In order to say that we know something to be true it is not necessary that we be able to support our claim by some independent checking procedure, or that we have independent reasons for our claim. All that is necessary is that in the situations where we make the claim, our belief should be empirically sufficient for its own truth. This point will be developed when we discuss the concept of knowledge in Part Two (Ch. 9).

It seems, then, that the doctrines of the incorrigibility of current introspective knowledge, or of the logically privileged access that we have to the contents of our own minds, are myths. Not only our own Materialist theory of mind, but the philosophy of mind generally, is freed from encumbrance.

XI. UNCONSCIOUS MENTAL PROCESSES

If the reasoning of the previous section has been correct, we are also forced to admit the logical possibility of our being in a mental state, but not being aware of being in that state. That is to say, we must admit the logical possibility of unconscious mental states. We must reject the view that our current mental states are 'self-intimating'.

If we consider such phrases as 'mental *experiences*' or 'inner *experiences*' then it is not unnatural to say that these are the tauto-logical accusatives of 'inner sense', just as 'sights' are the tauto-logical accusatives of the sense of vision. When we see we must see sights; when we introspect we must be aware of experiences. If this is correct, or if it is adopted as a rule of language, then it will make no sense to speak of experiences of which we are not aware.

But this only postpones the real question. For we can now ask 'Are the happenings of which we are introspectively aware—such things as pains, sense-impressions, mental images, etc.—neces-sarily experiences, or can they exist when we are not aware of them?' I think we ought to say the latter. For suppose that we decide that pains, sense-impressions, images, etc., logically must be apprehended, the logical possibility must still be admitted of inner happenings which resemble these mental states in *all* re-spects except that of being objects of introspective awareness. For if introspective awareness and its objects are 'distinct exist-ences', as we have argued, then it must be possible for the objects to exist when the awareness does not exist. And once we concede this, we have every reason to call such states pains, sense-im-pressions, etc.

Nor need we restrict ourselves to bare logical possibility, for there are plenty of empirical cases which can be naturally in-terpreted as implying the current existence of mental states of which we are not aware: states which do not intimate themselves. Consider the case of the patient who screams and struggles when having a tooth extracted although under the influence of nitrous oxide. He is not conscious of pain. But he is exhibiting pain-behaviour, and it is at least a natural induction to say that this is caused by a mental state which resembles the ordinary mental state of being in pain, except for the fact that it is not experienced. To say that nothing but mere pain-behaviour can possibly be involved seems to be only an exhibition that one is prisoner of a dogma. I am not arguing that pain must be present, but only that its presence is one possible way of explaining the facts. A final decision might only come when we know far more about the working of the brain than we do now.

Again, consider the interesting case of the chicken-sexer. He can, more or less accurately, say that a chicken will grow up to be a cock or a hen, but he does not know, and nobody else knows, what visual cues he is using. (Chicken-sexers are trained by being shown photos of chicks whose later career is known. They are told when they guess correctly, and they gradually come to guess better and better.) It is natural to say that female and male chicks give rise to different sense-impressions in the chicken-sexer, and that these impressions are responsible for the sexer's choice, but yet that the sexer has no direct awareness of these impressions. And they might have every property of 'ordinary' sense-impressions, except that of being objects of awareness.

It seems, then, that any theory of mind ought to admit the possibility, and, indeed, the actual existence, of unconscious mental states. We shall assume the existence of such states in what is to follow. (*A fortiori*, we shall assume that mental states of which we are aware may have mental properties of which we are not aware.)

But although our conclusion is independent of the Materialist theory of mind, the Materialist theory allows a peculiarly simple theory of the nature of unconscious mental states. For the materialist will say that, as a mattter of empirical fact, they are simply physical states of the brain. Now most modern philosophers would admit that in such cases as the patient struggling under nitrous oxide, or the chicken-sexer sexing a chick, there are brain-processes going on which are responsible for, or at any rate closely connected with, this behaviour. Now if we are forced to admit the possibility of unconscious mental states anyway, it will be a great economy to say that they are nothing but brain-processes.

I do not think we can overestimate the importance for the philosophy of mind of a completely ungrudging acceptance of the possibility of introspective error and of unconscious mental states. Again and again, the Cartesian picture of our own mind as something perfectly transparent to us stands in the way of philosophical progress. We must see our cognitive relation to our own mind as like our cognitive relation to anything else in nature. We know in part, guess in part, in part we are mistaken and in a large part we are simply ignorant. Being in a mental state entails nothing about our awareness of that state.

XII. FURTHER OBJECTIONS TO OUR THEORY

I have emphasized that the argument put forward for a Materialist theory of mind involves two steps. In the first place, it is argued that a mental state is a state of a person apt for the bringing about of behaviour of a certain sort. This is intended to be a piece of logical analysis. In the second place, it is argued on general scientific grounds that this inner cause is, as a matter of fact, the brain. Some objections to the second step of the argument—in general, objections of an empirical nature—I shall leave until Part Three of the book, where they will be briefly treated.

(i) I begin with the relatively frivolous objections: those that are based on a failure to understand the position being attacked. In the first place, it may be objected that the theory has the absurd consequence that, when a person is aware of having a pain and at the same time a brain-surgeon looks at his brain, the two of them may be aware of the very same thing.

The objection is frivolous, because the consequence is not absurd at all. The patient and the surgeon may be aware of the same thing, but they are aware of very different characteristics of it. An analogy would be: one person smells the cheese, but does not taste it; the other tastes it, but does not smell it. The patient is aware that there is something within him apt for the production of certain behaviour, the surgeon is aware of certain intrinsic characteristics of this something. And, unlike the case of the cheese, it needs a theoretical scientific argument to show that what each is aware of is in fact one and the same thing.

(ii) It is equally frivolous to object that a yellow after-image cannot be a state of the brain because, when we have a yellow after-image there is nothing yellow, or need be nothing yellow, in the brain. For the theory does not assert that after-images are states of the brain. It asserts that statements like 'I am having a yellow after-image' are to be analysed along the following lines: 'I am in a certain state apt for the bringing about of certain sorts of behaviour (roughly, yellow-discriminating behaviour).' Now there may be all sorts of doubts whether an analysis of this sort is satisfactory, and, indeed, until we have given a detailed account of the concept of perception, it cannot be developed and defended properly. But it is the state mentioned in the proposed analysis that is to be (contingently) identified with a state of the brain, and not the after-image. If the proposed analysis, or anything like it, is correct, there is no yellow thing involved in 'having a yellow after-image' at all.

The same reply can be made to those who point out that after-images are not in space, or lack electrical charge.

(Having made this point that it is the whole situation 'the having of an after-image' and not the after-image itself which constitutes the mental state that is contingently identified as a brain-state, I shall hereafter feel at liberty to *speak* in the less accurate way where it is convenient to do so. It will often avoid a wearisome prolixity if we can refer to after-images, pains, intentions, etc., as states of the person apt for the production of certain sorts of behaviour, when, strictly speaking, it is the *having* of such things that should be said to be such states.)

(iii) But now it may be objected that even if it is 'the having of an after-image', and not the after-image, that is to be identified with a state of the brain, it still does not make sense to say that this having of an after-image is taking place in some part of the brain.

Here I would simply deny that such statements fail to make sense. They are only unfamiliar. They resemble odd-sounding but perfectly sensible statements like 'Pass the sodium chloride'. If the mind is the brain, then they may be true.

(iv) It may still be objected that when we are aware of our mental states we are directly aware that they are things that are non-spatial in nature.

This is an observation-claim, and if it is correct, of course it refutes my view. But I see no reason to grant that it is true. (In the next section we will see why it seemed so plausible to say that the introspective data were non-physical.) My position is greatly strengthened here by the rejection of the dogma of the indubitability of consciousness. Once this dogma is rejected, as it was in Section X, it can be said that the objector is simply mistaken about what introspection reveals.

It must be admitted, however, that when we are aware of our own mental states we are not aware of them as having any spatial properties. But it does not follow from this that mental states have no spatial properties. This would only follow if we assumed that mental states cannot have properties of which we remain introspectively unaware. But this is the doctrine of the self-intimating nature of mental states, which we rejected in the previous section.

(v) Now to come to more serious objections. It may well be questioned whether it is really possible to carry out the analysis of all mental occurrences purely in terms of the bodily behaviour that they are apt for bringing about. But the only way to answer this question is to produce a detailed analysis of all the main concepts falling under the concept of mind. This task we shall begin to undertake shortly, but for the present let us dodge this general doubt. Notice, however, that we can be very sanguine in advance about the success of our programme, because we shall inherit all the astonishing progress made by Analytical Behaviourism in unfolding the nature of the mental concepts, without having to accept the doctrine that proved the downfall of Behaviourism: the denial of inner mental states.

(vi) We have spoken vaguely of inner states apt for the causing of behaviour *of certain sorts*. But now we may be challenged to say what sort of behaviour we have in mind. Unless we can mark off this behaviour from other physical behaviour, it may be said, our definition is perfectly empty.

However, I do not think that we need be too worried by this objection. Exactly the same objection might be brought against the Behaviourist doctrine that to have a mind is to behave, or be disposed to behave, in certain ways. I think the Behaviourist could answer this objection by simply *pointing* to that medley of types of behaviour which we normally think betoken the presence of a mind in the creature that exhibits such behaviour. He can make some general remarks about the nature of such behaviour. He can say, for instance, that it is behaviour that involves a peculiar flexibility of response to external stimuli. But he cannot define the behaviour except by pointing to typical instances, and saying that behaviour expresses the presence of mind when it more or less resembles these typical instances. For 'behaviour that betokens mind' is a loose family of cases.

Now the Behaviourist answer here will also serve for our theory.

(vii) We cannot say that every state of the person apt for the production of certain sorts of behaviour (behaviour of the 'mind-expressing' sort) is a mental state. A certain state of the liver, for instance, may be apt for the production of ill-tempered behaviour. Yet it is not a mental state.

This objection forces us to say that not all states of the person apt for the production of certain sorts of behaviour are mental states. What marks off the mental states from others? If we consider the secretions of the liver it is clear that, considered as causes, they lack the complexity to bring about such complexities of behaviour as are involved even in ill-tempered behaviour. It is not until the chain of causes reaches the brain that processes of a sufficient complexity occur. Only then do we get processes which are sufficient to produce and sustain ill-tempered behaviour.

We are handicapped here by the absence of any widely accepted logical analysis of the notions of complexity and simplicity. Nevertheless, we do have some clear intuitions in this matter. It is quite clear that a motor-car is a more complex mechanism than a bicycle—and not simply because the car has a greater number of parts. It is because of this complexity that the car is more difficult to design and manufacture. Equally, it is quite clear that the brain is a more complex object than the liver. And the complexities of the brain are necessary if the secretions of the liver are to issue in such a sophisticated effect as ill-tempered behaviour.

I think we can therefore form the notion of an 'adequate' cause of ill-tempered behaviour. The secretions of the liver bring about happenings in the brain which bring about actions. Only when the causal chain reaches the brain can we call the series of causes 'adequate', because only then does it have a complexity adequate to the complexity of the behaviour it initiates. The 'adequate' cause in the series of causes is what we call the mental event. Of course, it is a purely empirical question where that 'adequate' cause is to be found. It is not contrary to reason to suppose it to lie in the liver. Modern physiology simply happens to locate it elsewhere.

It may be objected that it is only a contingent fact that complex behaviour should have an inner cause of comparable complexity. We can imagine complex states of affairs arising from less complex causes. However, I think it can be replied that our concept of a *mental* state is the concept of a cause whose complexity mirrors the complexity of the behaviour it is apt for bringing about. If it were discovered that complex behaviour did not spring from equally complex causes, then this would amount to the discovery that this complexity of behaviour was not an expression of *mind*. It would simply be an accidental complexity, like twigs falling to the ground and forming an intricate and meaningful pattern.

If this answer is unsatisfactory, the problem can perhaps be dealt with in another way. Earlier, we noticed Brentano's view that 'intentionality' was a peculiar mark of mental processes. Mental processes 'point' to states of affairs that may or may not exist in a way that, it seems, no physical thing or processes could do. It is possible to argue that there are mental states that lack intentionality: perhaps objectless depression is an example. But mental states typically have intentionality, and states that lack intentionality (if there are any) might be defined by their resemblance in other respects to the more typical cases.

Now Brentano thought that intentionality was an ultimate, unanalysable, property of mental processes; Central-state Materialism, on the other hand, must give an analysis of the notion on pain of contradicting Materialism. But to analyse is not to analyse away. Why should not the Materialist appeal to intentionality to help mark off mental states from other states of the person? Why should he not say that a mental state is an intentional state apt for the production of certain sorts of behaviour or, if it is not intentional, that it is very like some intentional state in other respects? An analysis of intentionality must follow later, but, until then, perhaps, this answer will suffice.

I hope that enough has now been done by way of answering various objections to our version of Central-state Materialism. The final section of this chapter will be devoted to a consideration of some advantages of the theory.

XIII. ADVANTAGES OF THE THEORY

(i) In the first place, it is not one of the least merits of the theory that it explains why an anti-Materialist theory of mind and body is so intuitively plausible.

Philosophers such as Descartes correctly realized that statements like 'I am thinking now' entail that some event is going on now in the thinker. (They would have correctly rejected an account of thinking in terms of dispositions conceived of in an operationalist way.) They also realized correctly that such statements do not entail that some physical process is going on in the thinker. (As Descartes says, truly I have argued, it is conceivable that I should think although I have no body.) They very excusably jumped to the conclusion that such statements entailed that something non-physical is going on in the thinker. The conclusion was only invalid because they failed to notice that, while such statements do not entail that something physical is going on, they equally do not entail that something non-physical is going on. The statements can have this peculiar property because, according to our doctrine, in speaking of mental states we do not in any way judge the question of their intrinsic nature. In this respect, statements like 'I am thinking now' are, as J. J. C. Smart puts it, *topic-neutral*. They say that something is going on within us, something apt for the causing of certain sorts of behaviour, but they say nothing of the nature of this process. (Is it too fanciful to suggest that the Dualists who reasoned thus vaguely apprehended the point that we can give the mind no positive description, but went on to mistake this 'logical transparency' for the 'immateriality' of spiritual substance or events?)

The Dualist mistake was all the more excusable because, until very recently, it hardly seemed possible that man contained within his material body a mechanism complex enough to account for the whole of his behaviour. As so often happens, the logical possibility of Materialism failed to be noticed because the hypothesis had no empirical plausibility. Only a few seers such as Hobbes and Spinoza would set no limit to the powers of the brain. (Descartes might seem to have less excuse than some others, because he did hold that animals were mere machines. But I have the impression that his doctrine of the brute-machine was adopted in an attempt to reconcile certain features of his doctrine of mind with Catholic theology, and did not correspond to any profound conviction.) After all, it is only recently that biologists have even been able to discern the outlines of a purely physicalist explanation of the behaviour of plants. While it still seemed necessary to postulate an immaterial principle to explain the growth of a tomato, it was all the more necessary to have a spiritual principle to explain the behaviour of man.

(ii) Closely linked with this first point is the difficulty that philosophers have always felt about saying what mental states are *like*. It has always been felt to be a matter of peculiar difficulty to give any description of the intrinsic nature of mental states. (This, of course, has been a source of aid and comfort to the Behaviourists.)

Now, if the concept of a mental state is simply the concept of a state apt for the production of certain sorts of physical behaviour, it is clear why it has been so hard to give any account of what a mental state is in its own nature. And yet it is not necessary to accept Behaviourism.

(iii) In the third place, our theory enables us to understand, and in some degree sympathize with, a curious doctrine of St. Thomas Aquinas concerning the soul. In his *Summa Theologica*, Pt. 1, Q. 89, Art. 1 he says of the soul that '. . . to be separated from the body is not in accordance with its nature . . .' At the same time he holds that '. . . it is possible for it to exist apart from the body . . .'.

Now if we take the view that a mental state is a state of the person apt for the causing of certain sorts of behaviour, but, contrary to Materialism, go on to say that the intrinsic nature of the mind is not material, Aquinas' view becomes perfectly intelligible. For if the mind is only known to us as that which has certain effects on the body, then it is easy to go on to say that it is naturally united with the body, although at the same time, if it is itself a spiritual object, it is capable of existence independently of the body.

(iv) The fact that Central-state Materialism has to be defended by an argument involving two steps enables us to understand, and to explain, the existence of two widely different traditions of opposition to a purely Materialist view of the mind.

There are some philosophers, particularly those associated with British empiricism or with modern empiricist and analytical philosophy, who think that the great objection to a Materialist theory lies in the existence of perceptions, sensations and mental images. These mental items seem to them to be irreducibly non-physical. Arguments based on purpose, thought or the creative activities of man impress them much less. On the other hand, there are other philosophers, associated with more conservative traditions of thought, and in particular with Thomism, for whom the great objection to Materialism is not perception, but the 'higher' activities of man, in particular: thought.

From our point of view, each group may be said to have seized upon what is indeed the main difficulty for the different steps of the argument.

Those who insist on the difficulties for our theory posed by perceptions, sensations and images may be said to be pointing to the great difficulty of giving an analytical account of these particular sorts of mental happenings as inner states that are apt for, or are capacities for, certain storts of outward behaviour. They are objecting to the logical or analytical step in the argument. And, as we shall see, they have this much justification: a logical analysis of the perceptual concepts that is compatible with our general formula is the most difficult analytical task to be undertaken in this work.

On the other hand, those who insist on the difficulty of giving an account of thought and the 'higher' activities of man that is compatible with Materialism, may be said to be pointing to the greatest difficulty in the second step in the argument: the step where the 'inner states' are identified with ordinary physical states of the brain. For while it may seem to be (relatively) simple to give an account of physical happenings in the brain which will account for things like perceptions, the problem of how a mere physical mechanism could think creatively is obviously much more difficult to solve. If any inner states are to be denied to be purely physical states of the brain on the grounds that no physical mechanism could be adequate to produce behaviour of such sophistication, then, clearly, it must be the 'higher' mental activities.

So both schools of thought have seized on a real difficulty for an identification of mind and brain, but they are difficulties for different steps in the Materialist argument.

(v) Finally, let us note that our account of the nature of mental states makes the problem of our knowledge of the existence of other minds peculiarly easy to solve.

Notice in the first place that our rejection of any sort of logically privileged awareness of our own minds means that there is certainly nothing wrong with the traditional argument from analogy. Given awareness of our own mind together with perception of our body and the bodies of others we can certainly say that there is some probability that there is a mind standing to the other body as our mind stands to our body. The inferred object is unobserved, but it is not logically unobservable, so the case is a quite uncontroversial case of inductive inference.

In introspection we have direct, non-inferential, awareness of our own mental states. We have no such direct, non-inferential, awareness of the mental states of other people. It is, however, perfectly conceivable that we should have direct awareness of the mental states of others. In Materialist terms, we have scanners that can scan some of our own inner states, but no scanners that can scan the inner states of others. However, I take the claim that telepathic knowledge exists to be the claim that we do in fact have some direct awareness of the mental states of others. Ignoring pedants who might accuse us of self-contradiction, we can say that telepathic knowledge is introspective awareness of other people's mental states, or, if preferred, that introspection is telepathic knowledge of our own mental states.

We are therefore in a position to understand how we could teach children to speak about mental states, and how we, as children, learnt to speak about such states. If a child cries, and has a splinter in its finger, I can assume on an inductive basis, ultimately based on my own case, that the child feels a pain in its finger. If its eyes are open, it has red spectacles on and is looking at a white object, then I can assume that, in all likelihood, it is having sense-impressions as of something red. I can therefore use such phrases as 'pain in your finger' and 'looks red to you, although it is not really red'. Further testing of the child in similar situations will tell me whether or not the child has 'caught on'.

Once we are fairly sure that the child can respond with correct descriptions of its mental state in such situations, then the way is open for it to describe its inner state in the absence of observed injuries or normal 'red-look-producing' conditions. We will have no direct check on such descriptions, nor will the child, but we can trust the child, and it can trust itself, because of its successful performance in the other cases, where there was a check.

It is true, nevertheless, that an argument from analogy is a rather slender basis for our complete assurance about many things that go on in the minds of others. So it is interesting to realize that an account of mental states as states of the person apt for the bringing about of certain sorts of physical behaviour makes the problem of our knowledge of other minds still more tractable.

Suppose a human body exhibits the right sort of behaviour.

Given our analysis of the nature of mental states we need only three premisses to infer the existence of a mind that this behaviour is an expression of. (i) The behaviour has *some* cause; (ii) the cause lies in the behaving person; (iii) the cause is an 'adequate' cause—it has a complexity that corresponds to the complexity of the behaviour. Given only these quite modest assumptions, the existence of another mind is necessary. Thus although our knowledge of other minds is inferential, the inference is more secure than that provided by the Argument from Analogy.

Part Two

THE CONCEPT OF MIND

7

THE WILL (1)

IN this Part of the book an attempt is made to give an account of all mental states as states of the person apt for the bringing about of certain sorts of physical behaviour. Classical theories of mind saw it as an inner arena. In Hegelian terms, this is the Thesis. In reaction, Behaviourism saw the mind as outward act. This is the Antithesis. We see the mind as an inner arena identified by its causal relations to outward act. This is proposed as the Synthesis.

Recent philosophical work has shown that a detailed account of all the mental concepts will involve almost indefinite complication. This means that, even if the proposed account of the mental concepts is correct, in actually working it out omissions will be inevitable, and errors all too likely. In general, the discussion in this part will be confined to those sorts of mental states that anti-Materialists, particularly anti-Materialists in the analytic tradition, have thought to raise special difficulties for Materialism.

Some modern philosophers may think that one has no business to be putting forward a general theory of mind in this way until the results of innumerable detailed investigations into particular mental concepts are at hand. But this rests upon a false view of what is the most effective method of discovery in philosophy. As a result of the work of Karl Popper, it is now widely conceded by philosophers that, in most scientific investigation, the putting forward of hypotheses precedes the making of observations. It is not always seen that the same is true in philosophy, even where our concern is with nothing but logical analysis. If we try to arrive at large conclusions by painstakingly making and putting together minute observations concerning particular mental concepts, one of two results is likely. We will either end in complete confusion, or we will select the evidence unconsciously in order to fit a model of the mind that was leading an underground, and so unexamined, life in our thought.

The riskier, but potentially more rewarding, course is to put forward some quite general hypothesis about the nature of the mental concepts, and then to see whether plausible analyses of particular concepts can be produced which will fit the hypothesis. The hypothesis will both be a guide through the conceptual labyrinth, and will run the gauntlet in the labyrinth. That is to say, it will suggest particular accounts of individual concepts, accounts which can then be examined for plausibility on independent grounds, thus testing the hypothesis. And if the examination given to the accounts by the propounder is insufficiently rigorous, as is psychologically all too likely, this deficiency can, as Popper emphasized, be remedied by his critics. Philosophical inquiry is a co-operative endeavour to reach truth by mutual criticism.

Now that we are embarking upon a detailed examination of the individual mental concepts it will be useful to introduce distinctions between *states*, *processes* and *events*. I propose these as stipulative definitions only, but they are definitions meant to correspond reasonably closely to an ordinary meaning of each word.

A state endures for a greater or a lesser time, but it exists entire at each instant for which it endures. Heat is a physical state. If a body is hot for a certain time, it is hot at every instant of that time. Anger is a mental state. If a person is angry for a certain time, he is angry at every instant of that time.

The word 'state' can be used more loosely. A man can be said to be in an anxiety-state all week, yet have carefree moments during that time. But in such a case he must be in a state of anxiety, in the strict sense of 'state' just defined, for a good part of that week.

States may be contrasted with processes. A process is not entire at each instant that the process is occurring. A process takes time to complete, and at any instant while the process is going on a certain amount of the process has been completed while a certain amount remains to be completed. Running a race is a physical process. It takes time to complete, and at any instant during that time a certain amount of the race has been completed. 'Calculating in one's head' is a mental process. It takes time to complete, and at any instant during that time a certain proportion of the calculation has been completed.

Sometimes the word 'event' is used to mean a process. But we shall use 'event' only to mean the coming to be or passing away of a state, or the initiating or terminating of a process. In this sense, winning a race is a physical event. It is the terminating of a physical process. Becoming angry is a mental event. It is the coming to be of a mental state.

In dealing with the various mental concepts we will consider whether they are concepts of states, processes or events. But, unless explicit reference is made to this threefold classification, the use of one of these words, or words like occurrence or happening, is not meant to bear such an exact sense.

It is convenient to begin the account of the mental concepts with a discussion of the Will. When I speak of 'the Will' I intend the phrase to be taken in the broadest possible sense. It is intended to cover every sort of mental process that is of the conative sort, as opposed to the cognitive sort, or any other sort there may be. It is a label for a whole great department of mental activities. The philosophy of the will has received a good deal of attention in recent years, but these discussions, valuable as they have been, have in some respects only left the subject in deeper obscurity. I believe that the root of the trouble is the dismissal, on inadequate grounds, of the view that the will is an inner cause. Here is the open door that we have only to go through, and an account of notions such as intention will not prove so very difficult to give.

11. PURPOSIVE ACTIVITY AS ACTIVITY WITH A MENTAL CAUSE

I begin by asking what it is for a human being, or other animal with a mind, to act purposively. The words 'to act purposively' are to bear a wide sense. If somebody raises his arm with the intention of striking another, then he raises his arm with a purpose. But if he raises his arm with no further action in mind, simply because it comes into his head to do so, we may not always wish to say that he has any purpose in raising his arm. But *here* the phrase 'acting purposively' is intended to cover both these cases.

It is a mistake to think that all purposive acting is a matter of a train of physical, as opposed to mental, happenings. Working out a long division sum in one's head is as much a case of purposive activity as deliberately striking somebody. Modern philosophy has shown a tendency to ignore the cases where the purposive train of events is purely mental. Doubtless this is due to the Behaviourist orientation of modern philosophical psychology, with its tendency to deny the existence of, or at any rate the importance of, inner mental happenings. However, simply for convenience of exposition, I propose for the present to concentrate on cases where the activity is physical, or primarily physical.

Wittgenstein has given us a classical formulation of the problem of purposive activity. To say that I raise my arm entails that my arm rises. But my arm can rise without my having raised it. What must be 'added' to the rising of my arm to give the raising of my arm? In the terminology introduced in the previous chapter, what must be 'added' to mere physical behaviour to give 'behaviour proper'?

The answer to be defended here was rejected by Wittgenstein, and following him, by most modern analytical philosophers. (It was rejected with particular contumely by Ryle.) But before Wittgenstein it was unchallenged orthodoxy. It is the simple and natural view that my raising my arm is distinguished from the mere rising of my arm by the fact that, in the former case, my arm rises as a causal result of a certain sort of antecedent in my mind. When my arm merely rises *this* sort of causal antecedent is lacking.

Now it is at once clear that not every train of physical events caused by something in my mind is a case of acting purposively. The main problem for the 'causal' theory of purposive activity is therefore to suggest marks which will distinguish between trains of purposive activities, on the one hand, and trains of events that are mentally caused but which are not purposive activities, on the other. The solution to this problem is the key to the account of the will to be defended in this work. The solution will be sketched in the fourth section. In this present section, and the next, all that will be attempted is to answer arguments which have had wide currency in recent philosophy: arguments designed to show that purposive activity cannot possibly be the effect of a mental cause. In answering these arguments, we shall see the quite special power of an analysis of mental occurrences in terms of 'states of the person apt for the bringing about of certain behaviour'.

Before doing so, however, we may briefly take note of the objection that not all 'behaviour proper' need spring from a purpose. Is it not possible for somebody to raise his arm, and for this to be something more than the mere rising of his arm, but for this action to involve no purpose, not even the purpose of raising his arm? May not the action be *quite* idle, yet be an *action*, be 'behaviour proper', for all that?

I agree that this is possible. But I think that such cases of 'behaviour proper' are logically secondary. The logically central cases of 'behaviour proper' involve purpose. If there was no purposive behaviour there could be no 'behaviour proper' that lacked purpose. An account of purposive behaviour will therefore be given first, and in the final section of this chapter the secondary cases will be briefly considered. I proceed now to examine the arguments against the view that purposive activity is the effect of a mental cause.

The first argument to be examined is a very persuasive one, and at one time it seemed to me to prove conclusively that purposive activity could not be accounted for as behaviour caused by something mental. Consider, for instance, the case where I form an intention to strike somebody, and then do so. Can we consider the forming of the intention to be a mental cause that brings about the physical happenings that follow? Contrast with this case, a case of an ordinary physical causal sequence, such as the thrust of a piston against the air in a cylinder. The piston's thrust is one event, the compression of the air (or lack of compression of the air if the thrust is insufficiently vigorous) is another distinct event. We can characterize either event without reference to the other. But how can we characterize my intention to strike except by mentioning the state of affairs that would constitute its fulfilment: my striking the other person? Again, it is clear that the connection between the piston's thrust and its effect, or lack of effect, is a contingent one. It is a matter of fact, to be discovered by experience, that the piston's thrust does, or does not, succeed in compressing the air. But is the connection between the intention and the occurrence of the thing intended a purely contingent one? Admittedly, the intention does not logically necessitate the occurrence of the thing intended. But is it just a contingent fact that having the intention to strike somebody is fairly regularly followed by hitting the person and only irregularly by the purchase of postage stamps? Might it have been otherwise in a less ordered universe? There seems to be some logical bond between intention and the occurrence of the thing intended that there cannot be between ordinary cause and effect.

But the argument loses much of its persuasiveness if we consider a parallel case that we have already discussed. It may be argued that brittleness cannot be a cause of, or a causal factor in, the subsequent breaking of the glass. For, in the first place, the notion of brittleness cannot be characterized independently of its putative 'effect': the glass breaking. In the second place, although the brittleness of the glass does not logically necessitate the subsequent breaking of the glass, it is no mere contingent fact that brittle things regularly break.

But there is in fact nothing in these points to prevent us from arguing, as we argued in Section VI of the previous chapter, that brittleness is an actual state of the glass, and so a causal factor in its subsequent breaking. Although speaking of brittleness involves a reference to possible breaking, the state has an intrinsic nature of its own (which we may or may not know), and this intrinsic nature can be characterized independently of its effect. And it is a mere contingent fact that, in suitable circumstances, things with this nature break. Now may not the relation of the intention to the occurrence of the thing intended stand in much the same relation as brittleness stands to actual subsequent breaking? And, if so, intentions may still be causes of the occurrence of the thing intended.

Suppose I form the intention to strike somebody. My mind is in a certain state, a state that I can only describe by introspection in terms of the effect it is apt for bringing about: my striking that person. It is a mental cause within me apt for my striking the person. In the order of being it has a nature of its own. According to Central-state Materialism, it is a material state, according to anti-Materialist theories it is an immaterial state. Whatever its nature, it is simply a contingent fact that that sort of thing is apt for bringing about the striking of the other person. But, if we turn to the order of knowledge, my direct awareness of this mental cause is simply an awareness of the sort of effect it is apt for bringing about. It is this that prevents us from being able to characterize the mental cause, except in terms of the effect it is apt for bringing about, and which gives the appearance of a quasi-necessary connection between cause and effect.

The peculiar 'transparency' of such mental states as the having of intentions, our inability to characterize them except in terms of the state of affairs that would fulfil them, is thus explained without having to give up the view that purposive activity is the effect of a mental cause, and an ordinary contingent cause at that.

Before going on, it may be wise to clear up a possible misunderstanding. It must not be thought that our awareness of our own aims and intentions is built up inductively. We do not notice a certain sort of disturbance in our minds, find that it is followed by striking somebody, and then make inductive use of this experience in further introspections. This would imply that introspection could characterize mental states independently of the behaviour they are apt for bringing about, which is what has been consistently denied. Rather, we are directly, that is to say, non-inferentially, aware of something 'apt for bringing about the striking of X'.

This does not imply that a capacity for direct awareness of our aims and intentions is born in us. It may well take a long time, and long experience of the world, to develop such awareness. But what time and experience bring to birth is not inductive knowledge of correlations, but non-inferential awareness of causes. The position is similar to the visual perception of distance. It seems that, despite Berkeley, at least some visual perception of distance does not rest upon the conscious or unconscious perception of 'cues', but is non-inferential. All the same, it takes time and experience for a baby, or a person blind from birth and newly made to see, to develop this direct awareness of distance.

It is not being maintained that this non-inferential awareness is necessarily free from error. In Part One (Ch. 6, Sect. X) it was argued that there is always at least the logical possibility of being mistaken about the nature of our own current mental states. Purposes are no exception. At the beginning of a train of actions I may be convinced that my aim is to help somebody. Later on it may become clear to the world, and perhaps to me also, that my real aim was to hinder him. We do not have to accept the findings of psycho-analysis in an uncritical way to agree that they have pointed to cases where people have deceived themselves about what their purposes were. And if it is said that in simple cases, such as going to strike somebody, I can hardly be mistaken in what my aim is, the answer is that mistakes in such cases may well be empirically impossible. It is only maintained that error is logically possible. For instance, the following sequence is conceivable. I go to hit somebody (as it seems), but the action ends with my patting him gently on the back. One way we could explain this sequence would be by saying that I only thought I meant to hit him.

Should having intentions, and having purposes generally, be classified as states, processes or events? It seems clear that it is the coming-to-have of a purpose or intention that is an event, and not the having of the purpose or intention itself. So the question reduces to 'Are havings of purposes and intentions states or processes?' Now the train of actions, physical or mental, that are the effects of purposes and intentions are certainly processes. They are not entire at every instant that the train of actions is taking place. But what of the purposes and intentions themselves? Suppose we consider the stretch of time from the moment a purpose or intention is formed up to the moment it is fulfilled or abandoned. At each moment we have the purpose or intention. We cannot be said to be half-way through having the purpose or intention, we can only be half-way through the activities that constitute its fulfilment.

So it seems that the having of purposes and intentions are not events, or processes, but are *states* of our mind. They are states with causal powers: powers to initiate and sustain trains of physical or mental activity. There may be, indeed there undoubtedly are, processes associated with the maintenance of these states, and with the causal operations of these states. But they themselves are states, not processes.

III. RYLE'S INFINITE REGRESS

But there is a second argument, of inferior but still of considerable persuasiveness, which has seemed to many philosophers to be another good reason for rejecting the 'causal' theory of purposive activity. It is the 'infinite regress' argument proposed by Ryle in *The Concept of Mind*.

Like all infinite regress arguments it has the form of a *reductio ad absurdum*. Let us suppose that purposive activity is activity caused by an 'act of the will'. Now is an act of will itself a piece of purposive activity? If it is, the act requires to be caused by a further act of will, and so *ad infinitum*. But this is absurd. The alternative is to say that the act of will is not itself a piece of purposive activity. This is equally absurd. (Ryle uses an exactly parallel argument to prove that intelligent action is not action that is caused by intelligent mental activity.)

First, let us note that there is something that Ryle's argument proves incontestably. It proves that not all purposive activity can be the effect of such things as *deliberating*. Deliberating what to do is itself purposive activity: purposive mental activity that has as its object the forming of a purpose to undertake some further action. So if deliberation is required for purposive action, prior deliberation will be required for deliberation, and so *ad infinitum*.

But does the argument prove that purposive activity is not activity with a mental cause? A causal theory of purposive activity can take the second horn of Ryle's dilemma. We must in the first place distinguish between *acts* of the will and mere operations or motions of the will. An act is something that we do as opposed to something that merely happens. An act springs from our will. An act of the *will* is therefore something that is itself brought into existence *by* the will. An intention formed as a result of deliberation would be an example. It follows that not all our acts can spring from acts of will, but that we must in the end come to acts that spring from mere operations of the will. Operations of the will are mere happenings. They have causes, no doubt, but these causes do not lie in the will.

Now operations of the will are not purposive in the same sense that actions are. Actions are purposive in the sense that they are caused by the will. Operations of the will are purposive in the sense that they cause actions. Only *acts* of *will* are purposive in both senses. So there is no regress involved in saying that actions are caused by the operations of the will.

IV. THE NATURE OF PURPOSIVE ACTIVITY

Purposive activity, then, is behaviour with a mental cause. But not all behaviour brought about by a mental state is purposive activity. Anxiety may produce a rapid heart-beat, but the beating of the heart is not a purposive activity. What marks off purposive activities? This section will attempt an answer.

It may be said that the beating of the heart is merely a bodily happening, while striking somebody on purpose is an action. But this seems to give no more than verbal satisfaction if we want to uphold a 'causal' theory of purposive activity. For we cannot say what the difference is between mere bodily happenings and actions proper, except by saying that actions are physical events that are caused in a certain way.

In order to give a real, as opposed to a verbal, solution of the problem let us begin by an analysis of the way that a simple goal-seeking mechanism, such as a 'homing' rocket, reaches its target. It will serve as a simple model that is a first approximation to the complex phenomenon of purposive activity. The analysis has become familiar to philosophers and others in recent years as the concept of 'negative feedback'. Its importance to the argument here must excuse repetition.

In order that a homing rocket may reach its determined target there must first be a thrust of some sort which propels it towards the target. For the sake of the analogy let us suppose that the thrust is wholly contained within the rocket, that is, that the rocket provides its own power. Clearly, however, the continuous operation of such a thrust will not, by itself, suffice to get the rocket to the determined target except by sheer chance. For the vicissitudes that the rocket encounters in its flight—winds blowing across its path, for instance—will gradually change the direction in which the thrust is impelling it. In order that such vicissitudes may be overcome, there must first be some way in which 'information' about changes of course can be registered in the rocket as they occur. This might consist in a gyroscopic compass in the nose of the rocket which registered the amount and direction of the deviation of the rocket from the course that would take it to the target. Then comes the essential thing. The registration of the deviation must have power to react back upon the thrust that is propelling the rocket, so that the thrust is modified in such a way that the rocket is brought back on to its proper course. The 'information' about deviation is fed back to the thrust, which is modified correspondingly. In general, if the nose of the rocket falls away in one direction, the feedback will have to operate so that the thrust compensates by favouring the opposite direction. The feedback is therefore 'negative'. The homing rocket is a relatively elementary mechanism, and when it reaches its target it simply explodes. In a more complex goal-seeking mechanism the reaching of the goal would have also to register as 'information' in the machine, and this 'information' would have to feed back to the thrust with the causal result that the thrust ceased to operate.

Now to consider a case of purposive activity directly. Suppose, for instance, I form the intention to go out for a drink, and proceed to execute it. My having the intention must get me to the bar despite doors being shut, people blocking my path, heavy traffic in the road I have to cross, and other obstacles. Of course, the intention will not ensure that I reach the bar in all circumstances. It will not do so if I am told on the telephone that my house is on fire, or if I am knocked down in the street on my way to the hotel. But many different things could happen to me on the way to get the drink, and I would still get the drink. Now, if I am to bring off this feat, things like the shut door, the obstructing persons, the traffic, must all be things that I become aware of, and this awareness must have the effect of adjusting my behaviour so that, despite the obstacles, I still get to the bar.

The parallel between the purposive activity and the homing rocket should now be clear. Purposive activity, we may say, is a train of activities initiated and sustained by a mental 'thrust' or causal state. At the beginning of the activity, and as the activity develops, perceptions of the current state of the agent and his environment occur. Where the information (or mis-information) contained in the perceptions is relevant, it feeds back to the causal state, modifying the latter in a way suitable (or believed by the agent to be suitable) for the achievement of the 'end' of the activity. The 'end' is simply the state of affairs such that perception that it has been reached feeds back to the sustaining causal state and stops the causal state operating. Purposive activity is a train of activities, initiated and sustained by a mental state, and controlled from beginning to end by perception acting as a feedback cause on the mental state. To put forward a slogan: a purpose is an information-sensitive mental cause.

In the case of getting the drink, perception that the objective has been achieved may extinguish the causal state completely.

But it is possible to have cases where what is sought is not some particular event, but a continuing condition ('keeping warm', for instance, or 'a session of drinking'). In such a case, the extinction of the causal state is a contingent extinction: contingent upon my body-temperature remaining up or there being beer in my glass. If actual conditions start to fall away from the continuing condition sought, and if that falling away is perceived, then the mental cause begins to operate again. The model here is a thermostat rather than a homing rocket.

The essential role of information in purposive action that enables us to understand a phenomenon very clearly brought out by Miss Anscombe in her book *Intention* (Blackwell, 1958): the fact that behaviour can be intentional behaviour under one description, and yet not be intentional behaviour under another description. Suppose that I am pumping water to a house, and that the motion of my arm is throwing peculiar shadows on the ground. It may be a true description of my action, *qua* physical event, that I am pumping water, and also that I am throwing peculiar shadows on the ground. But, it may be also, although my action is intentional under the first description, that it is in no way intentional under the second description.

Now if I am pumping the water intentionally, I am aware that the water is being pumped. This awareness reacts back upon my state of mind, and, as a causal result, my arm keeps on moving up and down. If I suddenly noticed that my actions were failing to pump any water, the causal result would be that I would stop moving my arm. It is these facts that make my action intentional under the description 'pumping water'. But, in the matter of the peculiar shadows, I may be quite unaware that I am making the shadows, so that there can be no question of any feeding back of information to the mental cause. And even if I am aware of the shadows, the awareness will have no effect upon what I do. If the shadows are not formed because the sun is obscured, nevertheless I will not stop moving my arm up and down. It is these facts that make my action not intentional under the description 'casting shadows'.

It is of great importance that the feedback cause should be a matter of perception or some other form of awareness. It sets a distinction (not an absolute distinction, as we shall see when we come to give an account of perception) between purposive activity and the mere simulation of purposive behaviour that we find in the case of the homing rocket. In such mechanisms there must be what engineers call 'information' fed back to the thrust. But unless genuine *information* is involved, of the sort that is given by perception, for instance, we do not have genuine purposive activity. Such beliefs or information may of course be sub-verbal, for animals and small children, who cannot speak, acquire information in perception.

Now this means that the notion of purposive activity involves operating with *concepts*, even if often sub-verbal concepts. For it is only in so far as we bring objects, events, etc., under concepts, that is to say, it is only in so far as we take them to be instances of things of a certain sort, that we acquire information or beliefs about them. The mental cause which initiates and sustains the purposive activity must therefore, so to say, be concept-sensitive. There must be something in the mental cause which is fit for the operation of information upon it so that the cause is then modified in some appropriate manner. In particular, the cause must be sensitive to the reception of that particular information which has the effect of 'turning off the power'. The state of affairs conveyed by this piece of information is what is called the end or objective of the particular mental cause.

The statement that concepts are essentially involved in the operation of those mental causes which steer our purposive activities may lead to misunderstanding. It may be thought that I am saying that, if purposive activity is to be purposive, the mental cause must involve knowledge of its objective *as its objective*, and that when the objective is reached it must be recognized not simply as a situation of a certain sort (say, drinking a glass of beer), but *as the objective*.

In fact, however, it seems that this view must be rejected. It is true that in purposive activity of any complexity and sophistication knowledge of objective, and recognition of the objective *as* the objective, is regularly present. Going out for a glass of beer would be a case in point. But such knowledge of the objective cannot be part of the *notion* of purposive activity.

For if we say that purposive activity necessarily implies knowledge of the objective *as the objective*, then we shall be involved in vicious circularity. Our account purports to give an analysis of what it is for something to be the objective of purposive activity.

If the account involves as a necessary condition that we be aware of the objective as the objective, then we are introducing the notion of 'objective' into our explanation of what an objective is. We are then in the same absurd position as one who tries to explain what a cat is by saying it is the offspring of two cats.

The only way I can see out of this difficulty for those who still wish to say that purposive activity entails knowledge of the objective as the objective is to distinguish between two notions which we may call 'goal-directed activity' and 'purposive activity'. Goal-directed activity will be what we have up to this point been taking to be purposive activity. Goal-directed activity will have goals, but knowledge of the goal *as a goal* cannot be involved in the notion of goal-directed activity. But once the notion of goal-directed activity has been introduced, it will be possible to introduce the notion of a more sophisticated activity. This new activity demands not only goal-directed activity, but knowledge of the goal *as the goal*. We can then restrict the phrase 'purposive activity' to this sub-species of goal-directed activity, and we can bestow on the goal of this sort of goal-directed activity the special title 'objective'.

It should be clear, however, that at this point the question has become one for verbal decision. It is now simply a dispute about how sophisticated a certain type of activity must be before we call it purposive activity. And since I can see no particular advantage in keeping the description 'purposive activity' for goal-directed activities where the subject is aware that he has the goal, I propose to allow the notion of purposive activity without knowledge of what the objective of the activity is.

Now, however, we must consider a serious difficulty. The mental state that initiates and sustains purposive activity does not cease to operate solely as a result of recognition that a certain situation (its 'goal') has been achieved. A purpose may be abandoned because circumstances are or seem to be such that it cannot be fulfilled. A purpose may be abandoned because a more attractive or compelling line of conduct suggests itself. Now, by what criterion do we pick out the cases where the mental cause ceases to drive because the thing purposed has been achieved? To put the point succinctly, since other situations besides the goal terminate the operation of the mental cause, how is the goal to be marked off from these?

In order to solve this difficulty, we must consider not only what actually happens when I set my face towards the public-house, but what might have happened if the empirical circumstances had been different. Consider, particularly, differences of circumstances of the sort that might reasonably be expected. Consider what might have happened, if, at various points along the route, the moveable parts of the environment had been at different places, alternative ways of fulfilling the purpose had presented themselves and so on. It is obvious that many circumstances could have been changed, yet I would have still arrived at the one place: the public-house. Despite the changes in circumstances, the line of my life would still have passed through the one point, and perception that I was at that point would have extinguished the mental cause. But now consider those changes in my environment, or in me, which would have led, either voluntarily or compulsorily, to the abandonment of my purpose. The points in time on these hypothetical lines of life where the mental cause ceased to drive would show no such tendency to cluster around the same happening. So they are not said to be the 'goal' of the activity. The logical situation can be illustrated by a diagram:

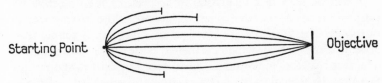

Starting Point   Objective

(The short vertical lines indicate the point where the drive ceases to operate.)

This distinguishes the 'goal' or 'objective' from the other points at which the operation of the mental cause may terminate. We now have a criterion for what constitutes the *objective* of purposive activity.

This account of what it is for something to be the objective of purposive activity is very close to, and indeed derives its inspiration from, R. B. Braithwaite's account of goal-directed behaviour in Chapter X of his *Scientific Explanation* (Cambridge University Press, 1953). But, for the behaviour to be purposive behaviour, our account demands more than a tendency to arrive at exactly the same point under diverse possible circumstances, which is all that Braithwaite's account requires. We also demand that the behaviour be initiated and sustained by a mental cause regulated by perceptual and other informational feed-back.

We have given an account of what it is to be the objective of purposive activity in terms of the outcome of the activity in normal circumstances. This implies that there is a logical connection between persons having objectives and their actually achieving their objectives. It is clear, of course, that having an objective does not entail achieving the objective. But unless objectives were regularly achieved, there would be no place for the notion of objective. I do not think that there is anything very mysterious here. The notion of a homing-mechanism (as opposed to something that somebody *meant* to be a homing-mechanism) is the notion of a mechanism that, when it operates, regularly homes on some target. Now we have argued that purposive activity is activity initiated and sustained by a mental cause operating like a homing-mechanism. Of course, men do pursue purposes that are quite impossible of fulfilment in any circumstances. But, it seems plausible to argue, we can only understand what it is to have a purpose of this sort in terms of its resemblance to purposes of the sort that are regularly achieved.

It will be seen that in giving an account of the objective of purposive activity we have given an account of the *intentionality* of purposes. The 'intentional objective' of a purpose is simply that state of affairs towards which the mental cause drives the organism. The fact that the 'intentional object' may not exist is simply the fact that the mental cause is not *always* sufficient to bring the objective to pass. We may think of the mechanism that drives a homing-rocket as having a first crude approximation to intentionality. The rocket contains a cause apt for bringing about the rocket's arrival at a certain target. So the cause 'points' to the target. Yet, at the same time, the rocket *need* never reach the target.

V. THE 'IMMEDIATE ACTS OF THE WILL'

Since we have accepted the classical view that purposive action is action initiated and sustained by a mental cause, we are also committed to the view that the causal chain involved begins in the mind (whether or not this is identified with the brain), that impulses then travel along the nerve-paths, changes occur in the muscles, then in other parts of the body, and finally in objects outside the body.

Reflection on these facts gives rise to a well-known antinomy, which some philosophers have used as a reproach to the causal account of the will. If I switch on the light it is natural to say that I do it by moving my arm. But it is not at all natural to say that I move my arm by doing anything at all. I simply move my arm. Yet the physiological evidence seems to show that I move my arm by means of a complex mechanism. Ordinary thought drives us one way, physiology another.

It is an important verification of our analysis of purposive activity that it can resolve this antinomy very simply. The movement of the arm is the first perceived link in the causal chain that begins in the mind. The previous links in the chain between mental cause and movement of the arm have to be discovered by arduous physiological research. Now, given our analysis of purposive activity, the first *perceived* result of the mental cause has quite peculiar importance. For here we have the first point at which we can acquire knowledge of what the mental cause has brought about, knowledge which can react back on the mental cause so that the direction in which the cause drives is adjusted in the light of circumstances. For only where perception begins can the characteristic mode of operation of the will emerge. Before that point, the causal chain is, as it were, an inflexible one, one that does not adjust itself to its own effects by any feedback. So the first perceived effects of the mental cause can quite properly be called 'the immediate acts of the will'.

When perception of the movement of a limb is spoken of here, it must not be understood as involving only conscious perceptions: perception of whose occurrence we are aware. It may involve perceptions of which we are unaware, including those subliminal perceptions of which we are not even capable of making ourselves aware, but which psychologists have shown to exist and to play a vital part in enabling purposive activity to occur. (As a sequel to our discussion of the alleged incorrigibility of introspection we saw that perceptions of which we were not aware are perfectly respectable, logically speaking. Cf. Ch. 6, Sect. XI.) Given a certain purpose, it is clear that the cognitive feedback that regulates the carrying out of the purpose is, to a great extent, something we are not directly aware of. For instance, the minute physical adjustments involved in trying to return a tennis-ball over the net are largely determined by perceptions of the developing situation that we are quite incapable of becoming aware of except by long and difficult scientific investigation. We could, if we thought it valuable, distinguish between the 'immediate conscious acts of the will', where conscious perception is demanded, and the 'immediate acts of the will' where the demand that we must be introspectively aware of the perceptions involved is dropped.

The 'immediate acts of the will' are more or less the same in all men. That is to say, each of us has in his immediate power more or less the same range of bodily movements. Of course, there are some differences. Some people can waggle their ears, or raise only one eyebrow, while others cannot. In some cases people acquire new powers. That is to say, they bring bodily movements that were previously not potential immediate acts of their will under its sway. Presumably this can only occur where potential 'circuits' already exist between the brain and the part of the body to be moved. How these powers develop—whether they grow up spontaneously, or are brought into existence as a result of deliberately going through certain procedures—experience alone can decide.

It is imaginable that the first perceived effect of the operation of a mental cause should be something quite other than a movement in our own body. It might be a movement in another body, or in an inanimate object. But it is an important fact about our concept of 'immediate acts of the will' that such things do not occur. (Notice that 'willing something to move', even if successful, would not be such a case. For here the immediate act of the will is something mental: the concentration of one's mind that constitutes the ritual of 'willing'.) If movements of this sort occurred in another body, or in inanimate objects, then our concept of what constituted our body would tend to expand. For it is part of the concept of our body that it is that which is under the immediate control of our will. Of course, not all bodily happenings are under the immediate control of the will, indeed most bodily happenings are not. But the only movements that are in fact under the immediate control of our will are all located in the unitary physical object that is our body.

It is true that we do have an independent criterion for what constitutes our body: viz., the place where we locate our bodily sensations. If we located a pain in a region outside our body, the concept of 'our body' would also tend to expand to include this region. But there is a connection between the criterion involving immediate acts of the will and the criterion of the location of bodily sensations. For, as will be argued in Chapter 14, bodily sensations are simply bodily perceptions: perceptions that may or may not correspond to physical reality. It is bodily sensation, then, that acquaints us with current bodily happenings, including those bodily movements that constitute the immediate acts of the will, thus allowing the possibility of purposive bodily action.

VI. MEANS AND ENDS

In the case of most of our achieved objectives, it is possible to ask by what *means* the objective was achieved. How was the car started? By turning on the ignition, and pressing a certain button. Starting the car is, in turn, a means to driving in the car which may be a means to further objectives. Someone learning to drive may ask by what means the ignition is turned on, and be answered by being shown that it is done by inserting a key in a certain place and turning it.

It would seem strange in ordinary discourse to speak of inserting a key, turning a key and pushing a button as all being (subsidiary) acts, and then asking by what means they are achieved. Nevertheless, it is a perfectly intelligible question and has a perfectly intelligible answer. It is a matter of grasping the key in a certain way with the hand, making certain motions with the hand and so on. Our answer is beginning to become vague—we begin to speak of 'a certain way' or 'certain motions'—but I do not think that this means that the question has become senseless. All it means is that it is becoming difficult for us to *say* how it is we achieve these simple ends. The matter might be investigated, in a time-and-motion study for instance, and an answer found. The question by what means we achieve ends becomes senseless (as opposed to pointless or uninteresting) only when we reach those bodily doings which are 'immediate acts of the will'. (No time-and-motion study would go beyond *these* doings.)

'Knowledge of means', then, is involved in the simplest pursuing of objectives, but it is regularly a knowledge that we cannot put into words. To use Ryle's now classical distinction, it is a 'knowing how' and not a 'knowing that'. To possess knowledge of this sort is to possess a certain skill. The skill stands to a verbal description of the skill something as a perception stands to a verbal description of the perception. (In both cases the verbal description is more explicit, but less rich, than that which it describes.)

This makes it clear that our original account of purposive activity in Section IV is a little too simple. We must now say that the mental cause which initiates and sustains progress towards the objective is able to operate because we have certain skills (normally acquired, rather than innate). Given that we know how to get from state A to state B, and given that we are in state A and intend to be in state B, the mental cause will initiate and carry through the skilful behaviour. (This implies a mechanism in the brain or spiritual substance whereby the mental cause gains 'access' to the skill in suitable situations.) The skill or knowledge how is something within us—a state of our minds—but it is said to be the skill it is by virtue of the behaviour it gives us the capacity for. Purposive behaviour involves the actual manifestation of such capacities in the service of some objective.

The conscious thinking about means, or calculation of means to end, which occurs in the course of sophisticated purposive activity, is more complex. Here the thought or calculation is itself a piece of purposive mental activity which is a means of achieving the ultimate objective. But in order to make use of the thought or calculation it will have to be applied to the current situation, and, as Ryle has insisted, such application cannot in the end be a matter of thought or calculation on pain of a vicious infinite regress. The thought or calculation is simply followed by the appropriate application.

At the beginning of this section we saw that it is arbitrary how many actions we say are involved in the carrying out of a certain purpose (for instance, starting a car). There is no established way of carving up the continuum of action here. This enables us to answer one of Ryle's criticisms in *The Concept of Mind* of the notion of 'acts of will' which are the causes of purposive behaviour. Ryle points out that it is impossible to say how many 'acts of will' occur during a given period of time, and he thinks that this fact is a reproach to the doctrine. But if 'acts of will' are defined by the purposive behaviour they initiate and sustain, and if there is no one natural way of dividing this behaviour into units of action, then this uncertainty about the number of 'acts of will' is exactly what we should expect.

Notice, however, that our doctrine should not have been stated in terms of *acts* of will, as Ryle states it, but simply in terms of operations of the will. For to speak of mental acts suggests that they are themselves things that we *do*: purposive mental activities. But not all the mental causes that initiate and sustain purposive activities can themselves be purposive activities. I have, of course, spoken of 'immediate acts of the will' in the previous section. But these are the first perceived *effects* of the mental cause, not mental *causes* as 'acts of will' are supposed to be.

VII. INTENDING AND TRYING

If an agent has a certain objective it may not be right to say that he *intends* to achieve this objective. For it may be that he can do no more than *try* or *attempt* to achieve this objective. How do we mark off the having of intentions from the having of purposes or objectives generally?

It seems that we call an objective an intention provided that the objective is something the agent thinks to be within his power. It is not necessary that other persons should share the agent's opinion before they can speak of his *intending* to do something. We can say 'He intends to come', even although we know that it is quite impossible for him to achieve his objective, provided only that *he* thinks it is within his power to come. The agent can look back on his past performance and say 'I intended . . .' although he now realizes that it was quite impossible for him to have achieved his objective. An intention is a purpose the agent thinks to be within his power at the time of having the purpose.

The existence of the concept of intention is, presumably, due to the special usefulness of statements of intention, as opposed to mere statements of objective, in everyday life. Such statements enable us to let other persons know what may be expected: in particular, what we may be expected to do. If X says to Y 'I intend to be there' then Y can have considerable confidence that X will in fact be there. If we exclude the possibility of insincerity of speech, which is a possibility involved in all discourse, or X making a mistake about his own mental state, there are only three reasons why X should not be there: (i) X may think that being there is within his, X's, power when in fact it is not. But in general people will have a good idea of what is or is not within their power. (ii) X may simply change his mind. (We may analyse such a change of mind as a case where the mental state initiating and sustaining the purposive activity ceases to exist before the purpose is fulfilled, but not because the agent comes to believe that the purpose cannot be fulfilled.) But X can exclude this alternative by saying that he has a *firm* or *settled* intention. (iii) Untoward circumstances may frustrate X's intention. But, by definition, such circumstances are relatively unlikely. So statements of intention have a predictive force, and are correspondingly useful in ordinary affairs.

Suppose, however, that the agent has an objective, but, although the agent does not think that the objective is impossible of fulfilment, he does not think that it is something definitely within his power. We can then only speak of trying or attempting, and not of intending. The objective may in fact be well within the agent's power, but if he does not believe that this is so, then he and we can only speak of his trying or attempting. Thus, the agent may believe that he will be lucky if he succeeds in moving a previously paralysed limb when he sets himself to move it, although we know that his enterprise will present no difficulties. We cannot say that he intends to move the limb, but only that he will *attempt* to do so, an attempt which will present no difficulty. Contrariwise, the fact that an objective is either empirically or logically impossible does not prevent an agent from attempting it, provided the agent *thinks* that success is possible. (Hobbes *attempted* to 'square the circle', and, indeed, thought he had succeeded.)

Why are the notions of intending and trying linked to what the agent *thinks* about the chances of success, and not the actual chances? The answer lies in the fact that the will is an *information-sensitive* mental cause: a mental cause where operation is controlled by what the agent believes to be the case.

The fact that the will is an information-sensitive cause explains why, if the agent believes or comes to believe that the objective is impossible of achievement, he cannot even be said to try to achieve it. (He can only be said to want the objective.) For such a belief, feeding back to an information-sensitive cause of behaviour, must inhibit action. If activity 'directed towards' the objective is nevertheless undertaken, then either the agent does not fully believe the objective is impossible, or he believes it but his belief is not influencing his conduct, that is, his behaviour is irrational.

Before concluding this section, a final question may be canvassed. If I am acting with the intention of achieving a certain objective, X, can I be said to be trying or attempting to achieve X?

The reason for thinking that this entailment does hold is that even purposive activity with a certain intention may fail of its objective, and in such a case we say that the agent tried or attempted to fulfil the objective. But it seems strange to say that the agent tried or attempted *only* if he subsequently failed. Perhaps the clearest case here is that of the man who goes to move his arm, and, utterly unexpectedly, finds it paralysed. We can certainly say that he tried to move his arm. Yet the mental cause that here fails to move the arm might be exactly the same as the mental cause that, in an ordinary situation, initiates and sustains the moving of the arm. (The paralysis, let us suppose, is simply due to damage in the arm.) So it seems natural to hold that, even in an ordinary situation, we still *try* to move our arm.

It must be admitted, of course, that it will be quite unnatural to *speak* of trying to move our arm in ordinary circumstances. But I think that this is only because there is a rule of candour operating in such situations which forbids us to say *less* than what we think is the case. If I have ten pounds in my pocket, then I have five pounds in my pocket, but if I *say* I have five pounds in my pocket it will be taken that I have five pounds in my pocket *and no more*. Equally, if I say I will try to move my arm, then it will be taken that I do not believe that the action is definitely within my power.

VIII. DESIRES WE DO NOT ACT FROM

It is possible to have desires to act in a certain way, and yet not act in that way. The most obvious case here is where the desire is not enacted because of a stronger, contrary, desire to do something incompatible. Let us consider what account we can give of this situation.

Suppose I have a great desire to go out and get a drink, but instead I carry out an earlier-formed intention to write a lecture. What account shall we give of the desire that was not enacted? After what has been said about purposive activity, the solution is fairly obvious. When I have a desire to go out and have a drink I am in a certain mental state (as distinct from a process or event), a state that is describable by introspection solely as a cause apt for initiating and sustaining a certain line of conduct: the whole process of going out and getting a drink. But this cause is restrained or inhibited by a more powerful pressure which impels me instead (in the characteristic way that purposes impel) down the path of duty. The desire to go out for a drink would have controlled my conduct but for the stronger mental cause which impelled me to write the lecture. In giving voice (if I do give voice) to my unfulfilled desire for a drink, I am simply paying tribute to this suppressed cause.

What is being proposed here is thus a return to the old model of a man's desires as so many causes acting upon him (but causes that lie within his own mind, and so form part of him in the most intimate sense), the cause that actually prevails being the desire from which a man acts.

What we must reject is the idea that, over and above desires, there are further mental states or processes which are responsible for the translation of desires into action. Desires are essentially action-producing although they may be inhibited or prevented from producing action by other desires. In old-fashioned language, the Will is not a separate faculty from Desire. Our purpose is simply the desire that is dominating our conduct.

To anyone who denies this we may put the following traditional dilemma. Either the will is determined solely by our desires (or, in case of conflict between desires, the 'strongest' desire), or it itself initiates or prevents courses of action. But in the former case it is an idle wheel, not worth postulating. Yet if it initiates or prevents behaviour it is itself purposive. And is it not then just another desire?

However, we do talk of acting in a way contrary to our desires. What do we mean by this? We may merely mean acting contrary to our immoral impulses. But normally, I think, we are referring to a semi-formal distinction in the nature of our desires: between desires that are not prudential and those that are, between desires that take no account of what the results of action will be in the long run and those that do take account, between the warm and the cool passions as Hume put it. When I act contrary to my desires (which I may do for moral, immoral or amoral reasons), some or all of my short-term or impulsive desires are inhibited by desires that do not have this character.

Of course, just as a number of physical pressures acting on a material object may issue, not simply in the object moving along the line dictated by one of the pressures, but rather along a line determined by a sum of all the forces at work, so competing desires may produce action that is a compromise between the different lines of action that each desire would have initiated if it had been alone in the field. This is one instance of the phenomenon that Freud called 'compromise-formation'.

Desires may wax and wane in strength, and to experience a pang of desire is to become aware that a desire has suddenly and temporarily increased in strength (perhaps coming to be from nothing at all). What does it mean to speak of the strength of a desire? There seem to be at least two different criteria, loosely connected. In the first place, a desire is strong to the extent it affects or might affect one's conduct. In this sense of 'strong', we necessarily act from the strongest desire. Thus, a pang of desire may result in incipient movements towards doing the thing desired. The stronger the desire, the more that has to be done to control it, if it is controlled at all. In the second place, a desire is strong to the extent that it creates, or tends to create, a condition of bodily agitation. A desire that is strong in the first sense is not necessarily strong in the second sense, and *vice-versa*. Introspective estimates of strength of desire (in either sense) may be more, or less, reliable.

It may be said that in this account of desire I have given the word 'desire' a very wide sense in order to make what I say true by definition. There is some, but only some, truth in this. The word 'desire' may be said to be a concertina-word: it moves between narrower and wider senses. But the widest sense, which I have employed, is a perfectly legitimate sense. There is *a* perfectly good sense in which everything which we do, meaning to do it, is what we want to do, and in which all desires to act which we do not act from are also things we want to do. This sense has the great advantage of bringing out the similarity between the purpose we act from and the desire that we do not act from. We can say: purposes are desires that we act from; or we can say: desires we do not act from are inhibited purposes.

IX. WANTS AND WISHES

The account of the previous section may serve for the desires that would guide our conduct but for the presence of other, stronger, desires. But what of cases where the things that we desire are completely unobtainable, or, if obtainable, are things that we can do nothing to obtain? What about desires to live forever, or to know everything there is to know? What about a desire that certain political actions be taken by groups over which we have no control at all?

In giving an account of desires of this sort, it may be helpful to draw a parallel between the relation of sense-perception to beliefs, on the one hand, and the relation of desire to action, on the other. In the first place, we have those central cases of perception which involve acquiring beliefs, whether true or false, about the current state of the physical world. To these we may compare the havings of desire which bring about trains of action, some of which achieve their goal and some of which do not, that is to say, mental causes of purposive activity. In the second place, we have perceptions which we do not accept as veridical, but which we have some inclination to think are veridical, an inclination held in check by a stronger contradictory belief. To these we may compare desires which press to be expressed in action, but which are held in check by a stronger inhibiting desire. These are the cases discussed in the last section. In the third place, we have perceptions which we do not think are veridical, and which we have no inclination to think veridical, but of which it is the case that, but for independent knowledge that we have, we would take to be veridical. They are perceptions about which a true counter-factual statement can be made: 'If I did not know, on independent grounds, that my perception is not veridical, I would take it to be veridical.'

I suggest that a parallel account can be given of those wants and wishes which do not govern our actions, or even press towards governing our actions. Let us make the contrary-to-fact supposition that a certain want or wish of this sort can be quite easily satisfied by actions on our part. Would it not follow that, under such conditions, we would attempt to fulfil such wants and wishes, or, at any rate, that they would become desires that pressed towards fulfilment? If they did not, would it not follow that the want or wish was not a real one?

So perhaps we can make the truth of such counter-factual statements the criterion for the existence of such a want or wish. To have a want or wish concerning things known to be beyond our power is to be in a mental state such that, if we were to believe the objective of the state could be easily fulfilled by certain courses of action, we would attempt to fulfil it, or, at least, there would be a tendency to attempt to fulfil it.

Suppose, for instance, I wish that I had attended the first night of *Twelfth Night*. My mental state is such that, if I had lived in Elizabethan England, but known something of what is known of Shakespeare today, I would have at least had some impulse to attend this performance. One might, on occasion, have justifiable confidence that such a counter-factual statement was true of oneself. I can know that my current state is such that, if *per impossibile* I was put in a suitable Elizabethan context, I would have an active desire to attend this first night.

Wants and wishes that we can do nothing to satisfy may nevertheless be satisfied as a result of other causes. Perception that the desired state of affairs obtains extinguishes the mental state that is the having of the want. It may be, of course, that the coming to be of the desired state of affairs 'gives no satisfaction'. This is parallel to the case where a certain objective is pursued, but then, being achieved, is not found to be what is still wanted. There is nothing paradoxical in either case. There is no reason why our purposes and our wants should not change in the new situation which arises when the purpose is achieved or the want satisfied. (These cases are different from the cases, which are also possible, where we are mistaken about what we want. In the former cases we really did want to get X. It is simply that, having got it, we no longer wanted it any more. In ordinary language there is an inclination to label both sorts of case 'not really wanting something'.)

To return to the comparison with perception. May there not be some perceptions, or at any rate perceptual experiences, of which it is not true that they would give rise to belief that veridical perception was occurring, but for the possession of independent beliefs to the contrary? They would not be belief-laden, nor even potentially belief-laden. (This will become of the greatest importance when we come to deal with mental images.) Now, in the same way, might there not be entirely 'idle' wants and wishes which we would not attempt to pursue, or be tempted to pursue, even if it seemed to us that such an attempt was quite easy? (And it would be quite easy to mistake such 'idle' wants and wishes for genuine ones, and *vice-versa*, because it is seldom an easy business to be sure of the truth or falsity of an empirical counter-factual).

But this raises a difficulty. The analyses we have given of the having of intentions, purposes and desires have all been in terms of states of the person apt (in their different ways) for the production of certain sorts of behaviour. But if an 'idle' want or wish can occur which is in no way tied to the production of possible behaviour, how can it be fitted into our scheme for the analysis of the mental concepts?

What we must say, I think, is that entertainings of 'idle' wants and wishes are states that *resemble* the action-producing or potentially action-producing states, but which themselves are not even potentially action-producing. (Perhaps they may give rise to playing with words, or the forming of fantasies, but if they are really 'idle' they will not be even potential pressures towards the fulfilment of their ostensible objectives.) But what does 'resemble' mean here? Mental states, according to our theory, are given solely as states apt for the production of bodily behaviour. The states under discussion are not so apt. So what is the force of saying they resemble such things as the having of desires?

The following series of imaginary cases may cast light on the question. Suppose somebody has the following power. He can put any liquid to his lips and then pronounce confidently whether or not it is poisonous. He is always right. But his knowledge that a particular sample of liquid is poisonous is non-inferential. (Which is not to say that there would be no causal process involved in the coming into existence of the knowledge.) He simply knows that the liquid is 'apt for causing death if it is drunk'. This is conceivable.

Now to refine the case. Suppose that some solutions of poison are mixed with an antidote. Suppose that the taster can non-inferentially pick the difference between (i) non-poisonous liquid *simpliciter*; (ii) poisonous liquid; (iii) poisonous liquid that contains an antidote. In the case of the poisonous liquid that contains an antidote, he can correctly identify it as liquid 'apt for causing death if drunk but for an inhibiting substance'. This is parallel to the case of one who is introspectively aware that he has a certain desire to which he does not propose to yield for other reasons, or which he is aware cannot be fulfilled. He is aware that a mental pressure apt for causing certain behaviour is inhibited by another mental pressure, or is inhibited by the known impossibility of satisfying the desire.

Now for a third refinement. Suppose that some very weak solutions of poison are mixed. Suppose the taster can correctly mark these off by saying 'poison, but in too weak a concentration to poison'. He is non-inferentially aware that these samples of liquid resemble poisonous liquid. The liquid is describable by him as 'containing what is apt for causing death if drunk, but in too small a concentration actually to cause death'.

I suggest that this is parallel to the case of one who has an 'idle' want or wish. He is aware of a state within himself which is in fact (whether he realizes this or not) not operating at sufficient strength to produce behaviour, even if inhibition were removed and/or circumstances were perfectly favourable. But it is a state of the sort that, if it operated more strongly, would be at least a potential producer of purposive activity. Unlike a purpose, such a state is at a great 'logical distance' from behaviour. But we can still give an account of it in terms of its relations to behaviour. It is a ghost of the Will.

Before concluding this section we may note that purposes, desires, wants and wishes may be in what we may call a 'mobilized' or not in a 'mobilized' state. 'At that time his purpose was to overthrow the government.' 'All that year the boy wanted a bicycle.' These remarks do not imply that the revolutionary's purpose was guiding his conduct at *every* moment during that time, nor that the desire was active in the boy's mind at every moment of that year. They imply only that the revolutionary and the boy were continuously in certain states which, from time to time, under the stimulus of suitable circumstances, brought it about that the purpose of overthrowing the government guided the man's conduct to a greater or lesser extent, or caused a desire for a bicycle to become active in the boy's mind.

I think the words 'mobilized' and 'not mobilized' captures the distinction intuitively. Formally, I think, it is a matter of the purpose, desire, want or wish being or not being *currently causally operative in our minds*. The revolutionary eats a meal. His current actions are not caused by the current operation of his political purpose. His purpose is not in a mobilized state. The boy looks into a bicycle shop window, or thinks about bicycles. His desire for a bicycle is currently operating to affect his actions or his thoughts. His desire is in a mobilized state.

Two words of caution here: In the first place, to say that a purpose or desire is currently causally operative in the mind is not to say that we are necessarily *conscious* of their current operation. In the second place, it seems clear that a sharp division between being and not being currently causally operative will often be over-simplified. A purpose or a desire might be more, or it might be less, currently causally operative in the mind, and, according to the degree to which we thought it to be currently operative, we might treat it as mobilized or not mobilized.

I believe that this distinction between a mobilized and a not mobilized mental state of this conative sort is very important, not so much for itself, but for the light it casts upon the relation between simply believing a proposition, *p*, and actually *thinking* of *p*. In the chapter on thinking it will be argued that to believe *p* without currently having *p* in mind is to have a belief, but not to have it in a mobilized state. But if we not only believe *p* but we are currently thinking of *p*, then the belief is in a mobilized state.

X. DELIBERATING AND DECIDING

Given that our mind has not existed from eternity, the mental causes that initiate and sustain our purposive activity cannot all have come into existence as objects of prior purposive activity on our part. Not all such causes can be mental *acts*. We must therefore distinguish between cases where a purpose simply comes into being, and the cases where we come to have a purpose as a deliberate result of prior purposive activity. The second sort of case sub-divides in its turn. There are rather peculiar cases where we embark upon some course of action with the objective of forming a purpose whose objective is completely given by the original purpose. These cases will be discussed in the next section. But the more usual cases are those where we embark upon some course of action—in particular, mental action—with the objective of forming a purpose whose objective is not given, or not completely given, by the original purpose. It is this course of action that we call *deliberating*; and, if the deliberating results in the agent coming to have a purpose, we call the result *coming to a decision*. This section is concerned with deliberating, and so with deciding.

But first a word about a relatively sophisticated sort of purpose which need not, however, involve prior mental activity. It is possible for purposes to refer to future conduct. I may form the intention to go out for a drink *in a few minutes*. Here we have the coming to be of an inner cause, which, however, then 'keeps on ice' until it begins to operate. A delaying mechanism in a time-bomb is an obvious if over-simple mechanical analogy. Clearly, in order for such relatively sophisticated mental causes to initiate and sustain activity it is necessary that we be able to recognize, and so have the concept of, 'the passage of a few minutes'. The drive must be inhibited until it is recognized that a few minutes have passed.

Such an intention, since it is a sophisticated case, is regularly the product of deliberation. And at the time set for the intention to be enacted, there will regularly be subsidiary deliberation before enactment begins. But there is no logical necessity that such purposes should involve any deliberation at any stage.

Now to consider deliberation. As has been said, deliberation is itself a purposive activity, although a purposive activity that, for the most part, involves mental not physical actions. It is an activity with an objective: the objective of forming another objective, which will then be pursued (perhaps after a time has elapsed).

Deliberation about what to do has two aspects: an intellectual and a practical one. In order to see the first aspect in a pure state consider the case of looking for a checkmate in chess. The deliberation may involve nothing but the solving of an intellectual problem: what moves by White will constitute a checkmate of Black here? Once this problem is solved, action can follow. (It is interesting to notice that faced with purely intellectual questions we can also speak of *deliberating* followed by a *decision* that the answer is so-and-so.)

The practical aspect may be exhibited in a pure state by considering an expert at chess playing a beginner. The expert may understand the position 'inside out'. He may still deliberate what to do. Shall he win quickly, or shall he prolong the game for the beginner's instruction or satisfaction? He deliberates over the practical problem: 'What course of action shall I pursue?' The process here is one of bringing possible courses of action before the scrutiny of the mind, with the object that one of them should become the action undertaken. He *thinks of* or *considers* various alternative courses of action that he can pursue. An arena is, as it were, set up containing the possibilities, and, as a result of their being scrutinized, one is pursued. That is to say, one alternative emerges as the object of the 'strongest' desire, in the sense of 'strongest' that relates to the causing of action. The purpose that emerges from such a process of deliberation we call the decision.

In most actual deliberation, of course, the intellectual and the practical aspects are almost inextricably intertwined. Notice also that in this analysis of deliberation we have appealed to such notions as 'calculating consequences' and 'considering possible courses of action'. A full account of these notions must be postponed until the chapter on thinking.

It may help to illuminate this account of deliberation if we discuss a point canvassed by Stuart Hampshire in his *Thought and Action* (Chatto & Windus, 1959). Hampshire argues that it is impossible that I should know in advance what I am going to decide. For if I know now, then I have already acquiesced in that decision *and so have already decided*. Hampshire thinks that this has far-reaching implications for the question of the freedom of the will. Richard Taylor has pursued a similar line of thought in a vigorous article 'Deliberation and Foreknowledge' (*American Philosophical Quarterly*, Vol. 1, 1964). He argues that neither I nor anyone else (even God) can predict what I will do as a result of deliberation.

Now, although I think Hampshire and Taylor are pointing to a real logical peculiarity involved in the notions of deliberation and decision, their conclusions about the breakdown of the causal principle in this field seem quite unwarranted.

Consider first the intellectual calculation that is regularly involved in deliberation. It is clear that if we could know the result of such calculation in advance, the calculation itself would be pointless, or would have been already performed. So a man cannot predict the result of his calculations. But the reason is obvious and uninteresting. Such calculation is a matter of going through certain steps with the object of making an intellectual discovery of some sort. Now it is necessarily true, but trivial, that a man cannot predict the *discoveries* he will make. It follows from the meaning of the word 'discovery'.

This will aid us in considering that scrutinizing of alternatives which is the other aspect of practical deliberation. Here we, as it were, set up the alternative courses of action in an arena, with the object that one should be adopted as a result of the contemplation of them. To the extent that we know in advance which course we will adopt, to that extent we have not set up a mental arena with the *object* of seeing which course of action will emerge from the arena victorious. And to that extent we have not *deliberated*. If we foresee a struggle between our various desires, but know quite well which desire will be victorious, our full notion of 'trying to come to a decision', that is to say, deliberating, has not been done justice to. So the unpredictability by the agent of the result of true deliberation is wholly analytic.

But this does not mean that a spectator would be logically unable to predict the results of the agent's deliberation. The simpler case of calculation is helpful here. I cannot predict the result of the calculation I am engaged on, provided that I am really calculating. But someone else may very well predict the result that I will arrive at.

It is true, however, that there is one sort of prediction by a spectator which would count against saying that the agent was really calculating. Suppose the spectator could predict accurately, on the basis of the agent's present state, the answer that the agent would arrive at, and that, according to his prediction, the agent's 'calculations' were totally irrelevant to the agent's arriving at the answer. Whether the agent 'calculated' or not, he, the agent, was going to come up with the answer *p*. Such a prediction would prove that the agent's 'calculation' was not really calculation. For it is part of the notion of calculation that it is a process that *has the effect* of getting the answer. If the calculation does not play an intermediate role in the causal chain from question to answer, it is not really calculation.

Now, in exactly the same way, if the agent's 'decision' is determined in advance *independently of the nature of his deliberations*, then the agent only appeared to deliberate. For it is part of the notion of deliberation that it is a process that *has the effect* of bringing about the decision. To be deliberation, it must lie within the causal chain that leads to the decision. Provided, however, that the spectator's prediction does not deny the causal efficacy of the agent's deliberations, there seems to be no reason why the agent's deliberations and their upshot might not, in principle, be predicted by the spectator.

The outcome of deliberation may, of course, be the 'decision to do nothing'. What happens here is that, as a causal result of the deliberative process, every relevant impulse to action is inhibited.

Notice finally that although the mental cause that initiates and sustains deliberation is a mental *state*, the occurrence of the deliberation itself is not a state but a *process*. This process issues in an *event*: the coming to a decision.

XI. MENTAL ACTIONS

What distinguishes mental activity from a mere succession of mental happenings? As has already been argued, we can give exactly the same account of mental activity as we have of purposive physical behaviour. An intention to work out a certain long-division sum purely in one's head is a mental cause that initiates and sustains mental activity. We are informed of the results reached at each stage of the activity by introspection (just as in the case of physical action we are informed by perception). The introspectively acquired information reacts back upon the mental cause, so that further steps in the calculation are made in accordance with the currently reached mental situation. Finally, recognition that the answer to the sum has been obtained 'switches off' the sustaining cause of the activity.

Here, perhaps, our theory of purposive activity yields us a most welcome bonus. It enables us to give an answer to the question asked again and again by so many biologists and psychologists 'What is the biological function of consciousness?'

The problem has already come up briefly in Chapter 6, Section IX, where it was suggested that if we knew that we were in certain states apt for the production of certain behaviour before that behaviour occurred, it might be possible to anticipate and control the behaviour. But now for a further suggestion.

Let us begin by considering what is the biological function of mind. Mental processes, biologically speaking, are those that fall between the stimulus and the response. Their biological function is to make the response more sophisticated, and so more efficient. Now, if what goes on in the mind between stimulus and response is itself something that has a directed or purposive character, this may well aid the agent to make the best response. For instance, in a problem-situation, various possible responses may be tried out 'in the imagination' in order to see which response will best fulfil the agent's purposes. As a causal result, the response may be much more efficient.

If the train of mental states between stimulus and response is to be a *purposive* affair, as in trying out possible responses in the imagination, then the conditions for the operation of the will must be satisfied. As we have seen, the most important condition that must be fulfilled is that there be some method whereby information about the current state of affairs can be fed back to the driving force behind the teleological sequence. But if the teleological sequence in question is a sequence of events in the mind, this means that the agent must become informed of what is currently going on in his mind. So if our mind is to work purposively between stimulus and response we must have awareness of our minds, that is, there must be introspection. There must be some form of self-consciousness, in however unselfconscious a form. It is implied by this that any animal that solves problems mentally must have some introspective powers, however rudimentary. Introspection is therefore a logical precondition of teleological mental behaviour. So we have given a 'teleological deduction' of the existence of introspection.

Philosophers who reject the notion that mental states are simply physical states of the brain, but who accept the Parallelist thesis that there is a one–one correlation between mental states and brain states, may object that I have given a 'teleological deduction' not of introspective *awareness*, but simply of the existence of a self-scanning physical apparatus in the brain. If their view of mental processes is correct, I agree that this is all that I have done. (It is still something.) But, on their view, the existence of any

sort of *mental* processes, as opposed to brain-processes, is teleologically inexplicable anyway. They just emerge 'alongside'
physical processes in the central nervous system when the physical processes reach a certain level of complexity. The existence of
the physical processes may be explained teleologically as the result
of biological adaptation, but a 'teleological deduction' of the
mental is impossible. This point, however, would seem to be a
difficulty, and not an argument, for Parallelism.

But at this point we must consider a more serious objection to
this 'teleological deduction'. On occasion, we can solve quite
complex problems during sleep, or while our mind seems to be
otherwise occupied. If this is possible, where is the need for
awareness of our own mental state in purposive mental
activity?

The first point to be made here is that if such phenomena are to
constitute any difficulty for our thesis, they will have to be trains
of mental events that are genuinely purposive. A calculation that
followed a fixed rule and so which simply drove on from one step
to the next would not suffice. A computer that is quite incapable
of goal-seeking behaviour can do this, and so might the brain
without benefit of self-awareness. Only a mental process that required for its successful prosecution a continuous feedback of
information to the cause that initiated and sustained the process
would pose any difficulty for our suggestion.

But suppose the evidence is such that seems to require genuinely purposive thinking during sleep or when the mind seems
otherwise occupied. What must we say about such cases? Well,
we have already seen that there is no logical objection to unconscious perception, that is to say, perception which occurs but
which we are unaware of. What is more, 'subliminal perception'
seems to be an actual case of such perception. Suppose, then, that
on a particular occasion we are aware of a particular mental state,
but suppose that this awareness is not linked up very closely with
the rest of our mental life. Suppose, that is, that we are introspectively aware, but unaware of that introspective awareness.
(We might call it 'subliminal introspection'.) Such 'unconscious
self-consciousness' might provide the feedback required for
teleological mental activity that goes on without our being aware
of it.

If this reply is satisfactory (I am not sure that it is), then the

existence of unconscious purposive mental activity does not refute the 'teleological deduction' of introspection.

But now we must consider a special problem posed by mental
as opposed to physical activities. If having an intention (for instance) is a mental state which initiates and sustains purposive
behaviour, then the coming to be of an intention is a mental
event. But if the coming to be of an intention is a mental event,
then, it seems, it ought to be possible to bring it about intentionally. If I can find the answer to a sum as the causal result of an
intention-state, I ought equally to be able to bring an intention-
state into existence as the causal result of an intention-state. But,
it is alleged, this is what cannot be done. The conclusion is that
intentions cannot be mental states. Plausible arguments of this
sort are used by Ryle and Miss Anscombe against the classical
doctrine of intentions and purposes generally as mental states
initiating and sustaining activity.

The first thing to be done here is to generalize the problem,
by seeing that it can be raised in connection with many other
mental states besides purposes. The acquiring of sense-impressions, of bodily sensations, of dreams, of emotions, of desires, of
beliefs, seems to present the same problems as intentions. It is just
as plausible to say that I cannot induce these states 'at will', as to
say that I cannot induce intentions 'at will'. Indeed it is only in the
case of thinking, of the direction of attention and the summoning
up or dismissing of mental images, that we have mental events
that *are* 'under the control of the will'.

Having generalized the problem, we can now attempt to solve
it. The first point to be made about all these mental phenomena
which are alleged to be beyond the power of the will is that, in
one clear and obvious sense, they are *not* beyond its power. If
I want to have certain sense-impressions or bodily sensations, there
are courses I can pursue to get them: courses that may be attended with success. There are procedures for working ourselves
up into, or working ourselves out of, emotional states of various
sorts. Dreams are in practice almost impossible to control, but
we can imagine the future discovery of recipes for producing the
dreams that we want. There is something strange about following
procedures designed to generate a certain belief in ourselves (a
strangeness that we shall explicate shortly), but nevertheless it is
a thing that can occur. And, finally, there are things that we can do

to make it likely that we shall form intentions of a certain sort in the future.

This quick survey, however, has revealed that there is frequently one simple source of absurdity in talking about an *intention* to have a certain mental state. As was argued in Section VII, an intention is not simply a mental cause which initiates and sustains purposive activity. It is a cause of this sort, but it is in addition one where the agent considers that the objective of the activity is within his power.

To speak of intentions is to speak of purposes which the agent believes to have good prospect of success. Now since we normally do not count on coming to have certain perceptions, sensations, emotions, dreams, beliefs, desires and intentions when we try to have them, it is inappropriate to speak of *intending* to bring about these mental states in ourselves. But it is perfectly possible to *attempt* to get ourselves into these mental states.

If I stand undecided on the high dive, I can (as a matter of empirical fact) hardly have the *intention* of working myself up to the point of diving intentionally. For I am not sure that I will be able to work myself up in this way. But I can *attempt* so to work myself up. And we could at least imagine that I might have, or think I have, an *assured* recipe for bringing myself to the point of diving, although unable to dive 'cold'. I could then *intend* to work myself up to diving.

Perhaps I still could not embark upon a course of activity with the intention of *coming to a decision* to dive. But this point is covered by the discussion of Hampshire's paradox in the previous section. To come to a decision involves prior deliberation, and we have seen that it is analytically involved in the notion of deliberation that we cannot predict the result of our own deliberations. But having an intention involves thinking that our objective is definitely within our power, and so involves a conditional prediction. An intention that the outcome of our deliberations should be such-and-such a decision would falsify our notion of deliberation and so our notion of coming to a decision.

So it seems that all mental states, although not all subject to the will in the sense that they are *clearly* within our power, can be objects (that is, objectives) of the will. We can attempt to bring them about. What, then, is the paradox that Ryle and Miss Anscombe are pointing to?

I do not see what they can say in reply except to appeal to the distinction drawn in Section V between the immediate and the mediate acts of the will. 'The raising of my arm', say, is an immediate act of the will, because, in the train of processes leading from the mental cause to the arm's being raised, it is the first step in the chain which is perceived. This perception is capable of feeding back to the mental cause and adjusting it so that the ultimate objective is achieved. But 'moving a matchbox' is not an immediate act of the will. What Ryle and Miss Anscombe will have to say, therefore, is that, while on the one hand thinking, direction of attention and the raising or dismissing of mental images are all immediate mental acts of the will, on the other hand the coming to have perceptions, sensations, dreams, emotions, desires and intentions are no better than mediate mental acts of the will.

But once the difficulty has been stated in this way, it begins to look far less formidable. For a similar situation exists in the case of physical activities. The immediate mental acts of a man's will are his own thoughts, the direction of his attention, and the summoning up or dismissing of mental images. Other mental states of his are only mediate objects of his will. The immediate physical acts of a man's will are the motion of his limbs. Other physical states of his (for example, a rise in the temperature of his body) are only mediate acts of his will. In both cases, the nature of the immediate acts of the will tends to be written into the *concept* of the will. As a result the attempt to raise one's temperature in the way one raises one's arm seems nonsensical. Equally, the attempt to summon up an emotion or create an intention in the same direct way that we summon up a mental image seems nonsensical.

It may still be objected that we can at least imagine being able to raise one's body-temperature in the way one raises one's arm. Can we do the same in the case of the mental states that are not immediate acts of the will? But I do not see why not. We can certainly *want* to be angry, or *want* to want something, or *want* to have certain intentions. Now if such wants were immediately succeeded by the mental state wanted, and if perception that the state wanted had come into existence could extinguish the original want, would not the want have become a mental state capable of bringing about a certain objective? And would not the states brought about have become 'immediate acts of the will'?

XII. BELIEF AND THE WILL

There is, however, a special peculiarity involved in the attempt to create a state of belief in oneself.

Suppose that I believe not-p, or suppose that I do not know whether p is true or not. But suppose that I embark upon a certain way of life in the attempt to bring myself to believe p. From the point of view that I *start* from I am trying to induce in myself the false, or at least the irrational, belief that p. The position is therefore much the same as if I try to persuade somebody else to believe p falsely or irrationally. If I am attempting either of these tasks, I shall be unwise to tell that person what I am attempting. For unless he does not believe or forgets that I am making such an attempt, or unless he can be induced to believe both p and not-p simultaneously, my attempt must fail. Now when I try to induce in myself the belief that p is true, *and if I know that that is what I am doing*, I am in the same position as one who has told his intended victim what he was going to do. Only if at some point I can manage to forget the initial situation or else come to believe p and not-p simultaneously, can my purpose be accomplished.

The strangeness of trying to create a belief in myself therefore comes to this: the activity is incompatible with a continued clear consciousness of the nature of the activity. We have pointed out, of course, that it is possible to pursue purposes without being aware that they are being pursued. If my attempt to persuade myself that p is true is an attempt of which I am not aware of being engaged in, there is no logical obstacle to its being accomplished. But if I know what it is that I am doing the whole time, including the time at which I acquire the belief, this knowledge must make my activity absurd. ('Trying to forget p' has the same sort of peculiarity. It is fatal to realize that one has succeeded in forgetting p!)

Furthermore, some of the mental states which are 'mediate acts of the will' involve belief. To have a sense-impression as of a red ball normally involves believing that there is actually a red ball before me which I am seeing. To have a pain in my hand normally involves believing that there is some bodily disturbance at the place of the pain. My anger with you may be sustained by my belief that you injured me. In so far as such states involve belief, it is impossible to bring them into existence clearly knowing what we are doing at the time the beliefs are brought into existence. Dreams also normally involve the (unselfconscious) belief that the experiences we seem to be having are really happening. (But since a dream would be unlikely to be accompanied by any belief about the way the dream had been induced, there would be no difficulty in dreams being mediate objects of the will.)

This impossibility of creating a belief in ourselves while knowing just what we are doing supplies a further reason why there seems to be absurdity in some attempts to bring certain mental states into existence in our own mind.

XIII. NEED ALL ACTIONS BE PURPOSIVE?

I will conclude this chapter by asking whether all our actions, as opposed to those bodily and mental events that simply occur, spring from a purpose. Must all 'behaviour proper', as opposed to mere physical behaviour, be behaviour that springs from a purpose? Must all mental action, as opposed to mere mental happening, spring from a purpose?

It is clear in the first place that many of our actions involve no further purpose beyond the doing of the action itself. They are actions done with no purpose in the sense that they are not done as means to further ends. But such actions are still purposive in a wider sense. I may shout 'for no reason'. But my action may still be an expression of my will although all I was attempting to do was to shout. The interesting question is whether there can be actions that spring from no purpose, not even the purpose to do the action in question.

Obvious possible candidates are some of the things we 'do idly', such as twiddling one's hair. We would be disinclined to say that this was mere physical behaviour. But must it be purposive activity, even allowing that the only purpose involved may be to twiddle one's hair?

I think such doings *need* not involve any purpose at all. But in order to account them genuine actions or 'behaviour proper' it must be the case that we could have *refrained* from doing them if we had purposed *not* to do them. I twiddle my hair. My behaviour is not informed by any purpose. But if I had attempted not to twiddle my hair, but instead tried to sit still, I would not have twiddled my hair. So twiddling my hair can still be called 'behaviour proper', even although it is strictly a logically secondary case.

Intermediate cases are clearly possible here. If a face at the window makes me start is this an action on my part or mere physical reaction? Our difficulty in answering the question reflects our difficulty in answering the question 'Could I have refrained from starting if I had wanted so to refrain?'

Some psychologists, notably the Freudians, hold that even the most trivial action that appears to have no purpose behind it is, nevertheless, the effect of an unconscious purpose. Their claim amounts to saying that, as a matter of empirical fact, all actions are purposive actions. Whether or not the Freudian evidence is good enough, this is a claim that can be entertained, and perhaps finally accepted. Of course, we would have to beware of getting this result simply by stretching the notion of unconscious purpose so that such purposes are automatically postulated whatever the nature of the behaviour observed. As is well known, such a charge can be brought against Freud, and still more against the Freudians. But here we have only been concerned to argue that not all action *need* be purposive action.

If the argument of this chapter has been correct, we have elucidated the distinction between 'behaviour proper' and mere physical behaviour. More generally, we have elucidated the distinction between action and mere happening. The rising of my arm is the *raising* of my arm provided that it is part or the whole of a pattern of behaviour that has an objective or (to cover the case of *mere* action) a pattern of behaviour that resembles in the way described above behaviour that has an objective. Behaviour that has an objective may in turn be defined as behaviour initiated and sustained by a mental cause, a cause whose operation is affected by information, and, in particular, is affected by perception of the developing situation in such a way as to facilitate the bringing about of a certain situation. This situation is called the objective. Perception that the situation which is the objective has been attained acts to extinguish the mental cause.

8

THE WILL (2)

I. MOTIVES

A GREAT deal of the previous chapter is of central importance to the further course of the argument. In this eighth chapter three further topics that stand in more or less intimate relation to the topic of the will are discussed, but if the reader is not interested in these particular questions he could omit it without loss.

What are we doing when we explain purposive activity (or in some cases desires to act that are not expressed in action) by reference to motives? A motive, language suggests, is something that *moves*, that is to say, is a cause. It will come as no surprise to the reader to find it argued here that to assign a motive to purposive activity is to give a *cause* of that activity.

But although in giving motives we give a cause of purposive activity, not all causes of purposive activity are motives. Motives are a certain sort of cause of purposive activity, or, as it turns out better to say, they are certain *sorts* of cause of purposive activity.

Miss Anscombe has suggested a three-fold classification of motives into 'forward-looking', 'backward-looking' and 'motive-in-general' (*Intention*, Sect. 13). It will be convenient to consider her three classes in turn.

Giving a 'forward-looking' motive tells us a further purpose for which a thing is purposively done. Miss Anscombe speaks of 'intention' instead of 'purpose', but her term seems too narrow. 'Why is he pumping the water?' 'His motive is to poison the inhabitants.' 'He (purposely) pumps the water *with this further purpose.*'

Here the mental cause or purpose which initiates and sustains the pumping activity is explained by saying that it came into existence as a causal result of a further mental cause or purpose which has as its objective 'killing the inhabitants'. The pumping is a means to an end, and the agent's having the end causes the activity that is the means to the end. If the agent did not have this end, he would not be pumping. The difference from other sorts of causal explanation, and so the reason why we speak of a 'motive', is simply that the cause of the mental cause or purpose that initiates and sustains the pumping is *itself* a similar sort of mental cause, working in the characteristic way that purposes work, a way of working bound up with all sorts of knowledge and belief.

'Backward-looking' motives are to be dealt with somewhat differently. Miss Anscombe gives as examples revenge, gratitude, pity and remorse. 'Why did you kill him?' 'My motive was revenge', or 'To be revenged'. Here, as Miss Anscombe points out, we must not think of being revenged as an end to which killing him is a means. Ends and means are, of necessity, distinct happenings, but my killing him *is* my being revenged. (The killing might be called 'Armstrong's revenge'.) It is true that we might explain why a man was pumping water by saying it was 'for revenge' (he knew the water to be poisoned). Here the agent's action is only a means to his being revenged. But the first example shows that assigning the motive of revenge to an action is not *necessarily* assigning a further purpose for which a thing is purposively done. So revenge at least *need* not be a 'forward-looking' motive.

Let us examine the nature of revenge more carefully. If A acts with the purpose of revenging himself on B, then he takes his act to be, or to be a means to, an injuring of B. But although necessary, this is not sufficient. Suppose that we now add that A's action was preceded by A's coming to believe that B had injured him, A. This is still not sufficient. For, suppose that evidence is produced which convinces us that A's action was not the result of A's acquiring that belief (or any similar belief). We will automatically deny that A's action is motivated by revenge. So it seems that if we are to call A's action 'revenge', then the purpose of injuring B must be caused, and sustained by, A's belief that B injured him. (The phrase 'sustained by' calls attention to the fact that if A ceased to believe that B had injured him, yet went on with his attempt to injure B, then he would no longer be acting with the object of revenging *that* putative injury that B did him.) This special role of the acquiring a *belief* in the causing of A's conduct marks off this case from 'forward-looking' motives. Gratitude, pity and remorse also involve beliefs in the same way.

But we have still not given sufficient conditions for A's acting 'from the motive of revenge'. For suppose that, in attempting to injure B, A, as we say, 'had no animus against B', but merely wanted to dissuade B from injuring him, A, a second time. This would not be a case of revenge. In order to eliminate such possibilities we must say that A's attempt to injure B, brought into existence and sustained by A's belief that B had injured him, A, is attempted *for the sake of injuring B*, and not for some further end that injuring B might be a means to. If the injuring of B springs from a 'forward-looking' motive, to that extent A's motive is not revenge.

In suitable circumstances, then, the purpose of injuring somebody is the motive of revenge from which we act. (Or the desire of injuring somebody is the motive of revenge from which we desire to act.) And a purpose (or desire), we have already argued, is a certain sort of mental cause. It is the fact that acquiring a belief that another has injured one *regularly* causes people to acquire the purpose (or at least the desire) to injure in return simply for the sake of injury, that is responsible for there being a *single* word 'revenge'. A similar analysis can be given of the other 'backward-looking' motives.

The class of motive that Miss Anscombe calls 'motive-in-general' must be dealt with differently again. She gives as examples vanity, admiration, spite, friendship, fear, love of truth, despair, and adds that there are 'a host of others'. She also points out that these examples *can* be 'forward-looking' motives, or be mixed cases.

Asked 'Why did he tell those lies about himself?' we can answer 'His motive was simply vanity'. But against Miss Anscombe, it seems that this particular case is a matter of a 'forward-looking' motive. He lied as a causal result of his desire to secure the admiration and envy of others. This desire led to telling lies, which the agent took to be a means to his end. The only difference from the previous case of a 'forward-looking' motive (poisoning the inhabitants) is that, because the desire to secure the admiration and envy of others is a common desire in human beings, we have the single word 'vanity'.

A better case of 'motive-in-general' might be this: 'Why did he lend him the money?' 'Out of friendship.' Here there is no question of a desire to be friendly (the end) initiating the money-lending behaviour (the means). For to lend money is a form of assistance and to assist a person is part of the conduct that *constitutes* 'being a friend to him'. The motive-explanation merely serves (i) to rebut the suggestion that the action was a means to some further end; (ii) to indicate that the mental cause, the motive, behind the action was that cause that leads to *friendly acts*, acts of which lending money is an instance.

Instead of 'motive' we can normally say 'reason'. Where the causal explanation of a man's conduct is not in terms of motives that he has, the word 'reason' at once becomes inappropriate. 'The sight of a face at the window made me jump.' It sounds distinctly forced to say that the sight of the face was the reason for my jumping, and quite wrong to say it was '*my* reason'. For the jumping is not an action initiated and sustained by a purpose. The best we can say about it is that it is something I might have tried to control. If, instead of simply jumping, I had rushed out of the door in order to confront the intruder, this would have been purposive behaviour, and it would have become natural to speak of my reason for my action.

But although we can normally substitute 'reason' for 'motive', the substitution seems to be most appropriate in the case of 'forward-looking' and 'backward-looking' motives. Consider a case of 'motive-in-general'. Somebody does something hurtful to another. On asking the motive, we are told that it is simply spite. But suppose instead we had asked for the reason for the action. Would it have been completely appropriate to say that the reason was simply spite? The locution would be permissible, no doubt, but equally the reply might have been 'He had no reason, it was simply spite'.

Why does the word 'reason' as a substitute for 'motive' tend to gravitate towards 'forward-looking' and 'backward-looking' motives? I think it is because the real home of the word 'reason' is in the intellectual, not the practical, sphere. Now, as we shall argue in the next chapter, to have a reason in the intellectual sphere is to have a belief that causes us, or tends to cause us, to acquire a further belief. It is a belief that causes further belief. Now in both the case of 'forward-looking' and 'backward-looking' motives we have beliefs that act as causes, although what they bring about in these cases, or press towards bringing about, is not the acquiring of further beliefs but the carrying out of actions. In the case of 'backward-looking' motives there are beliefs of the sort 'He injured me'. In the case of 'forward-looking' motives, where something is done in order to fulfil a certain further purpose, there is the belief that this thing is in fact a means to the desired end. (In neither sort of case, of course, need the beliefs involved be *verbal* beliefs.) I suggest that it is the presence of *beliefs* among the causes or causal conditions of action in such cases that makes the use of the word 'reason' seem specially appropriate.

A final point about motives. It is clear that one who has a certain motive is in a certain mental *state*. For to have a motive is to have a certain purpose, or at least a certain desire, and havings of these are states, not processes or events.

II. PLEASURE AND PAIN

Pleasure and pain are not sensations. There are certain sensations that *give* us pleasure, and which are therefore called pleasurable sensations. But, as will be argued again in the discussion of bodily sensations in Chapter 14, it is simply a fact, which might have been otherwise, that sensations of a particular nature give us pleasure. Pleasurableness is a *relational* property of sensations. The point may not be so obvious in the case of pain. There is certainly an asymmetry in our language: we call a certain class of bodily sensations 'pains', but 'pleasures' is not the name of a class of bodily sensations. Nevertheless, even in the case of bodily pains, the painfulness of pain resides not in the bodily sensation itself, but in the peremptory mental reaction that the bodily sensation evokes. The fact that we call a class of bodily sensations 'pains' is simply a tribute to their special power of making us miserable. The word 'pain' derives from the Latin *'poena'*, a punishment, and bodily pains are called pains because they are, upon the whole, the worst 'punishment' that human life affords. To say that a pain becomes worse is to say that it becomes a worse punishment. This point will also come up again in the chapter on bodily sensations.

Shall we say, then, that pleasure and pain are feelings? 'Feeling' is the most ambiguous of all the words in our psychological vocabulary and the difficulty is not so much that there are specific objections to this suggestion, as that of understanding what the suggestion comes to. We do speak of 'a feeling of pleasure' and even of 'a feeling of pain'. But what is the force of these phrases? If somebody has a 'feeling of pleasure' does this mean anything more than that he has become currently pleased about something, and, perhaps, that he is aware that he is pleased? Anything more seems an inessential accompaniment. If so, talk of 'feelings' yields no advance in understanding.

Pleasures and pains are not sensations, and it is not helpful to call them feelings. Instead, a quite simple account may be suggested. A man is enjoying himself, or is taking pleasure in what he is doing or in what is happening, if, or to the extent that, what he is doing is what he wants to be doing or what is happening is what he wants to be happening. A man's state is painful, if, or to the extent that, what is happening to him, or what he is doing, is something he wants not to be happening or wants not to be doing. If I am doing what I want to do and if I lack any desire to be doing anything else; if my situation is as I would wish it to be and I have no wish that it should be different; is not my state perfectly pleasant? And if my situation is as I would wish it not to be, and/or if I have to do what I do not want to do, is not my state painful? And, all other things being equal, the stronger the desires satisfied or frustrated, the greater the pleasure or pain.

Here we have an account of pleasure and pain in terms of the satisfaction and lack of satisfaction of desires, wants and wishes. And we have already given an account of these notions in the previous chapter (Sects. VIII–IX).

The account of pleasure and pain that we have given is fairly obvious. In modern philosophy, it has received the endorsement of Ryle, at least for the cases where being pleased is a matter of enjoying or liking, and where pain is a matter of disliking. He wrote:

> To say that a person has been enjoying digging . . . is to say that he dug with his whole heart in his task; *i.e.* that he dug, wanting to dig and not wanting to do anything else (or nothing) instead. (*The Concept of Mind*, p. 108)

However, dominated by his Behaviourist model, Ryle goes on to make the extraordinary statement, 'His digging was his pleasure . . .'. This, of course, is a most unnatural way of speaking. It would be natural to say that his digging *gave* him pleasure, that is to say, that this piece of behaviour had the effect of satisfying his desires at that time.

There can, of course, be cases where pleasure or pain does not involve the 'whole heart'. Sensual pleasure accompanied by guilt would be an example. Here, perhaps, we have a case where strong sensual desires are fully satisfied, but the desire to conform to a certain code of conduct is not satisfied. We can still talk of pleasure here, but it is clear that for the individual concerned the total pleasure in the situation (as opposed to the sensual pleasure) is automatically the less.

If we are to give an account of pleasure and pain in terms of fulfilment and non-fulfilment of desires, wants and wishes, then it follows that we are always pleased or pained *by* something. For desires, wants and wishes necessarily have intentional objects. In pleasure and pain, therefore, there must always be situations which we perceive to obtain or are introspectively aware of, which are situations we want or do not want. We need not always be conscious of our wants, or be aware of the perceptions of our situation that satisfy or fail to satisfy them, but the wants must have 'objectives'. I think that this is what is correct in Ryle's contention that enjoyment involves heeding, or paying attention to, something that is enjoyed (*The Concept of Mind*, p. 132).

What, then, are we to say about the cases where we feel pleased, but can give no reason for being pleased, or cases where we feel sad or depressed, but can give no reason for being sad or depressed?

In the first place, it is possible that we are simply unaware of what is pleasing or displeasing us. However, it does not seem that this must necessarily always be the case with 'objectless' pleasure or sorrow. Suppose it is not the case. What account should we give of such a situation? I suggest that to be in such a state is only to be in a state where almost anything will please one, or where almost anything will pain one. (Compare: 'It is in such a state that almost anything will make it explode.') And even in such situations there will be certain perceptions or acquiring of information possible which will arouse at least some displeasure in the abnormally cheerful man, or at least some pleasure in the man who is sad.

Suppose, however, that while in a state of euphoria, I am unbeknownst injected with a drug which quite changes my mood. In this case I stop feeling pleased with the world, but not as a result of any cognition. However, this case does not cause any real difficulty. The drug does not fail to satisfy my desires: it simply *changes* them so that what previously made me happy no longer makes me happy. (Compare: 'As a result of the removal of the detonator, it is no longer in such a state that almost anything will make it explode.')

It will be noticed that, on this account of pleasure and pain, there is no direct logical link between pleasure and pain, on the one hand, and *behaviour* on the other. The direct logical link is to desires, wants and wishes, which are themselves then causally linked to behaviour, sometimes in rather indirect ways. This point is relevant when we consider fashionable talk about the intimate relation of physical pain to 'pain-behaviour'. When we are in physical pain we have a bodily sensation of a certain sort, and a most peremptory desire to be rid of it. This peremptory desire entails that, if we know any way to be rid of the sensation or to minimize it, we shall be powerfully impelled to take that course of action. But cryings, groanings, writhings, etc., although natural concomitants of bodily pain (or even of great mental distress), hardly seem to bear any logical relation to it. Certainly, these are things that we are irresistibly impelled to do when we are in great pain (perhaps they have the biological function of *distracting* us a little from the pain itself?), but they do not seem to be involved in the notion of physical pain. Their usefulness in teaching a child other-person pain-language ('He is in pain') seems simply due to the fact that they are empirically reliable signs of pain.

There is a wide vocabulary connected with pleasure and pain. We can, for instance, be elated, joyful, happy or contented. We can be hurt, sorrowful, depressed or sad. And this is only to mention a few such words. An investigation into the species of pleasure and pain might show that what has been said in this section is a mere rough and perhaps misleading sketch. But here I shall excuse myself such an investigation. (Some further points will emerge in the discussion of the emotions in the next section.)

One final point about pleasure and pain. They are clearly mental states rather than processes or events. If one is pleased or pained, one's pleasure or pain is entire during each instant that it endures.

III. THE EMOTIONS

To finish our account of conative (as opposed to cognitive) mental processes, let us give some account of the emotions or passions. It is not very clear what counts as an 'emotion' or a 'passion', and what does not. For the purposes of this discussion let us simply say that the class is defined by the examples that will be treated of in this section, together with any sufficiently similar mental item.

Like pleasure and pain, the emotions seem clearly to be states rather than processes. But these states are to be defined by reference to *processes* of certain sorts: certain causal patterns of mental and bodily states. Let us begin by considering the nature of these causal patterns.

The *cause* involved is always a belief that the individual has acquired, or a perception that he has. Thus, if A is *jealous* of B, then a certain effect has been produced in A's mind by acquiring the belief that B stands in a certain relation to some other person or thing, C. If A is *disgusted* by the toadstool, a certain effect has been produced in A's mind by the perception of (or perhaps the description of) a toadstool.

There is, therefore, a possibility in all such cases that the belief is false, or that the perception fails to correspond to reality. If this is the case, the emotion is, in one possible use of the term, 'unjustified'. Cf. Errol Bedford, 'Emotions' in *The Philosophy of Mind*, edited V. C. Chappell, Prentice-Hall, 1962:

> ... if the claim that our emotion word makes about a situation is not satisfied, this is often indicated by saying that the emotion is unjustified, or unreasonable. The attribution of the emotion, that is to say, is not withdrawn but qualified. (p. 120)

Part of the intentionality of an emotion, therefore, is the intentionality of belief or perception.

These beliefs or perceptions have two effects: a bodily and a mental. In the first place, there are characteristic bodily happenings. Grief and sorrow involve weeping and crying. Fear involves trembling, paling and movement of the hair on the scalp. So may anger. Shame and embarrassment involve blushing. Disgust involves a heaving of the stomach. Of course, these bodily happenings are not involved in every instance. Nor is it even true that there is a distinguishable syndrome of bodily happenings regularly associated with each distinguishable emotion. Nevertheless, in typical or paradigm cases of emotion the initiating beliefs or perceptions do give rise to more or less typical sorts of bodily happening.

Now these bodily happenings in turn give rise to bodily sensations. Thus arises what is for the subject an introspectively conspicuous element in emotion: a pattern of bodily sensations. It was this element in the causal pattern that was seized upon in the James-Lange theory and wrongly taken to constitute the essence of emotion.

I suspect that this close connection between emotion and bodily sensation explains why we speak of 'feeling' emotions. The etymologically original sense of the word 'feel' seems to be that connected with tactual and bodily perceptions (see *O.E.D.*). Bodily perceptions (that is, sensations) are phenomenologically conspicuous in first-person experience of emotions, and so we speak of *feeling* angry. (And where the sensations are absent, it is natural to speak of *being* angry, but not *feeling* it.)

In the second place, the initiating beliefs or perceptions have an effect upon the will. The word 'will' must be taken in its widest sense here. Certain impulses to act may be involved: thus, the perception of a fearful object may evoke the impulse to flee. But in some cases no more may be involved than the evoking or satisfying of a want or wish. Thus, grief for someone who is dead may involve no impulses to action because all action is perceived to be futile. There may simply be a vehement wish that what is recognized to be so should not be so; a frustrated wish that is *ipso facto* painful. The fact that impulses, desires, wants and wishes have intentional objects gives a second dimension of intentionality to emotions. If A is jealous of B on account of C, then A believes that B stands in a certain relation to C and wishes that B should not stand in that relation to C. Thus A's belief and wish each have different, although related, intentional objects.

The fact that the beliefs or perceptions involved have two distinct (although intertwined) effects: one bodily and one mental, means that there are two distinct criteria for the *strength* of emotions. (This point has been made by Anthony Kenny, *Action, Emotion, Will*, Routledge, 1963, p. 35 f.) There is firstly the question of how much bodily agitation is produced, secondly the question of how much the agent's will is affected, either in terms of strength of impulses to act or strength of desires aroused. A conflict of criteria for the 'strength' of an emotion is therefore possible.

How can this analysis accommodate 'objectless' emotions, such as a feeling of dread which the subject cannot identify as dread *of* anything? In the first place, it may simply be that the subject is unaware of some part (or whole) of the pattern. He may be unconscious of what belief or perception has affected him, or may be unaware of what he is impelled to do, or what he wishes for, as a causal result of the belief or perception. In the second place, it may be that the dread has an object but a completely unspecific object. The belief may simply be 'that something dreadful (something very unpleasant for the subject) is going to happen'.

Nevertheless, it seems at least logically possible that somebody might have 'feelings of dread' that do not involve unconscious or unspecific intentional objects. What account can we give of such feelings? I think that Kenny's suggestion is correct here. A 'feeling of dread' which is not dread *of* anything, even anything unspecific, is simply awareness of a pattern of bodily sensations characteristic of the emotion of dread *without any actual dread*. (The sensations might be caused solely by some bodily malfunctioning.) It is a 'feeling of dread' only by courtesy.

The emotions themselves may be now identified with the *mental* effect of the initiating belief or perception. As we have seen, this effect is typically two-fold: there is an effect on the will, and there is bodily sensation. If we are in a certain conative state, and are having certain bodily sensations, and both have been brought about in the appropriate way by the appropriate set of beliefs or perceptions, we are in a certain emotional state. The fact that emotions are mental states that are *effects* of certain causes gives a rationale to the word 'passion', with its etymological implication of passivity.

So much for a general account of emotion. The pattern sketched is a *typical* one, not one that holds exactly for every sort of emotion, or every instance of any sort. It may now be supplemented by a more detailed account of the causal patterns involved in individual emotions, without, however, any claim being made for comprehensiveness. Some of the work here seems to have been already accomplished, or at least sketched: expecially in Hobbes' *Leviathan*, Pt. I, Ch. 6.

Let us consider first fear, anger, hate and disgust.

In *fear* the evoking belief is the belief or suspicion that something will happen to the subject, or to persons or things the subject is identified with, of a sort that the subject desires should not happen. A paradigm case is the belief that something in one's environment may do one bodily harm.

In typical cases, the evoking belief gives rise to characteristic bodily states: paling, trembling, screaming, loosening of the stomach, bristling of the hair. These bodily states in turn give rise to unpleasant bodily sensations.

The effect of the evoking belief on the will is that, where avoiding action is thought to be in one's power, there is an impulse towards such an action. Where avoiding action is thought to be futile, there is simply the strong desire that the thing anticipated should not occur. In some cases of extreme fear, impulses to avoiding action can be thwarted by a bodily manifestation: paralysis of the limbs. But the *desire* to take avoiding action is still present in such a case.

It would be possible for somebody to believe some thing or situation to be dangerous, for this belief to evoke the characteristic sensations of fear, for the subject to take avoiding action, and yet claim that, although he was afraid, he had mastered his fear. In order to support such a claim he would have to show that (i) he believed that such avoiding action was the most effective way of meeting the situation, but that (ii) if he had believed that the most effective way of meeting the situation was not to avoid it, but to confront it, then he would have taken such action. If both these claims were true, and in addition he lacked the bodily symptoms and sensations of fear, he could even claim to be fearless. His fearlessness, moreover, would not be marred by foolhardiness!

The opposite of being afraid is being fearless. It is not being courageous. Being courageous is perfectly compatible with being afraid, provided that the fear is mastered. To be courageous, a man must actually act in a certain way in the presence of danger, or it must be true that if certain dangerous situations arose, he would so act. I think that it is this conceptual link with actual *action* (which might, in some cases, be purely mental action) which makes us reluctant to say that courage is an *emotion*. For an emotion demands only an impulse or desire to act.

It will be convenient to treat *anger* and *hate* together, because the distinctions between them are relatively fine. In both cases there must be some evoking belief or perception. If your insulting of me is to make me angry with you, I must become aware of your insult. If I hate you, I must at least have come to be aware of your existence. (Even to hate a fictional character I must have become aware of the character's existence-in-fiction.) But it is very hard to set any *a priori* limits to the sorts of thing one can be angry with or hate, and, parallel to this, it is hard to set any *a priori* limits to the sorts of belief or perception that evoke anger or hatred.

In the case of anger, the belief or perception involved characteristically evokes certain bodily states. More importantly, it evokes an impulse to overt aggressive action towards some object that figures in the evoking belief or perception. (This object is the 'thing one is angry at'.) Or, where no behaviour is possible, there is a desire that such action should be taken, or that the object should be injured in some way. This aggressive action is action that is aggressive for its own sake: in so far as the aggression served some further purpose it would not be anger, or at any rate anger at the original object. It is characteristic of anger, however, that where aggressive behaviour towards the original object is not possible, or not prudent, that there will be at least impulses to find surrogate objects of aggression.

In hate, the bodily effects of the evoking belief or perception play a much lesser role than in the case of anger. 'Convulsed with anger' is a quite natural conception, 'convulsed with hate' somewhat less so. Contrariwise, the effect on the will in the case of hate is much more clear-cut than in the case of anger. In hate, the ill-will evoked towards the object of the emotion is both firmly directed towards that object (it is not easily deflected), and there is no necessity for an impulse towards the *open* display of aggression that is characteristic of anger.

The importance of bodily state in the notion of anger, and its relative unimportance in the case of hate, connects with the point that to speak of current anger is characteristically to speak of a mental state that is currently causally active in the mind, while there is no such implication in speaking of current hate. It is true that we can say that A has been angry with B for days without implying that A's anger was causally active in his mind all that time. Equally, we can speak of a brief and single spurt of hate towards a person one loves. But anger normally involves a relatively brief state, causally active in the mind during that time, while hate normally involves a settled ill-will that may be causally active in the subject's mind only from time to time.

In *disgust*, the perception of some object, or, in less typical cases, simply thinking of the object, produces firstly a characteristic bodily effect (turning over of the stomach, etc.) which in turn produces certain unpleasant bodily sensations, and secondly a desire that the perception or thought should cease.

We pass on to a group of emotions all of which involve love in some way.

In the case of love itself, perceptions of, or beliefs about, some object or state of affairs give rise to the desire to possess the object in some way, or bring the state of affairs about. In the case of *disinterested* love, there is simply a desire for the good of the object. In the case of sensual love there are characteristic pleasurable bodily effects, but in the other cases bodily effects are most typically involved in love frustrated.

Grief and sorrow are species of love, or desire, frustrated. The belief or perception involved is that something loved is unavailable to one. Since a desire is frustrated, the emotions are painful ones. The belief or perception evokes characteristic bodily states (weeping, etc.), especially in grief, which is violent sorrow. If it is thought that any action can be taken to relieve the frustration there will be an impulse evoked to take such action. But very often the situations that evoke grief and sorrow are thought by the subject as unalterable, or, at any rate, as unalterable by actions of the subject. In this case, all that is evoked is a want or wish that things should be different.

Pity is a species of sorrow. It is evoked by the perception of, or belief about, the misfortunes of others. The perceptions or belief gives rise to characteristic bodily states and sensations ('the bowels of compassion'), and to an impulse to do something to remove the misfortune, or, where the agent lacks power to alter the situation, a wish that the misfortune might be removed.

Remorse is a very particular species of sorrow. A belief that a past action of the subject was wrong (and done from a wrong motive) evokes 'pangs of remorse' and a wish that he had not done the action. The subject's *moral* condemnation of his action is essential for his emotion to count as remorse.

Regret is not so specific as remorse. The belief characteristically involved here is that we or somebody else acted in a certain way (or even that certain things happened in the world of nature), a belief which evokes a wish that this action or happening had not occurred. But we can also regret what is now happening or even what will happen.

Now for an account of shame, embarrassment, pride and humility.

In *shame* the evoking belief is that some characteristic possessed by the subject, or by something with which the subject identifies himself, is not up to some standard set by others, or even by the subject. But such a consciousness of shortcomings, even if it evokes the desire that the shortcomings might not be so, is insufficient for shame. To yield shame there must be a fear and a dislike of these shortcomings being brought to the knowledge or attention of others. It is for this reason that shame involves the impulse to conceal or not draw attention to the thing one is ashamed of. It is when shortcomings are made the object of attention by others that the characteristic bodily states, such as blushing, are evoked.

This account of shame may seem not to cover the shame involved in nakedness, bodily functions, etc. But for shame to be involved here, it must be the case that the subject considers certain states or activities as inferior, as not coming up to some standard. A person can be ashamed of being seen naked by accident only if he thinks of his situation as falling below some standard. He must think of his nakedness as a shortcoming: although not necessarily as a moral shortcoming. If this is not his view, he cannot be said to be ashamed, but at most to be embarrassed.

In *embarrassment* the evoking belief is that certain things about the subject, or some person or thing he identifies himself with, are the subject of other people's observation. The belief evokes a normally unpleasant bodily agitation—often tending to produce further a certain inefficiency of conduct—and a desire that this observation should cease.

With *pride* the evoking belief is that something which is in some sense 'one's own' is superior to something of the same sort belonging to others. Bodily changes evoked by this belief do not play any very important part in our notion of pride, although we do speak of 'swelling with pride'. The belief satisfies a desire for superiority, and so pride involves *pleasure* in this superiority. The belief also characteristically evokes impulses to actions that make a public demonstration of that superiority.

In the case of *humility* (in so far as it is an emotion and not a pattern of action) the evoking belief is that something that is in some sense 'one's own' is inferior to something of the same sort belonging to others. But, unlike shame or embarrassment, this belief evokes no more than a willingness to accept publicly the claims of others to superiority.

Finally let us consider hope and despair, which are perhaps only dubiously emotions.

Hope involves a lack of knowledge that something is so, but a belief that it is at least a real possibility, together with a desire that the thing should be so. (Hope does not imply that the thing hoped for lies in the future. We can say 'I hope he *arrived*' as well as 'I hope he will arrive'.) There seems to be no necessity for a causal relation between the belief and the desire.

Despair is the certainty that something is not so which the subject wishes was so. The typical case is the extinction of a prior hope by the certainty that the thing hoped for cannot be so.

I hope that what has been said here at least shows that a plausible account can be given of the emotions which consorts with our Causal analysis of the mental concepts in general, and our theory of the will and allied notions in particular. No attempt has been made to cover the whole range of the emotions. There has also been an important *lacuna* in the analyses offered. Evaluative notions such as 'good' have been employed without giving any account of what is involved in such concepts. This is because space forbids an account of ethical and evaluative concepts in this book.

9

KNOWLEDGE AND INFERENCE

IT has proved a relatively simple task to give an account of the 'conative concepts' in terms of inner causes of behaviour. This may be contrasted with the agonizing difficulties encountered by those modern philosophers who have set their faces against a causal account. Beside the will, the other great central topic for the philosophy of mind is perception. But before considering perception it will be convenient to give an account of two notions: that of knowing something to be true, and that of inferring one proposition from another. The analysis will not go all the way: in particular the notion of *belief* will be taken as an undefined term, and an attempt will be made to give an account of knowledge and inference in terms of belief. For this reason, the theses of this chapter will be neither sufficient nor necessary for a 'Causal' analysis of the concepts of knowledge and inference. But the simplification involved will stand us in good stead in the course of later chapters.

1. PLATO'S PROBLEM

We are concerned here simply with knowing that something is the case and not with knowing how to do something.

Although the matter is not entirely uncontroversial I propose to assume that to say A knows *p* entails two things:

(i) A believes *p*;
(ii) *p* is true.

But it is possible to be right by accident, and so not every case of true belief is a case of knowledge. This enables the problem 'What is knowledge?' to be formulated thus: 'What must be added to true belief to give knowledge?' This is the way Plato finally formulated the problem at the end of his *Theaetetus*.

The classical answer is that knowledge is true belief together with *good reasons* for that belief. And there is no doubt that in the case of much of our knowledge this is a good preliminary answer. But there is also a classical difficulty (mentioned by Plato himself) in applying this formula to all cases of knowledge. To say I have good reasons for a proposition, *p*, is to say that I *know* other truths, *q*, which constitute good reasons for *p*. (If I did not *know* *q*, my reasons would not be good.) This new knowledge will itself require the possession of further good reasons, and so to infinity. The vicious infinite regress exposes the concealed circularity in the proposed definition of knowledge: knowledge is true belief, together with knowledge of good reasons for that belief.

This difficulty makes it clear that, if knowledge is a meaningful notion at all (and I propose to assume that it is), all knowledge based on good reasons must terminate in knowledge that is not based upon any reasons at all. Let us call such knowledge *non-inferential*. The first problem that we may usefully consider, then, is 'What constitutes non-inferential knowledge?' It is clear that non-inferential knowledge is something more than true belief without any reasons for the belief. The problem may therefore be reformulated as 'What must be added to true belief without reasons to give non-inferential knowledge?'

The classical reaction to the difficulty about the regress of reasons was to search for a special class of propositions such that, once we contemplate them, it is logically impossible to be mistaken about their truth. Within this class there would be no distinction between knowledge and mere true belief, and so they could serve as the ultimate foundations of knowledge. It is thus that we have Descartes' clear and distinct propositions, or modern philosophy's incorrigible statements about our current mental state.

Now we have already argued in Chapter 6, Section X, that the notion of knowledge which it is logically impossible to be mistaken about is incoherent. The classical solution to the difficulty is therefore barred to us.

II. THE NATURE OF NON-INFERENTIAL KNOWLEDGE

The solution to be advanced here is suggested by some of the things said by Wittgenstein in the *Philosophical Investigations* (cf., for example, Section 324), but never, I think, made explicit. A similar view is briefly set out by John Watling in an article 'Inference from the Known to the Unknown', *Aristotelian Society Proceedings*, 1954–5.

If somebody had a true belief that logically could not be false, that would certainly be knowledge. But we have argued that this is logically impossible. But suppose that he had a true belief that *empirically* could not be false? A belief that empirically could not be false would be an absolutely reliable belief. Would it not give everything that was required for knowledge?

This suggests the following definition of non-inferential knowledge:

A knows *p* non-inferentially if, and only if, A has no good reasons for *p* but:

(i) A believes *p*;
(ii) *p* is true;
(iii) A's belief-that-*p* is empirically sufficient for the truth of *p*.

(Since if *x* is necessary for *y* then *y* is sufficient for *x*, condition (iii) can also be written:

(iii) The truth of *p* is empirically necessary for A's belief that *p*.)

To take an example. Suppose A knows non-inferentially that his legs are now crossed. This simply means that he truly believes that his legs are crossed, and that he empirically could not have had that belief unless his legs were crossed in physical fact.

The formula can be simplified. Given (i) and (iii) it is entailed that *p* is true. So condition (ii) is redundant, and we can write:

A knows *p* non-inferentially if, and only if, A has no good reasons for *p* but:

(i) A believes *p*;
(ii) A's belief-that-*p* is empirically sufficient for the truth of *p*.

There is absolutely no need that A *know* that condition (ii) be satisfied; all that is necessary is that it *be* satisfied. So there is no vicious regress. (It follows from this, incidentally, that A may know without knowing that he knows. This is indeed usually the case when A is a dog or a small child. The point will be taken up again in the last section of the chapter.)

It is important to understand exactly how the formula is to be read. In saying that A knows non-inferentially that his legs are crossed if and only if (i) he believes his legs are crossed and (ii) this belief is empirically sufficient for his legs being in fact crossed, the second condition must not be interpreted to mean that *whenever* A believes his legs to be crossed, then they are in fact crossed. For it might well be that when suitably drugged, say, A may come to believe non-inferentially that his legs are crossed when they are in fact not crossed. Yet this would not make us want to deny the possibility of an undrugged A *knowing* that his legs were crossed. What is being asserted, rather, is that *in this particular situation* A's belief that his legs are crossed is empirically sufficient for his legs being crossed in fact. Suppose, on a particular occasion, a stone hits a window and breaks it. We do not imply that all stones that hit windows break them. We imply only that *in this particular situation* the impact of the stone is empirically sufficient to break the window. This is a model for the sufficiency of A's belief-that-*p* for the truth of *p*. The impact of the stone is, of course, a *cause* of the window's breaking while A's belief-that-*p* is not a cause of *p*. But in both cases we have something that is, in that particular situation, empirically sufficient for something else.

What further account we should give of such empirical sufficiency is a further matter. I would argue that it is a matter of being able to subsume the situation under a covering law of a certain form, a law which, however, may be quite unknown to us even although we are certain that the situation before us is a case where something is empirically sufficient for something else. But I deliberately refrain from making this part of the analysis of what it is to know something non-inferentially. The notion of something being empirically sufficient for something else in a certain situation is, I think, an intuitively clear one, and we expose the minimum of flank if the analysis is rested simply on this notion.

It may be noticed incidentally that non-inferential knowledge can survive even the possession of bad reasons. Provided the conditions of the formula are satisfied, A may have perfectly specious reasons for his belief. It is only if the true belief is sustained solely by the reasons (undermine A's reasons and you undermine his belief), that A lacks knowledge.

If somebody denies our account of non-inferential knowledge, he may be challenged to say whether he thinks that there can be such knowledge without the second condition obtaining. Suppose, in the situation A is in, A's belief that his legs are crossed is not empirically sufficient for his legs being in fact crossed. There would then be an *empirical* possibility of error in the situation, and, faced with such a possibility, how could we say that A really *knew*? If you (empirically) can be wrong, your belief is not perfectly reliable, and you do not know.

So I think it must be admitted that at least our formula states a *necessary* condition for non-inferential knowledge. Opponents may therefore be challenged to say what must be added to give necessary and sufficient conditions. What will they say? Must A have gone through the 'proper procedures', or have had the proper organs suitably stimulated? Apart from any difficulty of specifying these conditions any more concretely, it seems that the only reason to accept such conditions would be that, as a matter of empirical fact, in such circumstances truth was obtained. But this is simply to repeat the second condition. There are procedures for gaining non-inferential knowledge, with which we are all familiar; for instance, exposing oneself to suitable stimulation of the sense-organs. But it is simply their truth-gaining value that recommends these procedures.

Now, however, to consider objections.

(i) In the first place, it may be said that the proposed definition of non-inferential knowledge is useless. In order to know *p*, my belief must be of the sort that, in that particular situation, is empirically sufficient for its own truth. But then, in order to know that *p* is true, I would have to discover the empirical connection between believing *p* and the truth of *p*. But how could I know that there was such a connection?

This objection shows how hypnotized we can be by the idea that the distinction between knowledge and true belief is a *mark* that can be used in the search for knowledge. To ask for such a mark is to ask for a reason to support a claim to knowledge, which resurrects the classical difficulty we have tried to evade. The proposed distinction between non-inferential knowledge and mere true belief without good reasons is not intended to be such a mark, and so the objection has missed the point. In similar fashion, it is no objection to the semantic theory of truth ('Snow is white' is true if, and only if, snow is white) that it does not tell us whether snow is in fact white. A definition of truth need be no recipe for gaining truth. A definition of knowledge need be no recipe for gaining knowledge.

It is true, however, that there is a point to this objection. No acceptable definition of knowledge should lead to scepticism. It ought not to leave hanging in the air our ordinary claims to knowledge. Now, it may be said, it is not clear that our proposed analysis escapes such scepticism.

I think the point is properly taken. But the answer to it must be reserved until the end of the chapter.

(ii) In the second place, it may be objected that even if the definition of non-inferential knowledge is along the right lines, it is insufficiently permissive. Suppose that there were in fact no situations in which A's belief-that-p was empirically sufficient for the truth of p. But suppose there were situations in which A's belief-that-p gave a very high probability of p's being true. If, in one of these situations, A believed p, might we still not say he *knew p* to be true?

I think that this objection has some force. What has been done so far is to define a strict sense for non-inferential knowledge. We could also admit a looser sense in which there was demanded no more than a high probability of A's belief being true.

This enables us to understand, and to some extent sympathize with, those now much brow-beaten philosophers who used to say that empirical knowledge was nothing more than belief that was very probably true. They went on to err, because they were not prepared to allow even the logical possibility of empirical knowledge that transcended very probable belief. Thus they themselves destroyed the contrast that they sought to draw in the empirical field between belief that is very probably true and knowledge strictly so-called. But we can understand their contention without adopting their arguments, and so without finding ourselves in their difficulties.

(iii) The account of non-inferential knowledge that has been given may be granted to have some plausibility in the case of knowledge of such situations as that of my legs being crossed. But what of knowledge of other sorts of fact? What, in particular, of knowledge of general truths, such as 'Arsenic is poisonous' or of logically necessary truths, such as '$7 + 5 = 12$'? What would it mean to say that a belief that arsenic was poisonous was empirically sufficient for arsenic's being in fact poisonous, or that a belief that $7 + 5 = 12$ was empirically sufficient for $7 + 5$ being in fact equal to 12? My belief that my legs are crossed and my legs being in fact crossed are two particular states of affairs. One can therefore be empirically sufficient for the other. But no such relationship is possible in the case of general laws and necessary truths.

My reply is that what I have been discussing is *non-inferential* knowledge. Now it seems plausible, on general Empiricist grounds, to say that the only things we can know non-inferentially are particular matters of fact concerning our environment and ourselves. But it is precisely this sort of non-inferential knowledge with which our formula is well equipped to deal. So I suggest that all other knowledge is knowledge based on good reasons. In order to draw a distinction between knowledge of general truths and logical necessities and mere true beliefs about such matters it is essential to refer to our possession or lack of good reasons for these beliefs.

However, I do not think that the conclusion that there can be no non-inferential knowledge of general truths implies that there cannot be non-inferential knowledge of singular causal sequences. For we regularly recognize that certain sequences are causal ones without being able to subsume the sequence under any law. (We believe, of course, that there is some law under which such sequences can be subsumed.) There seems no reason why A's belief, on a particular occasion, that an object is pressing on A's body and causing the latter to move should not be empirically sufficient for the truth of this belief. And this would be non-inferential knowledge of singular causal sequence.

III. THE NATURE OF INFERRING

Non-inferential knowledge has now been defined without appealing to any *psychological* concept except belief. We have now to give an account of knowledge based upon good reasons.

In the first place, it must be recognized that there is an important ambiguity in the notion of knowledge based upon good reasons. It is possible to have once had good reasons for believing that p was true, but to have now forgotten the reasons. Are we to say that this entails that we no longer know p to be true? This seems very severe. Are we to say that the knowledge was once based upon good reasons, but is now non-inferential? This also sounds very strange.

What I think we ought to say here is that p is now 'based on good reasons' in one sense of the phrase only. We were *led* to our knowledge of p by good reasons, but we do not now *have* any reasons. For the reasons that once led us to the knowledge need not be reasons we still have. Contrariwise, the reasons we now have for knowing something to be true need not be reasons that led us to that knowledge. We may begin by asking what it is to be *led* to know something for good reasons. But it will be convenient to precede this question by a more general one: 'What is it to *infer* one proposition from another?' So in this section we shall be concerned solely with the nature of inferring.

We are not concerned here with logicians' questions about inference, but solely with the psychological process of inferring. The primary sense of the word is that in which it involves acquiring a belief on the basis of a belief already held. There are other senses. A speaker may say 'And so I infer . . .', and then come out with a statement he has believed, and has argued for, for many years. Again, someone may assume that a proposition is true for the sake of seeing 'what can be inferred from it'. But these are secondary uses which can be explained after the nature of the sort of inferring that involves acquiring beliefs has been elucidated.

The account of inferring defended here was held at one time by G. E. Moore (see his *Commonplace Book*, Allen & Unwin, 1962, ed. C. Lewy, p. 7). It has recently been revived by Max Deutscher, from whom I learnt it. As T. A. Rose has pointed out to me, it is essentially Hume's theory of the nature of inferring, divorced from Hume's theory of the nature of belief.

According to this view, to say that A infers p from q is simply to say that A's believing q *causes* him to acquire the belief p. And the sense of 'cause' employed here is the common or billiard-ball sense of 'cause', whatever that sense is.

There is no difficulty here in the fact (as I take it to be) that belief is a dispositional concept. For, as has been stressed again and again in this work, every possession of a disposition implies that the thing that has the disposition is in a certain non-dispositional *state*. Now there is no objection to the non-dispositional state with which the disposition can be identified being causally efficacious. So if beliefs are dispositions, and if holding a belief causes another belief to be acquired, one such state brings about another.

But there is a difficulty for this account of inferring that Moore himself perceived. He pointed to the following case. I think that there is somebody in the house, which causes me to open the door, which causes me to believe that there is nobody in the house. Here my belief that there was somebody in the house caused me to believe that there was nobody in the house. But nobody wants to say that I inferred the second proposition from the first, even invalidly. (No importance attaches to the fact that the second proposition contradicts the first. The point would be the same if what I discovered when I opened the door was that the staircase had fallen down.)

Moore tried to solve the difficulty by saying that in this case the causation is not 'direct'. This solution is either false, or hopelessly vague. What is the criterion for 'direct'? If I come to know q, it may still take many days, and much thought, to infer p from q. Is the causation then 'direct', or not?

In order to solve the problem, let us contrast Moore's case with another one. Detective A perceives that there is a blood-stained handkerchief on the floor. This so rattles him that he is caused to drink a glass of whisky. (If he had not seen the handkerchief, he would not have drunk the whisky.) This so stimulates his brain that he comes to believe that B has committed a murder. (If he had not drunk the whisky, he would not have reached this belief.) Unlike Moore's case, we want to say that this is a case of inference, an inference assisted by whisky. What is the difference between the two cases?

In Moore's case, once I open the door *as a result of whatever cause* I learn that there is nobody in the house. My original belief becomes irrelevant. But, in the second case, if A does not see the handkerchief but still drinks the whisky, he does not come to believe B was a murderer. His belief is acquired as a result of the *joint* action of whisky and knowledge that he has just previously perceived a bloodstained handkerchief.

So we can say that, if A is to infer *p* from *q*, it is essential that A's belief *q* be causally relevant right up to the time that A acquires belief *p*. (Unless A had believed *q* up to the time of acquiring belief *p* he would not have come to believe *p*.) Of course, once A has acquired belief *p* he can forget *q*, yet still have inferred *p* from *q*.

However, what of a somewhat different case, proposed to me by G. C. Nerlich? A believes the time-table to be reliable. So, wishing to find out the time of a train, he looks up the time-table. As a result, he acquires the belief that the train goes at 3.30. Here it was A's belief that the time-table was reliable that caused him to look up the time-table, and so caused him to acquire the belief that the train left at 3.30. And A's belief that the time-table is reliable is causally relevant for his acquiring the belief that the train goes at 3.30 right up to the instant that he acquires the latter belief. Yet A does not infer that the train goes at 3.30 from the reliability of the time-table.

In this case, however, although A's belief that the time-table was reliable was causally relevant right up to the moment that A acquired the belief, *it was not the only belief that was causally relevant.* It was necessary also that A acquire perceptually the belief that the time-table said 3.30. Now we *would* be prepared to say that the belief that the train left at 3.30 was an inference from the *joint* premisses: (i) the time-table is reliable; (ii) it says that the train leaves at 3.30. When we speak of inferring we must take the premiss of the inference to be *all* those beliefs which are causally relevant right up to the moment of the arriving at the conclusion. It is true that the belief that the time-table is reliable may be the only belief that is causally relevant to the acquiring of the belief 'that the time-table says 3.30'. For only if A thought the time-table was reliable would A have looked it up. But this case is simply a variant of Moore's case. Once A has looked at the time-table, his belief that it is reliable is causally irrelevant to his acquiring the belief that it says 3.30.

However, our account of inferring is still not quite correct. For suppose A's belief *q* causes him to believe *p*, and he then forgets *q*, but, nevertheless, believing *p* later causes him to believe *o*.

Has he not inferred *o* from *q*? Yet he did not believe *q* at the time he arrived at belief *o*.

But we can get over this difficulty by saying that what we have been defining up to this point is the notion of 'directly infers'. A 'directly infers' *p* from premisses *q* provided that the inference is directly from *p* to *q* and not *via* some intermediate set of propositions which A infers from *p* and then uses as premisses to infer *q*. An inference of the latter sort is a non-direct inference, and can be defined as a series of direct inferences.

With these qualifications, it seems that our causal account of inferring can stand.

This work is written to argue for, and defend, a materialist theory of the mind. But if the reader is antecedently sympathetic to the identification of mind and brain, this 'causal' theory of inferring will naturally appeal to him. For consider what the analogue of inferring will be in a computer, say. It will be the bringing into being of a new state of the computer (the 'inferred' information) as a causal result of the existence of a previous state of the computer (the original information). Now if the mind is the brain, it will be natural to construe inferring as a similar causal process in the brain. (At the same time, of course, nothing in our account of inferring here in this section entails a materialist theory of the mind. It is simply an account that is *compatible* with materialism.)

Should we say that inferrings are processes or events? If an inference were a process, it would make sense to speak of such things as 'being half-way through an inference'. Such an idiom seems at the very best strained. As soon as we are in a position to say 'I infer' (and we do not say 'I am inferring') we are in a position to say 'I have inferred'. So it seems that an inference is a mental *event*, the acquiring of a belief—an acquiring of a belief that is a causal result of a belief already held.

We may now deduce some consequences from this doctrine of the nature of inferring.

In the first place, since we can always be unaware of, or mistaken about, a causal sequence, it follows that we may be unaware that we inferred *p* from *q*, or think we inferred *p* from *q* when we did not. There seems to be nothing objectionable here. It is the merest commonplace that we are sometimes unaware of, or hold false beliefs about, the beliefs that led us to certain views we hold.

We have previously argued for the possibility of unconscious mental states. If we allow unconscious beliefs, that is, beliefs we hold but are unaware of holding, it will follow that totally unconscious inferring is possible.

It follows also that we must be prepared to accept as cases of inferring perfectly fantastic transitions from one belief to another, provided only that one causes the other in the appropriate way. If it was my belief that Socrates is mortal that made me acquire the belief that the moon is made of green cheese, then I inferred the second proposition from the first. Again, there seems to be no particular objection to this consequence. It fits in well with what psychologists tell us about the darker workings of the mind. There is no reason why we should not speak of 'utterly unreasonable inferences'.

But now it may be objected that any piece of inferring must proceed according to some *principle of inference*. The principle of inference need not be a logically necessary one. 'If a human being's head has been cut off, then he is dead' is a perfectly good principle of inference, although decapitation does not logically imply death. Nor need we be always aware of what our principle of inference is. The chicken-sexer infers from visual cues to the sex of the chicken, but neither he nor anybody else knows what these cues are. All the same, it will be said, must there not be a principle of inference according to which any inference proceeds? But if inferring is *merely* a matter of one belief causing us to acquire another belief no principle of inference is involved.

My answer to this objection is that the principle of the inference is given by the nature of the causal sequence involved. Thus, suppose I am told that Jim, an Australian, had his head cut off. I infer that he is dead. Now it is clear that learning that he was a male, that his name was Jim and that he was an Australian played no causal role in bringing about the belief that Jim was dead. Only the belief that his head had been cut off did that. So the principle of my inference is clear. Again, suppose I hear that X has been passed over for appointment, and I infer he will be very angry. It may be clear that if my information had been about Y then I should not have been caused to come to the same conclusion. So the principle of inference is certainly not 'Those who have been passed over for appointment become angry'. It might perhaps have been 'Those who have been passed over for appointment and who have a certain nature and are in certain circumstances (exemplified, as I took it, by X) become angry.' I might not be able to specify the nature and circumstances, but it would be possible, at least in theory, to discover just what it was in my 'impressions of X' that caused me to believe that *he* would become angry if passed over for appointment on that occasion. And that would be my 'principle of inference'.

It is the simplest matter to say what makes a principle of inference a good one. If the principle of inference is 'if *q*, then *p*' then it is a good principle if this proposition is *true*. (It may be true of logical necessity or simply contingently true.) One who infers in accordance with such a principle makes a good inference.

Suppose, however, that there can be found propositions *r* and *s* whose conjunction is logically equivalent to *q*. And suppose it is the case that if *r* is true, then *p* is true, but it is not always the case that if *s* is true, *p* is true. Suppose it is also the case that *s* was causally essential for A's inference to *p*. If A had simply believed *r*, and not *q* which is the conjunction of *r* and *s*, he would not have acquired the belief *p*. The principle of inference 'if *q*, then *p*' is still a good one. But I think it should be said that A did not infer in accordance with a good principle of inference. For acquiring the belief *s* was essential to A's inference, yet 'if *s*, then *p*' is not a good principle of inference.

We may now give a brief account of the secondary sorts of inferring. The man who says 'And so I infer . . .' although his conclusion and argument is no novelty to him, is simply rehearsing an argument. He is claiming that a certain proposition follows from another proposition. Perhaps we can say that he is also going through the *motions* of an information-acquiring inference.

The cases where a proposition is inferred from another proposition, but we do not believe the premiss, may be dealt with as follows. The cause is the entertaining of, or considering, a certain proposition, *p*. (The notion of entertaining a proposition is still to be elucidated in the chapter on thinking.) The effect is the acquiring of a belief that *if q* is true, then a further proposition, *p*, is true. This whole causal sequence is called 'inferring *p* from *q*'.

In elucidating the notion of inferring we have done something towards elucidating the complex and polymorphous notion of thinking. Now it is sometimes argued that if everything, including the mind, is subject to causality, a valid inference is not really possible, and so objective thought is not possible. Causes are blind, and if my thoughts are caused, my 'thought' is blind and irrational. This argument has relatively little currency with professional philosophers, but it is often used by those on the fringe of philosophy.

But we can now see that, at any rate as far as inferring is concerned, the very reverse is true. In order to infer, either validly or invalidly, the premiss of my inference must be the cause (in the appropriate way) of the belief that I arrive at. So far from causality making inferring impossible, causality is in fact a logical precondition of the possibility of inferring.

Before leaving the topic of inferring I must mention an ingenious counter-instance that was put to me by Michael Rohr. I do not know what to say about the case, and can only hope, like Hume on a celebrated occasion, that the instance is 'so particular and singular' that it 'does not merit that for it alone we should alter our general maxim'.

Following Kant, I have spoken of awareness of our own states of mind as 'inner sense'. That is to say, I have compared introspection to perception. Now, as I shall argue in the next chapter, in perception the thing perceived is causally responsible for the perception of it. To say that I see a table entails that the table brought about my perception of the table. So, since I compare introspection to perception, I am committed to saying that in introspection the mental state we are aware of is causally responsible for our awareness of it.

Suppose, then, that I believe p. Suppose, further, that this belief does not remain unconscious, but I introspectively acquire the belief that I believe p. Here the belief-that-p causes me to acquire the belief *that I believe p*. Now nobody would want to call this a case of inferring that-I-believe-p from p, yet it seems to fulfil all the conditions for this inference laid down in this section.

IV. INFERENTIAL KNOWLEDGE

We are now in a position to give a simple account of knowledge to which we have been *led* by good reasons (as opposed to knowledge for which we only *have* good reasons).

A knows *p*, and has been led to this knowledge by good reasons *q*, if and only if:

(i) A believes *p*;
(ii) A knows (or knew) *q*;
(iii) A inferred *p* from this knowledge *q*;
(iv) A inferred in accordance with a good principle.

A's knowledge-that-*q* may either be non-inferential or knowledge to which A was led by good reasons, but in the end we must get back to non-inferential knowledge. And to say that A's belief-that-*p* was inferred from A's knowledge-that-*q* is to say that the belief-that-*p* was acquired as a causal result of the knowledge-that-*q* (with the qualifications made in the last section). And given both that *q* is true, and that the principle of the inference was a good one, *p* *must* be true.

Instead of saying that A is *led* to believe *p* by good reasons *q*, we can also say that A knows *p* *because* he knew *q*. It has been fashionable in modern philosophy to deny that the 'because' here is the 'because' of ordinary causality. If our account has been correct, the 'because' is simply the ordinary causal 'because'. We speak of 'reasons' not in virtue of the special relation that the knowledge *q* bears to the knowledge *p*, but simply in virtue of the special nature of the cause (viz. it is the acquiring of knowledge). In the case of non-inferential knowledge, the causes that bring the knowledge into existence are (presumably) a chain of physical processes that are not mental processes. But, in the case of knowledge to which we are led by good reasons, the causal chain that brings the knowledge into existence includes one or more pieces of knowledge.

It might, however, be a little too linguistically simple-minded to say that reasons which lead me to adopt a certain belief are causes of my acquiring that belief. It is not natural to say that somebody's reason for believing *p* is *that he believes q*. It is the proposition that he believes, viz. *q*, that is naturally said to be his reason, although, to be sure, it is the fact that he believes it, and the fact that this belief has led him to the belief *p*, that makes us call proposition *q* his reason for believing *p*. Now if a reason is a proposition it is not a cause, for propositions cannot be causes. All this, however, seems to be merely a linguistic subtlety. A's belief-that-*q*, or his acquiring the belief-that-q, can perfectly well be spoken of as a cause.

(It may be advisable to insert a word about propositions here. If A believes or entertains p he can be said to believe or entertain the proposition, p. But this does not mean that A stands in a certain relation, the believing or supposing relation, to an entity, p. A's-believing-p and A's-entertaining-p are mental states which do not contain detachable portions called propositions. But, at the same time, the two mental states do resemble each other—a resemblance which may be rendered by saying that they have as their object the same proposition. Propositions may be said to be the *intentional* objects of such mental states. If I desire to do x, then 'the doing of x' is the intentional object of my desire. My desire 'points' to this state of affairs, which, however, need not exist. If I believe p, then the proposition p is the intentional object of my belief. My belief 'points' to this state of affairs, which, however, need not exist. Our account of desire has claimed to give an account of the intentionality of desire that is compatible with a purely materialist view of man. Our account of believing and entertaining, when we come to give it, must also give an account of the intentionality of these states that is compatible with materialism. Notice that, as the term is used in this book, 'propositions' have no special connection with *language*. There can be sub-verbal beliefs—animals and young children have beliefs—and in such cases 'what is believed' will be said to be a proposition.)

It is now time to discuss the question what it is to *have* a good reason for a certain piece of knowledge, although possession of this knowledge did not lead us (did not cause us) to acquire the knowledge.

It seems clear that if A has good reasons q for knowledge-that-p, but q is not a reason which led to this knowledge-that-p, then it is entailed that:

(i) A knows p;
(ii) A knows q;
(iii) 'if q, then p' is a good principle of inference.

But these three conditions can hardly be jointly sufficient. Is it not possible that these two pieces of knowledge, p and q, exist alongside each other in A's mind without standing in any relation to each other? And could q be called a reason then? One might try to answer this by saying that in such a case A has a reason for believing p, but fails to realize that he has a reason. And in support of this it may be pointed out that we do say of people that they have reasons for believing something even although they do not realize that they have such reasons. Nevertheless, this reply does not quite satisfy. It is not just that A fails to realize that he has a reason for p. If the knowledge-that-q bears no relation to the knowledge-that-p in A's mind the 'reason' is not really *acting* as a reason. It is a reason only by courtesy.

This suggests that we should add a fourth condition, a condition that has the great advantage of bringing out the parallelism between our account here and the previous account of reasons that actually *lead* to the acquiring of knowledge:

> (iv) A's knowledge-that-q is a *potential cause* of A's acquiring knowledge-that-p.

The notion of 'potential cause' may be explicated by means of the following comparison. We may think of reasons that actually operate to produce knowledge as a stamp that makes a certain impression (the knowledge) in the wax of the mind. Good reasons that we have for a piece of knowledge, but which are reasons that did not lead to the knowledge, may be thought of as a stamp that fits into the impression left by the first stamp. It would have brought the knowledge into existence, except that its work was already done.

There are, however, two objections to this fourth criterion which leave me a little uneasy.

In the first place, is it not possible that the first three conditions should be fulfilled, and even that A be prepared to *adduce q* as a reason for p, and yet that, for some psychological or physiological reason, knowledge-that-q is not even a potential cause of A's acquiring the knowledge-that-p? Yet in such circumstances it seems we would be prepared to count q as one of A's reasons for p.

But must not A at least believe his knowledge-that-q to be something that is capable of bringing about the knowledge that-p in A and in others? And if this is so, perhaps we can say that q is one of A's reasons in an extended or courtesy sense, where simply to take a thing to be a reason makes it a reason.

The second difficulty has been pointed out to me by Douglas Gasking. It seems possible to offer as a good reason for accepting a claim to current knowledge a run of past successes in similar circumstances. (Consider the case of the skilled judge of distances who nevertheless does not know how his feat is accomplished. He might back up his claim to current knowledge by pointing out that he has been right in the past.) Now these 'reasons' are not even a potential cause of the current knowledge, because unless the current knowledge was already in existence it would not be possible to back up the claim to current knowledge in this way.

But is the 'reason' really a reason for the person who possesses the current knowledge? Might he not say, if challenged to give reasons for his current claim, 'Strictly, I have no *reasons*, but you will find I have never been wrong about such matters.' The reason is only a *reason* for his hearers. Learning of his past successes might lead them to the knowledge that he now had knowledge. But it is not a reason for him.

If these answers to the two objections are satisfactory, we have given an account of what it is to have reasons for a piece of knowledge, where these reasons did not lead us to the acquiring of the knowledge.

V. FURTHER CONSIDERATIONS ABOUT KNOWLEDGE

If we have succeeded, an account has been given of the closely connected notions of knowledge, inferring, and having reasons for a belief without appealing to any specifically *psychological* concept except that of belief. This is an important simplification. But before leaving the topic of knowledge I shall append three further considerations.

In the first case, it is clear that knowledge may cease to be knowledge with the passing of time. We may simply lose the knowledge, but the more interesting case is the one where the knowledge does no more than degenerate to mere true belief. What account shall we give of this?

Consider in the first place non-inferential knowledge. We said that A knows p non-inferentially if:

(i) A believes p;
(ii) A's belief-that-p is empirically sufficient for the truth of p.

Now in the case we are considering, after a lapse of time it is no longer the case that A's belief-that-p is still sufficient for the truth of *p*, although A still truly believes *p*. A's belief is now such that it cannot be absolutely relied on. That this sort of thing happens is a commonplace. When I am present at a scene, or shortly afterwards, it may be empirically impossible that my beliefs about what is happening, or has just happened, should be false. But a day later it may be only a piece of luck that my beliefs about what happened correspond with reality.

In the case of knowledge based on good reasons, if we still have good reasons (and they are still good reasons for us), then we automatically have the knowledge. Suppose, however, that we have forgotten the reasons. Have we still got knowledge? Again, this depends on whether our current belief is or is not empirically sufficient for its truth. I believe that the earth is round, but I have forgotten the reasons that originally led me to believe it. Do I know the earth is round? Well, is it empirically impossible for me, in the situation I am in, to have that belief unless the earth is in fact round? If it is empirically impossible, I know.

In the second place, it is clear that, if our account of knowledge is correct, A may know *p but not know that he knows p*. This is not a paradoxical result, although it does conflict with the prejudices of many philosophers. To find such cases in ordinary life, we do best to go to animals and smaller children. They know many things, but, since they lack self-consciousness, they do not know that they know. But even adults may know without knowing that they know. I may deny that I know the answer to a certain problem, to be told that I really do know the answer, and find to my surprise that I do know it. We also have such idioms as 'I think I know . . .' and 'I wonder if I know . . .?'. It may be said that these are just sloppy ways of saying 'I believe . . .' and 'I wonder if I can guess . . .?' *Prima facie*, however, these idioms are to be taken literally.

Normally, however, we not only know, but know that we know. Anybody who has learnt to use the word 'know', and who applies it truly to himself on a particular occasion will, very likely, not simply know but know that he knows. What is it, then, for A to know that he knows *p*? It is simply for A to believe he knows *p*, and for it to be empirically impossible in that situation that he should have this belief that he knows unless in fact he does know.

It may be true that the phrase 'I know *p*' is not ordinarily used solely to make a descriptive statement about the speaker, but to perform a variety of other tasks: including, for instance, pledging the authority of the speaker that *p* is true. But such a linguistic pledging of authority surely presupposes that the speaker believes a descriptive autobiographical statement to the effect that he knows *p* to be true.

In the third place, we must consider whether this whole account of knowledge that we have advanced does not lead to scepticism. According to our doctrine, to have knowledge is for a certain sort of empirical connection to hold between a belief and the fact that it is true. How then, it may be asked, can we *pick* an instance of knowledge? Not by establishing that the empirical connection exists, for to establish this we must know that our procedures for establishing the connection are reliable, so that knowledge will be required to establish the existence of knowledge. And according to our view there are no incorrigible truths about which it is logically impossible to be wrong. So, given the purely formal definition of knowledge that we have argued for, it seems impossible to find any ground for saying that any of our beliefs constitute knowledge.

The only possible reply to these sceptical doubts is that we must, logically must, start from the beliefs that we are in fact certain of. Given we have not the slightest reason to think something is false, and given that we are absolutely certain it is true, *we cannot but take it that we know it*. Nor is this just a 'pragmatic' piece of wisdom. A belief cannot but be judged innocent unless there are reasons for thinking it to be guilty. This is involved in the concept of belief, because to believe something is to believe it *to be true*. And to say that I am absolutely certain that something is true entails claiming that I know it to be true. So, given for instance that I am absolutely certain that my legs are crossed, I must, logically must, accept it as true that my legs are in fact crossed.

Is it then being argued that certainty constitutes a reason for accepting a belief as true? It is not. Complete certainty is compatible with being wrong. All I am saying is that we must start from complete certainty because the notion of 'complete certainty' *entails* that this is in fact where we do start from! Perhaps this is no answer to the sceptic. But, if so, has he not asked an unanswerable question?

We may sum up the view of knowledge put forward in this chapter by saying that knowledge is a belief which it is impossible we should be wrong about. 'If you know, you cannot be mistaken.' But the impossibility must not be interpreted as *logical* impossibility. That was the error of those who sought to found knowledge on self-evident or logically indubitable truths. The impossibility of mistake is an empirical impossibility. Nor is this 'impossibility of being mistaken' any sort of *recipe* for the discovery of truth.

10

PERCEPTION AND BELIEF

WE come now to an account of the concept of perception. Here I have been unable to see any way of presenting the position except by an analysis that has two stages. In the first stage, it is argued that an account of perception can be given in terms of the acquiring of beliefs about the physical world. Many of the *traditional* problems of the philosophy of perception can be solved at this stage. Such an account, however, must take as primitive the psychological concept of belief. It is therefore incomplete from the point of view of the attempt to give an account of mental states simply as states of the person apt for the production of certain physical behaviour, or states apt for being brought about by certain physical objects or situations. The second stage of the argument tries to show that the acquirings of belief involved in perception are susceptible of this sort of analysis.

The present chapter is solely concerned to give an account of perception as the acquiring of belief. The account is along the same general lines as that proposed in my book *Perception and the Physical World* (Routledge, 1961), especially Chapters 9 and 10. But I hope I have been able to correct various errors, and, as a result, present a more acceptable view. Readers who are antecedently sympathetic to this view of perception, or who are prepared to grant it for the sake of argument, could go straight on to Chapter 11.

Perception and Belief

I. PERCEPTION AS ACQUIRING OF BELIEF

It is clear that the biological function of perception is to give the organism information about the current state of its own body and its physical environment, information that will assist the organism in the conduct of life. This is a most important clue to the *nature* of perception. It leads us to the view that perception is nothing but the acquiring of true or false beliefs concerning the current state of the organism's body and environment. 'True belief', here, is meant to cover both knowledge and *mere* true belief. (In the previous chapter the attempt was made to define knowledge without recourse to any psychological concept except belief.) Veridical perception is the acquiring of true beliefs, sensory illusion the acquiring of false beliefs.

The beliefs involved must be conceived of as sub-verbal beliefs. Animals can perceive, sometimes, we believe, better than we can, but they lack words entirely. And we ourselves are often hard put to translate our perceptions into words. If we think of the wealth and subtlety of the information that we gain by our eyes, to take one example only, we see that much of it eludes the relatively coarse mesh of the net of language.

The word 'belief' is a stumbling-block. To talk of beliefs may seem to be to talk in a very sophisticated and self-conscious way, quite unsuited to such an unsophisticated thing as perception. Do animals have beliefs? It may seem a strange way to talk about them. But the difficulty is to find another word. 'Judgement' is even worse than 'belief'. A word like 'awareness' would be nearer the mark in some ways, but it has the most serious disadvantage that it is linguistically improper to speak of false awareness. Yet any theory of perception must cover both veridical perception and sensory illusion. Perhaps one could say that perception is a continuous 'mapping' of what is going on in our body or our environment, for mapping can be correct or incorrect. It is certainly useful to think of our sensory field at any one time as a partial and sometimes faulty map of our body and its environment. But to talk of mapping may be to err in an opposite way to talking of believing. It suggests that it is just a matter of our body and our environment registering upon, or making an impression upon, our minds. A map, after all, is just a physical object which we have to *use* to tell us where things are. But perceptions are not like that. If they are maps, they are maps that essentially refer beyond themselves to the objects they claim to map. Unlike ordinary maps, perceptions have intentionality.

One useful alternative to the word 'belief' is the word 'information'. It has in fact already been employed in this section, and will be employed again in future. It has the advantage that we can then speak of sensory illusion as 'misinformation'. However, the word does have one misleading association. It is often natural to think of information or misinformation as something distinct from the true or false beliefs one acquires as a result of the information or misinformation. Spoken or written words are often naturally spoken of as information, and they are distinct from the beliefs which the words create in hearer or reader. But when perception is spoken of in this work as the acquiring of information, it must be clearly understood that no distinction at all is intended between the information and the beliefs to which it gives rise. Information and beliefs are identical. Given this warning, the term 'information' will often be convenient.

If perception is the acquiring of beliefs or information then clearly it must involve the possession of concepts. For to believe that A is B entails possessing the concepts of A and B. But since perception can occur in the total absence of the ability to speak, we are committed to the view that there can be concepts that involve no linguistic ability. More will be said about perceptual concepts in the next chapter.

I have spoken of perception as the acquiring of true or false beliefs about the *current* state of our body and environment. It may be objected that it is possible to see, in the literal sense of 'see', that somebody came in with muddy boots last night. However, such a case can always be regarded as a case of inference, even if quite unself-conscious inference, an inference based upon perception of some current state of the environment (the bootmarks). I acquire the belief that there is a certain muddy pattern of marks on the floor now, and this causes me to acquire the further belief that somebody came in with muddy boots last night. (See the discussion of inferring in the previous chapter.) It is significant that in such cases we speak only of seeing *that*. It would be improper to say we saw the person or the muddy boots.

If perceptions are acquirings of beliefs, then the correspondence or failure of correspondence of perceptions to physical reality is simply the correspondence or failure of correspondence of beliefs to the facts. And the intentionality of perception reduces to the intentionality of the beliefs acquired.

II. THE ROLE OF THE SENSE-ORGANS

It is tempting to include a reference to the sense-organs: the eyes, ears, nose, etc., in the logical analysis of perception. That is to say, it is tempting to say that seeing is the acquiring of true or false beliefs as the causal result of the operation of the eyes, hearing is the acquiring of true or false beliefs as the causal result of the operation of the ears, and so on.

But the suggestion involves a number of difficulties. In the first place, it is difficult to say what is the organ of *touch*. Most of the body is tactually sensitive. Perhaps this difficulty can be met by saying that touch does not involve a special organ but rather a special procedure: objects coming into contact with the flesh. This procedure causes certain sorts of beliefs to be acquired, and we call such acquirings of beliefs tactual perceptions.

In the second place, there is one form of perception where it does not seem possible to specify even such a procedure for acquiring beliefs. This is bodily perception. Where I perceive the motion or position of my limbs and body, or the heating up or cooling down of parts or the whole of my body, there is no process, and still less no organ, that I can point to from my ordinary knowledge as causally responsible for such perceptions. Of course, there are in fact mechanisms in the body which are involved in bodily perception, but only physiologists know anything about them. There is nothing we ordinarily say we perceive the motion of our limbs with.

In the third place, it is possible to have experiences resembling ordinary perceptions which do not involve stimulation of sense-organs, known or unknown. If the central nervous system is acted upon in various ways (for instance, by continuous drinking or by a probe being stuck in certain brain-areas), the subject may have visual or other sorts of hallucination without any stimulation of the sense-organs.

In the fourth place, even if we waive all these objections, it is imaginable that we should have much the same perceptual experiences that we have now, even although we could discover nothing that we could identify as sense-organs. Again, we can imagine that stimulation of particular sense-organs might produce quite different perceptual experiences from those that are actually produced. Stimulation of the ears, for instance, might lead to what we now call visual experiences.

But even when all these points have been admitted, it still remains true that the sense-organs play a part in our concept of perception, or, perhaps it would be better to say, in our 'picture' of perception. Quite early in life we learn that the acquiring of certain very complex and idiosyncratic patterns of information about the current state of the world is bound up with the operation of certain organs or combination of organs. In a loose sense of the word 'presuppose' our concept of perception comes to presuppose such knowledge. If we started to acquire beliefs about the current state of our body and environment in a way that did not conform to established patterns, we might start talking of a new sense, or even of a new faculty different from sense-perception.

It is this knowledge that the acquiring of certain patterns of information about the environment is bound up with the operation of certain organs that makes us talk, for example, of *visual* hallucinations even when no stimulation of the eyes is involved. Macbeth, while considering the hypothesis that the dagger is a mere hallucination, says 'It is the bloody business which informs thus to *mine eyes*' in the very process of putting forward the suggestion that it is *not* any stimulation of his eyes that is responsible! His way of talking strikes us as natural. The pattern of misinformation involved is so like the patterns of true and false belief actually acquired as a result of the stimulation of the eyes that it is easy to think of it as caused by stimulation of the eyes.

We can therefore say, if we like, that perception is the acquiring of true or false beliefs about the current state of our body and environment *by means of the senses*. But we must remember that the final phrase, although helpful, has not a full right to appear in a definition.

What is our concept of a sense-organ? One mark of a sense-organ is obvious: it is a portion of our body which when stimulated produces a characteristic range of perceptions. A further important mark has been pointed out by Anthony Kenny in his *Action, Emotion, and Will* (p. 57). It is a portion of our body which we habitually move at will with the object of perceiving what is going on in our body and environment. The two criteria seem to be jointly necessary and sufficient for calling something a sense-organ.

The receptors involved in bodily perception fulfil the first criterion for being sense-organs, but not the second. In this work, however, it will sometimes be convenient to talk about the 'stimulation of the sense-organs' in contexts where bodily perception is included. In that case we will be using a relaxed test for 'sense-organ' where only the first criterion is required.

The second criterion has the interesting consequence that not all perceptions can arise as a result of the use (as opposed to the mere stimulation) of our sense-organs. We saw in Chapter 7 that the operation of the will is logically bound up with the occurrence of perceptions acting as 'information' which suitably modify the direction of the causal influence of the will. Now this entails that if we are to move our sense-organs at will we must be able to become perceptually aware of what happens to them during the time that they are being moved. If this perceptual awareness is gained as a result of the use, as opposed to the mere stimulation, of a sense-organ we are faced with an incipient vicious infinite regress. So there must be some perceptions that do not arise as the result of the *use* of the sense-organs.

This result consorts well with, although it does not actually entail, the point that there are no organs of bodily perception in the *full* sense of the word 'organ'. For normally, at any rate, we become aware of a change in the state of our sense-organs by bodily perception. We should therefore expect that there was no organ we *use* when we come to have bodily perceptions themselves.

III. BELIEF IS DISPOSITIONAL, BUT PERCEPTION IS AN EVENT

To say that A believes *p* does not entail that there is anything going on in A's mind, or that A is engaged in any behaviour, which could be called a manifestation of A's belief. It makes sense to say that A believes *p*, but that A is asleep, or unconscious. It is true that there must be some difference in A's state of mind if he believes p from his state of mind if he does not believe p. But we need not know what that difference of state is, any more than we need know what is the difference in state between brittle glass and glass that is not brittle. Belief is a dispositional state of mind which endures for a greater or lesser length of time, and that may or may not manifest itself (either in consciousness or in behaviour) during that time. But perceptions are definite events that take place at definite instants and are then over. How, then, can perceptions be beliefs?

The answer is that perceptions are not beliefs, and so not dispositional states, because they are *acquirings* of belief. The acquiring of a dispositional state is not a state, nor a process, but an event, in the sense of 'event' explained at the beginning of Part Two (Ch. 7, Sect. I). If a glass becomes brittle at t_1, that is an event even although brittleness is a dispositional state.

Now perception is an event, in this sense of the word 'event'. It is not a process which happens to occupy a very short stretch of time (an event in another sense of the word). Up to a certain moment the perceiver has not yet perceived a certain state of affairs, from that moment on he has perceived it. This we interpret as meaning that up to a certain moment the subject has not yet acquired a certain belief, and that after that moment he has acquired it.

We owe the recognition that perception is an event to Gilbert Ryle. He put the point, rather unhappily as we shall see in a moment, by saying that verbs of perception are 'achievement-words'. His view is sometimes attacked by pointing out that we can perceive an unchanging scene for a period of time. To espy a robin may be an achievement, but where, it is asked, is the achievement involved in going on staring at the robin? However, if we think of perception as the acquiring of beliefs, and if we remember that we cannot look at a robin without time passing, this objection is easily met. At t_1 we acquire the information that the robin is there at t_1. At t_2 we acquire the information that the robin is still there at t_2. This is new, even if monotonous, information. And so for the whole stretch of time that we are looking at the robin.

It may still be objected that looking at a robin is a continuous performance, quite unlike spotting one. However, some achievements are continuous. If I hold a heavy weight aloft for some time, this is a continuous performance which is also a continuous achievement: keeping the weight there. Each new instant is, in a way, a new achievement. Looking at the robin is also a continuous achievement, continually yielding new, although monotonous, information.

But to talk of verbs of perception as 'achievement-words' is to invite us to conflate the notion that perception is an event with no less than three other notions.

In the first place, an achievement is ordinarily thought of as the outcome of some train of purposive activity. Now although many perceptions are the outcome of trains of purposive activity, in particular trains of activity involving the use, as opposed to the mere stimulation, of sense-organs, this is not the case with all perception. Some perceptions simply occur, without our having done anything to bring them about.

In the second place, to talk of achievement implies that what is brought about, or comes about, is some sort of *success*. Now we do normally use the phrase 'perceive that' and its determinates 'see that', 'hear that', etc., to imply that the perception reported is veridical. If I perceive that x is y, then indeed x is y. We might call this the 'success-grammar' of these phrases. So to perceive that x is y might be called an achievement, even if it is not the outcome of a train of purposive activity, because it is the coming to be of a success. But although all perceptions are events, that is, they are the coming to be of states, they are not all the coming to be of *success*-states. For some perceptions are illusory. When we perceive, we do not always 'perceive that . . .'.

This point about the 'success-grammar' of 'perceive that' is in turn easily confused with another point. When verbs of perception are followed by the name of an object, process or event (as *opposed* to a 'that' clause) they normally have what we might call 'existence-grammar'. If A is said to see a bush, then there must be a bush to be seen. This is *not* the point about 'success-grammar' because to say that A sees a bush does not entail that his perception is veridical. A may see the bush, but quite fail to see that it is a bush. (In passing, it may be noted that not *all* perceptions logically imply the existence of something perceived. In hallucinatory perception there need be no existent object that can be said to be perceived.) This feature of the grammar of verbs of perception is easily, but mistakenly, assimilated to the notion of achievement or success.

In view of these ambiguities we do best not to say that verbs of perception are 'achievement-words'. But it is important to see that all perceptions, of whatever sort, are *events*. These events, we have said, are acquirings of true or false beliefs.

IV. PERCEPTION WITHOUT BELIEF

But there are cases where perception occurs, but there is no acquiring of true or false beliefs.

In the first place, as has often been pointed out, it is possible to have perceptions that do not correspond to physical reality yet quite fail to be deceived by them, that is, quite fail to acquire false beliefs. In the case of visual perception, this is a familiar experience. When we look into a mirror, the visual appearance that we are presented with is that of a mirror-*doppelganger* behind the glass. Yet, whatever may be the case for anybody unfamiliar with mirrors, mirror-images do not normally deceive us.

The same thing can happen, although it is rarer, in the case of veridical perception. If I am told that the conditions under which I am viewing a certain pond are such that, although it is in fact round, it looks elliptical to me, then I may believe it is round although it looks elliptical. It may nevertheless be the case that viewing conditions are perfectly normal, and the pond really is elliptical. Here we have veridical perception, but no acquiring of true belief.

In the second place, there are cases where we cannot speak of *acquiring* true or false belief because we already have that true or false belief. Here the normal cases are those involving veridical perception. Thus, if I am looking at a red book, I may know with perfect certainty that it will continue to be red in the next instant. So when my eyes still rest upon the book during that instant, I cannot be said to acquire the true belief that it is now red, because I already knew it would be red during that instant.

It is possible, although less common, to have the same sort of thing occur in the case of sensory illusion. If a pond looks to me to be elliptical, and I believe it to be elliptical, although in fact it is not, I may be perfectly certain that it will be elliptical the next instant. And if I look at the pond at that instant, I cannot be said to acquire a false belief because I already falsely believed that it would be elliptical during that instant.

The first set of cases may be called 'perception without belief', the second 'perception without acquiring of belief'.

All these cases seem to show that we ought to make a distinction between the beliefs that we acquire in perception, and the perceptual experience on which these beliefs are based.

How is this perceptual experience to be conceived? Suppose I have the perceptions that we associate with looking at a red ball. It is clear that I might have had exactly the same perceptions without there being any red ball in physical reality. When we reflect on this point it is very tempting to say that what is involved is some relationship between my mind and a non-physical red item: a sense-impression or sense-datum. Now it is clear that if there are such items involved in perception, then it is false that perception is simply a state of the person apt for the bringing about of certain physical behaviour or a state of the person apt to be brought about by certain physical stimuli. The 'Causal' analysis of the concept of perception would be false. We must therefore give an account of perception, and in particular of 'perception without belief' and 'perception without acquiring of belief', which does not involve non-physical sensory items.

One way to do this would be to admit the notion of perceptual experience as something quite distinct from the acquiring of beliefs about the environment, but go on to give an account of perceptual experience that was compatible with a Causal analysis of all the mental concepts. I have been unable to see how this can be done, and so I will attempt to give an account of perception in terms of the acquiring of beliefs.

But before this task is attempted, those who accept the existence of sensory items may fairly demand that cause be shown why their intuitively plausible view should be rejected. What justification is there for proposing elaborate analyses where a straightforward and simple account in terms of sensory items is available?

In the first place, as has been shown again and again, the view that all perceptual acquiring of belief is based upon some relationship that the mind has to non-physical sensory items leads to one of two very unsatisfactory alternatives. In the Representative theory, the mind is confined to non-inferential knowledge of its own sensory items, and has to make an inference to the existence of physical things. The Phenomenalist alternative, which gives an account of physical reality as nothing but an elaborate construction out of the sensory items themselves, is even less satisfactory.

Some modern philosophers, aware of these difficulties, have tried to reduce non-physical sensory items to mere phenomenological facts, mere accompaniments to our acquiring beliefs about the current state of our body and its physical environment. Yet surely this is a thoroughly artificial view? If there are non-physical sensory items, they surely could not stand in this quite external relation to our perceptual beliefs. If one espouses sensory items at all, does one not want to say that we believe there is a red ball before us *because* there is a certain non-physical item in a certain relation to our mind?

These objections to the postulation of sensory items are rather general. So now let us consider a much more specific difficulty. It is the paradox about the non-transitivity of the relation 'exact similarity in a given respect' with regard to the alleged sensory items.

If A is exactly similar to B in respect X, and B is exactly similar to C in respect X, then it follows of logical necessity, that A is exactly similar to C in respect X. 'Exact similarity in a particular respect' is necessarily a transitive relation. Now suppose that we have three samples of cloth, A, B and C, which are exactly alike except that they differ very slightly in colour. Suppose further, however, that A and B are *perceptually* completely indistinguishable in respect of colour, and B and C are *perceptually* completely indistinguishable in respect of colour. Suppose, however, that A and C can be perceptually distinguished from each other in this respect.

Now consider the situation if we hold a 'sensory item' view of perception. If the pieces of cloth A and B are perceptually indistinguishable in colour, it will seem to follow that the two sensory items A_1 and B_1 that we have when we look at the two pieces *actually are identical in colour*. For the sensory items are what are supposed to make a perception the perception it is, and here, by hypothesis, the *perceptions* are identical. In the same way B_1 and C_1 will be sensory items that are identical in colour. Yet, by hypothesis, sensory items A_1 and C_1 are not identical in colour!

There are two ways in which a defender of sensory items might try to deal with this paradox. In the first place he might take the heroic course adopted by Bertrand Russell, and say that this only shows that exact similarity in a certain respect is not necessarily a transitive relation. I think this is a somewhat staggering defence. It is nearly as bad as if we had demonstrated to a philosopher that there was a contradiction in his argument, and he had asked, 'What is so wrong about a contradiction?' If it is not obvious that exact similarity in a certain respect is transitive, what is obvious?

A more hopeful line of escape is open if the upholder of sensory items is prepared to abandon the view that we have incorrigible knowledge of the nature of the items at the time of having them. He can then say that in the case described it cannot really be true that sensory items A_1 and B_1 are identical in colour, so are B_1 and C_1, but A_1 and C_1 are not identical in colour. We must have made an error concerning the nature of our perceptions at some point, and so made an error in the nature of the sensory item present.

But although this way of escape is not logically absurd as Russell's suggestion seems to be, it is nevertheless most implausible. The phenomenological facts seem clear: piece of cloth A looks to be exactly the same colour as piece of cloth B, which looks to be exactly the same colour as piece of cloth C. But A looks to be a slightly different colour from C. There seems to be no reason to suggest that any phenomenological error has occurred, except the fact that the case clashes with a certain theory of the nature of perception. It seems rational to back the case against the theory. After all, those who support the analysis of perception as involving sensory items, regularly allege that it is their view, and their view alone, that does phenomenological justice to the perceptual facts. It will be ironic if they, faced with a difficult case, turn round and assert that there is a phenomenological error involved in the case!

It seems, then, that the defender of sensory items has no easy escape from this paradoxical case involving the apparent non-transitivity of the relation of 'exact similarity in a certain respect' in the case of sensory items. We shall see shortly that an analysis in terms of belief deals with this case with the utmost ease.

A second difficulty for an analysis of perception as involving non-physical sensory items is provided by the indeterminacy of perceptions. The classical case is that of the speckled hen. I may be able to see that it has quite a number of speckles, but unable to see exactly how many speckles it has. The hen has a definite number of speckles, but the perception is a perception of an indeterminate number of speckles. However, this indeterminacy is present in perception generally, perhaps in all perception. For instance, when I see or feel that one object is larger than another, I do not perceive exactly how much larger the first object is. The first object's size bears a perfectly definite relation to the second object's size, but the perception does not yield that definite relation. It yields something much less determinate. What is being referred to here is not simply what can be *verbalized* in our perceptions. If we completely abstract from the way we verbally describe our perceptions, they still remain indeterminate.

Now the difficulty that this indeterminacy of perception creates for a theory of sensory items is that it seems to imply that the items will have to be indeterminate in nature. The non-physical item that exists when we perceive the physical speckled hen will have to have an indeterminate number of speckles. Again, of the non-physical items that exist when we perceive that one physical object is larger than the other, one will have to be larger than the other without being any determinate amount larger. And how can any object be indeterminately larger than another?

Once again, there are two lines of escape available to the defender of sensory items. In the first place, he may argue that, although in the physical sphere to be is to be perfectly determinate in character, this rule does not hold for non-physical sensory items. Among sensory items, there can be speckled surfaces with a non-definite number of speckles, or one item can be larger than another without being any definite amount larger, and so on.

This reply seems to have something of the same character as Russell's reply to the difficulty concerning the transitivity of 'exact similarity in a certain respect'. It simply proposes to suspend the rules for objects in the case of mental objects. It asserts that in the sphere of mental objects there can be determinables without determinates. Against this no more can be said except that it is obvious that to be is to be determinate.

The alternative reply would be to say that the sensory items do have perfectly determinate characteristics, but that we are only *aware* of something less. The sensory item has a perfectly definite number of speckles, but we are only aware that it has *a large number* of speckles. But this has the paradoxical consequence that objects specially postulated to do phenomenological justice to perception are now credited with characteristics that lie quite outside perceptual awareness. The theory is now postulating (i) speckled physical surfaces with perfectly determinate characteristics; (ii) speckled sensory items with perfectly determinate characteristics; (iii) indeterminate awareness of the speckled sensory items. But have not items (ii) become redundant? Why not simply postulate the speckled physical surfaces and indeterminate awareness (perception) of those surfaces? It is hard to see that the sensory items are now doing any work in the theory.

We shall see shortly that, by contrast, an analysis of perception in terms of the acquiring of belief accounts for the indeterminacy of perception with the greatest ease.

Now I do not claim that these difficulties for the analysis of perception as involving sensory items are quite conclusive. But they do show that the theory is involved in strange paradoxes. The first move in the analysis may seem simple and obvious, but the consequences are far from simple or obvious. Since this is so, the attempt we are about to embark on of explaining cases of 'perception without belief' and 'perception without the acquiring of belief' in terms of those cases where belief *is* acquired cannot be rejected out of hand as a quite artificial manoeuvre. It will emerge, incidentally, that our own analysis does not reject the notion that perception involves the having of sense-impressions. All it rejects is the notion that sense-impressions are perceived items or objects.

We shall now attempt a positive account of 'perception without belief'.

In the first place, in cases where such perceptions occur there may still be an inclination to 'believe our senses'. If a thing looks to be a certain way, although we know on independent grounds that it cannot actually be that way, we may still half-believe, or be inclined to believe, that it is as it looks. And this inclination to believe can persist even when we clearly recognize that the inclination is irrational. What is an inclination to believe? I think it is nothing but a belief that is held in check by a stronger belief. We acquire certain beliefs about the world by means of our senses, but these beliefs are held in check by stronger beliefs that we already possess. So there is nothing here that is recalcitrant to an analysis of perception in terms of the acquiring of beliefs.

But, it will be objected, there are plenty of cases where 'perception without belief' occurs and no inclination to believe is acquired. One case already mentioned is the perceptions normally involved in looking at a mirror.

Nevertheless, we may reply, in such cases of perception without belief and even without inclination to believe, it is possible to formulate a true counter-factual statement of the form 'But for the fact that the perceiver had other, independent, beliefs about the world, he would have acquired certain beliefs—the beliefs corresponding to the content of his perception.' We do not believe that our mirror-double stands before us *only* because we have a great deal of other knowledge about the world which contradicts the belief that there is anything like the object we seem to see behind the surface of the glass. When our vision blurs, it is *only* because of our knowledge of the ways of the world that we do not acquire the belief that our environment is actually becoming misty and that the outlines of objects are actually beginning to waver. And so on for other cases of 'perception without belief'.

It is to be noticed here that only in a relatively small number of cases are we actually moved to *utter* such counter-factual statements. We might actually say, among high mountains: 'If I had not been told of the effects of a clear and rarefied atmosphere I should have believed the mountain was quite near.' The corresponding remark about a mirror-image will not be made in ordinary contexts. However, this seems to be of little importance. The situations in which a certain remark would be true form a much wider class than the situations in which the remark would be natural or called-for. We actually *assert* such counter-factual statements in cases where we think it was a relatively near thing that we were not deceived. But such counter-factual statements might still be true in cases where there was absolutely no risk of deception, even if there was no point in asserting them in the course of ordinary chat.

Now, in Chapter 6, we have argued for what we called a 'Realist' as opposed to a 'Phenomenalist' account of dispositions. This means that we are committed to saying that, if up to T_1 a certain counter-factual statement is not true of A, but after T_1 it is true, then some actual event took place at T_1. We may not know the nature of this event, but we know that such an event must have occurred. We have also argued that ordinary perception is the acquiring of a belief, which is a mental event as opposed to a process or a state. In cases of 'perception without belief', we can now argue, an event still occurs in our mind, an event which can be described as one that would be the acquiring of belief but for the existence of other, contrary, beliefs that we already hold. The event might perhaps be called the acquiring of a *potential belief*. We come to be in a certain state which would be a belief-state but for the inhibiting effect of other, contrary, beliefs. In this way, perception without belief or inclination to believe might be fitted into our analysis. Introspective awareness of such perception would be awareness of the acquiring of such potential beliefs.

But dissatisfaction may remain. It may be objected that it is at best a contingent fact of psychology that 'perception without belief' is an event that would be the acquiring of belief but for the possession of other, independent, beliefs. We can quite well imagine the occurrence of perceptions that involve no acquiring of belief at all, even although contrary beliefs about the world are quite absent. Now if this is so, the objection goes on, it does not pertain to the essence of perceptual experiences that they involve either belief or even 'potential belief'. So perception is something more than our analysis allows.

In answer to this I say that, if perceptions did occur which were not even the acquiring of potential beliefs, we could only describe such perceptions by reference to the central cases where beliefs are acquired. They would be events *like* the acquiring of beliefs or potential beliefs about the world. What is the force of 'like' here? We have already discussed the problem in connection with wants and wishes (Ch. 7, Sect. IX). It will be remembered that we compared purposes that we actually act from to those central cases of perception where true or false beliefs are acquired. Desires which press towards action, but which we do not act from, were compared to perceptions which involve the acquiring of inclinations to believe held in check by stronger contrary beliefs. Then we argued that wants and wishes which do not press towards any fulfilling action were nevertheless potentially action-producing. If circumstances were to occur that seemed to the agent to give some promise of fulfilling the want or wish by the action of the agent, there would be at least some pressure in the agent's mind to take such action. These we may compare to those cases of 'perception without belief' which are acquirings of 'potential beliefs'.

Finally we called attention to the possibility that there might be 'idle' wants and wishes which neither pressed towards action nor were even potentially pressures towards action. Such mental states, we said, might be described as *like* real wants and wishes although lacking even the potential power to initiate action. In order to understand the force of 'like' here an imaginary case was envisaged. In this case a man had the power to say truly when he tasted a liquid, on the basis of no evidence at all, that it 'contained poison, but in insufficient quantity to poison'. It was then suggested that introspective apprehension of the likeness of 'idle' and ordinary, real, wants and wishes was parallel to the taster's apprehension of the likeness between this liquid and genuinely poisonous liquid.

Our account of the nature of perception without even the acquiring of potential belief should now be clear. It is exactly parallel to the account of 'idle' wants and wishes. The event involved is of the belief-acquiring sort, but, like the poison insufficiently concentrated to poison, not even potential belief is acquired. It is an 'idle' perception.

If our account of 'perception without belief' has been correct, it will be easy to give an account of 'perception without *acquiring* of belief'. It is clear that in all normal cases here a true counterfactual will hold. If I had not already known 'that the book would be red at T_2', then I would have acquired the belief 'that the book was red at T_2'. The event is one that would have been the acquiring of belief if belief had not already been acquired. Like the case where we discover good reasons for what we already know, the perception is like a seal stamped on wax that already bears the impression of that seal. Nothing further is done, because the seal simply fits into an imprint already made. Information is duplicated. And if it is said that it is imaginable that in some cases this counter-factual may not hold true of the perceptual event, then it is an 'idle' perception, and we can give an account of it like that given in the previous paragraph.

In considering 'perception without belief' and 'perception without the acquiring of belief' it is particularly helpful to think of perception as the acquiring of true or false *information*. A perception which involves an inclination, but no more than an inclination, to believe, may be conceived of as the acquiring of information which we have some tendency, but no more than some tendency, to accept. A perception which involves mere potential belief may be conceived of as the acquiring of information that, because of other information that we already possess, we completely discount. An 'idle' perception may be conceived of as information that is completely disregarded, but, incredibly, not because of any other information that we already possess. 'Perception without the acquiring of belief' may be conceived of as a case where the information received simply duplicates information that is already at our disposal.

It must now be shown that our account of perception can deal with the paradoxes about the non-transitivity of exact similarity in a given respect with respect to perceptions, and with the indeterminacy of perceptions.

Consider first the problem about similarity. Looking at samples of cloth A and B, I acquire the belief that they are the same colour. Looking at B and C, I acquire the same belief. But looking at A and C I acquire the belief that they are slightly different in colour. This forces me to realize that A and B cannot really be exactly the same colour, and neither can B and C. These two beliefs become mere 'potential beliefs'. There is no difficulty at all here, no question of the rules for the transitivity of exact similarity in a certain respect having broken down. The reason why we prefer the third perception to the first two is that we have discovered by experience that where we seem to perceive small differences between things the differences are usually real, but that where we can perceive no difference there often are small unperceived differences all the same. So we acquire the belief that all three colour-samples differ slightly in colour.

Again, there is nothing puzzling about beliefs being indeterminate. I may believe, and believe truly, that Jupiter has a number of satellites, yet not have any belief about their exact number. My belief is indeterminate in that respect. Equally, when I turn my eyes towards the speckled hen, I acquire the belief that it has a great number of speckles, but I do not acquire any belief that it has, say, ninety-three speckles. My belief is indeterminate in that respect. When I compare two objects in size by means of the hand or the eye, I acquire the belief that one is larger than the other. I do not acquire any belief about their exact proportion. My belief is indeterminate in that respect.

It seems, then, that when we are introspectively aware of our perceptions, we are aware of a stream of mental events: acquirings of beliefs about the current state of the world, or events which resemble such acquirings. Perception is a flow of information, a flow that goes on the whole time that we are not completely unconscious. Perceptual *experience*, as opposed to mere perception, is simply this flow in so far as we are conscious of it, that is to say, are introspectively aware of it. The content of our perceptions, which so many philosophers want to turn into a non-physical object, is simply the content of the beliefs involved.

Our perceptions, then, are not the basis for our perceptual judgements, nor are they a mere phenomenological accompaniment of our perceptual judgements. They are simply the acquirings of these judgements themselves. Our perceptions do not stand between our mind and physical reality, because they *are* our apprehensions of that reality.

It may be objected that ordinary discourse provides evidence for saying that we treat our perceptions as evidence or grounds on which we base conclusions about the physical world. 'How do you know that there is a mouse in the cupboard?' 'I saw it just then.' Here I seem to be appealing to my visual data to support a judgement about the contents of the cupboard.

However, this dialogue can be understood quite differently, and in a way compatible with our analysis. In saying I *saw* the mouse I am (besides begging the question by using the word 'see', thus assuming the mouse was there) indicating that I acquired the belief that there was a mouse in the cupboard *by using my eyes*. Now it is a known fact that beliefs of that sort acquired as a causal result of the use of the eyes are pretty reliable beliefs. So I have provided my questioner with a reason for believing that there was a mouse in the cupboard. The position is the same as that of the man who estimates a distance by eye, and then defends his claim to knowledge of the distance by pointing out that he regularly gets such estimates right. The only difference is that the ability to gather reasonably reliable information about mice by using the eyes, as in the first case, is an almost universal ability.

Perception and Belief

Verbs of perception take two sorts of accusative. Sometimes we speak of perceiving things, events, or processes: seeing a horse, for instance. At other times we speak of perceiving that something is the case: seeing that there is a horse before us, for instance.

Now the second idiom fits in very well with the analysis of perception as the acquiring of beliefs. To say A sees that there is a horse before him can be quite plausibly construed as asserting that A, as a result of the stimulation of his eyes, acquires the (sub-verbal) belief that there is a horse before him. It is true that to speak of 'seeing that' carries the further implication that there actually is a horse before him. 'Seeing that' has 'success-grammar'. But this only means that in speaking of 'seeing that' it is entailed that the belief acquired is *true*. This entailment could be cancelled by saying something like 'A sees, or thinks he sees, that there is a horse before him.'

But the first idiom, where we speak of perceiving things, events or processes, may seem to present problems. Suppose it is said that A perceives a horse. This implies that there is a horse there to be perceived. Phrases of the form 'perceives an *x*' have 'existence-grammar'. But the idiom does not signal a cognitive success on A's part, as in the case of 'perceiving *that* . . .'. For there is no contradiction in saying that A perceives a horse, but does not perceive that it is a horse.

Indeed, it would not be going too far to say that philosophical accounts of perception may be classified according to whether they seek guidance from the one or the other sort of idiom. Corresponding to talk of perceiving things we have what might be called the 'searchlight' view of perception. According to this view, perception is an act that lights up for the perceiver a particular finite portion of the world, or, at any rate, certain aspects of a portion of the world. Perception is a two-term relation holding between the mind and a portion of physical reality. It is this view that it is natural to call a 'Direct Realist' theory of perception, and I now think that I said something potentially misleading in *Perception and the Physical World* when I spoke of my own theory as a form of Direct Realism. In the subjectivist form of the 'searchlight' view the beams reach no further than our own sense-impressions, yielding either a Representationalist or a Phenomenalist theory. It is this subjectivist form of the 'searchlight' view that characteristically takes sense-impressions to be non-physical *objects*. It may be remarked, finally, that Russell's distinction between 'knowledge by description', on the one hand, and 'acquaintance' which is below all descriptive knowledge, on the other, is a distinction drawn under the influence of the 'searchlight' model.

Corresponding to talk of perceiving that something is the case we have what may be called propositional or 'information-flow' views of perception, of which the view being developed in this chapter is a specimen. This view agrees with Direct Realism in being a two-term theory: there is simply the belief and the physical situation that corresponds, or fails to correspond, to the belief.

Now since there are these two sorts of idiom, each associated with a particular picture of the nature of perception, I will here give an account of talk of perceiving *things*. This will remove any suspicion that an 'information-flow' account of perception cannot explain the other idiom.

When it is said that somebody perceives something, then the mental event that takes place is simply the acquiring of information and misinformation about the environment, information or misinformation that may be 'discounted', for one reason or another, by the perceiving subject. But the peculiarity of the idiom 'A perceives *x*' is that to speak in this way does not tell us exactly what the information or misinformation is. The idiom tells us that it is information or misinformation *about x* that is acquired but it tells us nothing more. To say that A sees a bush is compatible with saying that he acquires the false belief that the object before him is a bear.

Now, it is only to be expected that there should be such an idiom. For although to talk of 'perceiving that . . .' (or 'seeming to perceive that . . .') is a far more exact way of speaking, its very exactness makes it a hindrance on many occasions. Stimulation of the senses is constantly giving us a vast flood of information (and misinformation) about our environment, far more than we could ever hope to verbalize. What is more, this information varies from person to person even when their senses are trained upon numerically the same object. (Their experience, their interests, their sensory powers, their location and their posture may all be different; and this will normally mean that they acquire different information.) Under these circumstances, the non-committal nature of the idiom whereby we speak of perceiving things or events or processes is extraordinarily useful to us. It bridges the gap between one man's perception and the next's. If there is to be effective communication between person and person about their perceptions, there must be idioms to range over this vast mass of idiosyncratic information without attempting to be very specific. So we speak of perceiving things.

At this stage, however, it must be recognized that the account given so far of the perception of things is too simple. If A is truly said to be perceiving *x* this does not simply imply that A's perceptions include information or misinformation about *x*. It is also implied that *x* is the *cause* of these perceptions. We will consider this point in the next section.

VI. PERCEPTION AND CAUSALITY

If A is said to perceive an *x*, then it is entailed that *x* is the cause of A's perceptions, whatever these are.

Consider the following case. I have visual perceptions as of an orange before me. Suppose also there really is an orange before me, corresponding exactly to my visual perceptions. Does this entail that I am seeing the orange? If the question whether I can be said to be seeing something depends solely upon the *content* of my perception, this should be the most favourable case. But in fact it is still at least logically possible that I am not seeing the orange. For it is logically possible that I am having those perceptions *but not as a result of the action of the orange on my eyes*. (My brain was being probed in just the right way.) And if this possibility were fulfilled, we would not say I was seeing the orange. But if the orange brought about my perceptions, then I can properly be said to be seeing the orange.

(Perhaps we ought to add the further condition that the orange act upon our sense-organs *in the ordinary way*. Whether we make this addition or not will depend upon whether we include reference to the stimulation of the senses in our account of what constitutes perception. See Section II of this chapter.)

Again, if I have perceptions as of a bear, I can still be properly said to be perceiving *a bush*, provided that it is the bush that is bringing about my bear-perceptions. Remove the latter condition and I can no longer be said to be perceiving a bush.

This causal condition, although necessary for saying that A perceives an x, is, of course, not sufficient. If a probe in the brain causes a visual hallucination, we would not say that the perceiver saw the probe. It may be objected that in the case of the probe the stimulus does not act on the *senses*, but instead by-passes them, acting directly on the brain. But suppose a pin held before my eyes stimulates them in such a way that I have visual perceptions as of a full-size elephant. We will hardly allow that I can be said to be seeing a pin.

What must be added to the causal condition to give necessary and sufficient conditions for saying we perceive an x? I do not know the answer. A further necessary condition seems to be that there must be some *resemblance*, even if slight, between the perceptions had and the object said to be perceived. A bush and a bear do have *some* resemblance in visual properties.

Here, then, is the source of what, in Section III, was called the 'existence-grammar' possessed by idioms like 'A saw a bush', a feature easily but incorrectly confused with the 'success-grammar' of idioms like 'A saw that there was a bush before him'. 'A saw a bush' entails that there was a bush to see because it entails that A's perceptions, whatever they were, were *caused* by a bush. And for the bush to be a cause, the bush must exist.

So A perceives an x entails that x is the cause of A's perceptions. This is to be contrasted with perceiving *that* x is y. If A perceives that x is y it need not be the case that A has this perception as a causal result of the fact that x is y. For instance, A may see that it will rain. This is not a metaphorical use of the word 'see', as in the case where A 'sees' the point of a joke. Yet the future rain cannot be the cause of A's seeing that it will rain.

Often, of course, when A is said to perceive that x is y, he can also be said to perceive an x or a y. It would be very neat and simple if we could say that wherever A can be said to perceive that x is y he can also be said to perceive an x or a y, provided only that the x or the y brings about his perception. Unfortunately, however, this is incorrect. For instance, if I see smoke coming up out of a chimney, I can be said to see that there is a fire in the hearth, but cannot be said to see the fire or the hearth. Yet the fire in the hearth is causally responsible for my seeing that there is a fire on the hearth.

Here, however, we have been going into matters of considerable linguistic detail, and, we may hope, of relative unimportance for the argument of this chapter. It remains true that in what we may vaguely call the *central* cases of perceiving that *x* is *y*, we can also be said to be perceiving an *x* or a *y*. And this means that even in the case of 'perceiving that . . .' there is a close link between perception and causality.

To conclude this section. According to our general formula, the concept of a mental state is the concept of a state of the person apt for bringing about certain physical behaviour. It was also said, however, that in the case of certain concepts, notably perception, the state involved is also to be conceived as a state apt for being brought about by certain physical causes. (It will be remembered that Place and Smart, *op. cit.* Ch. 6, Sect. IV, tried to give an account of those mental concepts that they allowed to involve central states in terms of the physical stimuli that characteristically bring the states about.) The link between perception and causation that has just been brought out is clearly connected with this second feature of the concept of perception. For we have seen that to talk of perception is, in typical cases, to talk of a state brought about in a certain way. This matter will be developed further in the next chapter.

VII. UNCONSCIOUS PERCEPTION

In Chapter 6 it was argued that any mental happening could occur without our being aware of its occurrence. It follows that there can be perceptions of which we are not aware. These are unconscious perceptions.

Cases of unconscious perceptions are easy to find. I pass a hoarding, my eyes rest upon it, but I am not aware of seeing what it says. A little later on I am asked what was written on the hoarding, and, to my surprise, I find I know. It is natural to say that, although I was not aware of perceiving the writing on the hoarding, I did actually perceive it.

In this case I was not aware of the *acquiring* of the belief, but later became aware that I had in fact acquired a belief about what was written on the hoarding. But a case can be found where the unconsciousness is more complete. (A case suggested to me by Noel Fleming.) I am walking along deep in conversation, and, while doing so, step over a log that lies in my path, with every appearance of care and concentration. Yet I remain completely unaware that I have done so. I think we must say here that I saw that there was a log there, although I remain unaware both of acquiring any beliefs about the log, and of the behaviour in which the belief was manifested.

In both these cases, however, it is true that if I had attended I would have been aware of perceiving hoarding and log. The unconsciousness was not a deep unconsciousness, for there was potential consciousness. But 'subliminal perception' provides cases where the perception is not even the potential object of introspective awareness. Suppose a message is flashed on a screen, too fast to have been seen consciously, saying that there is an insect on the left sleeve of my coat. Suppose I then brush my left sleeve, but without consciously attributing any significance to this action. It seems reasonable to say that I saw the message, although I was not and empirically could not possibly have been, aware of seeing it. The belief was manifested in behaviour, but I was unaware of the belief, and unaware of the manifestation *as* a manifestation of any belief.

VIII. 'SMALL PERCEPTIONS'

There is an important doubt about an analysis of perception in terms of acquiring beliefs that may still remain in the mind of even a sympathetic reader. Is not talk of acquiring true and false beliefs, or even information and misinformation, too ambitious a way of characterizing much of our perception? In the case of objects that are the centre of our attention and interest, speaking of 'acquiring of beliefs' may seem quite appropriate. But many, perhaps the vast mass, of our perceptions are 'small perceptions' that hardly deserve such a description. Consider, in particular, the great flood of detail that is involved in our visual perceptions. Can we say it is all an acquiring of beliefs or information, or the occurrence of events like the acquiring of beliefs or information?

The words 'small perceptions' recall Leibniz's phrase '*petites perceptions*'. But I have deliberately not used the French words because I am not referring to the same range of phenomena. The 'small perceptions' I am referring to are not 'small' because we are unconscious, or only dimly aware, of them. In the case of the log that was carefully stepped over, the perception was unconscious, but I do not want to call it a 'small perception'. For in this case it is natural to say that fully-blown *knowledge* was acquired, even if only unconsciously. But, by contrast, even when we recall ourselves from practical concerns and force ourselves to become fully conscious of the profusion of detail offered by vision, we may still want to describe most of these perceptions as something less than the acquiring of beliefs or information.

The trouble seems to be that the impression made upon us is too evanescent. At a certain instant the perception occurs. This is an event, as opposed to a process or a state, but it is the event of coming to be in a new state. But this state disappears so rapidly—the impression fades so fast—that we may well be reluctant to describe it as a state of belief. The state is gone before there is any possibility of a manifestation of belief, and if there is no possibility of manifestation how can we speak of belief?

This very description of the phenomenon, however, shows that there is here no threat to our analysis. What happens in the case of a 'small perception' is that we acquire a certain state, a state which hardly persists for any time, but which, if it had persisted, would be a belief about the current state of our body or environment. There is no reason why we should deny this possibility.

IX. IMMEDIATE AND MEDIATE PERCEPTION

In *Perception and the Physical World* I fell into serious confusions in attempting to draw this distinction. (The difficulties of my position were pointed out by Noel Fleming in a review article 'The Nature of Perception', *The Review of Metaphysics*, Vol. XVI, No. 2, Dec. 1962.) The cause of my errors was the failure to appreciate the linguistic distinctions between talk of perceiving things and perceiving that something is the case. As a result, I wrongly attempted to distinguish between immediate and mediate *objects* of perception. In fact, the distinction, which I still think to be of great importance, should be drawn between immediate and mediate perceiving (or seeming to perceive) that something is the case. It must be drawn in terms of the acquiring of beliefs.

It is clear that at least some 'perceiving that . . .' involves inference. If I see that there is a cat's head poking out from behind a door, I can say with linguistic propriety and truth that I can see that there is a (whole) cat there. But it is obvious that the perception that there is a whole cat there involves inference. This does not mean that there need be any self-conscious or laborious transition from one belief to another. We saw in discussing the nature of inferring in Chapter 9 that (saving a few qualifications) it involves nothing more than the acquiring of a belief as a causal result of holding another belief. Given this causal relationship between beliefs, then we have inference, even where the transition is automatic and instantaneous.

Now since our knowledge of the current state of our body and environment *begins* with perception, and since we have rejected the view that perceptual beliefs about the world are based on the further evidence of perceptual experience, we must allow that, in every perception, some of the beliefs acquired are *non-inferential* beliefs. Such 'perceivings that . . .' may be called immediate perceptions. All other 'perceivings that . . .' may then be called mediate perceptions. Clearly, they must be inferred on the basis of the immediate perceptions, together with any other relevant beliefs we happen to have.

But the interesting question only arises when we ask 'What sort of "perceivings that . . ." involve no inference?' What sorts of perception are immediate? If we consult ordinary language we shall get the answer that beliefs acquired by means of the eyes like 'There is a cat's head over there' or 'There is a sheet of writing-paper in front of me' involve no inference. And it certainly sounds peculiar to say that they do involve inference. Do I not contrast the cat's body that I infer is behind the door with the cat's head that I do not infer, but perceive quite directly?

Now it is certainly possible to maintain without self-contradiction that when we see that there is a cat's head or a sheet of paper before us absolutely no element of inference is involved. Perhaps it is even the correct view. Certainly there is nothing in the analysis of perception given here which would rule the view out. Nevertheless, there do seem to be grounds which suggest that, despite ordinary language, there is a concealed element of inference in such perceptions. We do have the notion that, correlated with the sense of sight, there is a certain group of properties of objects that may be called the *visual* properties. This group is quite a small one, and exactly what its membership is may be a matter of dispute, but such properties of objects as colour, shape, size, position and motion seem to be visual properties. Now cat's heads are material objects, and material objects have other properties beside those included in the list of visual properties. For instance, because they are material objects they have a capacity to exert and to resist pressure, and these are certainly not visual properties. The problem then arises how it is that we can *see* that such objects are material objects. It is natural to solve the problem by saying that we see immediately that there is a thing having certain visual properties before us, and that this, by an automatic and instantaneous inference, produces the further belief that there is a cat's head or a sheet of paper before us. It is only the visual properties of things that can be immediately perceived by the eyes.

Now such an analysis involves splitting up what appears to introspection to be a single event in the mind—seeing the cat's head or the sheet of paper—into the acquiring of one belief which then brings about the acquiring of another. But we have followed Kant in comparing introspection to sense-perception, and have urged further that, like sense-perception, introspection can be mistaken and also that mental processes can occur of which we are not introspectively aware. Now once we have abandoned the idea that introspection is an infallible and all-seeing faculty we can say that the swiftness of the transition from belief to belief deceives the inner 'eye' just as the swiftness of the hand deceives the outer eye.

Of course, this does not prove the hypothesis. It merely shows that inspection of what happens in the mind, and ordinary language which records the result of that inspection, do not conclusively refute the hypothesis I am supporting. Positive proof would have to come from psychology, and in particular, I suppose, from neurophysiology. If, in the brain, visual perception began with a mere registration of colour and shape, and this registration goes on in normal cases to produce a more complex effect in the brain, an effect associated with acquiring beliefs about such things as material objects; then the hypothesis I am advancing would be confirmed.

The view I am putting forward is connected with the Aristotelian doctrine of the 'proper sensibles' that pertain to each sense. The list of visual properties (to take an instance) would however have to include certain properties that Aristotle classed as 'common sensibles'—shape and size, for instance—because he defines 'proper sensibles' as properties discernible by one sense *alone*.

On the view put forward here, there would be plenty of room for dispute about exactly what are the visual and other sensory properties, although to say that, *e.g.* colour was a visual property would hardly admit of dispute. For instance, there could be a dispute as to whether distance out from the eye was a visual property, or was always an inference from other perceptions. Since the identification of visual, tactual, auditory, olfactory and gustatory properties would be a matter of psychological theory, it is clear that there could be much dispute about just what should be included in the lists of such properties.

X. THE NATURE OF SENSE-IMPRESSIONS

If the distinction between immediate and mediate perception is drawn as in the previous section, light is cast on the notion of sense-impressions or sense-data. The concept of a sense-impression seems to be a narrower one than that of a perception. We can find cases where two perceivers have different perceptions, but it is conceivable that they have the same sense-impressions. Consider the case where two people look at a printed page, and one knows what the words mean while the other cannot read. It is reasonable to say that they have different perceptions. One sees meaningful words, the other nothing but marks on paper. But is it not possible (whether or not it is true) that they are having exactly the same visual sense-impressions?

I think the distinction between sense-impressions and perceptions can be made by appealing to our distinction between immediate and mediate perception. When we speak of sense-impressions we are speaking of our perceptions, veridical or illusory, but are confining ourselves to our *immediate* perceptions, the true or false beliefs that are acquired without any tincture of inference. The beliefs are therefore restricted to beliefs involving the sensory properties of the sense in question. (The sensory properties are the 'proper sensibles' of the sense in question, together with such 'common sensibles' as pertain to that sense.)

We can then understand talk about a person's *visual field* during a period of time as the totality of that person's visual sense-impressions, that is, immediate visual perceptions, veridical or illusory, during that time. 'Visual field' must then be distinguished from 'field of view'. The visual field, we may say, is something in the person's mind. But the field of view is that portion of physical space over which the person's seeing eye is able to range at that time. Parallel to the notion of visual field are the notions of auditory field, tactual field, etc. They are embraced in the general notion of the sensory or phenomenal field.

Our sense-impressions must not be conceived of as evidence for our non-inferential beliefs about the current state of our body and environment, for they are themselves the acquirings of these beliefs. (And those philosophers who said, or were tempted to say, that sense-impressions are *perceived*, were confusing introspective awareness of sense-impressions with perception.) But sense-impressions can be truly said to be the foundation of all our *further* perceptual beliefs about the environment.

I have said that the narrow compass to which I wish to reduce immediate perception is the consequence of a psychological theory, not a piece of logical analysis. If it is correct to tie the notion of sense-impression to immediate perception, it follows that, although there must be sense-impressions if there is perception, the particular content that sense-impressions have is a matter of psychological theory.

XI. PERCEPTION AND KNOWLEDGE

In those cases where perception involves the acquiring of belief, we have spoken of veridical perception as the acquiring of *true beliefs*, using the phrase 'true belief' neutrally to cover both knowledge and mere true belief.

In the previous chapter, we discussed the nature of knowledge: both non-inferential knowledge and knowledge to which we are led by good reasons. It is clear that the true beliefs acquired in veridical perception will regularly satisfy our conditions for knowledge. Thus, if by using my eyes I acquire the true belief that there is something red and round before me, this will constitute knowledge provided only that, in the circumstances I am in, it is an empirical truth that the physical existence of something red and round before me is a necessary condition of my acquiring that belief. If my belief is 'reliable' in this sense, I have acquired knowledge. And, since our knowledge of the physical world begins in perception, perception is the major source of our non-inferential knowledge.

But it is possible to have veridical perception that is the acquiring of *mere* true belief. One set of such cases has been already noticed in our discussion of perception and causality. If perceptions correspond with physical reality, but are not brought into being by that reality, we may have acquired true beliefs, but can hardly be said to have acquired knowledge. For it would be just an accident that perception and reality corresponded. (A possible exception might be where physical situation and perception both spring from a common cause.)

However, we may not be willing to count these cases as cases of veridical perception. We might want to say that they were simply perceptual illusions that happened to correspond to reality. The interesting cases of veridical perceptions that are acquirings of *mere* true belief are those where the causal condition is satisfied. One simple but ingenious case has been suggested by Max Deutscher.

An unsophisticated person watches a conjuror. The conjuror, using no deception at all, transfers a ball from one hand to the other. This means that the following conditions are satisfied:

(i) The spectator acquires the belief (by means of his eyes) that the conjuror transferred the ball from one hand to the other.

(ii) The transfer of the ball *caused* the belief that it was transferred to be acquired.

Let us consider what we should say about this case. In the first place, it is clearly right to say that the spectator saw the transfer of the ball. Is it also right to say that he saw *that* the ball was transferred? This is not quite so clear, but I am inclined to think that it is right. But, in the third place, although the spectator acquired a true belief, it is clear that he did not acquire knowledge. For we know that conjurors can easily deceive people in such matters, and so we think the spectator trusted his eyes in a situation where it was unwise to do so, even if, in his case, his trust was not misplaced.

If the notion of a cause was that of a *necessary* condition of its effect, then, of course, the conditions for knowledge would automatically be satisfied in every veridical perception which involved the acquiring of belief. But our ordinary concept of cause, which is the concept involved in our concept of veridical perception, is not the concept of a *necessary* condition. There can be a plurality of causes. Certainly the simplest way to cause A to have visual experiences as of a ball being transferred from a person's hand to his other hand is actually to effect such a transfer before A's open eyes. But a conjuror can cause A to have the same visual experiences without any actual transfer. The unsophisticated spectator's belief, although caused by actual transfer, thus lacks that reliable correlation with the facts that makes a true belief a case of knowledge.

The case of the magician is an unusual and striking one. But a more ordinary case can be found. Suppose that a blue ball in the far distance acts upon A's eyes, and, as a result, A acquires the belief that there is a blue ball in the distance. It may be the case that the object is too far away for reliable judgement. That is to say, it may not be that case that the presence of a blue ball in the far distance is a necessary condition of A's acquiring that belief in the circumstances that A is then in. In that case, A acquires a true belief, but not knowledge.

Nevertheless, in veridical perception the acquiring of *knowledge* is the standard case, the acquiring of mere true belief the relatively eccentric case. The reason for this will be indicated in the next chapter.

XII. THE NATURE OF THE PHYSICAL WORLD

I shall finish this chapter by showing that the analysis of perception in terms of the acquiring of beliefs, or the occurrence of mental events that resemble the acquiring of beliefs, can very simply solve pressing problems about our conception of the physical world.

There is a certain picture of the physical world that we all cherish in our hearts, although in our philosophical thinking we may consider ourselves forced to abandon it in a greater or lesser degree. According to this picture, the physical world, including our bodies, consists of a single realm of material objects, and perhaps other objects, related in space and enduring and changing in time. Material objects have shape and size, they move or are at rest, they are hot or cold, hard or soft, rough or smooth, heavy or light, they are coloured, they may have a taste, and they may emit sounds or smells. These properties of objects are, on occasion, perceived; but objects continue to have these properties in a perfectly straightforward way when, as is usually the case, the objects, or particular properties of the objects, are not perceived.

This is the picture of the physical world to which we are all instinctively drawn (even Berkeley was). We may think that relatively abstruse evidence garnered from scientific investigations forces us to modify this picture. But it is the picture we have gained through perception, and when we are not considering perception as philosophers, we do not think that the evidence of *ordinary perception* tends to overthrow it in any way.

But as soon as we start to think reflectively, difficulties for this picture begin to appear. Most of the problems arise in connection with vision, and the excessively familiar cases now to be mentioned are mostly, but not exclusively, visual. Consider first the case of mirror-images. When somebody looks into a mirror, the image that they see appears as far behind the physical surface of the glass as the thing that is imaged is in front of that physical surface. (The image, of course, also reverses the left–right relations of the thing imaged.) Now where are we to place the mirror-image in the physical world? There can hardly be an actual visual object of that sort behind the mirror's surface. The mirror may be backed by a thick stone wall which would certainly exclude such an object. (Two material objects cannot be at the same place at the same time. Neither can two visual objects, such as mirror-images or rainbows. Equally, it seems, a material object cannot be at the same place at the same time as a visual object.) Is the image really a two-dimensional picture temporarily formed on the surface of the mirror? It certainly does not look to be. But where else in the physical world can the image be located?

Or consider the case of the stick that looks bent when half-immersed in water. Does this mean that there is a bent visual object in the water at an angle to the physical stick? Does putting a stick into water split it into a visual and a tactual component which 'occupy' different parts of the water, each in their different ways?

Consider, again, a case mentioned by John Austin in *Sense and Sensibilia* (Oxford, 1962, p. 98). On the horizon a white dot can be seen. I say 'That white dot is my house'. Yet I would not be prepared to say 'I live in a white dot'. Where, then, shall we place the white dot in the physical world? And what is its relation to my house?

I see the bright disc of the sun. Yet what I see is far, far, smaller than the sun, and in any case is a perception of the sun as it was eight minutes ago. Where shall we place the bright disc that exists now? I see the blue dome of the sky. Yet no such blue dome exists in physical reality. The hole in my tooth feels far larger to my tongue than it looks to my eye. Are there two holes of different size in physical reality?

Such puzzles may be multiplied indefinitely, as is well known.

It is possible to preserve our picture of the physical world more or less intact by distinguishing between the physical world and non-physical immediate objects of perception. We can distinguish between our immediately perceived visual field, tactual field, and so on, and mediately perceived physical objects. The visual field contains mirror-images, visually bent objects, white dots, bright discs and blue domes, but nothing corresponds to these objects in the physical world. The tactual field contains a large tooth-hole, but nothing corresponds to it in the physical world.

To take this way out is to embrace the Representative theory of perception, with all its difficulties. The mind is locked in behind its own sensory field, and it becomes hard to see how we could have any reliable knowledge of the physical world that allegedly lies beyond it. And the Phenomenalist alternative, which tries to give an account of physical reality as an elaborate construction out of subjective sensory fields, faces still greater difficulties.

Another attempt to deal with the problem posed by these sensory phenomena that appear not to correspond to physical reality is to complicate our account of physical reality. Mirror-images, visually bent objects, white dots, bright discs, blue domes and tactually large holes are all given a place in the public world. One of the simplest ways to do this is to distinguish between visual, tactual and other sensory realms, each realm being conceived of as a *public* thing. The physical world is then conceived of an elaborate correlation or concomitance between these separate realms or 'spaces'. This view preserves our direct perceptual awareness of the physical world at the cost of complicating, indeed overthrowing, our ordinary picture of that world, a picture which seems to have been gained from perception.

Still other, more complex, solutions of the problem have been offered. But I think it is fair to say that all of them either (i) create a problem of how we can know of the existence of the physical world; or (ii) make that world depend for its existence, at least in some degree, on the perceiving mind; or (iii) destroy our ordinary picture of the physical world.

But if we conceive of perception as nothing but the acquiring of true and false beliefs about the current state of the perceiver's body and environment, or of mental events that resemble the acquiring of such beliefs, an extraordinarily simple and natural dissolution of the problem is possible.

Mirror-images can be excluded from our account of the physical world. There are no such *objects* as mirror-images, instead there are simply false beliefs of those who turn their eyes towards mirrors that there are things behind the glass that resemble the things in front of it. When we look at mirrors we acquire a false belief, just as a camera pointed at a mirror produces a false representation of the world. (And for the same reasons.) In time we learn about the deceptive properties of mirrors, and then the mental event involved is no more than the acquiring of a 'potential belief'. It is an event that resembles the acquiring of a belief, but of which we can say no more than that the state that comes to be would have involved belief but for the existence of contrary beliefs that we hold. However, because the image 'in' a good plane mirror corresponds point by point to the objects in front of the glass we can use mirrors to gain true beliefs about objects in front of the glass.

Again, when a straight stick is partly immersed in water, and it is looked at, it is a fact of nature that the observer acquires a false belief that the stick is bent, or else a mental event occurs like the acquiring of that belief without any actual acquiring of belief.

When I look towards my house when it is far away, I acquire the false belief that it is only a very small (dot-sized) white object, or else the corresponding belief-less event occurs. It *looks* like a white dot-sized object, although it is actually a house. But if I am familiar with this deception, and know that others looking at the house from the same place have the same perceptual experience, I can speak (loosely) of 'that white dot'.

When I look up at the sky I acquire the false belief that there is a smallish, hot, bright disc above me now. In fact, I later learn, this belief was caused in me by an enormously larger, but also enormously distant, object that existed eight minutes ago. (Given information of this sort, I can use this sensory illusion to acquire true information about the physical world, working back from the nature of the illusion to the nature of things.)

On a cloudless day I acquire the false belief that I am below the centre of a great, blue, dome-like object that encloses my field of view. When I put my tongue-tip in the hole in my tooth I acquire the belief that the hole is far bigger than it really is. If I do not acquire these beliefs, a mental event like the acquiring of belief occurs (a 'potential belief'), but no belief is acquired. And so on.

In this account there is simply the mind acquiring true or false beliefs (or else the occurrence of mental events resembling true or false beliefs), about the physical world of common sense.

This view treats the mirror-images, 'bent' sticks, white dots, hot bright discs, blue domes, etc., as species of *illusion*. One difficulty about this account is that they may not involve false belief. I hope that what has been said in Section IV of this chapter answers this difficulty. They do always involve the acquiring of misinformation, but, because of independent knowledge, this misinformation is often 'discounted'. A second stumbling-block is the *publicity* of the phenomena. This may be answered by pointing out that it is simply a consequence of the uniform operation of the laws of nature and the more or less uniform nature of human sense-organs. The same causes give rise to the same illusions in every perceiver. 'Public' illusions are logical constructions out of the illusions that everybody is subject to in certain circumstances.

But there is a closely-connected difficulty for our analysis that demands a little closer consideration. It may be argued that, so far from it being an illusion when the stick half-immersed in water looks bent, it would be a sign that the stick was not straight if it did not look bent in those conditions. Again, when a flat, round, object looks elliptical from certain oblique points of view, then so far from it being an illusion, it would be a sign that the object was not round if it did not look elliptical in that situation. In both

The Concept of Mind

cases, presenting just these appearances under just these conditions seems to be part of what makes the physical objects the objects they are. How, then, can these appearances be accounted illusions?

I think the answer to this is that our *primitive* concepts of straight sticks and round flat objects do not involve saying that they present these illusory appearances. But afterwards, it is discovered that these illusory appearances are, as a result of the laws of nature and the uniform nature of the human sensory apparatus, presented to all perceivers under certain conditions. Now there is always a tendency to pack widely-known facts about an object into the concept of that object. As knowledge increases, our concepts tend to presuppose more and more empirical facts. This is what happens in the cases we are considering. It becomes part of the concept of a straight stick or a round, flat object that they present certain illusory appearances to all observers under certain conditions.

This chapter has involved the discussion of many complexities. But a single, simple, thread has run through the argument. It is the contention that we can give an account of perception in terms of the acquiring of true or false beliefs or information.

II

PERCEPTION AND BEHAVIOUR

THE previous chapter has been nothing but a preliminary treatment of the topic of perception, for its account of perception in terms of the acquiring of beliefs or information is neither logically sufficient nor necessary for an analysis of perception as a state of the person apt for the production of certain behaviour. But it has accomplished a great deal of preliminary clearing of the ground. The present chapter attempts this further analysis of the concept of perception. It is indeed the central chapter of the whole book, for in giving an account of perception we will have to give a deeper account than that given hitherto of the other great central mental concept: the notion of purpose or will. The notions of perception and purpose, we shall find, are inextricably bound up with each other.

I. THE MANIFESTATION OF PERCEPTION IN BEHAVIOUR

Most modern philosophers accept the view that to say A believes *p* is to make a dispositional statement about A. I think it is clear that they are right. Now, if to say that A believes *p* is to make a dispositional statement about A, then, since we have rejected a 'Phenomenalist' or 'Operationalist' theory of dispositions, we are implying that A is in a certain *state*, even although a state that can only be described in terms of its *manifestations*. So, in terms of the 'information-flow' theory of perception advanced in the previous chapter, to say that A perceives that *p* is to say that A comes to be in a certain state, a state which can only be described in

245

terms of its possible manifestations. Now if we want to give an analysis of the concept of perception which is compatible with (without entailing) a Materialist view of man, we shall have to say that these manifestations are simply certain sorts of purely physical behaviour. (The state itself, which is causally responsible for the manifestations, may turn out to be a material or an immaterial state. The *concept* of perception entails no decision on this point.)

Let us consider a simple case. We place a number of blocks in front of a baby. To ordinary perception the blocks are identical except for the fact that some are coloured blue and some green. In this situation the child may be expected to make various movements, including perhaps reaching out for individual blocks. When the child happens to reach out for a blue block we reward it in some way; when it reaches out for a green block we do not reward it. Suppose that eventually the child reaches out for blue blocks, but never reaches out for green blocks. (This is B. F. Skinner's 'operant conditioning'.) Is not its behaviour a manifestation of a true belief, acquired by means of its eyes, that there is a difference in colour between the blue and the green blocks? And could it not be said to possess the *concepts* of blue and green, or at any rate the *concept* of the difference between blue and green, even if in a very primitive form?

It is true that certain doubts may be raised. Is the child really discriminating between the different *colours* of the blocks? Perhaps it is discriminating between some other feature in which the two sorts of block differ, such as the different brightnesses of the two sorts of surface? However, such a possibility can be eliminated by further experiment.

Can the child discriminate between *blue* and *green*, or is it simply discriminating between the particular shade or shades of blue and green painted on the blocks? Further testing with blocks of other shades of the two colours would be necessary. Again, even if this question is settled, has the child learnt to discriminate between blue and green, or simply between a *blue block* and a *green block*? Further tests would be necessary to decide whether the baby could tell blue things from green things generally.

There are also doubts of a slightly different sort. Was the child aware of the difference between the blue and the green blocks before the training procedure was undertaken, or did the training cause it to become aware of a difference that it had not been aware of before? This seems to be a perfectly real question, one that would be difficult, but by no means impossible, to answer on the basis of psychological or physiological evidence. Fortunately, however, it is not important for us to answer it here. (In the first case, the child already has true beliefs, and the experiment simply elicited manifestations of these beliefs. In the second case, the training gave the child new discriminatory powers, and so it was able to acquire new beliefs about the world. The decision between the two possibilities is, of course, of the greatest importance for *psychology*. But we can leave it an open question here.)

Now, despite all the doubts that may be raised about exactly what features of the situation the baby can perceive, the differentiated behaviour towards the blocks does provide good reasons for saying that it can perceive a difference between the blocks, and so can acquire true beliefs on this matter when its eyes are suitably stimulated by the blocks. And if we arrange that a green block be viewed under conditions in which it would look blue to the normal perceiver, and the baby reaches out towards the block (the rewarded behaviour towards a *blue* block) we have good reasons to think that it falsely believes that this is a blue block.

So the behaviour manifested is the reason for thinking that a certain belief has been acquired. But just how are behaviour and belief connected? In the traditional account of the matter, the perception involves no logically necessary reference to behaviour. The baby's actions in reaching out for blue blocks but not for green blocks are mere *signs* that it perceives a difference between the two. Behaviour and perception are contingently connected. On such a view, only an argument by analogy from our own case allows us to assume that the baby perceives at all. Behaviourism, on the other hand, rushes in alarm to the opposite extreme, and says that the baby's perception is to be identified with its behaviour. The Behaviourist admits there can be perception without behaviour, but says that such perception is a mere disposition to behave appropriately. The disposition is conceived according to the 'Phenomenalist' theory of dispositions, as not entailing the existence of a non-dispositional state. Against this view we are likely to protest that perception is an inner affair, and not a matter of behaviour, which seems to throw us back again on the view that there is a merely contingent connection between perception and behaviour.

But if we say that the baby's perception is the coming to be of a state of the baby apt for the bringing about of certain sorts of discriminative behaviour, we get the best of both realms. We preserve the 'inner' character of perception, yet at the same time we create a logical tie between the inner event and the outward behaviour.

What general formula can we find to cover all that behaviour of the baby which may be properly taken to be a manifestation that it can perceive the difference between the blue and the green blocks? The following formula looks hopeful. If, under certain conditions, a blue block acts on the baby's eyes, and if the baby follows this with one or many patterns of behaviour, *b*, which involve certain definite relations, *r*, to the blue block: and if, under the same conditions, when a green block acts on the baby's eyes, it does not follow this with behaviour of the sort, *b*, then this is a manifestation of perception of the difference between the blue and green blocks. That is to say, if the baby behaves towards the blue and green blocks in a systematically different way, then it has shown that it can perceive their difference. The *reaching out* for the blue blocks and not for the green is simply a particular case falling under this formula.

This case of the baby is intended to present a model of an account of perception as a state of the person apt for bringing about certain behaviour. But much still remains to be done. There are important objections that can be made to the account proposed. These objections can only be answered by further elucidating and deepening this analysis of the nature of perception. The rest of this chapter will be devoted to this task.

II. PERCEPTION A MERE NECESSARY CONDITION OF DISCRIMINATORY BEHAVIOUR

It is clear that perceptual beliefs can be acquired which are never manifested in behaviour. Nor need there be any pressure towards such behaviour. For I can perceive something yet be completely uninterested in what I perceive, and so have not the slightest tendency to manifest appropriate behaviour. The structure of the eyes of cats is said to be such that they should be capable of perceiving colour-differences. Yet no experiments have ever elicited any manifestation of such perceptions in their behaviour. But, all the same, may they not have colour-perception? It is at least an intelligible supposition. Perception is compatible with complete passivity. (Since this was written, experiments have been performed which claim to elicit manifestations of colour-discrimination in cats. See the *Scientific American*, Vol. 210, No. 6, June 1964, p. 59.)

This brings up a point that has already been touched upon in Chapter 6. The formula for a mental happening 'a state of the person apt for the causing of certain sorts of behaviour' cannot be understood in the same way for all mental items. The exact nature of the relation between mental happening and behaviour differs for different sorts of mental happening. In the case of the will, that is, in the case of such things as intentions and purposes, we have seen that the happenings are mental states that actually impel the organism towards a certain state—the state that we call the 'thing intended' or 'thing purposed'. The mental cause may not be sufficient to bring about the thing intended or desired, but it impels the organism in that direction. (If pressure is exerted on the rear end of a car standing on a level road, the pressure is a pressure towards making it move forward, as opposed to any other direction, even if the car does not budge.) Now, in the case of perception, there is no question of the inner event actually tending to bring about behaviour. What we must say, rather, is that perception supplies a *necessary precondition* for appropriate behaviour. If the baby can perceive the difference between a green and a blue block, then it is in a position to discriminate between them in its behaviour *if it should want to*. But the perception by itself does not involve any impulse towards such differentiating behaviour. As was suggested in Chapter 6, we can compare intentions and purposes to the physical pressures that are put on a door in the course of an attempt to open it. Perception can then be compared to acquiring a key to the door. If I acquire such a key, I have acquired an instrument which may be a necessary precondition for the opening of the door, even if I subsequently ignore the door completely. Perception enables discriminating behaviour, but does not impel towards that behaviour.

But this clarification only raises a further problem. It may be granted that if the baby is to be able to behave differently towards the blue and the green blocks a perception of their difference is necessary. But this is clearly not the only necessary condition. For instance, if the baby's limbs become paralysed it will be unable to respond to the blocks differently even if it can perceive their difference. So how do we pick out perception from among other necessary conditions for discriminatory behaviour?

Let us postpone the answer to this question until we have taken up another difficulty: the problem of what is meant by 'behaviour' in our formula.

III. WHAT IS DISCRIMINATORY BEHAVIOUR?

My environment is altering all the time, and, as a result, my physical state is altering. The same thing can be said of a stone. Many of the changes in the environment result in a more or less systematic alteration in my physical state. For instance, as the temperature of the environment goes up, so does my body-temperature. This also happens in the case of a stone, and still more obviously in the case of a thermometer, which is built to react in this way.

Now, when my temperature goes up because the temperature of the environment goes up, am I not behaving towards different environmental temperatures in a systematically different way? To a rise in environmental temperature I react with a rise in my body-temperature. And, if I do so, have I not fulfilled the conditions for manifesting a *perception* of rise in environmental temperature in accordance with the formula proposed at the end of Section I? And would not a thermometer be an even better 'perceiver' of heat than I am according to this formula? (A point once made somewhere by Whitehead.) But this seems to be a *reductio ad absurdum* of the formula. A mere rise in body-temperature, or a rising of the mercury within a thermometer-tube, is not a *perception* of heat.

But at this point one may protest: 'But if all that happens is that my body-temperature varies with the temperature of my environment, this is scarcely *behaviour*.' But why is it not behaviour? Why is reaching out for a coloured block 'behaviour' while a rise in body-temperature is not? Both are alterations of bodily state. By what criterion can we mark off one bodily alteration from another?

It is at this point we must appeal to the will. We must distinguish between mere bodily change, on the one hand, and purposive behaviour, on the other. The rise in my body-temperature is a mere bodily change; the baby's reaching out for a blue block under the stimulus of a reward is purposive behaviour. It is 'behaviour proper', as opposed to mere physical behaviour. And when we say that the baby manifests his perception of the difference between the blue and the green blocks only if he behaves towards them in a systematically different way, we mean 'behaviour proper'. The salivation of a dog in the presence of an unconditioned or conditioned stimulus, for instance, would not be behaviour in the sense of the word being employed here because salivation is not 'behaviour proper'.

But now the reader who remembers our account of purposive activity in Chapter 7 will object that this involves us in a vicious circularity. According to the analysis given there, purposive behaviour is a matter of a train of physical (and mental) events occurring as the result of the operation of a mental cause. This cause is an information-sensitive cause. It is modified in its operation by the information the agent receives (in particular as a result of the stimulation of his senses) about the current state of the environment. As a result, the agent's actions 'home' upon a certain situation. Receipt of information that this situation has been reached acts to extinguish the operation of the mental cause, such a situation being called the goal of the activity.

This description is not simply a description of any mechanism that is capable of 'homing' behaviour by means of 'negative feedback' corrections supplied by stimuli from the current environment. For we differentiate genuine purposive activity from mere mechanical goal-seeking activity by stipulating that genuine purposive activity demands that the 'feedback' be the work of *perception*.

But now this manoeuvre seems to rebound on our own head. For if we seek to give an account of the manifestations that count as manifestations of perception in terms of systematic difference of *behaviour* towards certain objects; and if we mark off 'behaviour' from mere bodily happenings by saying it is purposive behaviour; and if finally we mark off genuine purposive behaviour from a mere mechanical simulacrum by saying that in the former case the feedback involved is provided by *perception*; we have simply moved in a circle. We set out to elucidate the concept of perception, but were obliged to invoke it in the course of the so-called analysis.

We must therefore pause and take stock. Let us contrast purposive behaviour with self-regulating processes that we find in the body, such as those that control bodily temperature. In the latter cases, also, we have systems where a certain result is achieved by a feeding back of 'information' which enables the system to achieve or maintain a particular physical result. How do these systems differ from genuine purposive behaviour?

My suggestion is that they differ simply in the enormously greater complexity of the causal mechanisms involved in purposive behaviour. In genuine purposive behaviour we have a gigantic flood of 'information' of unbelievable complexity and subtlety. The cause that initiates and sustains such behaviour is sensitive to the whole range of such information, and the exact direction of the impulse it gives in any current situation will be modified in situations where such information is relevant. This, together with the modifications due to the *past* acquiring of information, also of inconceivable complexity, enables 'goal-seeking behaviour' to occur of a sort that is far, far, more sophisticated than any comparable bodily system. And when we get a system of this sort operating, we call the states the organism arrives at things *aimed at, purposed, or intended*, and we call the 'information' *perception*. Purpose and perception, then, cannot be defined independently of each other, nor can one be defined in terms of the other, because they are two sides of the one hugely complex process. (The logical interdependence of purpose and perception is grasped and defended in an intuitive way in a brilliant article by Brian O'Shaughnessy: 'Observation and the Will', *Journal of Philosophy*, Vol. LX, No. 14, 1963. But I think he would reject the *interpretation* of the interdependence that I have offered here, and, perhaps, as a disciple of Wittgenstein, any interpretation at all.)

The processes involved do not have to be of the same complexity and sophistication as those involved in human purpose and perception, for we allow that animals have purposes and can perceive. Just how complex and sophisticated they have to be is a linguistically uncertain matter. Confronted with facts about the functioning of lower organisms we may be as hard pressed to say whether or not they have purposes and can perceive as we may be to say whether or not a certain man is bald. But this, of course, is a verification of our Materialism, because, according to Materialism, there need be no *sharp* distinction between systems involving purpose and perception, and those that do not.

(This is not to say that a Dualist or anti-Materialist might not maintain that associated with purpose and perception are processes of a special, non-material, nature. All the argument is intended to show here is that in *defining* purpose and perception we need make reference to nothing but physical behaviour, and physical stimulation by the environment, of a special complexity.)

If physiology discovered a system in the body of this sort where the complexity and sophistication of operation equalled the system involving will and perception, we ought to be prepared to say that here was purpose and perception of which we had hitherto been totally unconscious. But, in fact, of course, we know that no such system is to be found.

It is vitally important to grasp the logical *inter*dependence of the concept of purpose and perception. We might say that they are 'package-deal' concepts: the introduction of the one entails the introduction of the other. There is nothing very mysterious here. The concepts of shape and size, for instance, are 'package-deal' concepts.

But for our purpose here, the relation of perception to purpose is better symbolized by the relation, say, of the notion of 'being in check', to the notion of 'the game of chess'. The concept of 'being in check' can only be understood in the context of the whole game of chess. And to understand what chess is, we must understand what it is to be in check. Nevertheless, and this is the important point here, we could apply the phrase 'being in check' in a logically secondary manner to a situation where no game of chess is being played. For instance, pieces set up on a chess-board at random might form a position where a king was in check. Such applications of the phrase 'in check' could not be paradigm applications: they must be logically secondary cases. But they are intelligible applications of the phrase.

In the same way, we can form a logically secondary conception of perceptions conceived of in abstraction from selective behaviour. Suppose, for instance, that we discovered the following biological freak. An organism is found to have something like our central nervous system on the perceptual side. That is to say, impulses come in from organs in much the same way that they come into our nervous system, and are sorted and classified in much the same way. But, let us suppose, these incoming impulses result in no outgoing impulses. (Let us waive the question how such an organism could come into existence or survive.) Perhaps we could say that such an organism has perception but no will. But this could be said only because of the likeness of these processes in the organism to the perceptual processes of us, who have *both* perception and will.

Now this enables us to make sense of the old distinction that philosophers and psychologists used to draw between sensation and perception, where sensation was taken to be perception at its most primitive, perception below all vestige of thought and belief. (Kant's 'intuitions'.) If we think of the stimulation of the mind by the world in complete abstraction from the further effects of this stimulation on behaviour or impulses towards behaviour, we might call this stimulation 'sensation'. But it is an abstraction from the whole process of perception-and-action.

But now, it turns out, here we gain deeper insight into the problem that gave us trouble in the last chapter: the problem of perception without belief. It seemed logically possible, we said, that there might be perception that involved no belief or even 'potential belief', meaning by the latter a state of mind that would be belief but for the possession of other, contrary, beliefs. How, we asked, was this possibility to be squared with an account of perception as the acquiring of beliefs? We can now see clearly what perception completely divorced from belief would be like. It would be a possible case, but, of necessity, a logically secondary case. For it would be perception divorced from the capacity for selective behaviour.

It should be noted that not only does the concept of perception involve reference to the concept of purpose, but also that we can only introduce the notion of *a* perception against the background of *further* perceptions. For perception is bound up with a capacity for discriminative or selective behaviour, and such behaviour is possible only if there is a whole flow of perceptions feeding back to the inner cause of the behaviour as it unfolds. A good model here is the concept of *a* soldier. A soldier *is* a soldier only in association with other soldiers: that is to say, as part of an army. Of course a soldier can have what is, *qua* soldier, a logically secondary existence outside an army. For instance, an army can be annihilated all except one soldier. In the same way, we can form the logically secondary conception of perceptions that occur in isolation from all other perceptions.

As well as gaining a deeper appreciation of the nature of perception that is divorced from belief, we are now also in a position to see the depth of the necessity that links perception of an object with the causation of the perception by that object. This causation was the theme of Section VI of the previous chapter, but there it could be only presented as a relatively isolated fact about the concept of perception. It is part of the notion of purposive activity that the organism takes account of the environment so that the direction in which the mental cause drives the organism can be modified appropriately, and the goal of the activity achieved. But the organism can take account of the environment only if the environment affects the organism: affecting it in different ways for different states of the environment. These affections are perceptions. So the fact that perceptions of the environment are brought into being by that environment pertains to the deepest essence of perception.

We are now also in a position to resolve our dilemma about perception in Section II of this chapter. We said then that perception was a necessary but in no way sufficient condition for the manifestation of discriminative behaviour. We were then at a loss to mark off this necessary condition from other necessary conditions (such as limbs being in working order). We can now see what sort of a necessary condition for discriminative behaviour perception is. It is that which supplies the 'information' enabling the goal-seeking activity to adjust to current circumstances. And since it is clear that incoming information may, on occasion, be perfectly irrelevant to purposes in hand, we can understand why some perceptions may quite fail to modify behaviour. At the same time, they are only perceptions because they have relevance to possible behaviour. It is this fact that perceptions may be irrelevant to current purposes that tends to obscure the logical dependence of perception on the will. The logical connection in the reverse direction—the logical dependence of will on perception—is simpler, and so less easily overlooked.

IV. DIFFERENCE IN PERCEPTIONS WITHOUT DIFFERENCE IN BEHAVIOUR

But now to consider an important objection to what has been said so far. It seems to be logically possible that some or all of my perceptions should be different from those of other people, yet all my behaviour (including speech) be exactly the same as theirs. To take the traditional example, it seems to be logically possible that when I look at pillar-boxes, and say they look red to me, in fact my perceptions are what other people would call pillar-boxes looking green to me. Similarly, I say cooking-apples look green to me, but if others had the perceptions I had they would say that they looked red to me. At the same time, it seems logically possible that there might be no evidence to show that my perceptions were reversed in this way.

But if we allow this as a logical possibility, it seems that there must be something wrong with the analysis of perception developed in the previous sections of this chapter. For if the content of perceptual beliefs is given by the capacity acquired to behave towards objects in certain ways; and if I and others behave, or have the capacity to behave, towards pillar-boxes and cooking-apples in exactly the same way; then it follows that all of us have acquired the same beliefs about the colour of pillar-boxes and cooking-apples. And if, as we have argued, perception involves nothing but the acquiring of beliefs or the occurrence of mental events that resemble the acquiring of beliefs, it follows that my perceptions and the perceptions of others are identical, which contradicts the supposition of the previous paragraph.

But first a note of caution. The supposition that my perceptions of the colour of pillar-boxes and cooking-apples are the exact reverse of other people's but my behaviour is exactly the same as theirs, is not quite as straightforward as it might seem. For instance, everybody would agree that red is a 'warm' colour, but green is a 'cool' one. Does this mean that the colour that other people call 'green' is, for me, a warm colour? If so, my eccentricity will be detected. Or do we have to assume that 'cool' and 'warm' are reversed in my tactual perception just as 'red' and 'green' are? Again, when I say that between red and yellow lies orange, *I* must mean that between the colour that other people call 'green' and another colour, lies a third, intermediate, colour. Now, what are these other two colours? It seems, at least, that there will have to be more than just a reversal of perceptions of red and green.

However, it may be that such difficulties in stating the colour-reversal case can be met. In what follows, at any rate, I propose to concede the possibility of a red–green reversal without differences in behaviour.

It must therefore now be shown that our theory can deal with the case of colour-reversal. C. B. Martin has argued that the most tricky case of all for a theory of the sort that I am defending is that where the population is equally divided: the colour-impression that one half would call 'green' being the colour-impression that the other half would call 'red', and *vice-versa*. For here we have no unique set of 'standard perceivers' to which to compare eccentric perceivers.

To half the population, pillar-boxes look to be red_1—which they simply call 'red'. To the other half of the population pillar-boxes look to be red_2—which they, too, simply call 'red'. To the first half, cooking-apples look $green_1$—which they call 'green'. $Green_1$ is in fact no different from red_2. To the other half, cooking-apples look $green_2$—which they too call 'green'. $Green_2$ and red_1 are identical.

The first point to be clear about is that to have, say, a $green_1$ (red_2) perception is not to have something $green_1$ (red_2) in one's mind. A perception is not a little coloured object. A $green_1$ (red_2) perception is a perception, veridical or illusory, *as of* something in the physical world that has that colour. To have such a perception is, typically, to acquire the belief that there is something $green_1$ (red_2) in our environment. Once this point is accepted, it can be suggested that systematic difference in the quality of perceptions is a systematic difference in the nature of the causes that enable the same behaviour in the two different groups. Suppose, for instance, that what is in one group the special sort of mental event that enables things that have the colour of pillar-boxes to be discriminated from their environment, is in the other the mental event that enables things that have the colour of cooking-apples to be discriminated from *their* environment. Suppose, that is, that relatively to each other, the wires in each group are crossed. We could then say that one group was attributing to pillar-boxes the colour that the other was attributing to cooking-apples, and *vice-versa*. And if the Materialist identification of mental processes with brain-processes is correct, such a crossing of the wires could in principle be discovered by comparative studies of the brains of the two groups.

In this solution of the problem it is assumed that red and green are objective properties of physical objects or physical surfaces. (The *nature* of such properties will be discussed in the next chapter.) If it is also assumed that nothing can be red and green all over at the same time (whether this is a logical or a physical incompatibility) then the colour-perceptions of at least one of the groups involve false colour-attributions. At least one of the groups has false beliefs about the world. Of course, *in the case as described*, where the population is evenly split, and behaviour is exactly the same, the evidence would not allow us to come to any decision as to which, if either, group was seeing the world rightly.

I believe this solution of the problem is correct, but it needs defence against a subtle objection. In order to grasp this objection it must be remembered that according to our account of mental processes in this book, there can be perceptions which the perceiver is unconscious of, or mistaken about. Introspection only makes us aware of some of our perceptions, and only those perceptions we are aware of can be called 'experiences'. Now, it may be said, the possibility that we ought to be considering here is the possibility that the different groups have reversed *experiences*. But, the objection goes on, according to our account of introspection in this book, what one is aware of in introspection is simply the occurrence of a state of oneself apt for the bringing about of certain sorts of behaviour. But, if this is so, the fact that the events in one group apt for the discrimination of the colour of pillar-boxes are in the other group events apt for the discrimination of the colour of cooking-apples, and *vice-versa*, goes for nothing. One group is aware of certain mental events apt for the discrimination of what are publicly called 'red' things, and other mental events apt for the discrimination of what are publicly called 'green' things. So is the other group. Since this is all that each group is introspectively aware of, on this account of introspection, it follows that each has exactly the same colour-*experience*. (The 'crossing of the wires' is not an object of experience.) But this is contrary to the supposition that colour-experiences might be reversed relative to each group.

I shall try to answer this objection by considering in turn three graduated cases where a reversal of colour-perceptions occurs in a perceiver. As before, perceivers are divided into two groups whose colour-perceptions are reversed relatively to the other group. Suppose, firstly, that I belong to one group, but my neural hook-ups are somehow altered so that *with respect to colour-perception only* my brain is brought to the same state as the other group. This switches my colour-perceptions. That such a switch has occurred will be evident both to myself and observers. I will find that pillar-boxes now look, as I say, 'green' and cooking-apples 'red'. The world will seem to me to have changed. Observers will find my behaviour altered. Suppose that at the time of the neural switch I am sorting red and green balls, putting red balls down one chute and green balls down another. The fact that the colour-switch has occurred in me will be betrayed to observers (whichever group they belong to) by the fact that what they call green balls start coming down the chute for what they call red balls, and *vice-versa*. And then, arguing from same cause to same effect, I can deduce from the fact that my perceptual neural hook-up is now that of the second group, and from my experienced change in colour-perception, to the conclusion that I am now seeing colours as the second group sees them.

Now for the second case. Let us assume that, after the switch has occurred in my perceptions, for some extraordinary reason it still seems natural to *speak* in the old way. The pillar-box and the cooking-apples seem to have exchanged colours, but I still *speak* of the first as 'red', and the second as 'green'. The questions must then be asked about this new case: 'Do I notice the change in my perceptions?' Let us suppose that I do notice the change. Then there must be some difference in my behaviour, or at least in my thoughts. There must at least be the thought: 'What I still call and treat as red things look to have become green.' And this implies things like 'If I still had my old verbal and other habits, I would match these balls with cooking-apples and not with pillar-boxes.' That is to say, the belief is present, or at least a 'potential belief', that changes in the colours of physical objects have occurred. Here, even on our theory of perception, and our theory of introspection, there will be introspective *experience* of the change.

In the final case there is not even a thought that a change has occurred in our perceptions and we simply go on as before. There is no *experience* at all of the change, it simply *occurs*. We have a different mental process, but have no experience of the difference. This case can be dealt with by the original suggestion about the 'crossing of the wires'.

The point of considering these three graduated cases is to lead up to the suggestion that in the case where the two sections of a population are equally divided, but their colour-perceptions are reversed relatively to each other, their perceptual *experiences*, as opposed to their perceptions, do not differ. For, when citizens from a different group have a perception of the sort they both call 'something looking red', then, by hypothesis, they both act, speak, think and feel about the object and the perception in exactly the same way. And if their reactions to the perception are identical, then, *ipso facto*, their experience of it is identical. There is certainly a difference in the mental state itself, but not in the awareness of it.

It may still be said that at any rate the two different groups acquire different beliefs about the world. For although both call pillar-boxes 'red' they attribute a different quality to them. And if we accept that the same physical object cannot have both qualities, at least one group will be making false colour-attributions. (Which one had the false view would have to be decided as a matter of scientific theory. And where a case like the present is given where all evidence is equally balanced, decision might be empirically impossible.) All this I am prepared to grant. But I point out that, because of the special nature of the case stated, this difference of belief will not be a difference of belief that anybody is in fact *aware* of.

If this argument is correct, the original suggestion about the 'crossing of the wires' suffices to solve the problem posed for our account of perception by the 'reversal of colour-perceptions' case.

V. THE INTENTIONALITY OF PERCEPTION

In discussing the case of a child who is able to discriminate between the blue and green blocks, we are discussing a very simple case: perception of qualitative difference. We could go on to build up an account of perceptual discrimination involving much more complex situations and much more sophisticated concepts. Behaviour can be described which would be a manifestation of (non-verbal) possession of concepts as abstract as the so-called 'logical constants'. An account of perceptual inference and also the non-inferential perception of causality can also be given. But since these developments of the argument are matters of industry rather than ingenuity, I will spare the reader the details. But before concluding this chapter, two problems require discussion.

We have said that a baby can discriminate between green and blue if, when confronted by blue and green objects, it has the capacity to behave towards these two sorts of object in a systematically different way. But there is a problem here that we have so far burked. Differences of colour will empirically necessitate other, correlated, differences in the perceptual situation. For instance, to the difference in colour of the objects there will (presumably) correspond a difference in the pattern of stimulation on the retina. Now is not the baby behaving towards the two sorts of pattern of retinal stimulation in a different, but equally systematic, way to the way it behaves towards the coloured objects? It behaves towards blue objects in manner r. It behaves towards green objects in manner s. Does this not mean that its behaviour bears the relation r_1 to blue retinal stimulation, and s_1 to green retinal stimulation? Yet it is absurd to say that the baby perceives its own retinal stimulation. So it seems that our account of perception in terms of selective behaviour lets in too much.

In order to begin the answer to this difficulty, let us consider a certain formal classification among those pieces of behaviour of a systematically discriminating sort that perceivers are capable of pursuing towards the objects that they perceive. Firstly, there is behaviour which is actually intended to *alter* in some way the state of the thing perceived. For instance, the blue block is picked up and put in a box, while the green block is ignored. The position of the blue block has been altered. Secondly, there is behaviour which, while it does not alter the state of the thing perceived, is intended to bring something else (for example, the perceiver's body) into some relation to the thing perceived. For instance, a finger is pointed in the direction of the blue block but not towards the green block. The blue block comes to have a certain relational property. Thirdly, there is behaviour that, while systematically correlated with the action of the perceived objects on the perceiver, has as its *objective* neither the alteration of the object nor the coming of anything into relation with the object. For instance, when the blue block is presented, the noise 'blue' is produced.

In the third case, the behaviour is prompted by the perceived object, but it does not have as its objective the alteration of some state, or relational property, of the object that prompts the behaviour. In the first two cases, the behaviour is not only prompted by the object but has as its objective some change, if only in a relational property, of the prompting object. There is a *causal circuit* that begins in the object, which in turn affects the perceiver, who then engages in behaviour that has as its objective some change, even if only in a relational property, of the perceiving object.

Now, it may be suggested, if we consider this sort of selective behaviour that 'returns to the object', we can solve our present problem. When the baby perceives the blue block, it has the capacity, if it should be so impelled, to pursue courses of conduct that have *as their objective* some change in the properties, relational or non-relational, of the blue block. But it cannot make a change in the retinal stimulation *an objective*. If the baby acts, there will *be* changes in the retinal stimulation. But the baby does not purpose to bring about such changes. In this way, we distinguish between the perceived blue block and the unperceived retinal stimulation.

Unfortunately, however, this solution is quite unsatisfactory as it stands. To see this, we have to remember the account we have given of the 'objective' of purposive behaviour. The 'objective' or 'thing purposed' is that situation of which the *perception* that it obtains has the effect of extinguishing the mental cause that initiates and sustains the behaviour. So, far from the notion of objective of purposive behaviour giving us a criterion to pick out the situations that are actually perceived, the notion of an objective presupposes that we can already pick out, independently of the objective, what is and is not perceived.

Nevertheless, some progress has been made. We can now see that the problem of what makes a certain mental event the perception that a certain situation obtains—the problem of the in-

tentionality of perceptions—is bound up with the intentionality
of the will. The notion of the intentional object of a perception is
bound up with the notion of objective. For suppose that I perceive
that there is a blue block in front of me. I might manifest my
perception by putting the block into a box marked 'blue'. Should
I say instead that the situation perceived is a certain pattern on my
retina? If I do, I must *also* modify my account of the behaviour
which, *as we ordinarily say*, has as its objective 'putting the blue
block into the box marked "blue" '. For I will have to say in
consistency that what will bring my purposive activity to a successful end will be the 'perception' of a *further* pattern of retinal
stimulation—that produced on the retina by a blue block being
put into the box marked 'blue'. And then we will have to say that
this retinal stimulation is the objective of the behaviour.

So the position so far is this. We can describe objectives of discriminatory behaviour in the ordinary way, and then we can say
that perceptions have the intentional objects that we ordinarily
say they have. Or we can describe both objectives and intentional
objects in terms of situations that are distinct from, although empirically correlated with, the situation that is ordinarily said to be
the situation perceived. Our problem is to say why what we would
ordinarily call 'the objective' of the discriminatory behaviour and
'the object' of the perception have a special right to be so called.

I suggest that this can be done in terms of the notion of the
causal circuit involved in purposive behaviour that has as its objective some change in non-relational or relational properties of
the object perceived. Consider the action of picking up the blue
block and putting it in the box labelled 'blue'. The situation must
begin with the blue surface of the block acting upon the perceiver. (Otherwise the object is not seen.) As a result of this effect
on the perceiver, he is able, if he is so impelled, to reach out, pick
up the block and put it into the box. Now what brings this train
of actions, initiated and sustained by a mental cause in the perceiver, to an end? It is the perception that the block is safely in
the box. But this involves the causal action of the *blue block in the
box* on the perceiver. So the thing perceived acts on the perceiver,
who in turn brings about some change in the non-relational or
relational properties of the situation, and this new situation in
turn acts on the perceiver to inhibit further action. This is the
causal circuit involved.

Suppose, now, that we try saying instead that the situation perceived to obtain is a pattern of retinal stimulation, and the objective of the discriminative behaviour is some further alteration of that pattern. We can certainly say truly that the retinal stimulation acts upon the perceiver; who, as a result, engages in certain behaviour; which has the result that the retinal stimulation is changed; which has the result of terminating the behaviour. But we do not take in the *full* causal circuit. The circuit goes further out into the world: it goes as far as the blue block, although it goes no further. The blue block plays an essential role in the complex back-and-forth causal transaction, or, at any rate, the blue surface of the block does.

So I suggest that the criterion by which we pick out the *blue surface of the block* as the intentional object of the perception, and the *putting of the block into the box* as the objective, is that, by taking these, and only these, as object and objective we can close the causal circuit, and close it without bringing in anything causally irrelevant. With this 'object of perception' and this 'objective' we reach out into the world the full way that the circuit goes, without reaching processes which are causally irrelevant to the circuit.

The argument is most easily grasped if we consider an unsophisticated perceiver, such as an animal or a baby, but regard the situation from an other-person or observer's point of view. The baby, we say, sees a blue block and reaches out for it. But what is actually observed to happen, or, perhaps better, what does experiment discover to happen? A block comes to be before, and acting upon, the baby's eyes, and as a result the baby does something that affects the ball. The new situation affects the baby again, bringing the behaviour to a halt. If only happenings on the baby's retina and in its other sense-organs are considered, much that is causally relevant is left out. Contrariwise, if we go beyond the block, we come on happenings that are causally irrelevant to the complex causal circuit. So we have here a criterion for saying what is meant by 'situation perceived' and, with it, 'objective'.

Once again we are in a position to appreciate the absolutely central role of causation in the concept of perception. Unless we accept the point that perceptions are states of the person apt for being brought about by certain situations as well as states of the person apt for the bringing about of selective behaviour, we shall not be able to give a coherent account of perception in terms of capacities for selective behaviour.

It is at this point, I hope, that we have finally given a satisfactory account of the 'intentionality' of perceptions which is compatible with, although it does not entail, a purely physicalist view of man.

VI. PERCEPTUAL ILLUSION

Now for a final hurdle. Some readers will have noticed that so far the argument has been confined almost entirely to the consideration of *veridical* perception. This has enabled us to talk of perceptions as the acquiring of *capacities* for behaviour. But now it may be asked whether our account can be applied satisfactorily to illusory perceptions. In these cases, there is, by hypothesis, no systematic correlation of capacities for behaviour, on the one hand, with stimulation of the sense-organs by objects of a certain sort, on the other. But if a thing looks red when it is not red, then the 'capacity' acquired will be a 'capacity' for behaving towards the object as towards *red* objects. But since the object is not red, this simply introduces an element of randomness into the perceiver's selective behaviour. The 'capacity' is really an incapacity. Why is the 'random' behaviour a manifestation of perceptual illusion, rather than *mere* random behaviour?

(In this section we need consider only perceptual illusion that involves the acquiring of false belief. Once difficulties presented by this sort of case have been surmounted, it would be easy to go on to give an account of perceptual illusions that do not involve acquiring false beliefs.)

Now if we reflect upon the difference between false belief and sheer ignorance, we see that false belief depends on the possession of appropriate concepts. Somebody can only acquire the false belief that something is *x* provided he has the concept of *x*. But, confining ourselves to the field of perception, what manifestations would show that a person had the concept of red? Surely this: that the perceiver involved is, in some circumstances at least, able to behave in a systematically different way towards red objects, on the one hand, and objects that are not red, on the other, when that perceiver's sense-organs are suitably stimulated by red objects. This implies that perceptual illusion presupposes that there are circumstances in which the person subject to it is capable of veridical perception with respect to the property or properties about which he is deceived. Error logically presupposes a capacity for freedom from error on certain other occasions.

Nor is this all that is presupposed. Since discriminative behaviour involves the will, and since perception of the developing nature of the situation is logically involved in action directed by the will, the possession of the concept of red implies the possession of a number of further perceptual concepts (just which they are may be logically arbitrary) which permit such discriminative behaviour by supplying appropriate perceptual capacities.

So we can classify certain discriminative behaviour as a manifestation of perceptual illusion only because we grant that perceiver all sorts of capacities for discriminative behaviour which are capacities for veridical perception. The notion of perceptual illusion is deeply rooted in the notion of capacity for veridical perception. This gives a deeper force to the contention that 'perceive' is a success-word than the relatively trivial point that when we say we perceive *that* something is the case we imply that it is indeed the case.

However, we must be careful to define the limits of this optimistic and anti-sceptical conclusion.

(i) In the first place, this conclusion does not entail that, when a perceiver takes something to be red when it is not, this must be a statistically unusual occurrence by comparison with the perceiver's veridical perceptions that objects are red. All that is necessary is that there be *a set of circumstances of a certain sort* in which the perceiver is capable of veridical perception of red things. This set of circumstances need not be one that regular obtains. The circumstances need not even be ones that actually obtain at all. It must simply be empirically true that if they did obtain the perceiver would have veridical perception of red things.

It is true that if a perceiver only manifested successful selection-behaviour towards red objects in a certain very limited context, but proved unable to manifest such behaviour in most ordinary contexts, we should certainly want evidence that, outside this special context, he ever had mental experiences that could be properly described as objects looking red to him although they were not in fact red. But such evidence might be forthcoming. It might be that the perceiver acted in relation to certain objects that were not red in *exactly* the same way that he acted towards red things in that limited context where he successfully discriminated red things from other things. Or physical considerations might lead us to believe that he must be seeming to see something red: for instance, he might have red glass in front of his eyes. Another sort of good evidence, although not evidence that we are at present in a position to produce, would be evidence provided by a really reliable theory of the working of the brain. If it was clear that processes were going on in the perceiver's brain that were associated with correctly selecting red objects in the limited context where the perceiver was regularly successful, we might have good reason to think that the perceiver 'seemed to see something red'. Finally, with perceivers who have a good command of language, we can rely on their verbal reports. As we have seen in Chapter 6 in discussing the alleged incorrigibility of introspection, these reports are no more logically infallible than any other way of ascertaining what the perceiver's perceptions are. But with sophisticated language-users, they are in practice quite reliable.

In the same way, we can even imagine evidence that would show that a perceiver who never in fact had a veridical perception of something red, nevertheless did have perceptual illusions as of red objects.

However, this concession to scepticism must in its turn be strictly limited. For all these ways of discovering that somebody (ourselves or another) has been subject to perceptual illusion depend upon the assumption that, in respect of the evidence supposed to prove the occurrence of illusion, we are capable of perceiving correctly. We assume that we can perceive that a man is in fact behaving in a certain way, or that the subject has red glasses on, or that his brain is in a certain state, or that he is uttering certain words. Only against the background of the assumption that certain perceptions are veridical, can we identify particular cases as cases of perceptual illusion.

(ii) There is a second limitation to be placed upon the optimistic and anti-sceptical conclusion apparently yielded by our account of sensory illusion. The account may seem to support the now celebrated anti-sceptical Argument from Paradigm cases, as applied to sensible properties. In fact I do not think it does.

The ordinary Argument from Paradigm cases, as I understand

it, may be formulated in the following way. Suppose it to be the case that all users of a language agree in applying a certain descriptive word or phrase, '*x*', to a certain class of instances. Suppose these instances are just the sort of instances that we would use to teach a person or child ignorant of the word or phrase what it meant. Suppose, that is, that they are paradigm cases. Then it follows of logical necessity that these things are *x*'s, and so that *x*'s exist.

Now this argument has come under much criticism in recent years. There is, however, an almost exactly parallel argument applied to sensory properties, an argument which may be called the *Argument from Paradigm cases of sensory properties*, which still enjoys widespread underground support although it is seldom explicitly formulated. To normal perceivers a certain class of objects look red. This class includes ripe Jonathan apples, post-boxes in England and Australia, tomatoes, the flag of the Soviet Union and blood. These are the sort of objects used to teach a child, or an animal with colour-vision, 'what redness is'. The Argument from Paradigm cases of sensory properties asserts that, given these empirical facts, it follows of logical necessity that these objects are in fact red. We cannot admit the facts, yet refuse to attribute the property. Now it might seem that our argument has also led us to the same conclusion by a different, although not dissimilar, route.

However, I do not think we should accept this argument, nor do I think that the same conclusion is really entailed by our own argument. It would be possible (logically possible, at any rate) to teach an animal or child the difference between red and non-red things by presenting it with objects that simply *looked* red to it. Such a perceiver might acquire the *capacity* to discriminate between red things and non-red things, and so have the concept of red, although never having perceived a thing that was really red. Now, if this is so, why should we not admit the (logical) possibility that the so-called paradigm objects might turn out to be things that look red but are not? I cannot see how this is to be ruled out. But to admit such a logical possibility is to reject the Argument from Paradigm cases of sensory properties.

Of course, we can only have the slightest reason to think that *in fact* the 'paradigm objects' are not really red, but instead only look red to normal perceivers in normal conditions, provided there is good evidence for such a view. And that evidence must in the end be based upon perception, which means that we shall have to accept *other* perceptual paradigms if we are to have reason for suspecting the paradigms of red. We gain our knowledge of the world by perception, and so we can do no better than overthrow one section of the beliefs acquired in perception by a theory which is supported by appeal to another section of our perceptually acquired beliefs. But no *particular* set of paradigm objects is logically sacrosanct.

Despite these qualifications, it remains true that perceptual illusion is, of logical necessity, possible only against a background of at least a capacity for veridical perception.

Now a *capacity* for veridical perception implies that the veridical perceptions involved are acquirings of knowledge as opposed to mere true belief. For according to the analysis of knowledge in Chapter 9, if, in certain circumstances, one's beliefs about a certain matter are of empirical necessity true, then these beliefs constitute knowledge. But a *capacity* for veridical perception implies that there *are* possible circumstances where one's perceptual beliefs about a certain sort of matter are, of empirical necessity, true.

In the previous chapter it was pointed out (in Section XI) that veridical perceptions might either be acquirings of knowledge or of true belief. But it was said, without argument being offered, that the central cases were those where knowledge was acquired. It is now possible to see the logical basis for this. All perception, veridical or illusory, presupposes a capacity in the perceiver for veridical perception in certain circumstances. This entails that the perceptions in which the capacity is actualized are acquirings of knowledge.

If the argument of this chapter has been correct, then, we can give an account of the concept of perception solely in terms of states of the person both apt for being produced by physical situations in the body and environment of the perceiver, and also apt for discriminatory or selective behaviour directed towards these same physical situations. Such an account is at least compatible with a purely physicalist view of man.

12

THE SECONDARY QUALITIES

IN what we have said so far, it has been assumed that the 'secondary qualities'—colour, sound, taste, smell, heat and cold—are objective properties of physical objects or physical processes. We discover the colour of an object, or its taste, in just the same way that we discover its shape or its texture. But, it may be argued, such a naïvely realistic attitude to these qualities is indeed naïve. For modern science finds no room for such properties in its account of the physical world.

Some properties of physical objects and processes are susceptible of logical analysis in terms of other properties. Thus, we might give an analysis of hardness in terms of a disposition in the hard object not to change its shape or break up easily when under pressure. But colour, sound, taste, smell, heat and cold, even if no other qualities, seem to resist any such analysis. They seem to be *irreducible* qualities. Any connection that they have with other properties of physical objects seems to be a contingent one.

However, as is well-known, the conception of the secondary qualities as irreducible or unanalysable properties of physical objects or processes has led to the greatest problems. The difficulties have been with us at least since the time of Galileo, and have only become more pressing with every advance in physical knowledge. How are we to fit such irreducible properties into the physical world as it is conceived by physicists? For instance, modern physics pictures an ordinary macroscopic object as an indefinitely large swarm of 'fundamental particles' moving in a space that is, despite the numbers of these particles, relatively empty. Only in the densest stars, where matter exists in a 'collapsed' state, are the fundamental particles packed in at all closely. Now what can we predicate the secondary qualities of? They surely cannot be predicable of individual 'fundamental particles'. Are they, then, 'emergent' properties of the whole area or surface of the area 'occupied' by the particles? Perhaps this is a barely possible line to take, but it is not one that a physicist, or, I think, anyone else, could look upon with much enthusiasm.

In the excellent terminology of Wilfrid Sellars, there is a *prima facie* contradiction between the 'manifest image' of the physical world that ordinary perception presents us with, and the 'scientific image' of the world that physicists are gradually articulating for us. If the secondary qualities are taken to be irreducible properties of physical objects, they can be fitted into the manifest, but not the scientific, image of the world.

Some philosophers and scientists have sought to remove the contradiction by arguing that the 'scientific image' of the world proposed by physics is a mere *manner of speaking*. The real world is the world of the manifest image, and the 'scientific image' is an abstraction of certain features from the manifest world, or is a fiction that has only heuristic and predictive value. I have said what I have to say in criticism of this view in *Perception and the Physical World*, Chapter 12, Section 2. There is very forceful criticism in J. J. C. Smart's *Philosophy and Scientific Realism* (Routledge, 1963), Chapter 2. Here I will say only that I think the scientific image of the world has to be taken seriously. It has to be taken ontologically. If this is so, there is still a problem of how the secondary qualities can be fitted into the physical world.

But most philosophers and scientists who have tried to tackle this problem have reached a different conclusion. They have concluded that the irreducible *qualia* cannot really qualify the physical objects they appear to qualify. The *qualia* qualify items in the mind of the perceiver. To say that a physical surface is coloured cannot truly imply anything more than that this surface has the power of producing items having a certain irreducible quality in the mind of a normal perceiver.

But from this conclusion further conclusions follow.

In the first place, Berkeley was surely right in arguing that if the secondary qualities qualify mental items, then the other directly perceived properties are also properties of mental, not physical, objects. Colour and visible extension, for instance, are inextricably bound up with each other. If colour qualifies something mental, so does visible extension. And so we are led to the view that what we are non-inferentially aware of in perception is never a physical situation but a situation in our own mind: our own current sense-impressions, perhaps. We are forced to accept a Representative theory of perception, with all its difficulties, unless, indeed, we accept the still more desperate doctrine of Phenomenalism.

In the second place, we are back in that bifurcation of mental and physical reality which it is the object of a physicalist doctrine of man to overcome. Man's mind becomes a quite different sort of object from physical objects because it is qualified by, or in some way linked with, qualities that physical science need take no account of. To accept the view that the secondary qualities are irreducible *qualia* of mental items would be to abandon the whole programme of this work.

It is clear, then, that a Materialist account of the mind must offer some new account of the secondary qualities. In this chapter, therefore, I put forward the view that they are nothing but *physical* properties of physical objects or processes. Colours of surfaces, on this view, will be simply physical properties of those surfaces. And by 'physical properties' is meant the sort of properties a physicist would be prepared to attribute to those surfaces, the sort of properties that would figure in the 'scientific image' of the world.

Notice that it is a physical surface's *being* red that is being identified with physical properties of that surface, and not that surface's *looking* red. Something looking red is a matter of a person or persons having certain perceptions as a result of the causal action of that surface on their eyes. These perceptions, we have argued, are not themselves red, and so do not necessitate the postulating of any *qualia* at all. The perceptions are acquirings of belief, or 'potential belief', that something physical *is* red; or, at a deeper level of analysis, they are acquirings of capacities for selective behaviour towards particular red objects, capacities characteristically brought into existence by the red object. As we may put it, red objects are red, but red sensations are not red, save *per accidens*.

In what follows I will concern myself chiefly with the colours of surfaces. There are other physical things that are coloured, such as transparent cubes of coloured glass. There are also other secondary qualities. But in the case of colours of surfaces various problems for our identification come up in an especially acute form. So I do not think that this concentration of attention will involve any evasion of issues.

I will proceed by considering in turn two sorts of objection to a physicalist account of the secondary qualities: *a priori* objections, and empirical objections.

II. *A PRIORI* OBJECTIONS TO IDENTIFYING SECONDARY QUALITIES WITH PHYSICAL PROPERTIES

Objection 1. We knew what redness was long before we knew what physical properties are necessary and sufficient for redness of physical surface. So redness is not a physical property of surfaces.

Reply. The claim that redness is a purely physical property of surfaces is not intended to be a logical analysis of the concept of red. It is not a necessary truth that redness is a purely physical property of that surface. We have argued in this work that, as a contingent matter of fact, mental states are purely physical states of the central nervous system. In just the same way, it is now being claimed that, as a matter of contingent fact, redness is a purely physical property of surfaces.

Objection 2. The secondary qualities of things might be imagined to change completely, although the physical characteristics with which they are correlated did not change at all. (What is being imagined here is a change in quality that everybody *noticed*.) So the secondary qualities cannot be identified with physical characteristics.

Reply. The objection depends upon covertly treating the connection between the secondary qualities and physical characteristics as if it were necessary, and not contingent. It is perfectly possible, in the logician's sense of 'possible', that the redness of surfaces is not a physical property of the surface. And, if this is so, it is perfectly possible that the redness of a surface should begin to vary independently of the physical properties of the surface. Now to imagine a migration of the secondary qualities is simply to imagine that both these conditions are fulfilled.

Consider a parallel case. It is logically possible that the morning star is not the evening star. And if the morning star is not the evening star, it is also possible that one day the two should appear in the sky side-by-side. But, of course, *given that the morning star is in fact the evening star*, it is not possible that the two should appear in the sky side-by-side. In the same way, it is possible that redness of surface is not a physical property of the surface. If this is so, it is further possible that redness of surface should vary independently of the physical properties of the surface. But, of course, *given that redness of surface is in fact a physical property of that surface*, it is not possible that redness of surface should vary independently of the physical properties of the surface.

Objection 3. But if the identity of redness with some physical property of surfaces is a contingent one, then it must be possible to give an account of the meaning of the word 'red' in terms logically independent of any reference to the physical properties of objects or their surfaces. This explanation of meaning can only take the form of saying that 'red' stands for a unique, irreducible, property: redness.

Reply. I grant that we must give an account of the meaning of the word 'red' in terms that involve no reference to the physical properties of surfaces. But I deny that this explanation must take the form of saying that 'redness' stands for an irreducible property.

But before going on to develop my own account of the meaning of the word 'red', I will say that I think that this is *the* critical objection to the identification of secondary qualities with physical properties. If the identification is incorrect, this is the reason that it is incorrect. When the contingent identification of mental states with states of the central nervous system was proposed in Chapter 6, we considered the objection that this required a characterization of the meaning of the phrase 'mental state' in terms quite independent of any reference to physical states of the brain. This objection was taken to be an objection of crucial importance, and, indeed, our account of the concept of a mental state as a state of the person apt for the production of certain sorts of behaviour grew out of the attempt to answer this objection. Now the objection we are currently considering to the proposed account of the secondary qualities is essentially the same objection. We may suspect that it is an objection of peculiar importance.

A mental state is a state of the person apt for the production of certain sorts of behaviour, but the further nature of this state of the person is not given by our concept of a mental state. This blank or gap in the formula enables us to make sense of the assertion that these states are purely physical states of the brain. Physical states can, as it were, be plugged into the gap. Now if we want to make a contingent identification of redness with some physical property, must not our account of what redness is involve some similar blank or gap? There seems to be no other way to carry through a reductive programme.

But at this point it may seem that in the case of colour there is no hope of working the same trick that was worked with the concept of a mental state. It is plausible to say that the concept of a mental state is a complex concept, and so that the phrase 'mental state' admits of definition or unfolding. The blank or gap then appears within the definition. But a word like 'red' seems to be indefinable except by synonyms. In Lockean terms, the concept of red is a 'simple idea'. And so there is, as it were, no room for any blank or gap within our concept of redness.

But this line of thought has overlooked one possibility. Suppose that our concept of red is *all* blank or gap? May it not be that we know *nothing* about what redness is in its own nature? May it not be that we only know contingent truths about redness—such truths as that it is a property detected by the eye and possessed, or apparently possessed, by such things as the surface of ripe tomatoes and Jonathan apples? Then it would be possible to go on to a contingent identification of redness with a physical property of the red thing.

But if the concept of redness is all blank or gap, would it not follow that the word 'red' lacks a meaning, a conclusion which is manifestly false? By no means. Consider the following imaginary situation. Let us suppose that there is an indefinitely large group of people who fall into a number of quite distinct sub-groups: 'families' that do not overlap. Members of the same 'family' all have certain subtleties of feature and behaviour in common that set them off from the members of the other 'families'. Normal observers can be fairly easily taught to sort members of the group as a whole into these mutually exclusive sub-groups. Normal observers spontaneously agree that individuals picked at random belong in a particular sub-group. Nevertheless, because the differences between the sub-groups are very subtle, such observers can make no comment on, and, indeed, have no knowledge of, the way that they sort out these people. They simply sort individuals into groups in a spontaneous way as the result of the action of these individuals upon the perceiver's sense-organs.

Now under such circumstances, I suggest, observers would be entitled to talk about the differentiating properties, and bestow names upon these properties, *although they would know nothing at all about the intrinsic nature of the properties*. Certain persons are all put into one group. They can then be said to have a certain property P not possessed by those who are put in other groups. P is given the name 'p'. But what can the observers say about P? Only that it attaches to certain individuals and no others. But that it attaches to these individuals is surely only a contingent fact about P.

I suggest that this imaginary situation will serve as a model for our knowledge of redness. Red objects all have a property in common which all normal observers can detect. But we normal observers are not aware of the nature of this property. We can only identify the property by reference to the way it is detected (by the eyes) and by mentioning objects that happen to be red. What principally stands in the way of our accepting this solution is the illusion that perception gives us a through-and-through knowledge of, or acquaintance with, such qualities as redness. (There is also the objection that we seem to have a greater knowledge of the intrinsic nature of redness than this account would allow, an objection that will be considered and answered shortly.)

Our imaginary case can easily be developed so that it will parallel the various things that we want to say about redness. Here are two important parallels. It was argued in the previous chapter that an object, or class of objects, that normal observers in normal conditions take to be red, may not be red in fact but only appear so. This possibility can be duplicated in the imaginary model. A certain individual, or class of individuals, may look to everybody to belong to sub-group A. But investigators might discover that the objective physical characteristics of this individual or individuals are those of sub-group B, although, for some further reason, these characteristics, when they attach to these individuals, have the effects upon perceivers that members of sub-group A normally have. Here we have individuals that look to be A's but are in fact B's. And, because they look to be A's they would be just as useful as real A's in teaching somebody what an A was.

It was also argued in the previous chapter that it was meaningful to say that different observers might have 'inverted spectra' with respect to each other, so that one man's 'red' should be the other's 'green', and *vice-versa*, and so for all other colours, although this inversion is behaviourly undetectable. Again, this possibility can be duplicated in our model. Suppose investigators discover that individuals in group A affect some people in manner x. The objects stimulate their sense-organs, and then bring about processes in their brain, associated with perception of the sort x. Individuals in group B affect the same perceivers in manner y. But suppose there are other perceivers who are affected by individuals in group A in manner y, and by individuals in group B in manner x, although this inversion is behaviourly undetectable. It would follow that A's look to one group as B's look to the other group, and *vice-versa*.

Here, then, is an account of the concept of redness, and so of the meaning of the word 'red'. Now, if the account is correct, then, just as there arises the question what, as a contingent matter of fact, a mental state is, so there arises the question what, as a contingent matter of fact, the property of redness actually is. And here, just as in the case of mental states, various answers seem to be in good logical order. It is an intelligible hypothesis that redness is an irreducible property that is quite different from the properties considered by physicists. But, from the standpoint of total science, the most *plausible* answer is that redness is a purely physical property. In this way we solve the difficulties raised in the first section of this chapter.

If properties such as redness are not identified with purely physical properties, then, presumably they will have to be correlated with the physical properties. But every consideration of economy speaks in favour of the identification. If we take a Realistic view of the entities of physics, then we have the physical properties on our hands in any case. So why not identify the secondary qualities with the physical properties?

Objection 4. The attempt we have given to characterize redness as an *unknown* property of certain surfaces and objects, breaks down when we remember that redness is seen to have something in common with blue, green, orange, etc. They are all *colours*. If our eyes became sensitive to ultra-violet and infra-red radiation we might become aware of hitherto unperceived visual qualities. Yet we might recognize at once that they were colours, that is, that they resembled the known colours. How could we do this if perception gave us no acquaintance with the nature of colours? Again, we recognize that the colours resemble and differ from each other in certain complex ways. For instance, red is more like orange than it is like yellow. Does not this imply some acquaintance with the nature of the three colours?

Reply. This objection shows that there has been an omission in our account of redness in particular and colour-concepts in general. It is true that we recognize that red, green, blue, orange, etc., have something in common. To be precise, what we recognize is that they are all determinates falling under a common determinable. Calling them all 'colours' is a verbal acknowledgement of this recognition. But this does not mean that we have any concrete knowledge of what this determinable, colour, is. We simply recognize that red, green, blue, orange and the other colours are determinates falling under a single determinable, *without having any visual awareness of what that determinable is*. The particular colours are identified as visually detected properties of certain surfaces and objects. We recognize further that these properties are determinates falling under a common determinable. But further than this, perception fails to inform us.

In defence of this view, we may recall the notorious difficulty that philosophers have found in saying what it is that all the colours have in common. Any alternative view of the nature of colours, or other 'ranges' of secondary qualities, may be challenged to give an account of the uniting principle of such ranges. I am proposing to solve the problem by saying that, although we perceive that the individual colours, etc., have something in common, we do not perceive what it is.

Now we also recognize further similarities and differences between the colours besides the fact that they are all determinates falling under the one determinable. The perceived relationship between red, orange and yellow is a case in point. On our account, this is interpreted as a recognition that red things are more like orange things than they are like yellow things in a certain respect, unaccompanied by any awareness of what that respect is.

Our account is also able to give a solution of the problem of colour-incompatibilities. (It will be assumed here that the colour-incompatibilities are logical incompatibilities, that it is logically impossible for two different colours both to characterize the whole of a surface at the same time. If the incompatibility is empirical, then a similar line of solution applies, *mutatis mutandis*.)

Consider first a more straight-forward case of the perceptual recognition of an incompatibility. Suppose I can see that a line is of a certain length. In bringing the line under the concept of length x (which, let us say, I do simply by using my eyes) it is automatically given that the line is not of another length. If I failed to realize this, to this extent my concept of length would be defective. So in perceiving that the line is of a certain length I perceive that it cannot be of another length.

Now, in perceiving that a certain surface is red, I perceive that it cannot be another colour. Just as different lengths are incompatible, so are different colours. But if my account of our perceptual acquaintance with colour is correct, then, unlike the case of length, vision does not inform us what colours are. All that we know is that they are incompatible. So the perception that a red surface cannot simultaneously have another colour is a perception that it has an unknown property, a property incompatible with certain other similar unknown properties possessed by other surfaces. The solution of the colour-incompatibility problem is simply to recognize that, in this case, the awareness of the incompatibility of certain properties is unaccompanied by any knowledge of the nature of the properties.

But suppose that the contingent identification of colours of surfaces with purely physical properties of the surfaces were correct. Suppose, to make a simplifying assumption, that the physical property of the surface that constituted redness of surface was a relatively fine-grained grid, while the physical property of the surface that constituted greenness of surface was a relatively coarse-grained grid. A grid cannot be fine-grained and coarse-grained all over at the same time, and so the incompatibility would *turn out* to be a quite unmysterious incompatibility of physical properties. Perception, of course, does not inform us that the incompatibility is an incompatibility of this simple sort. It simply informs us that the properties are incompatible.

The position may be illustrated by a somewhat fanciful analogy.

Suppose that pairs of statements are put in separate envelopes, and suppose that some of the pairs are incompatible statements, although some are not. Now suppose that a clairvoyant has certain non-inferential knowledge concerning these statement-pairs. He always knows infallibly whether any given envelope contains a compatible or an incompatible pair of statements. But he never knows what the content of the statements is. This may serve as a picture of our knowledge derived from perception of the compatibilities and incompatibilities of the secondary qualities.

If the traditional view is accepted that properties such as redness and greenness are irreducible qualities whose whole nature is perceptually given, then some *other* account of how colour-incompatibilities are possible must be produced. The history of philosophical discussions of this problem shows that a satisfactory account is not easily found. It is a powerful argument for our view that it solves the problem.

Notice, finally, before moving on to consider the next objection, that the fact that colours are recognized to be different determinables falling under a common determinate enables a physicalist theory of colour to give worthy hostages to fortune. If the physical properties connected with the colour of surfaces did not turn out to be determinates falling under a determinable physical property, this would count against this theory of colour.

In the same way, we can predict that the physical properties connected with red, orange and yellow surfaces will be such that in some respect they form a scale, a scale on which the physical property connected with orange is the intermediate member. Such a prediction might be falsified.

Objection 5. Colour-surfaces are homogeneous. It is part of the essence of what it is to be a red surface that *each* part of that surface is also red. Contrast this with 'shaped like a grid'. Not every part of a grid-shaped thing is itself grid-shaped. Gridded surfaces are not homogeneous in this respect. Now the physical property of the surface with which the redness of the surface is to be putatively identified may not be a homogeneous property. But how can something homogeneous be identified with something that is not homogeneous?

Reply. May we not distinguish between relative and complete homogeneity? Consider a uniformly coloured surface. Now consider any *minimum visibile* in that surface, by which is meant here any smallest portion of the surface that we are able to discern in the conditions of observation then prevailing. This *minimum* must be coloured. But need we say that any proper part of this *minimum* is necessarily coloured? I do not think we need. Consider a parallel case. The larger parts of a quantity of water are themselves quantities of water. But when we get down to the molecular level we finally reach parts which are not quantities of water. Why should it not be the same with coloured surfaces?

The objection that can be brought against this answer, and which I used to think conclusive, is that proper parts of a coloured *minimum* can lack colour only if colour is a structural, or non-homogeneous, property of surfaces. We cannot divide water forever, and still reach quantities of water, because, it turns out, water is made up of water-molecules which have a certain complex structure: hydrogen and oxygen atoms linked together. But colour of surface seems to be something that lacks any such complexity of structure: in this respect it is a simple property.

On the view of colour being put forward here, however, we can evade this point by arguing that the 'simplicity' of colour is epistemological, not ontological. Colour may in fact be a 'structural' property of physical surfaces, but this is a fact that is not given to us in perception. *All* we are given in the perception of a uniform coloured surface is that the *minima* do not differ in colour-property. So, for all perception tells us, the property is a simple one as opposed to a structural one. But since, on our view, the property of colour is like an iceberg—the greater part of its nature is hidden from us—it *also* remains possible that colour is a structural property, not a simple one. Perception fails to inform us. What hinders us from seeing this possibility is the belief that perception gives us a through-and-through acquaintance with colour.

Objection 6. Colour, sound, taste, smell, heat and cold are the paradigms of *qualities*. Yet the proposed analysis is reducing them to mere theoretical concepts, mere 'that whiches' whose nature must be determined by further scientific research. Surely this is a topsy-turvey account of the secondary qualities?

Reply. On the view being argued for, it is part of the notion of a quality such as red that it has certain resemblances to, and differences from, other properties. Thus, in perception we are directly aware that all the colours are determinates falling under a single determinable. Again, we are directly aware that red is more like orange than it is like yellow. And so on. We are aware of many resemblances and differences between red and the other colours. So we are not completely in the dark as to the intrinsic nature of a secondary quality, even if all we perceive of this nature is its resemblance to, and difference from, other qualities. This, I hope, preserves the distinction between our concepts of the secondary qualities, on the one hand, and mere theoretical concepts, on the other.

Objection 7. If we 'reduce' the secondary qualities of objects to purely physical properties of objects, then it seems that we will not be able to form a coherent conception of a physical object. This is an argument I myself advanced in the last chapter of *Perception and the Physical World*. It is to be found in embryo form in Berkeley, and was very carefully worked out by Hume in a brilliant section of the *Treatise* (Bk. I, Pt. IV, Sect. 4).

I put the argument in the form 'How can we differentiate a physical object from empty space?' Mere spatial properties are insufficient, because physical objects share these with empty space. But if we look at the properties of physical objects that physicists are prepared to allow them, such as mass, electric charge, or momentum, these show a distressing tendency to dissolve into *relations* that one object has to another. What, then, are the things that have these relations to each other? Must they not have a non-relational nature if they are to sustain relations? But what is this nature? Physics does not tell us. It is here that the secondary qualities, conceived of as irreducible properties, are thrown into the breach to provide the stuffing for matter.

Reply. Whatever the solution to this difficulty—and it is a central difficulty in that complex of problems that constitute 'the problem of substance'—it is certain that appeal to the secondary qualities cannot solve it. Gregory O'Hair has drawn my attention to the following consideration, which seems quite decisive. I have said, although I have not argued it here, that we must take a Realistic as opposed to an Operationalist or Phenomenalist view of the 'scientific image' of the physical world. Now if we do this, then we must admit that such things as electrons are *individual objects*. But, in that case, the problem just briefly outlined must come up for individual electrons. Yet it seems madness to say that the electron has any of the secondary qualities. It would be plainly contrary to what we know of the physical conditions associated with the existence of the secondary qualities. So the problem of non-relational nature *must* be solved for electrons without bringing in the secondary qualities. And if the problem can be solved for electrons without appealing to the secondary qualities, surely it can be solved for physical objects generally without appealing to the secondary qualities?

What *is* the solution to the problem of the non-relational nature of physical objects? I do not know. In *Philosophy an Scientific Realism* Smart canvasses three suggestions (pp. 74–5). There are other possible solutions. But here we may excuse ourselves further consideration of the difficulty, on the grounds that it is a quite separate problem from the problems considered in this book.

III. EMPIRICAL OBJECTIONS TO IDENTIFYING SECONDARY QUALITIES WITH PHYSICAL PROPERTIES

So much for *a priori* objections to our physicalist doctrine of the secondary qualities. But what actual physical properties of objects are the secondary qualities to be identified with? In the case of the colours, the colour of a surface or the colour of an object such as a piece of amber may be identified with a certain physical constitution of the surface or object such that, when acted upon by sunlight, surfaces or objects having that constitution emit light-waves having certain frequencies. The sound an object emits may simply be identified with the sound-waves it emits. Heat and cold are the mean kinetic energy of the molecules of the hot or cold substance. The exact identification of tastes and smells is still a matter of controversy.

There are, however, still a number of empirical difficulties that can be raised against these identifications. As before, these difficulties centre chiefly around colour.

Objection 8. We have suggested that the colour of a surface is to be contingently identified with that physical constitution of surface which emits light-waves of certain frequencies when acted upon by sunlight. Now under sunlight surfaces assume one colour, under other forms of illumination they assume another. What we call a blue surface looks blue in sunlight, but it looks purple under fluorescent light. Yet we say the surface is blue, not purple. Why do we do this? Why is the colour presented in sun-light said to be the *real* colour? What privilege does sunlight con-fer, beyond the contingent fact that it is, at present, the natural form of illumination in our life?

Reply. It seems to me that we must admit that a real change in quality occurs at surfaces that, as we *say*, 'appear to change' when conditions of illumination are changed. I can see no ground for saying that such changes are in any way illusory or merely ap-parent. But it seems that there is room here for two different ways of talking about colours.

In one way of talking, the colour of a surface is determined by, and so can be contingently identified with, the actual nature of the light-waves currently emitted at the surface. In this way of talk-ing, the colour of a surface is constantly changing, really changing, as changes in conditions of illumination occur. Such a way of talking about colours is one that naturally commends itself to those who are concerned with the visual arts.

But in another, more usual, way of talking, colour is determined by the nature of the light-waves emitted under *normal illumination*: ordinary sunlight. It is therefore a *disposition* of surfaces to emit certain sorts of light-waves under certain conditions. And so, like all dispositions, colour, in this way of talking, can be identified with the state that underlies the manifestation of the disposition: certain physical properties of the surface. In this way of talking, of course, colour does not change very easily, and so this idiom is better suited to the demands of ordinary life.

The former way of talking is, however, less anthropomorphic, because it does not depend upon the conditions of illumination that are normal in the human environment. It is also logically the more fundamental, because we can give an analysis of colour in the second sense in terms of colour in the first sense: viz. colour (in the first sense) assumed under normal illumination. It may be noted that it seems natural to identify sound with the sound-waves being emitted. That is to say, our account of sound is parallel to our account of colour *in the first sense*. There is no way of talking about sound corresponding to the second way of talk-ing about colour, for obvious reasons.

These two ways of talking about colours may be compared with two possible ways of talking about tennis-balls. In one way of talking, tennis-balls are, from time to time, very far from being round. For instance, at the moment of being struck by a racquet they suffer great distortions of shape. They are only round under 'normal conditions': when they are under no particular pressure. But in another, more usual, way of talking, tennis-balls are never anything but round. If they became elliptical they would be discarded. The factory 'makes them round' just as a dyer 'dyes the cloth blue'. Yet we could give an account of this second, more usual, sense of 'round' in terms of the first, less usual, but logically more fundamental sense of 'round'.

This distinction between different ways of talking about colours enables us to solve Locke's problem about porphyry losing its red colour in the dark (*Essay*, Bk. II, Ch. 8, Sect. 19). In the first, or unusual, way of talking porphyry *does* lose its red colour in the dark. In the dark, the surface of the porphyry emits no light-waves at all. So, in this way of talking, porphyry is black in the dark. (Black surfaces emit no wave-lengths.) But in the second, or usual, way of talking the porphyry is still red. For restore normal conditions, that is, restore normal illumination, and the porphyry will reflect 'red' light-waves. It may be noted in passing that there is nothing here that does anything to show that colour is 'subjective', although this is the conclusion that Locke draws from the case.

Objection 9. But what of the fact that surfaces, etc., under constant illumination may still appear to have different colours in different surroundings and background conditions? The reply to the previous objection will not suffice here. For there may be no change in the light-waves actually emitted by the surface.

Reply. I think we should treat these appearances as mere *appearances*. The sun, or a sodium-vapour lamp, actually *act* on the visible surface, and so it is reasonable to think of them causing different effects at that surface. But the differences in colour exhibited by the same surface placed in different environments are not due, I presume, to the differing causal action of these environments. To some extent, of course, the 'differences' are just a matter of different relations to the environment. A dingy white surface placed against an even dingier background really is, and is seen to be, whiter than its background. Placed against a dazzling white background, it really is, and is seen to be, less white than this new background. There is no sensory illusion here. But where there really is change in the 'colour presented' because of change of background, we can treat this as a change in the *appearances* presented. An obvious analogy is the illusory distortions of visual size and shape that occur in certain sorts of perceptual situation.

Is colour-blindness a matter of being subject to illusions? This is less clear. Colour-blind persons are unable to make all the colour-discriminations that persons with normal sight can make. But mere failure to perceive something is not illusion. There is no necessity to think that any illusion is involved unless the colour-perceptions of the colour-blind are actually *incompatible* with ordinary perceptions. If, however, a surface looks grey to a colour-blind person but looks blue to normal perceivers, then, since grey and blue are incompatible colours, at least one of the perceivers is subject to illusion. The fact that ordinary perceivers make colour-discriminations where colour-blind persons do not (between blue and grey things, say) will then serve as a *reason* for thinking that it is the colour-blind person who is subject to the illusion. For, *in general*, if X perceives a difference between two sorts of thing, but Y perceives no such difference, then there really is a difference. Perception of differences points strongly to the real existence of such differences, failure to perceive differences points much less strongly to the absence of differences.

Objection 10. But what of the difficulties posed by microscopes and perception from a great distance? It is well known that, under these conditions, the colours exhibited by a surface are quite different from, and incompatible with, those exhibited to the unaided eye at an ordinary distance. Yet it is clear that no change in the physical state of the surface is involved. Man might have had microscopic eyes, or have been permanently at a distance from the objects that he sees. What warrant is there for taking the colours exhibited under normal conditions as the real colours? But if the colours exhibited under normal conditions are not the real colours, what are the real colours? Unless we can say what the real colours are we will not know which colour-appearances to correlate with the physical properties. And how then can we identify colour and physical properties?

Reply. In the case of objects at a great distance, the colour exhibited by the objects is largely due to the distorting influence of the air between the object and the eye. The nature of the light-waves that arrive at the eye is not the same as the light-waves *actually emitted at the surface of the object.* It seems reasonable, therefore, to speak of mere appearances, or illusions, in such a case.

But when the same surface presents incompatible colour-properties to the naked eye and to a microscope the problem is not quite so simply dissolved.

Let us begin by returning to the case of objects viewed from a great distance. The hills look blue in the distance, but the surface of the hillside is not really blue. This can be explained by pointing out that the intermediate air between the hills and the viewer filters out all light-waves except those waves or combinations of waves that are emitted by blue surfaces in sunlight. Notice, however, that, although the hills only look blue, this would remain a perfectly good case to use in building up correlations between blueness of surface and emission of certain packets of light-waves. For we could correctly correlate blueness of surface with the pattern of waves that actually enter the eye. For if the waves that get to the eye *and those alone* had been emitted in that pattern at the surface, then the surface would in fact have been blue. The 'information' that enters the eye has been selected and distorted by the intervening atmosphere. But the same 'information', if unselected and undistorted, would have been that transmitted by a blue surface.

This is relevant to colour-perception in ordinary situations. Even in optimum viewing conditions the eye is visually affected by only a portion of the waves actually emitted by the surface. Correlations can be set up between colour of surface and pattern of light-waves emitted by the surface, but they must be set up on the basis that what enters the eye is a fair sample of what was emitted by the surface. For what enters the eye determines the apparent colour of the surface. There remains the possibility, however, that what enters the eye is an *unsatisfactory sample* of what was emitted by the surface. And, if so, there remains the possibility of deciding that the real colour of the surface is different from the colour a thing looks to have to ordinary observers in ordinary situations. Yet it will be the very correlations between apparent colour of surface in ordinary conditions, and the light-waves that actually affect the eye in these conditions, that will force this revision of our common-sense attributions of certain colours to certain surfaces.

But, by comparison with the naked eye, microscopes do actually cause a more complete sample of the light-waves that leave a certain portion of a surface to be brought to, and to affect, the eye. So it is perfectly possible to favour the evidence of microscopes, rather than the evidence of the naked eye, in deciding what is the true colour of a surface. I have said only that this is 'perfectly possible'. The caution is deliberate. The microscope refracts and scatters rays as well as bringing a larger sample to the eye *per* unit of area. So it distorts as well as reveals. But the way seems open, *if detailed physical considerations should demand it*, to take the microscope as a better guide to the real colour of surface than the naked eye. Further than this a work of philosophy would be unwise to go!

Objection 11. But, even if certain colour-appearances are written off as mere appearances, is it really possible to find one sort of wave-length emitted by all surfaces of the same colour when illuminated by sunlight? In recent years, Smart has emphasized again and again that a huge and idiosyncratic variety of different combinations of wave-length may all present exactly the same colour to the observer. The simple correlations between colour and emitted wave-length that philosophers hopefully assume to exist simply cannot be found. Is this not a bar to an identification of coloured surfaces with surfaces that emit certain wavelengths under sunlight?

Reply. One possibility here is that all these different combinations of wave-lengths may be instances that fall under some general formula. Such a formula would have to be one that did not achieve its generality simply by the use of disjunctions to weld together artificially the diverse cases falling under the formula. Provided that such faking were avoided, the formula could be as complicated as we please. Such a formula could be tested, at least in principle, by making up new combinations of wave-lengths that nevertheless still obeyed the formula. If the surface from which these wave-lengths were emitted exhibited the predicted colour-appearance, the formula would be at least verified. Under these conditions, it might well be conceded that, because of its complexity and idiosyncratic nature, the physical property involved was not one of any great importance in physics. But it would still be a perfectly real, even if ontologically insignificant, physical property. Now I know of no physical considerations about colour that rule out such a possibility.

The Secondary Qualities

A parallel case here is the theory of smell recently put forward in an article in the *Scientific American* ('The Stereochemical Theory of Odor', John E. Amoore *et al.*, Vol. 210, No. 2, Feb., 1964). According to this view, smell is a matter of molecules of different *shape* fitting into differently shaped receptors in the sense-organ. In this way, the receptors sort out different chemical substances from one another. Now molecular shape is an idiosyncratic property. Chemicals of quite different nature may have the same molecular shape, while chemically similar substances may have different molecular shapes. Yet although molecular shape is not a property of which chemistry need take much account (it is 'ontologically insignificant'), it is a perfectly real property, and there would be no objection to identifying smells with the shape of the molecules of the substance that has the smell. Something similar, although more complicated, may be true of colour.

Suppose, however, that no such unifying formula can be found. Suppose it is simply a matter of *irreducibly* diverse causes in the physical surfaces bringing about identical colour-appearances for human observers. I think we would then have to conclude that colour is a pseudo-quality: a sorting and classifying of surfaces by means of the eye that has no proper basis in physical reality. For the surfaces that we classify together as a result of using our eyes could not be classified together on the basis of physical theory. But what objection is there to this possibility?

A physicalist is in fact already committed to saying something of this sort about heat and cold. Phenomenologically they are distinct qualities, no doubt due to the existence of distinct sets of receptors. But the physicist sees no reason to postulate anything except a *single* physical scale of temperature. So the physicalist must admit that temperature-*perception* involves a measure of illusion here. Why can we not say the same about colour?

Of course, the facts about heat and cold, and the putative facts about colour, might be used by an anti-physicalist to argue for the falsity of the identification of these qualities with physical properties of objects. But the general considerations in favour of physicalism are very strong. They outweigh any doubt created by a failure to produce a positive identification, in terms of the physical properties of objects, for every distinct feature exhibited by the secondary qualities.

Here, then, is a sketch of a physicalist account of the secondary qualities. The account is to be contrasted with the physicalist account put forward by J. J. C. Smart in *Philosophy and Scientific Realism*. There he says of the secondary qualities that they are 'powers to cause differential responses' (p. 88). Earlier he had spoken of giving 'an account of colours which depends on behavioural reactions' (p. 81). I reject this Operationalist view of the secondary qualities. We could say that Smart's view is a Behaviouristic Reductionism, while the view put forward in this chapter is a Realistic Reductionism. Realism about the secondary qualities accords with common sense, while Reductionism accords with findings of physical science, thus doing justice to both manifest and scientific image of the world. There is, indeed, an exact parallel here to the dispute between the Behaviourist and the Central-state account of mental states. I think that Smart's view of the secondary qualities is an unfortunate legacy from an earlier operationalist or behaviourist phase in his thinking.

13

MENTAL IMAGES

MENTAL images present an obvious difficulty for a Materialist theory of the mind. They were one of the more conspicuous reefs on which Ryle's argument foundered in *The Concept of Mind*. It will be an especial triumph if we can give a satisfactory analysis of what it is to have a mental image which is compatible with our general theory.

There is an extensive philosophical literature devoted to the subject of perception. But relatively little work has been devoted to mental images. It will therefore be wise to spend the first section of this chapter in preliminary investigations.

I. PRELIMINARY INVESTIGATIONS

It seems clear (*pace* Ryle) that there is the closest resemblance between perceptions (or perhaps we should say sense-impressions) and mental images. A good way to begin an inquiry into the nature of mental images, therefore, is by asking 'What are the marks of distinction between perceptions and mental images?' In Hume's terms, what is the distinction between impressions and ideas? Various suggestions will be examined.

Mental images, of course, are not to be restricted to *visual* images. The 'tune that runs through one's head' is an auditory image, and so it is a mental image. And it is possible to have tactual, somatic, gustatory or olfactory images. It is simply a fact of nature that people's mental images are mainly visual. Visual mental images must be distinguished from after-images, and still more obviously from mirror-images. After-images and mirror-images are simply particular species of visual perception or sense-impression that fail to correspond to physical reality. Some mental images are associated with memory. Unfortunately, however, space does not permit a discussion of memory in this book.

(a) Perceptions have 'greater force and vivacity' than mental images

The following suggestion may be made about the difference between perceptions and mental images. Mental images are dim, blurred and flickering. Perceptions, on the other hand, are clear, precise and steady. This seems to be at least one of the things Hume was referring to when he said that impressions had 'greater force and vivacity' than ideas.

However, this suggested criterion is unsatisfactory, as Hume himself pointed out. In the first place, some mental images can have as much 'force and vivacity' as perceptions. It is true that for most people the mental images associated with conscious thought are extremely woolly. But if, for instance, we consider the images that sometimes pass through our mind before going to sleep, these are much closer in character to perceptions. (Yet we are not tempted to call them illusory perceptions.) We must also recall the remarkable phenomenon that psychologists call 'eidetic images'. These are quite common in children, but can be found even in some adults. 'Eidetic images' are phenomenologically indistinguishable from perceptions. A child that has images of this sort may 'project' them upon physical surfaces and can 'read off' features of the image in just the same way that we can 'read off' features of our visual field. Yet they are not spoken of as illusory perceptions. (Although it is open to somebody to argue that they ought to be so spoken of.)

In the second place, some perceptions can have less 'force and vivacity' than some mental images. Consider the auditory experience of hearing or seeming to hear a faint cry in the distance. It is possible to hear, or seem to hear, a faint cry in the distance quite clearly and distinctly. But it is more probable that such an auditory perception will not be at all clear and distinct. And, if so, will it not have less 'force and vivacity' than some mental images? The same thing may be said of some fleeting visual impressions, or visual perceptions where the conditions of perception are adverse, for instance where there is little light.

So it seems simply a contingent, although no doubt convenient, fact that most perceptions have 'greater force and vivacity' than most mental images.

(b) *A distinction between sounds and auditory images*

Ryle has pointed out (in an unpublished paper) that we say that the shindy in the factory *drowns* my neighbour's humming, but do not say that it drowns the 'tune that is running through my head'. All the shindy can do in the second case is distract my attention, so that the tune no longer runs through my head.

But although Ryle is pointing to a real distinction in the way we speak about sounds and auditory images, there is no distinction here between auditory perceptions and auditory images. For the mental event of hearing, or seeming to hear, a sound is not something that can be drowned by a shindy in a factory either. A shindy can only drown another *noise*, and the hearing of a noise, or seeming to hear a noise, is not a noise. Once again, the shindy can only distract my attention from my auditory experience (by giving me another, more compelling, auditory experience). Ryle has only succeeded in pointing to a distinction between sounds, on the one hand, and auditory perceptions and auditory images, on the other. But we are looking for differences between auditory perceptions and auditory images.

(c) *The reference of perceptions is given by their own nature*

What is a particular mental image an image *of*? Sometimes, it seems, I can decide at will what my image is to be an image of, much as I might arbitrarily decide to make a rough diagram on a piece of paper stand for a ship rather than a house. And even in cases where there is no decision—cases where we just find ourselves treating a mental image as an image of a particular thing—nevertheless it is often intelligible to say that we might have treated that image as the image of something else. But, by contrast, it seems that what a perception is a perception *of* is, as it were, indelibly stamped on it. We are forced to take it as, say, a perception of a bent stick. If it were an impression of anything else, it would necessarily be a different impression. The intentionality of mental images is, as it were, arbitrary by comparison with the intentionality of perceptions.

This suggestion might perhaps claim the authority of Wittgenstein if there was any decision-procedure for settling claims to something so elusive. It is attractive at first hearing, but I think can be shown to be completely unfounded.

Suppose we see certain marks on a piece of paper. They may spontaneously strike us as forming the picture of a cat, or, again, we may take them as a cat only by a certain effort of the imagination. In either case we may be said to 'see the marks as a cat'. Now we can distinguish between our visual perceptions of marks on paper and this further matter of 'seeing the marks as a cat'. Whatever account we give of such cases of 'seeing as' (a discussion of the topic was omitted from Chapter 10 for reasons of space) it seems clear that they are to be distinguished from ordinary visual perceptions, such as perceptions of marks on paper, which such cases of 'seeing as' presuppose. For our temporary purposes here, we may distinguish between the 'content' of our visual perceptions—the 'content' of a perception of a bent stick being *a bent stick*—and what we 'see such contents as' in the sense of 'seeing as' that has just been referred to.

Now, in just the same way, it seems that we can distinguish between the 'content' of mental images and what such content is 'taken as'. For instance, just as we may see, or take, rough lines on paper 'as a cat', so an image that is quite schematic in 'content' may strike us, or be taken by us, as the image of a cat.

Now, when it is said that it is not arbitrary what perceptions are perceptions *of*, but arbitrary what mental images are images *of*, what is being compared is the 'content' of perceptions, on the one hand, and the things we take mental images to be images of, on the other. If, contrariwise, we compared the element of 'seeing as' in our perceptions (when it occurs) with the 'content' of mental images (in the case of visual images such things as shape and colour), the situation would be reversed. If this is correct, there is no essential difference between perceptions and images here.

It is true that there is a contingent difference. Many people use mental images as symbols in the course of their thinking. Images are regularly used in the way that such things as plans or drawings are used, and in such circumstances what they are taken for is more important than their actual 'content'. This is not generally the case with perceptions. With most perceptions their 'content' is the most important thing. But there seems to be no foundation here for any distinction of essence between perceptions and mental images.

(d) *Images are not images of located things*

But it may still be argued that, even if we restrict ourselves to the 'content' of perceptions and images, the former have a feature that the latter lack. If we take visual perceptions, for example, then we can say that they are perceptions of objects located in physical space: in particular, the physical space in front of our body. But if I summon up the image of a unicorn, it is not an image of a thing before me.

However, I am inclined to deny this point about the image of the unicorn. It is surely significant that one's image involves a 'point of view' just as visual perception does. The unicorn is imaged as 'from the side' or 'from the front'. The thing imaged, then, is imaged as located in a vague and imprecise way *vis-à-vis* ourselves. The visual impression, of course, is normally 'set' in a context of visual impressions which, all together, make up the perceiver's 'visual field'. Mental images often lack a context of other images, nor do they have a context of visual impressions, unless we allow that eidetic images 'projected' upon physical surfaces are counter-instances. But it seems that these differences between perceptions and images are contingent.

Notice that to say that the thing imaged is imaged as located is quite different from saying that images are located. The latter does not make sense, but then equally it does not make sense to talk of the location of visual impressions. I would maintain, of course, that it does make sense to say that the *having* of mental images and impressions are located happenings; although whether such statements are or are not true is an issue between Central-state Materialists and their opponents.

(e) *There are behavioural tests for the occurrence of perceptions*

The suggested marks of distinction between perceptions and mental images that have been examined so far have turned out to be valueless, and so our discussion has served only to clear the ground. The suggestions to be examined from now on do, I think, cast some positive light on the distinction between the two.

There are behavioural tests for determining what perceptions a perceiver is having. (Here 'behavioural' is being used to *contrast* with 'linguistic'.) Failure to pass the tests does not necessarily mean that the perception is absent, for the perceiver may be unwilling, or unable for other reasons, to go through that form of behaviour. But passing the tests may show almost conclusively that a certain sort of perception is present. It is these tests that have enabled us to determine to some extent the perceptual abilities of animals.

But what tests are there for determining what mental images, if any, are passing through another person's mind, except linguistic ones? How can one determine what mental images an animal is having? This has inclined some behaviouristically-minded philosophers to say that it is senseless to speak of animals having mental images. If this is true, it sets up a sharp distinction between perceptions and mental images, since everybody (except Descartes) agrees that animals have *perceptions*.

But to say that animals cannot have mental images seems intuitively wrong. And we can conceive of one sort of evidence that would convince beyond doubt anyone not debauched by behaviouristic philosophy that animals have mental images like ourselves. Suppose it were found that certain sorts of brain-processes were empirically necessary and sufficient for the having of mental images in men, and suppose it were also found that the same processes occurred in the brains of animals. We would be convinced that animals have mental images. So there are possible, even if not actual, non-linguistic tests for the occurrence of mental images in animals.

Nevertheless, there does seem to be a real difference between perceptions and mental images here. For there are no strictly *behavioural* tests for the occurrence of mental images, except linguistic ones.

Even this, however, does not draw an absolutely sharp line between images and perceptions. For if we consider the special class of perceptions where there is no accompanying belief or inclination to believe that a situation of the sort that seems to be perceived is occurring, then equally there are no behavioural tests except linguistic ones for discovering the existence of such perceptions in others.

(f) *The temporal priority of perceptions*

It seems to be a mark of perceptions that the having of them always precedes the having of the corresponding mental image. Impressions precede ideas.

But put so simply, this is false. We can have a mental image of a mermaid, without having had a veridical or illusory perception of a mermaid. However, a more cautious formulation can overcome this objection, and can overcome it without appealing to the dubious doctrine of 'simple ideas' adopted to solve the difficulty by Locke and Hume. Given that I am having a mental image of an x, then either I must have had a previous perception of an x, or I must have had perceptions which, if united to give a compound perception, would have yielded a perception of an x.

There does seem to be a real difference between perceptions and mental images here, but it is difficult to estimate its importance. In the first place, it is notoriously difficult to say whether this precedence of perception to mental image is a matter of empcirial fact, or is a logical necessity. In the second place, the difference will not serve to mark off perceptions from images. For suppose I have a perception of an x (my first), followed by an image of an x, and then a perception of an x again. There is nothing in the precedence of perceptions to images to inform us how to classify the last two mental items. All we know is that the first 'experience of x' must be a perception.

(g) *Mental images are centrally aroused*

Perceptions, it may be argued, arise only as a result of the stimulation of the sense-organs or receptors. Now the remote cause of the having of a mental image may be the stimulation of the sense-organs, but what such stimulation gives rise to in the first instance is a perception which only later causes us to have the mental image. We can therefore say that mental images, as opposed to perceptions, are *centrally* aroused. (Which does not entail that they are mentally aroused.)

Unfortunately, however, this simple method of distinguishing perceptions and mental images overlooks the case of *hallucinatory* perceptions. Extensive sensory deprivation, for instance, may cause severe hallucinations in the subject of the experiment, yet the whole point of the experiment is to avoid stimulating the sense-organs as far as possible. Now, although Hume, for example, seems to classify hallucinations as ideas rather than impressions, they must be treated as a species of perception. For, unless I have independent information, when I am hallucinated I take myself to be perceiving. For instance, I claim to see that there is a black cat before me. Even when I realize that I am merely hallucinated, it remains the case that I would believe I was perceiving but for independent beliefs that I hold. It is possible to argue that in all such cases we *mistake* a mental image for a perception. But it is an implausible and uneconomical suggestion. So I think we must allow that hallucinations are a species of illusory perception. Hence some perceptions are centrally aroused, and the proposed mark does not differentiate images and perceptions.

(h) *Perceptions are not dependent on the will*

Berkeley argued that mental images are under the direct control of the will, while perceptions are not. I can summon up or dismiss mental images at will, in the same direct way that I can raise my arm, but I cannot summon up or dismiss perceptions at will except by means of some other voluntary action, such as opening or shutting my eye-lids.

As it stands, this way of making the distinction is unsatisfactory, for if I try to summon up a particular image, or dismiss one that is in my mind, I may not be able to do so.

Nevertheless, even when I lack this direct control over my mental images, it makes sense to speak of so controlling them. Here is a possible field for the direct application of the will. In the terminology adopted in Chapter 7, Section V, the summoning up or dismissing of images are 'immediate acts of the will'. (See also Section XI, 'Mental actions'.) But to speak of having such direct control over our perceptions seems to be some form of nonsense. So there is a real distinction between perceptions and images here.

(i) *The special relation of perceptions to belief*

It is clear that the having of mental images does not involve belief. If having a mental image of a red ball involved the belief that the subject was currently seeing a red ball, the image would not be an image, but a perception. Perception, on the other hand, characteristically involves the acquiring of beliefs.

Of course, it is true that it is possible to have perceptions without having or acquiring any belief that anything corresponds to the content of these perceptions. But such cases characteristically involve what, in Chapter 10, we called 'potential belief'. It is only because we have independent information which assures us that things cannot be as they are perceived to be, that we discount our perceptions.

It does seem, however, that we can conceive of having a perception which neither involves belief nor even 'potential belief'. We can conceive that, despite the complete absence of independent information suggesting deception, we simply fail to believe that reality is as it perceptually appears to be. But now it may be suggested that if we did have such a perception, it would not *be* a perception but a mental image. Mental images, according to this suggestion, are simply *completely belief-free perceptions*.

At one time I thought that this was the solution to the problem of differentiating perceptions from mental images. But a counter-case was pointed out to me by Gregory O'Hair.

Suppose I have a train of completely belief-free perceptions, perceptions that do not even involve 'potential belief'. But suppose that these perceptions are brought into existence by the environment acting upon my sense-organs, and suppose that they correspond more or less to the nature of the environment, in the way that ordinary perceptions do. Despite the absence of belief or 'potential belief', would we not want to say that these mental happenings were perceptions, and *not* mental images? I think O'Hair is right here, and so it seems that mental images are not simply completely belief-free perceptions.

II. THE NATURE OF MENTAL IMAGES

The previous section has yielded tantalizing clues, without giving us any clear account of the distinction between perceptions and mental images. In this section it will be argued that if we take *two* of the putative criteria of distinction already considered, they will be seen to be jointly necessary and sufficient to mark off perceptions from mental images.

In ordinary perception, the environment acts upon the sense-organs, and gives rise to the perception. Even in illusory perception, when a bush is taken to be a bear for example, there is still the *bush* in the environment, acting upon the sense-organs and giving rise to a perception as of a bear. There are, however, exceptional cases of perceptions that are *centrally* aroused. These we call hallucinations.

Again, in ordinary perception, the perception involves the acquiring of beliefs. It is possible to have perception without belief, but it will normally be the case that belief is absent only because we have independent information suggesting that the perception is unreliable. So there will be at least 'potential belief'. It is, however, possible to imagine exceptional cases where there is perception but not even 'potential belief'. We might discount our perceptions for no reason at all.

But suppose we had a perception that was exceptional in both these ways. Suppose we had a perception that neither came into being as a result of the environment acting upon our sense-organs, nor involved any belief or 'potential belief'. I suggest that these 'perceptions' would not be perceptions but would be mental images.

Hallucinations are centrally aroused. But they involve belief or 'potential belief' and so they are still perceptions. There can be perceptions that involve neither belief nor 'potential belief'. But if they come into existence as a result of the environment acting upon our sense-organs, they are still perceptions. But if perceptions are doubly eccentric—if they are both centrally aroused and involve no belief or 'potential belief'—then they are mere mental images.

This account of mental images must now be linked with our reductive analysis of the nature of perception in Chapters 10 and 11. It was argued there that the logically central cases of perception are acquirings of knowledge or information about our environment as a causal result of the action of that environment upon the perceiver. We gave an account of the belief itself in terms of a capacity for selective behaviour towards those features of the environment that are the subject-matter of the belief. Now, if this is so, a 'perception' that involves neither belief, nor the action of the environment on the perceiver, must be a logically secondary case. It must be a mental event that is defined in terms of its resemblance to the central cases, much as a quite broken-down stove in a junk-yard can still be called a 'stove' only because of its resemblance to those central cases of stoves which can be, and are, used to cook food with.

Mental Images

It may be objected that this comparison is not a fair one. In the case of the broken-down stove we have descriptions of the stove independent of its dubious resemblance to stoves that work. It is, for instance, 'that twisted mass of old metal'. But, on our account of mental images, prior to their problematic identification with states of the central nervous system, they can be described *only* in terms of their resemblance to the central cases of perceptions.

We have met this difficulty before. It came up in the case of 'idle' wants and wishes, which can be defined only in terms of their objectives but which involve neither actual nor potential pressure towards fulfilling them on the part of the agent. The case was then suggested of a person who had the capacity, after tasting liquids, to pronounce truly, on no evidence whatsoever, that these solutions (i) contained poison; (ii) but that the poison was in too weak a concentration to do the job of poisoning. All that he would be able to say about the liquid was that it resembled the paradigm cases of poisonous liquid, although lacking an essential attribute of poisonous liquid: power to poison. Introspective awareness of 'idle' wants and wishes was compared to this imaginary case of non-inferential knowledge.

The comparison seems apt in our present case also. Mental images may be said to be 'idle' perceptions. They are events that resemble the acquiring of beliefs about the environment as the result of the action of that environment on the perceiver, although no belief or 'potential belief', nor any action of the environment, is involved. Our introspective awareness of mental images is an awareness of mental occurrences of this sort.

It remains to show that this account of mental images enables us to understand the other points of distinction between perceptions and images which emerged in the course of Section I of this chapter.

We saw that if we interpret 'greater force and vivacity' in a phenomenological way we can set up no distinction between perceptions and mental images. But if we interpret it as measuring the distance of the mental event involved from events that involve *belief*, then we can give it a good sense. Mental images lack force and vivacity in the sense that, of all perceptual events, they are the most completely divorced from belief.

It is clear why there are behavioural tests for ordinary perceptions but none for mental images, except linguistic ones. There are behavioural tests for beliefs, but none for mental events that resemble the acquiring of beliefs although no beliefs are acquired. It should follow, as is indeed the case, that there will be special difficulties in teaching people to speak about their mental images.

The priority of perceptions to mental images is also easily explained. The concept of a mental image, we have seen, can only be elucidated in terms of the resemblance that a mental image has to a fully-blown perception that involves belief. The essential thing about a mental image is its resemblance to fully-blown perceptions. The concept of perception is therefore logically prior to the concept of mental image, that is to say, we can have the latter concept only if we have the former concept, although we could have had the concept of perception without having the concept of a mental image.

This does not mean to say that we might not discover evidence to indicate that, for example, persons blind from birth but later made to see *had* visual images before they gained their sight. But if they lacked the notion of 'seeing' until they gained their sight, they could not be *aware* of the visual images because the concept of visual image can only be elucidated by reference to the concept of seeing. If, however, we allow that a man blind from birth can understand what sight is (perhaps by comparison and contrast with the other forms of sense perception), then we could allow that he could become *aware* that he was having visual images.

The fact that it makes no sense to speak of perceptions being under the direct or immediate control of the will, but that it does make sense to say this of mental images, is linked both with the criterion of distinction between perceptions and images involving belief, and with that involving causation. To the extent that perceptions involve belief it is impossible that they should be under the direct control of the will, because acquirings or losings of beliefs are not 'immediate acts of the will'. The causal criterion is involved in the following way. If the mental event is caused from without, as perceptions characteristically are, then it is not caused by something in the mind, and so, *a fortiori*, does not spring from the will.

These points do not show that the summoning up or dismissing of an image is an 'immediate act of the will', and I think it is just an empirical fact that images are regularly under the direct control of the will. But since images do not involve either belief, or external causation through stimulation of the sense-organs, the two features of perception that would certainly exclude direct control by the will are removed. It becomes *possible* that images are under the direct control of the will.

It seems, then, that an account of mental images can be worked out which is compatible with our analysis of perception and our general formula for mental occurrences. As compared with perception, relatively little philosophical work has been undertaken on mental images, after the pioneering efforts of the British Empiricists. But I think enough has been said here to show that mental images pose no insuperable problem for an account of mental concepts which will be compatible with (without entailing) a purely materialist theory of man.

III. DREAMS

For lack of anywhere else to place it, it will be convenient to end this chapter with a section on dreaming. If what has been said about perception has been along the right lines, the question of the nature of dreams can be very briefly dealt with.

Like mental images, dreams are idiosyncratic phenomena. One man's descriptions of his dreams may correspond to nothing in another man's experience, although he claims to dream too. However, for most people the core of dreaming seems to be the having of perceptual experiences. These perceptual experiences involve belief. During the dream, we take ourselves to be perceiving happenings in the world. This belief is entirely unself-conscious, it is a taking-for-granted and involves no anxious affirmation that we are really perceiving. Such a level of self-consciousness would be psychologically improbable in dreams, where the level of the mental life is of a very primitive sort. But the fact that unself-conscious belief is involved is shown by the fact that on waking we often say or think 'It was only a dream'. The force of the 'only' here is that it is not what we took it to be while the dream was going on: a perception of real happenings. The same conclusion is enforced by considering the reports of young children and primitive peoples. What we call their reports of dreams they treat as memories of real happenings. It is only very occasionally, usually when beginning to wake up, that we may think to our-selves *during the dream* that our current experiences are 'just a dream'. But this is a very sophisticated mental performance, com-parable to discounting a sensory illusion as a mere illusion while undergoing the illusion.

Now if the core of dreaming (for most people) is perceptual experience involving belief then it seems that we can say that such dreaming is simply *total hallucination occurring during sleep*. This fits simply into our account of perception. During sleep, certain mental processes occur. These are describable in the first place as illusory perceptions of things of a certain sort. These illusory perceptions can be further elucidated as the acquirings of various false beliefs about the nature of our current situation and en-vironment. These acquirings of false beliefs can be still further analysed as the occurrence in us of certain events which, in a real environment of that sort, would give us the capacity to discrimi-nate in a systematic way the various features of that environment. For the particular content of these mental events we have to rely on our very fallible memory that we have of them on waking. But psychological and physiological research is now learning more of the conditions of dreaming, and we can imagine finding out what a man is dreaming of while he is still asleep, simply by knowing what is occurring in his brain.

Other things occur in dreams: dream-thoughts, dream-emotions, and so on. I think that these can simply be treated as thoughts or emotions occurring during sleep, very often confused thoughts or emotions evoked by totally false beliefs about our current situation, but genuine thoughts and emotions none the less. In general, there is no call to treat dream-states as anything but ordinary mental events, states or processes which occur in the mind during sleep, and are sometimes remembered.

But before leaving the subject of dreams I will mention a sug-gestion put to me by Graham Nerlich. Nerlich starts from the position that we have also accepted: that introspective error about our current mental states is perfectly conceivable. If such error can occur, then we can think that we are in a certain mental state but be wrong. Now dream-states, as they yield themselves to memory, are certainly very strange in nature. Nerlich suggests that in dreams we only *think* we are having certain perceptions. On the analysis of perception given in this book this implies that we only *think* we are acquiring certain beliefs about the current state of the world. Nerlich does not deny that mental events occur in dreams, but he suggests that these events are not the mental events they seem to be, but are acquirings of false beliefs that such mental events are occurring. (A similar account to his account of dream-perceptions might be given of dream-thoughts and dream-emotions.)

Now there is no doubt that if we take the denial that introspection is incorrigible seriously, we must admit the logical possibility of Nerlich's suggestion being true. How, then, do we decide whether it is in fact true or not? More careful remembering of our dreams, and scrutiny of those memories, is clearly insufficient. The introspective data are simply not precise enough. Decision on the question, I think, would have to be based on some high-level psychological or neurophysiological theory. In the present state of these subjects, then, the question is purely speculative.

But whether Nerlich's suggestion is correct or not, dreams seem to pose no special problems for our account of the mental concepts.

14

BODILY SENSATIONS

LIKE mental images, bodily sensations are thought of by many philosophers to present a quite especial difficulty for a Materialist theory of mind. It will be argued in this chapter that such sensations are nothing but bodily and tactual perceptions, using the word 'perception' in the neutral sense that is compatible with failure to correspond to physical reality. If this thesis is correct, we can then appeal to our account of perception in terms of the acquiring of states of the person giving a capacity for certain sorts of (discriminative) behaviour. It will be a matter of capacities for discriminative behaviour towards one's own body. An account of bodily sensations will then have been given which is compatible with, although it does not entail, a purely Materialist account of man.

The account of bodily sensations given in this chapter is much the same as that put forward in my monograph *Bodily Sensations* (Routledge & Kegan Paul, 1962). In that work, however, I still half-heartedly accepted the view that first person reports of current mental states are incorrigible, a view which is repudiated in this book. Nor had I arrived at the view of the secondary qualities put forward in Chapter 12, a view which seems to cast light on certain problems connected with bodily sensations.

I. TACTUAL AND BODILY PERCEPTION

It will be well to begin by a brief discussion of the nature of touch and bodily perception.

By touch we gain information about the current state of our material environment and our body; by bodily perception we gain information about the current state of one particular material object: our own body. In both cases the English language uses the word 'feel'. We feel, that is to say, we perceive by touch, the pressure of the bandage on our leg, or the roughness of the material over which our fingers move. We feel, that is to say, we perceive by bodily sense, that our cheeks are hot, our limbs moving or our heart pounding. But besides the difference in the objects on to which the two sorts of perception are directed, there is a difference in the way in which the word 'feel' is used in each case. If we feel something by touch common sense can ask and answer the question 'With what do we feel this object?' The answer will be 'With the fingers' or 'With the tongue' or something of that sort. But suppose we ask 'With what do I feel that my arms are moving, or that my cheeks are hot?' The question can only be answered by a physiologist. This distinguishes touch and bodily perception.

Bodily perception has the peculiarity, remarked earlier in this book, which marks it off from all other forms of sense-perception: its object is private to each perceiver. Each of us has a way of perceiving what is going on in our own body that is denied to everybody else. I can become aware of some of the things that are currently going on in my own body without the aid of touch, sight, hearing, taste or smell. I have no such perceptual power with respect to another person's body. This privacy is purely empirical. If my nervous system were suitably connected with other bodies, and theirs with mine, the privacy would vanish. I have already suggested that in this respect bodily perception can serve as an excellent model by which to grasp the nature of introspection.

II. BODILY SENSATIONS AND BODILY FEELINGS

If asked what should be included among bodily sensations we might instance such things as sensations of pressure, warmth and movement, together with pains, itches, tickles and tingles. These seem to be different from such things as feeling tired, feeling fresh, feeling hungry and so on, which may be called 'bodily feelings'. 'Bodily feeling' is introduced as a term of art, simply because a distinction seems called for but no ordinary word or phrase is available to mark the distinction. Bodily sensations and 'bodily feelings' have close resemblances, and, as we shall see shortly, there seem to be intermediate cases. But there does seem to be a distinction between the two sorts of phenomena. Thus, it would not be natural to say that feeling faint *is* a sensation, even although it characteristically involves the having of sensations. Bodily feelings may involve sensations, but do not seem to be sensations.

The question then arises by what marks can we distinguish bodily sensations and bodily feelings? I think the answer is that bodily sensations are, but bodily feelings are not, *located* in particular parts of the body. We have sensations of pressure in the small of the back, sensations of warmth in the ears, sensations of motion at the joints. It is even more obvious that pains, itches, tickles, tingles and so on, are located in particular parts of the body. But feelings of hunger or freshness cannot be located in the same way. Hunger-pangs can be located, but not feelings of hunger.

However, there are phenomena that challenge this attractively simple criterion. In the first place, we do speak of feeling tired in the legs, or arms, or back. Perhaps this is not very important, because there is no question of our locating the tiredness in the precise way that bodily sensations can be located in the body. A more serious difficulty is that we do speak of *sensations* of giddiness and dizziness, yet we do not give them a location in our body. (Although 'dizzy in the head' may be a barely permissible idiom.) We shall see, however, that these two are intermediate cases, lying between the ordinary bodily sensations, on the one hand, and 'bodily feelings', on the other. For the present I shall set aside the question of the nature of bodily feelings. An account of their nature will be put forward in the last section of the chapter.

III. 'TRANSITIVE' BODILY SENSATIONS

But now to distinguish between two sorts of bodily sensation. Heat is not the same thing as a sensation of heat. My hand can be unusually hot, yet there be no sensation of heat in my hand. Contrariwise, I can have a sensation of great heat in my hand, although my hand is not unusually hot. The same thing can be said about pressure and motion. An object can be pressing on my body, yet there be no sensation of pressure. Contrariwise, I can have a sensation of pressure on a certain part of my body, although there is in fact no unusual pressure on that part of my body, or perhaps on any part of my body.

But in the case of pains, itches, tickles and tingles, it seems that no similar distinction can be made. We can distinguish between heat and sensations of heat, but not between pains and sensations of pain, or tingles and sensations of tingling. For a pain is a sensation of pain, and a tingle is a sensation of tingling.

Sensations of the first sort may be called 'transitive' bodily sensations, and sensations of the second sort 'intransitive' bodily sensations. The distinction is a preliminary one only, for it will shortly be argued that the 'intransitive' sensations do have a concealed transitivity. But it is a convenient one, because the 'transitive' sensations can be quickly and simply dealt with, and will then serve as a model for a similar, but more complex, treatment of the 'intransitive' sensations.

A simple account of the nature of the 'transitive' sensations will now be put forward. To have a sensation of heat in the hand is simply *to feel that our hand is hot*: a bodily perception that may or may not correspond to physical reality. To have a sensation of pressure in the back is simply *to feel that something is pressing into our back*: a tactual perception that may or may not correspond to physical reality. To have a sensation of our knee bending is simply *to feel that our knee is bending*, a bodily perception that may or may not correspond to physical reality.

If the 'transitive' bodily sensations are simply bodily and tactual perceptions, then we can give the same account of them as other perceptions. We can analyse the having of such sensations in terms of the acquiring of beliefs or of mental events that resemble the acquiring of beliefs. We can go on to give an account of acquiring such beliefs as the acquiring of capacities for behaviour of a 'discriminating' sort. In this case, it will be our own body and objects in contact with it which we become capable of behaving towards in this systematically discriminating way. For instance, we may become capable of discriminating between portions of our body that are at an unusually high temperature, and portions that are not. A manifestation of the capacity might be the removal of the affected portions from a source of heat.

The location of such sensations in the body is therefore an *intentional* location. To say that I have a sensation of pressure in the small of the back is to say that physical pressure *seems* to be occurring there. The situation is the same as with the visual field, where 'visual field' means the totality of my visual impressions at any one time. In my visual field, the mirror-image is behind the surface of the glass. That is to say, there *looks* to be something behind the surface of the glass which we know is in fact not there. This 'intentional' interpretation of the location of the 'transitive' sensations permits a very simple treatment of the problem of 'phantom limbs', and (transitive) sensations in these 'limbs'. If, after amputation, I have a 'phantom arm', and one day I have a sensation of heat in this 'arm', we can give the following account of the situation: it still feels to me that I have an arm, and, on a certain occasion, it feels to me that the hand of this arm has become unusually hot. I really do have a certain perception, but it is a perception to which nothing in the physical world corresponds. This is hallucinatory bodily perception, accompanied by the knowledge that the perception is hallucinatory. A mirror-image is a visual phantom, a 'phantom limb' is a bodily phantom.

IV. PROBLEMS ABOUT 'INTRANSITIVE' SENSATIONS

The question now arises whether we can give the same simple account of the 'intransitive' sensations: itches, tickles, pain, tingles and so on. If we can, we have reduced all bodily sensations to perceptions of bodily state, perceptions that may or may not correspond to the actual physical state of the body. There will then be no *special* problem of bodily sensation. But there are two important objections to taking such a view of the 'intransitive' sensations. In this section the objections will be stated; in subsequent sections it will be argued that the objections can be overcome.

In the first place, and less seriously, it is part of the nature of most of the 'intransitive' sensations that they involve characteristic *reactions* on the part of the person who has them. The word 'reaction' is not intended to be taken behaviouristically: it may involve no more than a change of mental state that is not translated into action. (Nor need it even be a change of mental state that we are *conscious* of.) Nor is it implied that, even in the case of those 'intransitive' sensations that characterically involve reactions, they do so in every instance. Some very mild pains, for instance, seem to involve no reaction at all. It is only implied that the *typical* or *paradigm* cases of such sensations do involve reactions, whether behavioural or purely mental.

Thus, it is of the essence of pains that in typical cases we do not like having them, although we are sometimes prepared to put up with them for the sake of what are judged greater goods. It is of the essence of erotic sensations that in typical cases they are pleasurable. An itching spot is a spot we want to scratch in order to stop the itching. A ticklish spot is one we want to rub. Hunger-pangs involve the desire to eat. Not all 'intransitive' bodily sensations involve such reactions: a case in point being tingles. But in most cases of 'intransitive' sensations such reactions are involved.

The question now arises how a mere perception could involve reactions in this way. Perceptions, we have seen, are essentially passive. They involve the acquiring of *capacities* for discriminative action, but involve no actual *impulse* towards discriminative action, or any other sort of action. How can those 'intransitive' sensations that involve reactions be a species of perception?

This difficulty, as we shall see, is relatively easy to answer. The second difficulty now to be discussed will demand rather more heroic measures. In the case of all perceptions, bodily or otherwise, we can distinguish between sensory appearances and physical reality. We distinguish between felt pressure and actual physical pressure, felt motion of the limbs and actual motion of the limbs. The felt pressure and felt motion are pressure-perceptions and kinaesthetic perceptions, which can correspond or fail to correspond to physical reality. Now if we want to treat sensations such as pain as perceptions we seem to be defeated by their 'intransitivity'. For we cannot distinguish between felt pain and actual pain, or felt itch and actual itch. A pain or an itch is a felt pain or felt itch, and an unfelt pain or itch is nothing. So the 'intransitive' sensations seem to lack an essential mark of perceptions.

It may be thought that here I am retracting what was said in Chapter 6 about the possibility of being unconscious of, or being in error about, any mental state whatever, including having a pain or an itch. But this is not so. A 'feeling of pressure', I take it, is simply a *sensation* of pressure. Now we can have a sensation of pressure and be perfectly unaware of having it: it will simply be an unconscious tactual or bodily perception of pressure. So there can be felt pressure we are unaware of feeling. In the same way, a 'feeling of pain' is simply a *sensation* of pain. Now we can have a sensation of pain and be perfectly unaware of having it. So there can be a feeling of pain that we are unaware of feeling: unconscious pain. But a feeling of pain, whether conscious or unconscious, still seems to defy the attempt to treat it as a perception in a way that a feeling of pressure does not. A feeling of pressure, conscious or unconscious, 'points' to physical pressure. But what does a feeling of pain 'point' to?

In face of these two objections, how can it be maintained that 'intransitive' sensations, such as pain, are simply bodily perceptions?

V. 'INTRANSITIVE' SENSATIONS AND REACTIONS

We must now show that the fact that the 'intransitive' bodily sensations are characteristically linked with particular reactions is no bar to considering them as species of bodily perception. The concepts of such bodily sensations are *portmanteau*-concepts, involving both what may be called a properly sensational component, which is a bodily perception, and a reaction of the mind to that perception. The bodily perception and the reaction are welded together by *causality*: the bodily perception characteristically *evokes* the reaction. It is a case of one mental event bringing about another mental event, in this case, a perception bringing about an affection. The fact that the perception invariably, or almost invariably, evokes the reaction, accounts for the fact that our ordinary concepts involve the concept of the whole causal sequence. Thus, in the case of pain, what is involved is a perception, which may or may not be veridical, of a happening in a certain part of the body (what sort of happening will be discussed in the next section). The perception at once evokes a peremptory desire for the perception to cease. In the case of pain 'in' an amputated leg, the peremptory desire is evoked by a perception that fails to correspond to reality.

This analysis of bodily sensations such as pain as 'bodily perceptions evoking reactions' fits in very well with a curious phenomenon that has attracted attention from psychologists and philosophers in recent years. Intractable pain can sometimes be removed by severing connections between the prefrontal lobes and the rest of the brain. But patients on whom this operation has been performed sometimes give very curious reports. They say that the pain is still there, but it does not worry them any more. It seems as if they are saying that they have a pain which is giving them no pain! This phenomenon can be very simply interpreted on the view that sensations of pain are 'bodily perceptions evoking reactions'. The operation has abolished the reaction without abolishing the perception. When the patient reports that the pain is still there, he is reporting that the same sort of thing feels to be going on in the same part of his body, but that this perception now gives him no concern.

A similar analysis can be applied to the case of exceedingly mild pains, itches and tickles. In these cases, also, we have the sensation without it evoking any reaction. That is to say, we have a perception of a certain sort of happening in our body, but although perceptions of the same sort are sufficient to evoke the characteristic reactions, this particular perception is insufficient.

It is very important to notice that the characteristic reactions evoked by these perceptions are, as a matter of empirical fact, pretty much unaffected by our knowledge of the correspondence or lack of correspondence of the perception to physical reality. If a man's leg has been amputated, the pain in the 'phantom limb' will cause him exactly the same distress as if it were a real leg. He has a non-veridical perception, unaccompanied by false belief, of bodily happenings in the place where the leg was, but this perception still evokes the mental reaction.

I will omit any discussion of the particular nature of the reactions characteristically evoked by different sorts of 'intransitive' sensations. Interested readers may consult *Bodily Sensations*.

VI. 'INTRANSITIVE' SENSATIONS AS BODILY PERCEPTIONS

But, as we have seen, the main difficulty in construing 'intransitive' sensations as bodily and tactual perceptions is the absence of any distinction between felt pain and real pain, felt itch and real itch, felt tickle and real tickle, to correspond to the distinction between feeling hot and being actually hot, or feeling that one's limbs are moving and the actual motion of the limbs. Perceptions correspond, or fail to correspond, to physical reality. How does a pain or a tickle correspond, or fail to correspond, to physical reality?

My answer is that, although there is no distinction between felt pain and real pain, or felt tickle and real tickle, nevertheless statements like 'I have a pain in my hand' may be translated without loss of meaning in such a way as to show that the statement as a whole is a perceptual statement. 'I have a pain in my hand' may be rendered somewhat as follows: 'It feels to me that a certain sort of disturbance is occurring in my hand, a perception that evokes in me the peremptory desire that the perception should cease.'

What is meant by 'a certain sort of disturbance' here? If we simply consult our *experience* of physical pain, its nature cannot be further specified. The situation here, I believe, is the same as our experience of colour and the other secondary qualities. In Chapter 12 it was argued that, while we recognize by sight that all red things have something in common, sight does not inform us what that common property is. In the same way, we recognize by bodily perception that the class of felt disturbances called 'bodily pains' all have something in common. But bodily perception does not inform us what that common feature is. All we can do by way of describing redness is to say what objects are, as a matter of fact, red. In the same way, all we can do by way of describing the bodily disturbance is to say that, *on the whole*, bodily perception of this disturbance happens to evoke a greater desire that the perception should cease than any other human perception.

We recognize by sight, of course, that red things have certain resemblances to and differences from things with other properties: in particular, the other colours. In the same way, we can recognize by bodily perception that the bodily disturbances associated with pain have certain resemblances to, and differences from, the disturbances involved in the other bodily sensations. In the case of the colours, however, we argued that vision gives us no information as to the nature of these recognized resemblances and differences. We may make the same claim about the bodily sensations. Again, we recognize by sight that red things differ among themselves in respect of redness. There are different shades of red. In the same way, certain pains resemble each other and differ from other pains. We recognize different sorts of pain. In the case of colours, however, we need not concede that vision informs us of the nature of the differences involved in being different shades of the same colour. In the same way, we need not concede that bodily perceptions inform us of the nature of the difference of bodily disturbance involved in the different sorts of pain. We are simply informed that the disturbances do differ in some respect.

In defence of this common treatment of the secondary qualities and the bodily sensations, it may be noticed that philosophers have frequently linked pain, itches, tickles, etc., with the secondary qualities proper. It seems plausible, therefore, to give the same sort of account of both.

If it is correct to say that pains (and other bodily sensations) involve a perception of bodily disturbance, but if no perception of the concrete nature of this disturbance is involved, then the physicalist can go on to make a contingent identification of the disturbances with purely physical disturbances in the body. The bodily disturbance perceived in the case of pain will simply be stimulation of the pain-receptors.

But notice that 'I have a pain in my hand' is to be rendered as '*It feels to me* that a certain sort of disturbance is occurring in my hand . . .'. The force of the word 'feels' in this formula is no more and no less than the force of the word 'feels' in 'My hand feels hot', where the latter sentence is so used that it neither asserts nor excludes my hand being hot in physical reality. But, in the case of the pain, what feels to me to be going on in my hand is not 'that my hand is hot' but 'that there is a certain sort of disturbance in my hand'. Now, while there is no distinction between felt pain and physical pain, there is a distinction between *feeling* that there is a certain sort of disturbance in the hand, and there actually *being* such a disturbance. Normally, of course, the place where there feels to be such a disturbance is a place where there actually *is* such a disturbance, but in unusual cases, such as that of the 'phantom limb', or cases of 'referred pain', there feels to be disturbance in a place where there is no such disturbance.

The problem of the 'location' of physical pains is therefore solved in exactly the same way as that of the location of 'transitive' sensations, such as sensations of pressure. In the case of pressure, the 'location' is an *intentional* location. There feels to be (physical) pressure at that spot, whether or not there is actual pressure there.

In the case of pain in the hand, the 'location' of the pain is equally an intentional location. There feels to be a disturbance of a certain sort in the hand, whether or not there is actually such a disturbance in the hand.

This account of the location of pain enables us to resolve a troublesome dilemma. Consider the following two statements: 'The pain is in my hand' and 'The pain is in my mind'. Ordinary usage makes us want to assent to the first, while a moment's philosophical reflection makes us want to assent to the second. Yet they seem to be in conflict with each other. But once we see that the location of the pain in the hand is an intentional location, that is, that it is simply the place where a disturbance feels to be, but need not actually be, it is clear that the two statements are perfectly compatible.

It is possible to have a very mild pain which does not evoke the pain-reaction. Equally, it is possible to have a very mild itch which does not evoke the itch-reaction. And it is possible to distinguish having a mild pain of this sort from having a mild itch of this sort. The following account of this situation may be given. In the case of the mild pain, we recognize that the disturbance that feels to be going on is the same sort of disturbance as that which, in typical cases, evokes the pain-reaction, although here it is evoking no reaction. In the case of the mild itch, we recognize that the disturbance that feels to be going on is that different sort of disturbance which, in typical cases, evokes the itch-reaction (desire to scratch, etc.), although here it is evoking no reaction. But in neither case are we directly aware of the intrinsic natures of the two sorts of disturbance. We are aware only that they are different. It will be seen that this account of very mild pains and itches is similar to the account already given of 'idle' wants and wishes, and 'idle' perceptions (mental images). In the two latter cases, introspective awareness of such mental happenings was compared to an imaginary non-inferential awareness that a certain liquid contained poison, but in insufficient quantity to poison. The comparison is once again apt in the case of introspective awareness of the having of mild pains and itches.

I will not discuss most other sorts of 'intransitive' sensation here, but a word is needed about the special cases of dizziness and giddiness. To feel *giddy* involves feeling that one is on the verge of falling, and this is a 'bodily feeling', not a bodily sensation. But there is also a bodily sensation involved. To feel giddy involves feeling that one's body and its environment are moving in relation to each other in that peculiar and idiosyncratic spatial relation that may be called the 'round-and-round' relation. Such a physical relation may in fact hold between the body and its environment, or it may not. It is the ('intentional') involvement of the *whole* body in this relation that makes it impossible to give giddiness a bodily 'location'.

To feel *dizzy* characteristically involves feeling in some degree faint, which is a 'bodily feeling'. It also characteristically involves some disturbance of visual perception. But in so far as it is an 'intransitive' bodily sensation, it involves feeling as if our *head* were moving in a peculiar and idiosyncratic way in relation to the rest of our body. Roughly, the head feels to move round and round in relation to the body. (In giddiness the whole body feels to move round and round.) This bodily perception is something that may correspond or fail to correspond to the actual physical motion of the head. It is because this sensation involves an apparent motion of the head that the phrase 'dizzy in the head' is a possible way of speaking. At the same time, because the head must be ('intentionally') involved for the sensation to be dizziness at all, the phrase is pleonastic. And so, while the phrase does not sound to be nonsense, it does sound forced.

VII. INTENSITY OF SENSATIONS AND INTENSITY OF REACTION

If we consider such bodily sensations as sensations of pressure, it is clear that we can distinguish between the felt degree of pressure (which conceivably may not correspond to the actual degree of pressure being exerted on the flesh), and any reaction that we may have to this felt pressure. Or if we consider sensations of heat, we can distinguish between the felt degree of heat, and the reaction we may have to such sensations. It is true that to say something feels 'very hot' is often not merely to say that the felt degree of heat is greater than normal, but also to indicate a further effect it is having on us, viz. causing us discomfort or pain. But felt degree of heat, on the one hand, and reaction to the thermal perception, on the other, are distinguishable. It is quite imaginable, at least, that something should feel to us to be exactly as hot as it felt to be on a previous occasion, but that on that previous occasion the feeling evoked distress, although it does not evoke distress now.

Turning now to the 'intransitive' sensations, we certainly describe tingles as more or less violent. What do we mean by this? We seem to be referring to the intensity of the disturbance in the flesh felt to be occurring, rather than any reaction to the felt disturbance. It is true that very violent tingling is likely to be unpleasant. But, over a wide range of lesser intensities, change in intensity seems to involve no necessary change in reaction. It seems correct to say, therefore, that the intensity is a felt intensity of disturbance, and not an intensity of reactions.

Now pain, itches and tickles normally involve both a bodily perception of a certain sort of disturbance in the body, and, evoked by the perception, a more or less peremptory desire for the perception to cease. There seems to be a possibility here, too, of distinguishing between felt intensity of the disturbance, and intensity of reaction. Now if these two intensities are distinct, then it is at least logically possible that the two intensities might vary independently, and that the sufferer might recognize the occurrence of such independent variations.

Should we *in fact* say we are aware of two intensities in the case of pain, itch and tickle: felt intensity of disturbance and intensity of reaction? To answer the question we can at present appeal only to the evidence of introspection, which, so far from being an indubitable faculty, leaves us here in the greatest doubt. We shall have to wait until much more is known about the neurophysiology of bodily sensation before we can have much chance of *settling* the issue. In the meantime, however, I will take a chance, and say that introspection does appear to distinguish between the two sorts of intensity in these cases.

Consider, in particular, the case of pain. It seems clear that, granted we are aware of two sorts of intensity, they normally vary together. If the intensity of the disturbance is felt to be greater, then the intensity of the reaction increases. But cases where this concomitant variation does not occur can be conceived and seem intuitively to be empirically possible. Consider the leucotomy patients who, after the operation, say that they still have the pain, but also say that they are quite unworried by it. Suppose that, on certain occasions, they reported both that the pain had increased, and that their reaction to it was quite unchanged. It would be natural then to say that they had perceived (veridically or non-veridically) that the disturbance had increased in intensity, but that the intensity of their reaction to the perception was unchanged. The opposite case, that of variation in intensity of reaction without variation in felt intensity of physical disturbance, actually seems to occur sometimes in ordinary life. For can we not sometimes notice that, of two pains, one affected us more than the other—*hurt* us more—although, *qua* sensation, there seemed to be no difference between them?

If we are only vaguely aware of two distinct dimensions of intensity in the case of pain and other bodily sensations, the reason for this vagueness is simply explained. It lies in the difficulty of finding any reliable public criteria for the intensity of the disturbance, which means in its turn that teaching procedures designed to improve our discriminations of such intensities are difficult to devise. For such intensity is presumably correlated with the degree of disturbance of the receptors in a certain area, but this disturbance is not well correlated with the amount of physical damage in the area, as ascertained by use of the other senses. Quite extensive physical damage may hurt less than apparently quite minor damage. Now without public checks on the success or failure of our perceptual discriminations, it is an empirical fact that they are not likely to become very reliable. In this case, they are so unreliable that there can even be doubt if these bodily perceptions do involve this dimension of awareness.

VIII. BODILY FEELINGS

There is much more that could be said about bodily sensations, but space does not permit. One important topic here omitted is the question of different sorts of pain. It may plausibly be contended that different sorts of pain involve perception of what are, phenomenologically speaking, irreducibly diverse sorts of happening at the 'place of the pain'. But if our account of the secondary qualities in Chapter 12 is along the right lines, the irreducibility of the pain-qualities need only be epistemological. We can go on to identify contingently the felt disturbances with purely physical happenings in the body. The pain itself will be the *perception* of these disturbances (a perception that may be non-veridical), and will be contingently identified, not with a physical happening at the 'place of the pain', but with an event in the central nervous system.

We will finish this chapter by briefly discussing what were earlier called 'bodily feelings': feeling tired, feeling fresh, feeling faint, feeling sick, feeling hungry and so on.

In the first place, a distinction should be drawn between the first four examples in the list just given, and such states as feeling hungry and thirsty. It will be argued that, like bodily sensations, the first four are perceptions of current bodily state. But this account will not fit feelings of hunger and thirst. Indeed, it may be best to exclude the latter two from the class of what we have arbitrarily called 'bodily feelings'.

The essential thing about feeling hungry is having the desire to eat, the essential thing about feeling thirsty is having the desire to drink. If any *perceptions* of bodily state are involved they are relatively incidental. Feeling hungry or thirsty is more like feeling angry than feeling faint. Feeling *tired* is perhaps an intermediate case. If, while I am running, my legs feel tired then this seems to involve a desire (not necessarily my *dominant* desire) to stop having to move my legs in this way. But it also seems to involve a perception of the current state of my legs. But feeling fresh, faint or sick do not seem to be desires for anything at all, even if they are mental states that very naturally evoke certain desires. It seems plausible, then, to treat them as bodily perceptions.

If these 'bodily feelings' are bodily perceptions, then *being* tired, fresh, faint or sick, as opposed to *feeling* tired, fresh, faint or sick, must be objective physical states of the body. This is in fact the case. After a period of bodily exertion, the body, or a portion of the body, may come to be in a state where it is increasingly difficult to sustain that exertion. This is being (physically) tired. The body may be in a state which normally precedes fainting, or being sick. This is being faint, or being unwell.

Again, if bodily feelings are bodily perceptions, it must be possible to feel tired, but not be tired, feel faint yet not be in the bodily state that precedes fainting, feel sick yet not be in the bodily state that precedes being sick. Equally, it must be possible to be tired without feeling tired, etc. And in fact we do allow of such possibilities.

If bodily feelings are perceptions of bodily state, a question arises whether they are perceptions that involve inference, or ones that do not. Are they like hearing a coach, or like hearing a sound? The traditional view among the few psychologists and philosophers who have discussed the question (mostly in the nineteenth or early twentieth century) was that these perceptions involve an inference from bodily *sensations*. The individual finds by experience that certain patterns of bodily sensations accompany or precede certain bodily states or happenings. Certain patterns of sensations accompany certain sustained use of the limbs, or bodily conditions where energy is high, or precede fainting or being sick. In the nineteenth century, philosophers and psychologists talked of *coenesthesis*, a perception of general bodily condition on the basis of obscure patterns of sensations. The fact noted in Section II of this chapter that it makes no sense to give a bodily location to bodily feelings can then be explained as the impossibility of giving a definite location to a whole pattern of sensations spread throughout the body.

The alternative is to compare these bodily perceptions to those immediate perceptions which involve no inference, such as the hearing of sounds. We simply have a direct (non-inferential) awareness (which, however, need not be a veridical awareness) that we are in a certain bodily state. In the case of feeling sick, for instance, we perceive that we are in that bodily state which regularly precedes actually being sick. The fact that it makes no sense to give a bodily location to bodily feelings has then to be explained by saying that the bodily perception involves no perception of the location of this state.

Modern philosophers, assuming that they are prepared to regard bodily feelings as a species of bodily perception at all, might be expected to object to the first or inferential view for two reasons. In the first place, it seems extremely difficult to give any precise account of the bodily sensations that are alleged to be the basis of the inference in each particular case. In the second place, there seems to be nothing like an inference that goes on. We simply find ourselves feeling sick or tired or fresh.

But if our analysis of perception has been correct, these two objections are clearly not conclusive. It is true that the first argument would be pretty well conclusive if, as is usually assumed, to have a sensation is to be aware of having it. But since our argument has allowed, has indeed asserted, the existence of sensations that one is unaware, or only marginally aware, of having, there can be no serious objection to saying that the inference is based on sensations of which we are only obscurely aware. And since we have allowed the notion of automatic and unconscious inference, it is equally no serious objection that we are unaware of the drawing of the inference.

Nevertheless, there are grounds for uneasiness. It is certainly suspicious that it is so difficult to describe the 'obscure patterns of sensation' on which the inference is based. In spite of this difficulty, however, I think we should accept the 'inferential' view, because the alternative seems even less plausible. The alternative, non-inferential, account makes the perceptions involved far too simple and 'transparent'. In many cases, we can only characterize the bodily state perceived by reference to future bodily states or happenings, future vomiting, for example. In all other non-inferential perceptions the states of affairs perceived can be characterized by reference to *current* happenings. Again, when we feel tired, sick or faint, there do seem to be current sensations involved, even if they are difficult to characterize and isolate. When one is about to be sick, for instance, there are characteristic sensations in the stomach and mouth. I am inclined, therefore, to take the 'inferential' view of the perceptions involved in 'bodily feelings.'

If we do take the 'inferential' view, there will be two different ways in which perceptual error can occur in 'bodily feelings'. Suppose I think I hear a coach, but am wrong because there is no coach there. I might have gone wrong in two different ways. I might have really heard a sound such as coaches produce, but in this case not produced by a coach. Or my error might have been more radical, because even the sound was not there to be heard. In the same way, I might have the pattern of bodily sensations *normally* associated with being tired or going to be sick, and these sensations, *qua* sensations, might be veridical perceptions, but I might not be physically tired, or be about to be sick. I take it that this is the usual way that perceptual error is involved in bodily feelings, whenever it is involved. But a still more radical form of error would be at least possible where even the patterns of bodily sensations themselves were non-veridical bodily perceptions.

15

INTROSPECTION

SINCE we have treated our direct awareness of our own mental states as 'inner sense', it is natural to deal with introspection immediately after perception. But because the nature of introspective awareness plays a vital role in our argument, a good deal has already been said on the topic. It may be advisable, therefore, to begin by recapitulating what has been dealt with elsewhere. This is the business of the first section.

I. RECAPITULATION

In sense-perception we become aware of current happenings in the physical world. A perception is therefore a mental event having as its (intentional) object situations in the physical world. In introspection, on the contrary, we become aware of current happenings in our own mind. Introspection is therefore a mental event having as its (intentional) object other mental happenings that form part of the same mind. Nevertheless, introspection may properly be compared to sense-perception, and Kant's description of introspection as 'inner sense' is perfectly justified.

The possession of language may alter, and make more sophisticated, our perceptions. but perception is not logically dependent on language for its existence, as is shown by the fact that animals and young children can perceive although they cannot speak. In the same way, there seems no reason to think that introspection is logically dependent on language. That is to say, introspection does not logically demand the making of introspective reports, or having the power of making introspective reports. It seems plausible to say that animals and young children do not merely have pains, but are aware of having pains. It seems perfectly possible that they not merely have desires, perceptions and mental images, but that they are aware of having such things. If so, they have the power of introspection, although they lack the power to make introspective reports. Incidentally, this is compatible with the view that there is a close empirical connection between the possession of any extensive introspective ability, and the power to use language.

In the case of perception, we must distinguish between the perceiving, which is a mental event, from the thing perceived, which is something physical. In the case of introspection we must similarly distinguish between the introspecting and the thing introspected. Confusion is all the more easy in the latter case because *both* are mental states of the same mind. Nevertheless, although they are both mental states, it is impossible that the introspecting and the thing introspected should be one and the same mental state. A mental state cannot be aware of itself, any more than a man can eat himself up. The introspection may itself be the object of a further introspective awareness, and so on, but, since the capacity of the mind is finite, the chain of introspective awareness of introspections must terminate in an introspection that is not an object of introspective awareness.

If we make the materialist identification of mental states with material states of the brain, we can say that introspection is a self-scanning process in the brain. The scanning operation may itself be scanned, and so on, but we must in the end reach an unscanned scanner. However, the unscanned scanner is not a logically unscannable scanner, for it is always possible to imagine a further scanning operation. Although the series logically must end somewhere, it need not have ended at the particular place it did end.

The distinction between the introspecting and the introspected state casts light on the much-lamented 'systematic elusiveness of the subject'. The 'elusiveness' of that mental state which is an awareness of some other state of affairs, physical or mental, is a mere logical elusiveness, the consequence of the fact that the awareness of something logically cannot also be an awareness of that awareness.

In the case of most forms of sense-perception we say that we perceive *with* certain parts of the body. These parts of the body we call sense-organs. The full concept of a sense-organ involves both (i) that perceptions of a certain characteristic range arise as a causal result of the stimulation of these parts of the body; (ii) that certain alterations in these parts of the body are under the direct control of the will, alterations which enable us to perceive different features of the environment. As we saw in discussing perception, it is logically impossible for every perception to be a perception gained by the deliberate use of some sense-organ. For the will can only function where there is perception; to alter deliberately the state of a sense-organ we must perceive what is happening to the sense-organ. If this perception itself demands a sense-organ, and so *ad infinitum*, we are involved in a vicious infinite regress. This argument does not identify those perceptions that do not involve the deliberate use of an organ, but in fact it seems that all bodily perceptions fall into this class. The so-called proprioceptors, stimulation of which gives rise to bodily perception, are not *organs* in the fullest sense because their operation is not under the direct control of the will. In bodily perception there is nothing we perceive *with*.

Bodily perception has the further peculiarity that its object—our own body—is private to each perceiver. If each of us were confined to bodily sense, there would be no overlap between our sense-fields, in the way that there is overlap in the case of the other senses. This privacy is purely empirical, and we can imagine having the same direct perceptual access to states of other people's bodies that we now have to our own.

These two features of bodily perception make it an appropriate model for introspection conceived of as 'inner sense'. In the first place, when we are aware of happenings in our own minds, there is nothing that we are aware *with*. (If there were an organ involved it would be something whose operation was under the direct control of our will. This, in turn, would demand a power of gaining direct awareness of the different states of this 'introspective organ'. At some point there would have to be a direct awareness that did not involve the use of an organ.) In the second place, our introspective awareness is confined to our own minds. It was argued elsewhere that it is only an empirical fact that our direct awareness of mental states is confined to our own mind. We could conceive of a power of acquiring non-verbal non-inferential knowledge of current states of the minds of others. This would be a direct awareness, or perception, of the minds of others. Indeed, when people speak of 'telepathy' it often seems to be this they have in mind.

When we perceive, there are many (indeed innumerable) features of our environment that we do not perceive. In the same way, when we are aware of our own current mental states, there are mental states and features of mental states of which we are unaware. These are mental states or features of mental states of which we are unconscious. Unconscious mental states stand to conscious mental states, in the realm of our own mind, as unperceived states of affairs stand to perceived states of affairs in the physical realm. In between the unperceived and the perceived there are those things which are just perceived, or are marginally perceived. In the case of introspective awareness there is a similar twilight zone.

Perception may be erroneous. We argued at length in Chapter 6 that, contrary to what might be called the Cartesian tradition, it is equally possible for introspection to be erroneous. This does not mean that introspective awareness may not *in fact* regularly satisfy the conditions for *knowledge*.

Eccentric cases apart, perception, considered as a mental event, is the acquiring of information or misinformation about our environment. It is not an 'acquaintance' with objects, or a 'searchlight' that makes contact with them, but is simply the getting of beliefs. Exactly the same must be said of introspection. It is the getting of information or misinformation about the current state of our mind.

It is the burden of this book that a mental state is a state of the person apt for the bringing about of certain bodily behaviour. So when I acquire by introspection the information that, for example, I am sad now or that I have a certain sort of perception now, this information is information about certain of my behaviour-producing or potentially behaviour-producing states. Now if introspection is conceived of as 'acquaintance' with mental states, or a searchlight that makes contact with them, it is difficult to see how all it can yield is information of such highly abstract nature about inner causes or potential inner causes. But if introspection as well as perception is conceived of as a mere flow of information or beliefs, then there is no difficulty.

We can even find an analogy for the sort of information acquired in introspection in the tactual perception of pressure upon our body. In such tactual perception we may be aware of no more than that something we know not what is pressing, with greater or lesser force, upon us. 'Pressing with greater or lesser force' here seems to mean no more than a greater or lesser aptness for producing a certain sort of effect: either the distortion or motion of our flesh.

The only further topic to be recapitulated is that concerning the biological value of introspection. We argued that without introspection there could be no purposive mental activity. As we have seen, purposive physical behaviour logically demands perception. For unless we can become apprised of the situation as it develops, so that this awareness can react back upon the cause that initiates and sustains purposive behaviour, there will be no possibility of the adjustment of behaviour to circumstances that is an essential part of such behaviour. And it is by perception that we become apprised of the situation as it develops.

If there are to be purposive trains of mental activity, then there must equally be some means by which we become apprised of our current mental state. Only so can we adjust mental behaviour to mental circumstances. For instance, if we are doing a calculation 'in our head' we will need to become aware of the current stage in the mental calculation that we have reached. Only if we do become so aware will we know what to do next. So there must be a way of becoming aware of our current mental state, which means that there must be introspection. The biological value of purposive mental activity is, of course, obvious. It permits of a far more sophisticated response to stimuli if we can 'think before we act'. But such thinking must be purposive thinking to be of real value.

This does not imply that purposive mental activity demands a highly self-conscious introspective scrutiny. Something far less may be, and normally is, all that is required. But without information of some sort about the current state of our mind, purposive trains of mental activity would be impossible.

II. INTROSPECTION AS INNER SENSE: OBJECTIONS

There are certain further objections to accepting the picture of introspective awareness as 'inner sense'. This section will be devoted to considering and rebutting them.

The first difficulty was drawn to my attention by C. B. Martin, although I do not know how seriously he takes it. He points out that although it is a commonplace that we can have perceptions without acquiring beliefs, there is no parallel occurrence of introspective awareness without belief. This sets a gulf between perception and introspection.

Belief-free perceptions occur only when we have both cast-iron reasons for believing that the perception fails to correspond to physical reality, and extensive experience of the deception. Such reasons and such experience are very largely acquired because of the empirical possibility of checking our beliefs by reference to the perceptions of others. Now, in the case of introspection, there is no overlap between person and person in the field of objects presented to each 'perceiver'. Correction of introspective 'observation' is therefore extremely difficult, and it is not easy to be certain that error has occurred. The result is that we do not often find cases where 'the deliverance of introspection' clashes with what we are quite certain are the facts about our current state of mind. However, we can very easily conceive that, in a future where far more is known than at present about the workings of the brain, it would be possible to be quite sure that certain introspections were illusory. I might appear to myself to be angry, but *know* myself to be afraid. So the difference between perception and introspection that Martin has pointed out seems to be a contingent one, and provides no reason to resist the assimilation of introspection to perception.

In discussing perception, we distinguish between 'perception without belief' and 'perception without acquiring of belief'. If a pond looks to me to be elliptical, but I know it to be round, this is a case of 'perception without belief'. If I gaze for a while at a red book, this will normally involve 'perception without acquiring of belief'. For since I know that the book will continue to be red during the next instant, I do not *acquire* any new belief about the book when that new instant arrives and I am still perceiving the book. Now Martin may be correct in saying that 'introspection without belief' does not occur. But, we have argued, it is only a contingent fact that it does not occur. It is worth noting, therefore, that introspective awareness without *acquiring* of belief certainly does occur. I may be directly aware that I am angry, and know that my anger will continue for some little while. So when, an instant later, I am introspectively aware of my current anger, I have not *acquired* any belief that I am angry now. In this case, then, the parallel between perception and introspection is complete, which strengthens the view that the lack of parallel pointed out by Martin is not significant for an account of the *concept* of introspection.

A second, closely connected, difficulty is raised by Peter Geach in his monograph *Mental Acts* (Routledge, n.d.). He argues that introspection is not a form of perception because, although there are mental images corresponding to perceptions, it is nonsense to speak of 'introspective images' which stand to introspections as mental images stand to perceptions. He dismisses McTaggart's view that there can be such 'introspective images', saying 'Of course McTaggart's idea is quite wrong, . . .' (Sect. 24, 'The Notion of Inner Sense').

Now we argued that mental images were what might be called a logically degenerate species of perception. They resemble perceptions, but lack essential marks of perception. In the first place, they are not brought into being by stimulation of the sense-organs, but rather by internal causes. In the second place, they involve no acquiring of belief or even 'potential belief'.

Now, assuming Martin to have been correctly answered, introspection without belief is at least a meaningful notion. Assuming our account of mental images to be correct, this gives us introspections which answer to the second criterion for images. It will then not be difficult to conceive of a sub-class of these belief-free introspections which fulfil the first criterion also.

The point about the stimulation of the sense-organs cannot, of course, be duplicated exactly in the case of introspection, but a parallel criterion can be formulated. If introspection is to be compared with perception, we must say that, where it is veridical, the mental state of affairs that we are aware of *brings about* the awareness of it. For, as we have argued, it is an essential mark of veridical perception that the situation that is perceived is the cause of the perception. And even where there is introspective error, in normal cases it will be some existent mental state that is 'mis-interpreted', and which has brought about the 'mis-introspection'. For in normal cases of misperception—taking a bush for a bear, for instance—there is an object which is the cause of the perception, and which is said to be the 'thing perceived'. In the introspective case, it may be, for instance, that our mental state is fear. This state is 'mis-introspected' as anger, that is to say, it is the mental state of fear that brings about the 'mis-introspection' that we are angry. (Notice, incidentally, that if introspection demands that the mental state introspected brings about our introspective awareness of it, then any Parallelist doctrine of the mind cannot explain our awareness of our own mental states.) Now, for 'introspective images', all we need to maintain a parallel with mental images is to say that, in addition to their being completely belief-free, they must not be caused by mental states in the fashion that ordinary veridical and illusory introspections are caused. Whether or not there are mental states answering to these criteria is another question, but all we are required to do against Geach is to show the intelligibility of the notion of 'introspective image'.

However, there is one phenomenon in our mental life which perhaps can be understood as involving such 'images'. I refer to the puzzling 'replicas' of emotion that we sometimes have when, for instance, we see plays performed or try to feel ourselves into the emotional situation of others, and which we can sometimes summon up in ourselves at will. When I am aware of 'feeling pity' for Lear, has it not some plausibility to say that my mental state stands to an introspective awareness of real pity much as mental images stand to perceptions? For I do not simply *think* that Lear is to be pitied. I am aware of a mental state that resembles pity. Yet I am not in fact pitying anybody, and I know I am not pitying anybody. (Unless, of course, Lear's plight moves me to real pity for humanity, or something like that.) Here we seem to have quite a plausible candidate for an actual case of an 'introspective image'.

Now to consider an argument of a different sort which is developed by Sydney Shoemaker (*Self-Knowledge and Self-Identity*, Cornell University Press, 1963, Ch. 3, Sect. 5). We have pictured introspection as resembling perception. We 'perceive' that we are in a certain mental state. Shoemaker argues that it is a contingent matter, to be settled empirically, whether a certain person is perceiving a certain object or not. I can perceive Jones, perceive a tree and perceive whether or not he perceives the tree. If we follow out this pattern with regard to introspection, it ought to be possible for me to perceive myself, perceive a particular mental state that I am in and perceive whether or not I am aware of that mental state. But this is not possible, Shoemaker argues. It is impossible that I should perceive that I was not perceiving the mental state, because I automatically must be perceiving it. So we must give up the comparison of introspection to perception.

The argument is undoubtedly ingenious, but it is an ingenuity that does not produce a great deal of confidence. It is reminiscent of Berkeley's ingenious but sophistical argument that a thing cannot exist unthought of because, when one tries to imagine such a thing, one is *ipso facto* thinking of it. Let us seek release by considering a third person instead of a first person case.

It is sometimes possible to perceive (mediately) that another person is in a certain mental state. Now we have allowed that a person can be in a mental state without being aware that he is in that state. So, having observed that the person is in that mental state, might we not seek to learn by further observation whether or not he was aware that he was in that state? And would it not be a contingent fact which of the two alternatives was the case? Here we have the parallel to the perception of Jones, the perception of a tree and the perception that Jones is or is not perceiving the tree. We perceive Jones, perceive his anger and perceive that he is or is not aware of being angry. There seems no shadow of incoherency in this third person case. This suggests that any incoherency in Shoemaker's case may not spring from applying the model of perception to the case of introspection.

It may be objected that this case is no real parallel to the case of introspection. For in the case of Jones our perception is clearly inferential. But introspection is supposed to be direct, that is, non-inferential, awareness of our own mental states.

But we can overcome this objection by constructing an imaginary case. Suppose I have telepathic powers with respect to Jones's mental states. On a certain occasion I acquire 'by telepathy' the knowledge that Jones is in a particular mental state. That is to say, I acquire the non-inferential knowledge that Jones is in a particular mental state. I am left in doubt whether Jones is or is not aware that he is in that mental state. But then, perhaps after further effort of concentration, I acquire non-inferential knowledge on this point also. Is this not a third person parallel to Shoemaker's case?

Emboldened by this, let us consider the first person case. Suppose I acquire a piece of unwelcome information. May I not scrutinize myself to see whether I have fully accepted the information? And may I not come to realize that a part of my mind has rejected it? (Supporting evidence might be the fact that I continued to act, or had impulses to act, in a way that was only appropriate if the information was false.) And if this occurs, is it not the very case that Shoemaker claims to be impossible? Part of my mind 'perceives' that another part of my mind fails to perceive the truth of certain information. Shoemaker may still object that since part of my mind perceives the truth, therefore *I* perceive the truth. This is true, but surely trivial. I perceive the truth, but I also do not perceive the truth. And I perceive that I do not perceive the truth.

It may be objected that this is a case of 'split consciousness'. This is true. If I accept the truth at all levels of my mind, that is to say, if my mind is not split on the matter, the situation cannot arise. But is not the inquiry into whether or not my mind is split in this way about a piece of information always a logically possible inquiry? And is this not parallel to the inquiry about whether Jones can or cannot see the tree that I see? So I do not think that Shoemaker's clever argument need worry us.

The final objection to conceiving of introspection as a form of observation stems from a point noticed by Hume. Wittgenstein once remarked:

'. . . if you go about to observe your own mental happenings you alter them and create new ones; and the whole point of *observing* is that you should not do this———' (I have lost, and have been unable to trace, the reference)

I do not think this argument has much weight. It is true that a careful and attentive scrutiny of our own current mental state will often serve to alter it. But the relatively 'reflex' awareness of our mental state, which is more usual, does not normally alter the state 'perceived'. In any case, I am quite unable to see how the argument can be stated without assuming the possibility of the very thing it is supposed to call into question. Wittgenstein himself speaks of attempting 'to observe your own mental happenings'. And how else could he identify the attempt? I am inclined to take the point, therefore, as Hume took it: a mere empirical difficulty for introspective observation.

III. INTROSPECTION AND BEHAVIOUR

We have argued that introspection is the acquiring of information (or misinformation) about our own current mental states. These mental states will be, *qua* mental states, states of the person apt in their various ways for the production of certain sorts of physical behaviour. So introspection will be the acquiring of information about current states of ourselves apt for the production of certain behaviour. But, of course, introspective awareness of mental states is itself a (distinct) mental state (more precisely, it is a mental event). So it, too, must be an aptness for certain behaviour: a certain sort of selection-behaviour towards ourselves. Now since the concept of a mental state is such a complex one, as compared to simpler concepts like 'red' or 'round', it will be advisable to spell out in more detail the sort of behaviour a person would have to exhibit to convince us that he had the capacity for introspective discriminations. This is the business of this section.

It may be helpful to consider an imaginary model first. What behaviour would convince us that a person could acquire a *non-inferential* knowledge that certain substances, such as untoughened glass, were brittle simply by putting their fingers in contact with the substance?

It will not be enough that the person was able to discriminate in a systematic way between material that is brittle, and material that is not brittle. Such behaviour will show that the perceiver can make a distinction between two sorts of material, a distinction that is in fact the distinction between being brittle and not being brittle. But does the perceiver perceive the distinction *as* the distinction between being brittle and not being brittle? The successful sorting does not demonstrate this.

What must be added? In the first place, the perceiver must be able to discriminate between those occurrences which constitute the manifestation of the disposition of brittleness and those which do not. For instance, a number of samples of material are struck sharply. Some break up, shatter or fly apart. Some do not. The perceiver must demonstrate that he can discriminate between the first sort of performance and the second sort.

This addition, although necessary, is clearly insufficient. The perceiver has still got to demonstrate that he understands the link between the first sort of discrimination (where nothing actually happens to the samples of material) and the occurrence or non-occurrence on other occasions of breaking, shattering or flying apart as a result of being struck. What sort of behaviour will demonstrate understanding of this link?

The answer is that the behaviour must have as its *objective* the actualization of the disposition or the prevention of the actualization of the disposition. Suppose the perceiver is rewarded when samples of material do not break, but punished when they do break. Suppose, after touching samples of material, the perceiver sorts them into two groups which are in fact the group of the brittle and the group of the non-brittle materials. Suppose furthermore that he treats objects in the two groups differently. The first group are handled very carefully, that is to say they are handled in a way that is, as an objective matter of physical fact, not conducive to their breaking. The other group are handled in a quite normal way, that is to say, a way that would as an objective matter of physical fact be conducive to their breaking if, contrary to the facts, they had been brittle. Does not such behaviour show that the perceiver perceives the connection between the original tactual discrimination and the brittleness or lack of brittleness of the samples? The perceiver has shown a capacity to link the original discrimination with later easy breaking and absence of easy breaking.

Let us now use this case as a model (over-simple and over-schematic perhaps) to unfold the behaviour that will betoken the making of non-inferential introspective discriminations. Let us take as our example the non-inferential awareness that we are angry.

We must in the first place exhibit a capacity to behave towards ourselves in a systematically different way when we are angry and when we are not angry. (Such behaviour, of course, must be something more than the behaviour the anger itself expresses itself in, if it does express itself. For this would allow no distinction between a mere angry state, and *being aware* that one was in an angry state.) To take a quite artificial example, we might exhibit the behaviour of pressing a button that lighted up a red light, when, and only when, we are angry.

(It is clear, incidentally, that the teaching and learning of such discriminations will be a rather tricky business in the case of anger that is not expressed in angry behaviour. Nevertheless, even if there are (empirical) difficulties in *checking* on whether discrimination has been successful, we can still have the possibility that it *is* successful and that in fact we light up the red light when and only when we are angry.)

This behaviour so far only shows that we can discriminate between the cases where we are in fact angry, and the cases where we are not. It does not show that we are aware of the distinction *as* a distinction between being angry and not being angry. What further capacities for behaviour must we exhibit?

In the next place, we must have the capacity to discriminate systematically between angry behaviour and non-angry behaviour in ourselves and others. When I say 'angry behaviour' here I do not mean behaviour that actually springs from anger, I mean angry *behaviour*. There can be angry behaviour that has not sprung from anger, and some behaviour brought about by anger is not what we would call *angry* behaviour. But there are certain typical sets of behaviours which occur when we are angry. (The relation of anger to its expression is more complicated than the relation of brittleness to its manifestations.) We must have the capacity to discriminate this sort of behaviour from other behaviour.

Finally, we must exhibit the capacity to link the original discrimination with angry behaviour. We must show ourselves capable of behaviour having as its *objective* the aiding or the inhibiting of the expression of anger. Suppose, for instance, we exhibit the following behaviour. After picking out those cases which are in fact cases where we are angry, we take action that has an inhibiting effect on anger but no similar effect on other mental states. We put our heads in cold water, or address soothing words to ourselves! We take no such action in the other cases. Have we not shown that the original introspective awareness was an awareness *of anger*?

No doubt what I have said here is oversimplified. But I think it has shown that there is no difficulty in principle in giving an account of the introspective acquiring of information about our own mental states as an acquiring of a capacity for certain sorts of discriminative behaviour. The parallel between perception and introspection is therefore maintained.

IV. MENTAL STATES AND THE MIND

One final topic remains to be discussed in this chapter. The account given in the last section would seem to be adequate for no more than an awareness of a current happening apt for the production of a certain sort of behaviour in a certain body. (If it is asked 'What body?', the answer is that the awareness is itself an acquiring of a capacity for discriminative behaviour by a certain body, and that the discriminative behaviour is directed towards that self-same body.)

Now if we consider a statement such as 'I am angry now' (taken as a purely descriptive remark), it seems to say more than is involved in the introspective awareness. For does not the use of the word 'I' here imply (among other things) that the current happening apt for the production of a certain sort of behaviour belongs to an organized set of happenings—a mind—all of which are happenings apt for the production of behaviour in the same body? The analysis of the last section does not do justice to this implication.

One might try to brush aside this difficulty by arguing that what is *meant* by 'a mind' is simply that group of happenings which are apt for the production of certain sorts of behaviour in a particular body. Unfortunately, however, this does not seem to be correct. For we can perfectly well understand the suggestion that something which is not *our* mind should have a capacity to bring about certain behaviour by our body of the sort that betokens mind. The notion of such 'possession' of our body seems a perfectly intelligible one, even if we think that in fact it never occurs.

What, then, does constitute the unity of the group of happenings that constitute a single mind? We are back at the problem that proved Hume's downfall. Is it a matter of the resemblance holding between the members of the group, or causal relations, or memory-relations (which are perhaps a sub-species of causal relation)? As we have seen in Chapter 2, it is possible to have mental happenings which we would be prepared to say were ours, yet which fulfilled none of these criteria.

I do not see any way to solve the problem except to say that the group of happenings constitute a single mind because they are all states of, processes in or events in, a single *substance*. Resemblance, causal relationship and memory are all of them important. Unless there were extensive relations of this sort between the different mental states that qualify the one substance we should not talk of the substance as 'a mind'. But the concept of a mind is the concept of a substance.

In taking the mind to be a substance, then, the Cartesian Dualists show a true understanding of the formal features of the concept of mind. Their view that the mind is a *spiritual* substance is, however, a further theory about the nature of this substance, and, while it is an intelligible theory, it is a singularly empty one. For it seems that we can only characterize the spiritual (except for its *temporal* characteristics) as 'that which is not spatial'. Modern materialism is able to put forward a much more plausible (and much more easily falsified) theory: the view that the mind is the brain. Mental states, processes and events are physical states of the brain, physical processes in the brain or physical events in the brain. (The Attribute theory also takes the mind to be the brain, but takes mental states, etc., as quite special, non-material, states of the material brain.)

But we must however grant Hume that the existence of the mind is not something that is given to unaided introspection. All that 'inner sense' reveals is the occurrence of individual mental happenings. This is the difficulty from which this section started. I suggest that the solution is that the notion of 'a mind' is a *theoretical* concept: something that is *postulated* to link together all the individual happenings of which introspection makes us aware. In speaking of minds, perhaps even in using the word 'I' in the course of introspective reports, we go beyond what is introspectively observed. Ordinary language here embodies a certain theory. The particular *nature* of this substance is a *further* theoretical question, but when ordinary language speaks of 'minds' it postulates *some* sort of substance.

The position, then, is this. Introspection makes us aware of a series of happenings apt for the production of certain sorts of behaviour in the one body. In a being without language, it may be presumed that introspection goes no further than this. Beings with language go on to form the notion that all these states are states of a single substance. This postulated substance is called 'the mind'. Once the notion of 'the mind' is introduced, there can be further speculation about its particular nature. (Just as, once the notion of the gene is introduced, there can be further speculation about *its* particular nature.) There is no absolute necessity for such a postulation of a single substance in the observed facts: it is simply a natural postulate to make. And sometimes, particularly in the case of primitive persons, a mental state of which we be-become introspectively aware may seem so alien to the other members of the 'bundle' that we may form the hypothesis that it is not a state of the same substance of which the other members are states. 'It is not I, but something alien.' Such an hypothesis is perfectly intelligible, even if it is not true, and even if it is a mark of maturity to recognize that everything we become aware of by introspection is part of the *one* mind: our own.

A *person* is something that has both body and mind. It will be seen, then, that when in the past we have spoken of a mental state as a state of a *person* apt for the production of certain sorts of behaviour we already presuppose the existence of *minds*. To that extent, this account of a mental state goes beyond the bare deliverances of introspection, and puts forward a *theory* about the objects of introspective awareness. But provided it is clear that we are doing so, there seems to be no objection to this procedure.

16

BELIEF AND THOUGHT

I. BELIEF

THIS section will be brief, but not because the topic of belief can be done justice in a short space. I have been unable to work out an account of the nature of belief in the concrete detail that would be desirable. 'Belief' here, of course, is not meant to exclude cases of knowledge, since it was argued in Chapter 9 that to know p is to believe p.

We have already given an account of perception as nothing but the acquiring of true or false beliefs (or 'information') about our environment as a result of the causal action of that environment upon our minds. To perceive that there is something red before us is to acquire the (true) belief that there is something red before us as a result of the causal action of that red thing on our minds. What are such beliefs themselves? It was argued that they are mental states apt for selective behaviour towards the environment. The perception of the red thing is the coming-to-be of a state that allows the perceiver to discriminate in his behaviour between this object and objects that are not red, if the perceiver should be impelled so to behave.

Beliefs involve concepts. Acquiring the belief that a particular object is red involves the possession of the concept of red. Possession of the concept entails a general capacity of the perceiver, in at least some set of circumstances, to differentiate between things that are red and things that are not red. And so a perceptual belief, which involves capacity for selective behaviour towards a particular object on a particular occasion, entails the possession of higher-order capacities: capacities for acquiring capacities for selective behaviour towards particular objects on particular occasions.

Now I wish to advance the view that these perceptual beliefs, and the concepts that they involve, are the logically fundamental beliefs, and the logically fundamental concepts. We can understand the notion of belief generally, and the concepts involved in belief generally, only in terms of these fundamental beliefs and concepts. This I take to be the truth enshrined, however confusedly, in the Empiricist doctrine of 'ideas' put forward in Book II of Locke's *Essay*. It is conceivable that a being should have none but perceptual beliefs. Presumably some organisms are actually in this situation. But, I am contending, it is inconceivable that a being that did not perceive could acquire or have any *other* beliefs.

What is the reason for such a contention? In the case of perceptual beliefs, there is the possibility of selective behaviour by the perceiver towards the perceived situation. Exhibition of a capacity for such selective behaviour is all the evidence needed for saying that the perceiver has acquired the particular belief. But now compare this with beliefs of a more abstract sort, or about situations that are remote from us in time and place. What behaviour can be specified which would be an unambiguous sign that the subject holds a certain belief?

The only behaviour that seems to have any very intimate relationship to such beliefs is *verbal* behaviour. My beliefs about Julius Caesar, or about philosophy, are expressed in words, and if I had no language it is impossible to see how they could be expressed at all. But, even if we ignore the possibility of insincerity of speech, what is it that makes the words I speak an expression of just the beliefs that they are an expression of? What ties the English sentence 'Julius Caesar was murdered by Brutus' to the particular historical happening that it records? In perception, or at any rate, in the logically central cases of perception, the behaviour that is an expression of the perception is brought into existence by the situation perceived and is directed towards just that situation, where 'directed towards' can be unpacked in terms of further causal relations between the perceiver and the situation (see Ch. 11). But in the case of Caesar's murder there is no such intimate tie between the linguistic behaviour that gives expression to the belief, and the happenings in 44 B.C. This suggests that perceptual beliefs are the logically fundamental sort of belief.

In the case of some non-perceptual beliefs, it seems that this difficulty might be overcome by invoking empirical counter-factual truths. If our position in space and time, or even our capacities and powers, were different, then it might be true that we would be able to carry out selective behaviour which would be appropriately tied to the situation believed to exist. And so we could make the truth of such counterfactuals *constitutive* of the possession of certain beliefs. But in the case of our more sophisti-cated and abstract beliefs such a simple resolution of the difficulty seems inadequate.

If we take the totality of our perceptual beliefs we can think of them as a complex structure that has a more or less continuing existence in our minds, and which constitutes a more, or less, complete 'map' of our environment. It is, of course, not a map in the ordinary sense of the word; it is not something we use, as we use ordinary maps, as evidence of the nature of the environment. It is a map which, as it were, does not have to be read, but which of its own nature points to the physical state of affairs that it maps. (Under the heading of 'perception' here I include intro-spection. The phrase 'the environment' is therefore to be under-stood as including our own body and our own mind.) The sen-tences in which we would express these beliefs (if we did express them) constitute a complex structure of sentences more or less accurately correlated with the perceptual 'map'. Now I want to say that our non-perceptual beliefs may be conceived of as *extensions of the perceptual 'map'*.

Let me try to fill this out. The perceptual 'map' of the world that we each possess may be thought of as a grid placed over a certain physical surface. Our environment, including our own body and mind, is represented by the physical surface. The whole linguistic structure in which we would express our perceptual beliefs, if we did express them all, may be thought of as another grid, roughly, at least, isomorphic with the grid that constitutes our perceptual beliefs.

Now the perceptual 'map', and the linguistic structure which is its verbal expression, are linked with the environment in a certain complex fashion. It is here that our perceptual *concepts* play a central role. It was argued in Chapter 11 that, if we possess a particular perceptual concept, then there must be at least some set of circumstances in which we can perceive correctly that certain objects fall under this concept. The relationship of perceptual concepts to objects in the environment, and in particular the relationship of perceptual concepts to objects under these cognitively successful conditions, are the backbone of the relationship between our perceptual beliefs (and the language we express them in) and the environment.

Suppose that we now think of the original grid as surrounded by extensions of the grid, extensions that project beyond the original surface that the grid was placed upon. These extensions represent our non-perceptual beliefs: those beliefs that are not expressible in selective behaviour towards features of our environment. Like our perceptual beliefs, these beliefs are to be conceived of as actual *states* of our mind. They are the beliefs that they are firstly, in virtue of the concepts that they contain and secondly, in virtue of the ordering of these concepts. The concepts themselves are either the concepts that are already involved in our perceptual beliefs, or else an account can be given of them that ultimately goes back to the perceptual concepts. The content of the perceptual concepts is fixed by their relationship to the environment. And so, indirectly, the content of our non-perceptual beliefs is fixed by this same relationship.

To our perceptual beliefs correspond the sentences in which the beliefs are expressed verbally, if they are expressed. In the same way, to our non-perceptual beliefs, correspond the sentences in which *they* are expressed, if they are expressed. And to the relations between perceptual and non-perceptual beliefs, and the concepts they involve, correspond the relations between the sentences used to express our perceptual beliefs and the sentences that express our non-perceptual beliefs, and the words they involve. But the verbal expression of our non-perceptual beliefs is of far greater importance than in the case of our perceptual beliefs. For in the non-perceptual case the verbal expression does not merely serve to communicate belief; it may be the only behaviour in terms of which the belief can be identified.

At the same time, of course, it is perfectly possible that we may have beliefs that we are unable to formulate verbally. It is a frequent experience to be unable to express ourselves but then later to find some form of words which seems to us to render our belief adequately. Granting that there is much room for self-deception in such matters, I think we can give a quite straightforward account of this situation. We really were in a certain mental state that involved certain concepts linked in certain ways. Given our language and its resources, then there was a certain verbal utterance that best served to communicate that state. At first we were unable to find this verbal formulation, later we succeeded. Of course, the conclusive verification and falsification of such claims about our beliefs might be impossibly difficult in practice. But a sufficiently powerful neurophysiological theory might be able to settle the matter, in principle at least.

This account of non-perceptual belief is sketchy, but it is the best I have been able to do. If it is on the right lines we see that the notion of a non-perceptual belief is very much a *theoretical* notion, not only when applied to the case of other people, but also in our own case. Such beliefs cannot simply be defined in terms of what we or another might say or do in certain circumstances, if impelled to act, although such possible behaviour has the closest connection with our holding such beliefs. Rather, in attributing a non-perceptual belief to another or to ourselves, we are postulating the existence in his or in our mind of a state with a certain formal structure. This structure has as its elements the same elements that form the structure of our perceptual beliefs. And so such states form a 'map' of reality that is an extension of the 'map' formed by our perceptual beliefs.

II. THINKING

The concept of thinking is a somewhat polymorphous one. But what I take to be the fundamental notion of thinking may be elucidated by the consideration of a case.

Consider the following situation. I talk to a friend and, as it happens, I have recently acquired certain information, p, which I know him to lack, but which I also know to be of great interest to him. I have no motive for failing to pass the information on. Nevertheless, I fail to give him the information.

Now, looking back on the incident, it would be natural for me to describe what happened by saying 'I failed to *think* of p at the time'. Such thinking need not involve any conscious contemplation of *p* before speaking. In order to see that conscious contemplation need not be involved, consider a case where I do pass the information on. What happens, let us suppose, is that I simply see my friend and straightaway launch into giving him the information *p*. Now would not such proceedings be sufficient to rebut an accusation that I failed to think of *p* at the time? 'So far from failing to think of *p*, I actually passed on the information!' So, in some clear sense, I did think of *p*, although there was no conscious contemplation of *p* before I spoke. This sense of thinking I take to be the fundamental notion of thinking. What account shall we give of it?

We can gain help here from a point made about purposes and desires in Chapter 7. There we asked what account was to be given of the difference in mental state between a boy who wants a bicycle, but is, say, currently asleep, and the same boy gazing into a bicycle-shop window. We offered the following simple account. When the boy is asleep, his mind is in a certain state, a state whose concrete nature we may not know, which constitutes his desire for a bicycle. But the state is not *currently causally active* in his mind. By contrast, when he is gazing into the bicycle-shop window, this state is currently causally active in his mind. It has caused him to embark upon a course of behaviour—gazing into the bicycle-shop window—which he would not have embarked upon unless he had the desire for a bicycle.

Now, when I failed 'to think of *p*' on meeting my friend, what failed to happen? The answer, I suggest, is simply that the knowledge-that-*p*, although a state of my mind, failed to be causally active in my mind at that time. In particular, it failed to act upon my will so that I imparted the information. And it failed to have any other effect within my mind.

An analogy with a computer seems very helpful here. After information has been fed into a computer, the information may be in one of two current states. It may be causally inactive: simply stored in the memory-banks. Or it may be causally active: either playing a part in producing a certain output on the tape, or else acting upon and changing other internal states of the computer. The first or inactive state is parallel to the case where I know that *p* is true but fail to tell my friend although I have every motive to do so. The second or active state is parallel to the case where I do pass the information on.

The knowledge-that-*p* may be currently causally active in my mind in all sorts of ways. It might cause me to acquire the belief-that-*q*. (Under suitable conditions this would be a case of inferring.) It might make me sad, or cause me to have certain mental images. Given only that it is currently acting on my mind so as to change my mental state, then, I am suggesting, we can speak of the thought-of-*p* being currently in my mind (although not necessarily *consciously* in my mind).

But now what of the case where, before I inform my friend that *p* is the case, *p* comes consciously before my mind? I think we can say that this is a *sub-species* of the wide notion of thinking that we have already defined. What is it for *p* to come before my mind in this conscious way? This is simply *introspective awareness* of the fact that I know *p*. Such introspective awareness is a particular case of the current causal operation of the knowing-*p* state within our minds. For we have earlier argued that introspective awareness may be compared to perception, and further that it is a feature of perception, and with it introspection, that the situation perceived or introspected actually brings about the perception or introspection of it. So introspective awareness that we possess knowledge-that-*p* is a current effect in our minds of the knowing-*p* state Here, then, we have a particular case falling under our general account of thinking as a belief that is currently causally active in our minds. In some cases it may be causally necessary that I become introspectively aware of my knowledge or belief-that-*p* *before* I am able to express this knowledge or belief in speech or other overt behaviour. It is such a case which we describe by saying that we have to think before we speak.

In terms of what has been said so far we can understand the familiar remark 'I know it, but I cannot think of it at the moment'. What is being claimed is that I do have certain knowledge, but that, contrary at least to my conscious wishes, the knowledge is not currently available to consciousness (introspective awareness), and, as a causal result of this unavailability, I am unable to manifest the knowledge verbally.

In the cases considered so far the subject already has certain knowledge (or belief), and it is a matter of this causally inactive knowledge (belief) becoming causally active in the subject's mind. But, of course, there are cases where thinking *p* is simultaneously *acquiring* the knowledge or belief-that-*p*.

The point here is that the moments after which one has acquired certain knowledge or a certain belief are frequently moments when the belief is causally active in one's mind. This is not a necessary truth. The acquiring of knowledge or belief may be unaccompanied by thought. All that happens in the mind may be the acquiring of a dispositional state. But, very frequently, the acquiring of knowledge or belief has immediate further effects in the mind. It is likely, for instance, that one who acquires knowledge or belief will simultaneously become *aware* that he has acquired this knowledge or belief. (How long one continues to 'dwell' on such newly acquired knowledge or beliefs is, of course, a purely empirical question.)

I think that this casts back some light on the nature of *perception*. We have given an account of perception as the acquiring of knowledge or beliefs about the environment as the result of the action of that environment upon the mind. Now, in very many cases, this knowledge or belief has further immediate effects within the mind of the perceiver. (The biological importance of our perceptions regularly having some such immediate result is obvious.) We may be moved to embark upon courses of action, or we may simply become aware that we are having the perceptions we are having. And since these perceptual beliefs are causally active in our minds at that time we can say that thought is present, even if thought in its most primitive form. Perhaps this helps to fill out the phenomenological picture of perception a little.

The mention of perception reminds us that there is no reason to restrict thinking to cases where the natural expression of the thought is in *words*. Suppose that in the past whenever an A has been perceived in circumstances B it has proved on investigation to be accompanied by C, and that a special policy has been found appropriate towards A's which are accompanied by C. Suppose, then, that a perceiver who knows all this perceives an A in circumstances B but at first fails to act towards it in the way judged appropriate. Suddenly, however, he does act towards it appropriately. May we not say that it has suddenly *struck him* that, in such circumstances, A's are invariably accompanied by C? And is this not a thought? Our account of what this thought striking him consists of will simply be that, at that moment, the belief that A's in circumstances B are always accompanied by C's had become causally active in his mind. But the point I wish to make here is

346

that the thought need not be something whose natural expression is linguistic. The perceiver may lack verbal concepts for A, B and C. He may even lack language altogether. Yet it still seems correct to say that a thought struck him.

Köhler's famous experiments with apes provide evidence of quite sophisticated thought on the part of animals. Suppose an ape is taught to get suspended bananas by putting a box under them, but that then the bananas are suspended still higher so that the ape can only reach them by putting one box upon another. If in this situation the ape first pauses for a time, and then does put one box upon another, it is clear that the ape has *thought* of a way to get the bananas. He has acquired a belief, which, if expressed in words, would be of the form 'If I take a box and put it on another then I can reach the bananas'. This belief at once influences his behaviour.

Notice, by the way, that just as we can distinguish between knowledge or belief that is currently causally active in our mind, and knowledge or belief that is not, so we can distinguish between practical skills or 'knowings how' that are currently causally active in our minds and those that are not. The actual utilizing of a skill on an appropriate occasion might be called 'practical thinking'. The cases where a person has consciously to summon up his 'knowledge how' before applying it to the task in hand may be analysed along the same lines as the parallel cases of theoretical knowledge or belief. It is a matter of becoming introspectively aware of what is involved in a certain skill, an awareness that then permits the accomplishment of the task in hand.

But now we must consider the difficulty that we can have thoughts where the thing thought is not something known or believed. There is the contemplation of mere possibilities. There are suppositions or imaginings that are known or believed to be contrary to fact. Our account of thinking up to this point will not suffice to cover such cases. In some cases, of course, although there is no belief, there is inclination to believe of greater or lesser strength. Such cases present no particular problem. The difficulty for our analysis is posed by thoughts that involve no belief at all.

Now such thoughts will, if they issue in words, issue in the words of the 'belief' that is not in fact held. But the words will be hedged around, either by explicit verbal devices or simply by the nature of the context, in a way designed to make it clear to a hearer that the hearer is not to think the speaker believes what is said. It is mere thoughts, not beliefs, that are being communicated.

What must be said is that 'mere thoughts' are logically secondary cases of thoughts (however important in 'the life of the mind'). When we make a supposition, but no belief or degree of belief is involved, then we are in a mental state that can only be characterized by its resemblance to the corresponding state of belief. But no belief is involved. The account already given of perception, and of the will, should make it easy to accept such an answer. Although we have given an account of perception in terms of the acquirings of beliefs about what is currently going on in our environment, we have called attention to the logically secondary cases of perceptions without belief or even without 'potential belief'. The latter sorts of perception can be defined only by their resemblance to those central cases of perception that do involve the acquiring of beliefs. In the same way, we have given an account of wants and wishes that involve no impulse to action, or even, in the case of 'idle' wants and wishes, that do not involve potential impulses to action, in terms of their resemblance to desires that actually steer our conduct. In the same way, when we make a supposition but no belief or degree of belief is involved, then we are in a mental state that can only be characterized by its resemblance to the corresponding state of belief.

What is the nature of this resemblance? If we believe p, then this mental state must have certain features which correspond to the content of the belief and mark if off from beliefs with a different content. So if we simply entertain the proposition p, then, since what is believed and what is supposed are the same thing, p, the mental state involved will have to have the same features that correspond to the content of the belief. The difference between the belief that p and the mere supposition that p is the role that the two states play in our mental life and behaviour. If the belief is one that can find expression in non-linguistic behaviour, then our preparedness to adjust our conduct in the light of the belief marks it off from the corresponding mere thought. If the belief is one that can only be expressed verbally, then it is marked off from the corresponding mere thought by the absence of those explicit or implicit linguistic qualifications which enable us to put forward a proposition without being committed to it. As mental images are ghosts of perception, and 'idle' wants and wishes ghosts of the will, so 'mere thoughts' that involve no belief are ghosts of belief.

Just as we can distinguish between beliefs that are or are not currently causally active in our minds, so, it seems, we can distinguish between mere suppositions that are or are not currently causally active in our minds. And when such a supposition *is* currently causally active, we can be said to be actually thinking that thought.

The notion that we have been elucidating is that of having a *single* thought. It seems plausible to say that this is the basic notion of thinking, in terms of which other notions can be explicated.

Besides speaking of the thought *that* something is the case, we also speak of thinking *of* something or someone. This linguistic distinction corresponds to the distinction between perceiving *that* something is the case, and perceiving things, events, etc. We said that the second perceptual idiom was, among other things, a sort of hold-all. It asserts that the perceiver said to be perceiving the thing or event is acquiring information or misinformation of a certain sort, without committing the speaker to saying exactly what the information or misinformation is. A similar account may be given of thinking *of* something or someone. To say that A is thinking of X, where X is some thing or person, is to say that he is having certain thoughts that something is the case, without specifying what these thoughts are except that they 'relate to X'. The non-committal nature of the idiom is just what makes it often useful.

A single thought may be contrasted with a sucession of thoughts. The latter may be a mere succession of thoughts. It may, however, be more than a mere succession, and be a *train* of thoughts. The notion of a train becomes clear if we consider a physical train, such as a train of gunpowder. A train of gunpowder is a train in virtue of the causal relations in which each successive portion of the train stands to the adjoining portion. In a train of thoughts, as opposed to a mere succession of thoughts, each successive thought brings about the next thought. On our analysis of thinking, this is a matter of the causal activity within the mind of a belief, inclination to believe, or supposition bringing about a further belief, inclination to believe or supposition, and so on.

A train of thoughts may be a *mere* train of thoughts. This is the phenomenon of 'association of ideas'. But it may be more than a mere train of ideas, as in the cases where we try to decide what to do, or we make a calculation. These differ from mere trains of thought by being *purposive*. They are trains of thought with an object: to come to a decision or to find an answer. On our view of purposive activity, this implies that they are trains of thought initiated and sustained by a mental cause external to them. But this does not mean that they are not still *trains*, because each step in the train is still causally essential for going on to the next thought.

Consider first trying to decide what to do. If the end is given, and the only question is what are the best means to this end, then the question is a purely intellectual one and the process reduces to one of calculation, or some similar species of thinking. But there may also be a question of ends as well as means: we may be undecided what ends to pursue. In Chapter 7, Section X, we argued that such 'making up our minds' is a matter of contemplating possible actions—our doing X, our doing Y—all in some degree attractive to us, with the purpose that, as a causal result of contemplating these alternatives, a purpose will form to do one rather than another. Now this 'contemplation of possible actions' seems to be simply the thinking of, and thinking about, certain possibilities, viz. certain actions currently within our power. Our account of that sort of thinking where the thing thought of is not believed will therefore cover this sort of contemplation.

In mental calculations we have a purposive train of thoughts where each successive thought comes into being as the result of a manipulation of the previous thought according to some fixed rule. In many cases, such calculation involves inference: the acquiring of new beliefs as a causal result of beliefs previously held.

This discussion of thinking concludes the account of the mental concepts. In each case, it has been argued, an account can be given of mental events, states and processes solely in terms of physical behaviour of the body and physical action upon the body. In the simplest cases, mental occurrences are definable as states of the person that are causes of certain bodily behaviour and effects of the action of the environment. In many cases, however, the relationship between mental state and behaviour, and mental state and stimulus, is much more complex than that of simple cause and simple effect. But it is always a relationship definable in terms of such causes and such effects. In this way, outward criteria are provided for inner processes. If such an account of mental happenings has been made good, the way is now open to argue that, as a matter of contingent fact, they are in their own nature nothing but physico-chemical happenings in the central nervous system. So we pass now from logical analysis to contingent identification.

Part Three

THE NATURE OF MIND

17

IDENTIFICATION OF THE
MENTAL WITH THE PHYSICAL

THIS final chapter will be brief. There are a number of reasons for this. In the first place, a certain number of arguments for the identification of the mental and the physical have already been mentioned in Part One. In the second place, this empirical step in our argument has already been defended at length, better than I could do it, by a number of writers. (See in particular J. J. C. Smart's *Philosophy and Scientific Realism*, Routledge, 1963.) I have almost nothing to add to what they have said, and so have judged it better to devote my energies to a task to which they seem to have paid less attention: an elucidation of the concept of mind and the particular mental concepts. In the third place, if the arguings in Part Two have been successful and the account of the concept of mind is on the right track, the contingent identification of mental with the physical seems neither particularly paradoxical nor particularly bold.

Nevertheless, I have given the chapter the dignity of a final Part of the book. My reason in doing this is to re-emphasize as sharply as possible the logical independence of this final step in the argument from what has gone before. Except for incidental remarks, nothing I have said in Part Two *entails* the truth of a materialist theory of mind. The best that can be said of Part Two is that in it the way has been made smooth for such an identification.

But now we can ask 'What objection is there to identifying

mental states with physico-chemical states of the central nervous system?' It has been argued that mental states are states of the person defined solely in terms of causal relations, of a more or less complex sort, to the objects or situations that bring the mental states about and the physical behaviour that constitutes their 'expression'. In the same way, genes are defined solely in terms of their causal relations to hereditary characteristics. (These hereditary characteristics could be said to be the 'expressions' of the genes.) There is good theoretical (as opposed to observational) scientific evidence to identify genes with the DNA molecule at the centre of living cells. *Assuming that our account of the concept of a mental occurrence is correct*, is there not almost equally good evidence to identify mental occurrences with physico-chemical states of the central nervous system?

Objections to the identification may be classed under two heads. In the first place, the identification may be resisted because it is thought that physico-chemical processes in the central nervous system are not in fact adequate to explain the whole range of human behaviour. In the second place, it may be granted that physico-chemical processes are adequate to explain human behaviour, but the identification of mind and brain may still be resisted for other reasons. Objections of the first sort seem to be intellectually serious, those of the second sort intellectually frivolous. The reasons for making this distinction will emerge.

When considering the first sort of objections it is convenient to make a further distinction: between objections drawn from those manifestations of mind which everybody grants to exist, and objections drawn from those manifestations whose existence is a matter of dispute. The first class will include everything from 'perceiving that there is an orange before us' and 'adding five to seven' up to 'writing the plays of Shakespeare' and 'making the discoveries of Newton'. The second class is the class of 'paranormal' manifestations. It includes such alleged facts as the occurrence of telepathy and clairvoyance. Let us begin by considering the former or incontestable manifestations of mind.

We are now moving in the realm of science and empirical fact, not in the realm of logical possibility that is appropriate to conceptual analysis. It must therefore be accepted without dispute that physico-chemical processes in the central nervous system are one of the factors that determine the behaviour of men and the higher animals. All that may be questioned is whether such processes are *wholly* responsible for behaviour.

If we consider the known activities of man, it is clear that such things as intellectual discovery and artistic creation, and in particular such transcendent facts as the discoveries of Newton or the plays of Shakespeare are the facts that present Materialists with greatest difficulty. For intellectual discovery and artistic creation may be said to be 'higher' activities of man in a perfectly objective sense: they are activities of greater complexity and sophistication than other human activities. It will be particularly hard to see how they can be products of a mere physical mechanism.

The anti-Materialist may here take his stand either on a stronger or on a weaker contention. In the first place, he may maintain that it is empirically impossible for *any* physical mechanism to produce such manifestations. In the second place, he may grant the possibility of a physical mechanism producing such manifestations, but may maintain that in fact man's body contains no mechanism that can undertake the task.

The first contention is being gradually undermined by the designing, and building, of machines that can duplicate an increasing range of human performances. It is true that no machine has yet been built which can be said to exhibit ingenuity or creativity in what it does. Present machines, for instance, can solve mathematical problems only if they are the sort of problem that can be answered by a set step-by-step procedure. But it is very unlikely that this represents the upper limit of the performances of machines, and suggestions already exist for the designing of a machine that will exhibit ingenuity. (Cf. Smart, *op. cit.*, Ch. VI, Sect. 3, 'Problem-solving ingenuity'.) And if the 'ingenuity-barrier' is broken it will be very arbitrary still to maintain that there are other expressions of mind that are beyond the powers of a mechanism to produce.

However, an anti-Materialist who concedes that a machine which could duplicate the expression of the full range of human mental activity is physically possible may still maintain that mental states are not physical states of the central nervous system because in fact no mechanism that has this capacity can be found in the human body. In practice, however, this line of defence is seldom taken. Once the anti-Materialist has been convinced of the physical possibility of a mechanism that can produce a certain range of mind-like manifestations, he generally concedes that such a physical mechanism, or something not too dissimilar, will be found at work in the central nervous system. (Indeed, the construction or projection of mechanisms that produce mind-like manifestations has turned out to be one of the best sources of fruitful hypotheses about the workings of the central nervous system.)

Nevertheless, someone may argue that the anti-Materialist has let himself be satisfied so easily only because our knowledge of the central nervous system is as yet so slight. It may be that a really detailed knowledge of the workings of the brain would make it clear that it was inadequate for the discovery of the Law of Gravitation or the writing of *King Lear*.

The possibility may be freely admitted, and it may be freely admitted that it is more than a bare logical possibility. But what reasons are there to think that it is a possibility that has any great probability? I am not aware of any such reasons.

There is an interesting compromise possibility here which falls between a pure physico-chemical Materialism and an Attribute theory of the mind. It is possible to argue that the whole range of man's behaviour springs causally from physical processes in his central nervous system, but still to say that some at least of these physical processes are not the sort of thing that can be accounted for in terms of the laws of physics and chemistry. That is to say, one can hold that certain processes in the central nervous system operate according to *emergent* laws, laws that cannot be deduced, even in principle, from the laws of physics and chemistry. As a result, behaviour occurs that could not be produced by something working according to purely physico-chemical principles. Such a view would still be a Materialism, for it would not demand any emergent qualities, still less an emergent substance, but it would not be a *physico-chemical* Materialism.

The most natural hypothesis here would be that these emergent laws were something that developed in *all* physical systems that reached a certain degree of complex interrelation. In this way one would avoid the arbitrariness of associating the emergent laws with a high degree of complexity in *biological* systems only. One might expect a man-built machine of the requisite degree of complexity to operate according to the emergent laws just as much as the central nervous system did.

Again, if one did accept an hypothesis of this sort one would need to be more sympathetic to the idea of emergent laws generally. One would expect to find that *all* biological systems, which, after all, involve much more complex interrelations of components than ordinary physical systems, operate according to laws that transcend the principles of physics and chemistry. It would be a surprisingly arbitrary feature of the system of scientific laws if the physico-chemical laws applied to all ordinary collections of matter and there was just one point where a jump to emergent laws occurred: with the emergence of mind.

As I have said already, I know of no compelling scientific reason to make us think that even the discoveries of Newton or the art of Shakespeare require that we postulate emergent laws of operation in the central nervous system. Nevertheless, if such reasons exist, or are later discovered, then falling back upon this 'Emergent-law' Materialism will be a quite natural and onto-logically quite economical move.

(It may be remarked here, in passing, that a Parallelist of any sort must agree that the workings of the brain are by themselves sufficient to account for the whole range of human behaviour, although it is true that he may take an emergentist view of the laws according to which the brain works. For according to the Parallelist, mental states play no part in the causation of behaviour. If one wants to say that the brain is insufficient to account causally for the whole range of human behaviour one will have to be a Dualist and an Interactionist about the mind.)

It may be objected to 'Emergent-law' Materialism that it could not be distinguished from Interactionist Dualism. Suppose that a physical event in the central nervous system is followed after a brief interval by another physical event, but the occurrence of the second event is inexplicable in physico-chemical terms. The 'Emergent-law' Materialist postulates emergent laws of matter to explain the phenomenon. But a Dualist could explain what happened by saying that the first physical event brought about changes in a spiritual substance which in turn brought about the second physical event. How could we choose between the two hypotheses?

In answer to this objection it must be pointed out that the Dualist view can be developed in two different ways. If developed the first way, there would be no possible experimental decision between Dualism and 'Emergent-law' Materialism. Considerations of economy, however, would favour the latter view. If developed in the second, more plausible, way, it would be possible in principle to decide the question empirically.

Suppose that the central nervous system is in a certain physical state. A physical event in the system brings about a spiritual event which brings about a further physical event. Is the causal efficacy of the spiritual substance on this occasion determined solely by the first physical event? Suppose firstly that it is. There are then laws to be discovered which permit us, given the current physical state of the central nervous system, to predict in principle the second physical event from the first physical event. Now how in this case do we decide that a spiritual event does play a part in the causal chain? How do we rule out the view that the first physical event gives rise to the second physical event directly, although according to 'emergent' laws? We cannot. There is no possible observational difference between the theories as they are presented. However, every consideration of ontological economy tells against the Dualist view.

Suppose, more plausibly, that what happens in the spiritual substance, and the nature of the second physical event, is determined not simply by the first physical event *but also by what has happened to the spiritual substance in the past*. No straightforward prediction from the first physical event to the second event will then be possible. The impossibility of such a prediction would then be evidence for the truth of Interactionist Dualism. Of course, given that the genesis and subsequent history of the spiritual substance is determined solely by physical factors in the central nervous system, it would still be possible to argue that the second physical event followed on directly, by 'emergent' laws, but without a spiritual event as intermediary, from the first physical event *in conjunction with other physical events in the past*. But the hypothesis would become so complicated that postulation of a spiritual substance that interacted with the brain would clearly be the better hypothesis. 'Emergent-law' Materialism can therefore be distinguished from Interactionist Dualism.

The Materialist also has another line of retreat available in face of evidence that appears to contradict a materialist view of the mind, that may be even more congenial to him. It is conceivable that the whole range of human behaviour can be explained as an effect of the working of the brain, but that that working cannot be explained in terms of the physical principles that we *now* have. It might still be explained by a recasting of physics. Instead of admitting the existence of emergent laws we might discover a new basis for physics in terms of which the apparently special way of working of the brain becomes something derivable in principle from the basic laws of physics, applied to the particular physical structure of the brain.

If new basic principles for physics could explain, and could pre-dict, ordinary (that is, non-mental) phenomena *at least* as well as those currently accepted, and if in addition they were able to pre-dict the anomalous behaviour of the central nervous system, then we could switch to the new physics in the interest of a unified scheme of explanation. Of course, it is easy enough to talk airly of a new physics when one is not faced with the task of actually producing one. But it is one way that the Materialist could defend his monistic vision.

Nevertheless, it is conceivable that it should prove impossible to explain some human activities—presumably the 'higher' activities—either in terms of emergent laws of working of the central nervous system or by recasting our physics. In that case Central-state Materialism would be false, although the *analysis* of the mental concepts put forward in Part Two—the Causal analysis—might still be true.

So much for those manifestations of mind that everybody grants to have been manifested. We may now consider 'paranormal' phenomena. These include telepathy, clairvoyance, precognition, psychokinesis (the direct action of mind on material objects) and disembodied existence.

The first great question that faces us here is whether these phenomena exist at all. If they do not, they constitute no objection to Central-state Materialism, for their mere logical possibility is no objection to a *contingent* identification of mind and brain. Now, not all those who have studied the subject closely are convinced of the occurrence of any of the alleged phenomena. (An article such as Michael Scriven's 'New Frontiers of the Brain', *Journal of Para-psychology*, Vol. 25, 1961, pp. 305–18, gives a physicalist a great deal of comfort.)

In considering this question, it seems reasonable to let the matter turn on whether *experimentally reproducible* phenomena can be found. Admittedly this is a rigorous criterion, but, since it is almost a logical precondition of the scientific investigation of the phenomena, it is one that it seems methodologically correct to make.

Now the amount of suggestive experimental material is not very large, but there is a small body of results which are, at any rate, difficult to explain except by admitting that some paranormal faculty is being exercised. In particular, there is some experimental evidence for telepathy, and/or clairvoyance, and/or precognition. (I have put the conclusion in this ambiguous way because the evidence is regularly susceptible of different interpretations. To give an over-simple illustration. Suppose that a subject appears to have precognitive knowledge of what card in a pack will be turned up two times ahead. If we were dealing with a pack that was not shuffled between turns the fact could equally well be explained by postulating mere clairvoyant knowledge of the card that is now two from the top. Given this clairvoyant knowledge, a perfectly ordinary inference will suffice to yield the apparently 'precognitive' knowledge.) And once it is allowed that the experimental material gives positive results, many of the alleged phenomena that did not occur under experimental conditions become plausible candidates for paranormal phenomena.

Suppose, then, that there are in fact paranormal phenomena. The question arises whether they stand in any necessary opposition to Central-state Materialism. Consider telepathy for instance. We might define telepathy as the gaining of non-inferential knowledge of what goes on in the mind of another. Or, to adopt a definition that is in better accord with the experimental facts, it is the making of guesses without evidence about what is currently going on in the mind of another, guesses that are significantly more successful than the results that could be attributed to mere chance. This phenomenon, if it exists, is 'paranormal' because the only normal way to discover what is going on in the mind of another is to make an inference from what his body does. But why does this phenomenon contradict Central-state Materialism? Could there not be some as yet undiscovered physical processes (perhaps processes of a perfectly familiar kind in other contexts) which link one central nervous system with another, and so permit the transmission of information? And similar suggestions might be made about other paranormal phenomena.

Such suggestions may turn out to dissolve the problem posed by these phenomena without in any way disturbing Central-state Materialism. Nevertheless, if we consider the particular nature of the alleged phenomena, then, if they actually occur, it is not easy to find explanations within the framework of physics as we know it. For instance, it is an initially not unpromising suggestion that telepathic communication of information is mediated by some physical radiation emitted by one central nervous system and picked up by another. This hypothesis can be tested by conducting telepathic experiments with subjects isolated from each other by radiation-proof containers. Now such experiments have actually been carried out in the U.S.S.R., and it is claimed that guesses made about what was going on in the other minds in such conditions were still significantly better than chance expectation. (*Cf. Experiments in Mental Suggestion*, L. L. Vasiliev, English translation: Institute for the Study of Mental Images, 1963.) If the experiments can be repeated, an explanation of telepathy in terms of radiation will seem very implausible. But, given the careful design of modern experiments, what other channels of physical communication between subject and subject can be suggested? We could say that the radiation involved is quite unlike the physical radiation blocked by 'radiation-proof' boxes. But then we are beginning to abandon the known structure of physics.

If precognition is a reality, it is still more difficult to explain. It is true that there is no particular difficulty in understanding the abstract possibility of non-inferential knowledge of the future. Suppose a system, S, is moving in a certain direction. Let us make the supposition that it is likely to be unimpeded, and that, if unimpeded, it will come to be in state S_1. It is easy to imagine that before the system comes to be in state S_1, a small portion of its energy 'hives off' and acts upon a mind, producing in that mind non-inferential knowledge that S will shortly be in state S_1. Any warning-system, such as the oil-light in a car, works on similar principles, although it produces a less sophisticated result: the turning on of a light, not non-inferential knowledge. Indeed, it is possible that we sometimes acquire information of the sort like 'I am going to be ill' not on the basis of any evidence, but simply as a result of the operation of such a mechanism producing in us non-inferential knowledge of our future bodily states.

But if we consider actual cases where precognitive ability is claimed, it is difficult to apply an explanation of this sort. For instance, suppose a subject guesses with better than chance results what sort of card will be turned up, but between each guess the pack is thoroughly shuffled by a random procedure. The physical causes that go to making a particular card turn up are incredibly many, and incredibly complexly interrelated. It then becomes almost impossible to see how 'information' could be transmitted from that concatenation of causes which would be correlated in any degree with the result that the causes are about to bring into existence. So this sort of precognition, if it occurs, seems to defy all accepted patterns of explanation.

It is true that this is not the end of the argument. The Materialist might still take one of the two ways of escape discussed in connection with 'normal' as opposed to 'paranormal' phenomena. He might try to work out an emergent materialism, with special laws for the central nervous system not derivable, even in principle, from ordinary physics. Or he might seek for a new physics which, within a unified set of principles, would explain and predict not only the ordinary capacities of matter and of men, but also the paranormal skills of men. But if these ways of escape prove unsatisfactory, Central-state Materialism cannot be the whole truth about the mind.

I consider that the claims of psychical research are the small black cloud on the horizon of a Materialist theory of mind. If there were no questions about paranormal phenomena to consider, there would seem to be little serious obstacle to the *complete* identification of mental states with physico-chemical states of the central nervous system. (This, of course, is assuming that the *logical* objections can be met.) The identification would be as certain as the identification of the gene with the DNA molecule. The apparent existence of paranormal phenomena must leave a small doubt. The upholder of any scientific doctrine has an intellectual duty to consider very carefully the evidence that seems most likely to undermine his view. So the Central-state Materialist has an intellectual duty to consider very carefully the alleged results of psychical research.

Finally, we may briefly consider the position of those who grant that the physico-chemical processes in the central nervous system are adequate causes of the whole of human behaviour, but who nevertheless resist the identification of mental states with states of the brain. It is this position I described at the beginning of this chapter as intellectually frivolous.

It is important, once again, to re-emphasize that in this chapter I am assuming the general truth of the account of the mental concepts given in Part Two. We may therefore ignore here the position of those who argue, for instance, that it is evident to introspection that mental states are something different from, or are something more than, states of the person apt for the production of certain sorts of behaviour. Now if one accepts an account of mental states in terms of their causal relations to behaviour; and at the same time one agrees that physical operations of the brain are adequate to bring about all human behaviour; and yet one still wants to resist the identification of mental states and brain states; there seems to be only one position one can adopt. One must say that physical processes in the brain give rise to mental processes of a non-material sort which in turn give rise to behaviour. The mental processes must be inserted into the causal chain at some point, although the chain unfolds in exactly the same way that it would unfold if there was no such insertion. (*Cf.* the quarrel between an 'Emergent-law' Materialism and a form of Interactionist Dualism where the interaction occurs in such a way that both theories yield exactly the same predictions.)

Now this is a logical possibility. It is logically compatible with the observed facts. But every principle of simplicity in science speaks against adopting the view. In order to see that this is so, consider another logical possibility. Perhaps it is the case that, at a certain point in the course of its operations, the DNA molecule brings into existence an immaterial principle. This immaterial principle in turn has further effects: the transmission of hereditary characteristics. The whole chain of causes operates exactly as if it were a physical chain, but in fact it contains this one immaterial link. One can see clearly that, although this hypothesis is a logically possible one, and logically compatible with the observed facts, it has nothing to recommend it. The same may be said of the parallel hypothesis about the mind.

This brings our long argument to an end. One of the great problems that must be solved in any attempt to work out a scientific world-view is that of bringing the being who puts forward the world-view *within* the world-view. By treating man, including his mental processes, as a purely physical object, operating according to exactly the same laws as all other physical things, this object is achieved with the greatest possible intellectual economy. The knower differs from the world he knows only in the greater complexity of his physical organization. Man is one with nature.

We must recognize, however, that even if the doctrine of mind put forward in this book is correct, a physicalist philosophy is not at the end, but rather at the beginning, of its problems. The clearing away of the problem of mind only brings us face to face with the deeper problems connected with matter. Such notions as substance, cause, law, space and time, remain in as much obscurity as ever when we have given an account of the local and temporary phenomenon of mind purely in terms of such concepts. A physicalist theory of mind is a mere prolegomenon to a physicalist metaphysics. Such a metaphysics, like the theory of mind, will no doubt be the joint product of scientific investigation and philosophical reflection.

INDEX

Absolute Idealism, 5
'Achievement-words' and perception, 214–16, 266
After-images, 79, 116–17, 291–2
Alexander, S., 12, 39
Amoore, J. E., 289
Analytical Behaviourism, *see* Behaviourism
Anderson, J., 12
Angels, 28
Anger, 131
  Analytical Behaviourism, 60–3, 66
  emotion, 183–4
  introspective awareness of, 334–5
  state, 130
Animals, 252
  beliefs, 202, 209
  cats and colour-perception, 248–9
  concepts, 141
  introspection, 95, 323–4
  knowledge, 205
  machines, 121
  mental images, 296
Anscombe, G. E. M., 140, 165–7, 171–3
Aquinas, St. Thomas, 28, 122
  see also Thomism
Argument from Analogy, *see* Other Minds
Argument from Paradigm cases, 267–9
Aristotle, 12, 38, 77, 235–6
'Association of ideas', 349
Attention, 165, 167, 177
Attribute theories of mind and body, 6, 11–14, 19, 37–48, 78, 89, 337, 357
Austin, J. L., 240
Ayer, A. J., 72, 102

Baier, K., 103, 106
Bedford, E., 179

Behaviour, physical behaviour and 'behaviour proper', 84, 132, 133, 169–70, 178, 245–69 *passim*
Behaviourism, 54–72, 90, 93, 118, 129, 132
  combined with other theories of mind, 13–14, 25, 37
  defined, 10
  disembodied existence, 19, 56
  dispositions, 57–9, 85–8
  perception, 247
  Place, U. T., 80
  Ryle, G., 54–6, 177
  Smart, J. J. C., 80, 290
  truth in, 68, 76, 92, 122
  Wittgenstein, L., 54–6
Belief, 339–43
  dispositions, 57–8
  emotions, 179
  indeterminacy, 225–6
  inferring, 193–204 *passim*
  knowledge, 187–207 *passim*, 237–9
  mental images, 298–300, 301–2
  perception, 208–69 *passim*
  'potential', 223, 225, 242, 254
  reasons, 174–5
  thinking, 158, 345–9
  will, 165, 168–9
  see also Inclination to believe, 'potential belief'
Beloff, J., xi
Berkeley, G., 240–331
  mental images, 298
  phenomenalism, 5, 7
  secondary qualities, 271, 282
  visual perception of distance, 135
Bodily feelings, *see* Feelings
Bodily sensations, 26, 147, 306–22
  emotions, 180–1
  will, 165

Index

Index